LITTLE VISITS
with
GREAT AMERICANS

OR,

Success, Ideals and
How to Attain Them

VOLUMES 1 - 3

Edited By

ORISON SWETT MARDEN

First published in 1905

This edition published by Read Books Ltd.
Copyright © 2019 Read Books Ltd.
This book is copyright and may not be
reproduced or copied in any way without
the express permission of the publisher in writing

British Library Cataloguing-in-Publication Data
A catalogue record for this book is available
from the British Library

CONTENTS

INTRODUCTION.................................13

VOLUME ONE
Inspirational Talks With Famous Americans

SUCCESS MAXIMS................................21

INVENTION
I. Hard Work: the Secret of a Great Inventor's Genius.....23

II. A "Down-east" Yankee who Dictates Peace to
the Nations..37

MANUFACTURE
III. A Poor Boy Once Borrowed Books Now Gives Away
Libraries..51

IV. A Good Shoemaker Becomes Detroit's Best Mayor
and Michigan's Greatest Governor....................67

COMMERCE
V. Determined not to Remain Poor, a Farmer Boy
Becomes a Merchant Prince..........................75

VI. Honesty, the Foundation of a Great
Merchant's Career..................................85

VII. A British Boy Wins Fortune and Title by American
Business Methods...................................97

FINANCE
VIII. A Self-made Man who Strives to Give others
a Chance 105

IX. Thrift, the Secret of a Fortune Built in a
Single Lifetime. 112

X. Cut Out for a Banker, He Rose from Errand Boy to
Secretary of the U. S. Treasury. 118

XI. A Young Millionaire not Afraid to Work
in Overalls. 123

TRANSPORTATION
XII. A Messenger Boy's Zeal Lifts Him to the Head
of the World's Greatest Telegraph System. 128

XIII. Enthusiasm for Railroading Makes a Section Hand
Head of the Metropolitan System. 135

LABOR
XIV. A Factory Boy's Purpose to Improve Labor Makes
Him a Great Leader. 145

PUBLIC LIFE
XV. A Puny Boy, by Physical Culture, Becomes the Most
Vigorous of American Presidents. 153

XVI. A Brave Volunteer Fights His Way to the Head
of the American Army. 165

XVII. Making the Most of His Opportunities Wins a
Coveted Embassy. 172

XVIII. A Village Boy's Gift of Oratory Earns Him
Wealth and Fame. 181

XIX. A Chance-Found Book the Turning Point in a
United States Senator's Career. 191

XX. Varied Business Training the Foundation of a Long
Political Career. 195

XXI. A Magnate, the Courage of His Convictions Make
Him a Reformer. 202

EDUCATION AND LITERATURE

XXII. A Backwoods Boy Works His Way through College and Becomes University President. 211

XXIII. A "Jack of All Trades" Masters One and Becomes the Poet of the People.. 218

XXIV. A Farm Boy Who Devoured Books Writes One of the Greatest Poems of the Century. 228

XXV. A Famous Authoress Tells Literary Aspirants the Story of Her Struggle for Recognition.. 236

XXVI. A Printer's Boy, Self Taught, Becomes the Dean of American Letters. 245

XXVII. A Famous Novelist Atones for Wasted School Days by Self-Culture. 255

XXVIII. A Social Leader, Having "Eyes That See," Earns Literary Laurels. 262

ART

XXIX. Painstaking, the Secret of a Celebrated Painter's Success. 267

XXX. A School Girl, Not Afraid of Drudgery, Becomes America's Foremost Woman Illustrator. 275

XXXI. A Schoolboy's Sketches Reveal the Bent of a Talented Illustrator.. 280

XXXII. Rebuffs and Disappointments Fail to Repress a Great Cartoonist's Genius.. 285

XXXIII. Being Himself in Style and Subjects, the Secret of an Artist's Wonderful Popularity. 291

XXXIV. A "Printer's Devil" Whose Perseverance Wins Him Well-Earned Reputation as a Fun-Maker. 299

XXXV. "A Square Man in a Round Hole" Rejects $5,000 a Year and Becomes a Sculptor. 303

XXXVI. During Leisure Hours He "Found Himself" and Abandoned the Law for Art. 309

AMUSEMENT

XXXVII. Deformed in Body, His Cheerful Spirit Makes Him the Entertainer of Princes. 313

XXXVIII. Energy and Earnestness Win an Actor Fame.. 319

XXXIX. A Father's Common Sense Gives America a Great Bandmaster. 323

PHILANTHROPY

XL. Blind, Deaf, and Dumb, Patient Effort Wins for Her Culture and Rare Womanhood. 329

XLI. Jay Gould's Chum Chooses "High Thinking, not Money Making," and Wins Success Without Riches. 338

XLII. A Millionaire's Daughter Makes Inherited Wealth a Blessing to Thousands. 347

XLIII. A Self-made Merchant Solves the Problem of Practical Philanthropy 353

DIVINITY

XLIV. A Varied Career Develops the Resourceful Head of a Great Institutional Church and College. 359

XLV. An Inspiring Personality Wins a Noted Preacher Fame. 364

XLVI. From the Forge to the Pulpit, a Life of Devotion and Application.. 371

CANADIANS

XLVII. Canada's Leading Conservative Extols "the Country of the Twentieth Century." 377

XLVIII. An Eminent Scholar Advocates the Union of Canada and the United States. 382

XLIX. After Failure as a Grocer, He Becomes the Ablest Administrator Quebec Has Ever Had. 386

L. Canada's Leading Economist Tells Her Sons To Seek Fortune in Her Own Domain.. 393

LI. A Distinguished Educator has Found Contentment in
the Simple Life.......................................400

LII. Beginning as Telegraph Operator He Built the
Canadian Pacific....................................405

LIII. An Immigrant Boy Becomes a National Figure
in Reform..414

LIV. A "Forty-niner" who Seized Opportunities Others
Failed to See.......................................424

LV. The Blind Yacht Designer Attributes His Conquests
to His Mother's Early Cares. 436

LVI. A Great Vocalist Shows that Only Years of Labor Can
Win the Heights of Song............................446

VOLUME TWO
Men And Women Who Have Achieved Eminence

SUCCESS MAXIMS...............................461

VOLUME THREE
Encyclopedic Biographies, Or The Romance Of Reality.

SUCCESS MAXIMS...............................531

Statesmen..533

Industrial Leaders..................................540

Manufacturers.....................................547

Transportation Leaders.............................555

Inventors. 562

Merchants. 569

Financiers...573

Political Leaders...................................579

Lawyers And Jurists................................585

Soldiers And Sailors............................592

Explorers..600

Educators..608

Editors..616

Publishers...623

Orators..631

Musicians..636

Singers..643

Actors...651

Actresses..659

Organizers And Lecturers..........................664

Canadians..671

Illustrators......................................676

Cartoonists.......................................679

Humorists...683

Journalists And Writers...........................687

Poets...692

Canadians...698

Authors...702

Novelists...706

Reformers...713

Philanthropists...................................720

Divines...724

Canadians...730

ILLUSTRATIONS

Infancy...62

Childhood.......................................115

Youth..169

Courtship.......................................222

Domestic Trials.................................349

Out Of Debt At Last.............................401

Statesmen.......................................464

Canadians Of Note...............................466

Canadians Of Note...............................468

Captains Of Industry............................470

Manufacturers...................................472

Transportation Leaders..........................474

Inventors.......................................476

Merchants.......................................478

Financiers......................................480

Political Leaders...............................482

Lawyers And Jurists.............................484

Soldiers And Sailors............................486

Explorers And Travellers........................488

Educators.......................................490

Editors...492

Publishers......................................494

Orators..496

Musicians..498

Singers..500

Actors...502

Actresses..504

Organizers And Lecturers............................506

Illustrators, Decorators And Sculptors................508

Cartoonists..510

Humorists..512

Journalists And Writers..............................514

Poets..516

Authors...518

Novelists...520

Reformers..522

Philanthropists.....................................524

Divines...526

SUCCESS

He has achieved success
Who has lived well, laughed often, and loved much;

Who has enjoyed the trust of pure women,
The respect of intelligent men and the love of little children;

Who has filled his niche and accomplished his task;
Who has left the world better than he found it
Whether by an improved poppy, a perfect poem or a rescued soul;

Who has never lacked appreciation of Earth's beauty or failed to express it;
Who has always looked for the best in others and given them the best he had;

Whose life was an inspiration;
Whose memory a benediction.

BESSIE ANDERSON STANLEY

INTRODUCTION

Apelles, the great artist, traveled all over Greece for years, studying the fairest points of beautiful women, getting here an eye, there a forehead, and there a nose, here a grace and there a turn of beauty, for his famous portrait of a perfect woman which enchanted the world. It was not a portrait, not an imaginary ideal head, but a composite, a combination from the most perfect features he could find. By combining the perfect points, the graceful curves, the lines of beauty of many individuals, he made his wonderful painting.

The great artist knew that all elements of beauty and perfection of physical form could not be found in one person. He knew, too, that some of the most perfect features and beautiful curves would be found in women who were on the whole anything but beautiful—perhaps repulsive.

The editors of this volume have been for many years in quest of the elements of a grand, healthy, symmetrical, successful man—the ideal man. They knew at the beginning that it would be impossible to find any one man who would illustrate all these points of perfection, who would combine in perfect degree all the success qualities, but they have found in scores of men who have achieved something worth while qualities which, put together, would make a composite ideal man, a man who, in the evolution of civilization, will, perhaps, sometime be possible. Usually, in men who have risen to eminence, some one quality or virtue shines conspicuous, often accompanied with defects, perhaps great weakness, which, to gain the lesson, we must ignore.

The editors have found here a man illustrative of perseverance, here one marked by undaunted ambition, there a life where grit overcame all obstacles, and another where the quick grasping of opportunities led to noble achievement.

They have interviewed successful men and women in the various vocations, trying to get at the secret of their success, the reasons for their advancement. These varied life stories will give the reader the material for constructing the composite character—the ideal man or woman—one that shall combine all the best virtues and qualities, whose imitation will help to insure a useful, profitable and honored life. This composite man will not be a one-sided specialist. He will not be a man cursed with any great weakness. He will be a man raised to the highest power, symmetrical, self-centered, equipoised, ever master of himself.

It does not follow that every man whose name appears in this book is a model in every respect. Napoleon was not a model character, and yet he exemplifies some success qualities in his career in an almost ideal degree.

What question, arising from individual experience, from family life, or from daily observation within the community, is of more poignant human interest than the query: "Why do some men succeed, while others fail?" and the allied question: "What constitutes success in life, and how may it be attained?"

An analysis of the ideals and achievements of these leaders in invention, commerce and finance, in public affairs, and in literature, the arts, and the professions, as set forth by themselves, seems to reveal certain salient life lessons well worthy of most careful consideration. First, it would appear that without exception every successful man or woman at some period of his or her life, whether early or late, has formed a life purpose, and has registered a solemn vow to achieve something more than ordinary in the world. An exception to this rule appears to obtain in the cases of men or women possessed of a strong natural bent or talent, the exercise of which is an instinctive craving that will not be denied. This determination to be or to achieve, or this instinctive bent of thought and action, appears to be the first indication of greatness, and the turning point in great careers.

The next most obvious lesson to be drawn from a careful

study of these interviews seems to be, that once a determination to succeed is made, and the first steps, however humble, have been entered upon in the new career, the subject commences to take an *interest* amounting to positive pleasure in the tasks and duties incident to his chosen life work.

The far-away goal of success, with its reward of fame, wealth, and all that money can procure, appears to fade from the worker's sight as he advances toward it, and the incitement to labor for material reward is lost in the joy of congenial labor for its own sake. The player loses sight of the hope of victory in the mere zest of the game. This note appears again and again in the life stories of great workers as revealed by themselves, and accounts for the spectacle, so puzzling to many, of the master of millions apparently grasping for more millions in his declining years. There can be no content with present achievement, however great, because all who have achieved great things have discovered that the ends sought are lost in the value of the faculties developed by the search, and they hence seek, not additional reward of toil, but rather the pleasurable exercise of the chase. The joy of labor will not permit men to lay down the harness and relinquish effort this side the grave.

A determination to succeed once formed, and a congenial career once chosen and entered upon, there commences a process of character-building by the formation of life habits. These solidify into personal characteristics, the varying assortment of which in the individual constitutes what we call his personality, wherein one man differs from another. Character, it has been wisely said, is the resultant of choices. It appears again and again in the reminiscences of those who have succeeded, that from time to time they have deliberately chosen a course of action which by force of habit has become a personal characteristic, and has earned them national, if not world-wide, reputation. The name of "Honest" John Wanamaker stands for a reputation having a commercial value of hundreds of thousands of dollars. The acorn from which grew this mighty oak was a young man's choice of honesty as the foundation of his career.

Books and essays by the score and hundred have been written by theorists upon the principles of success in life. Worthy as are many of the writers, their lives often illustrate the adage of the poet, "It were easier to tell twenty what were good to be done than to be one of the twenty to follow mine own teachings." Boldly contrasted with such writings are the flesh and blood maxims herein contained, stamped with the mint marks of great personalities, towering mountainous among their fellows, each coined from the life habits which have hardened into enduring character, and have left their impress upon the history of our times.

In a drawing-room or public assemblage he would indeed be unambitious and mean-spirited, who would not choose the company and conversation of the greatest and the best. Carlyle says, "Great men taken up in any way are profitable company." What privilege could promise equal pleasure and profit with a series of visits at the homes of the most notable personages our land contains, to consult with each on the great questions of success or failure, of what constitutes ideal success, and of how it may be attained?

Such is the privilege contemplated by this volume and freely offered to all who choose to avail themselves of it. Compared with the inspiration, the examples and the wise counsel contained within its covers, the cost of such a volume sinks into insignificance. Benjamin Franklin said that the reading of one good book made him what he was. Henry Clay testified, "to the fact that in the midst of her early poverty my mother provided her home with a few choice books, do I owe my success in life." Senator Dolliver, in the present volume, regards a chance-found book as the turning point of his career, and like testimony is all but universal. Let the young and the guardians of youth weigh well the thought that there are sins of omission, as well as of commission, and that it may be hardly a less criminal negligence to refuse fit books for the growing mind than food for the growing body.

Quite aside from considerations of profit and duty are the considerations of pleasure offered by a volume of this character. It is a truism that truth is stranger than fiction. The romance of reality is the most thrilling of all romances, and there is a peculiar fascination associated with those glimpses of the inner man which are revealed by a speaker who sets forth his own life story, and places his own interpretation upon it. From this view point, "Little Visits" possesses a wealth of suggestion and of information, alike valuable and interesting to readers of all ages and of every walk in life.

The dominant note of this book, is inspiration; its keynote, helpfulness.

We have tried to drive home every precept and lesson with stirring and inspiring stories of great lives which show that men and women are the architects of their own fortunes, and which will explode the excuses of those who think they have no chance in life. It shows that necessity has ever been the priceless spur that has urged man to struggle with his destiny and develop his greatest strength.

We think the reader will find in these pages the composite character, the all-round success. We have tried to show that there is something better than making a living, and that is making a life—that a man may make millions and be a failure still.

We have shown that a man to succeed must be greater than his calling, that he must overtop his vocation. We have tried to teach that the really successful man must be greater than the book he writes, than the patient he treats, than the goods he sells, than the cause he pleads in the courts—that manhood is above all titles, greater than any career.

THE EDITOR.

VOLUME ONE

INSPIRATIONAL TALKS WITH FAMOUS AMERICANS

SUCCESS MAXIMS

The tissue of the life to be
We weave with colors all our own,
And in the field of destiny
We reap as we have sown. —Whittier.

No man is born into this world whose work is not born with him.—Lowell.

If a man can write a better book, preach a better sermon, or make a better mousetrap than his neighbor, though he build his house in the woods, the world will make a beaten path to his door.—Emerson.

Character is power—is influence; it makes friends, creates funds, draws patronage and support, and opens a sure and easy way to wealth, honor and happiness.—J. Hawes.

To be thrown upon one's own resources is to be cast into the very lap of fortune.—Franklin.

There is no road to success but through a clear, strong purpose. A purpose underlies character, culture, position, attainment of whatever sort.—T. T. Munger.

Heaven never helps the man who will not act.—Sophocles.

The talent of success is nothing more than doing what you can do well, and doing well whatever you do, without a thought of fame.—Longfellow.

The longer I live, the more deeply am I convinced that that which makes the difference between one man and another—between the weak and powerful, the great and insignificant, is energy—invincible determination—a purpose once formed, and then death or victory.—FOWELL BUXTON.

In the measure in which thou seekest to do thy duty shalt thou know what is in thee. But what is thy duty? The demand of the hour.—GOETHE.

A strong, defiant purpose is many-handed, and lays hold of whatever is near that can serve it; it has a magnetic power that draws to itself whatever is kindred.—T. T. MUNGER.

INVENTION

I

HARD WORK:
THE SECRET OF A GREAT INVENTOR'S GENIUS.

TO discover the opinion of Thomas A. Edison concerning what makes and constitutes success in life is an easy matter, if one can only discover Mr. Edison. I camped three weeks in the vicinity of Orange, N. J., awaiting the opportunity to come upon the great inventor and voice my questions. It seemed a rather hopeless and discouraging affair until he was really before me; but, truth to say, he is one of the most accessible of men, and only reluctantly allows himself to be hedged in by the pressure of endless affairs. "Mr. Edison is always glad to see any visitor," said a gentleman who is constantly with him, "except when he is hot on the trail of something he has been working for, and then it is as much as a man's head is worth to come in on him." He certainly was not hot on the trail of anything on the morning when, for seemingly the tenth time, I rang at the gate in the fence which surrounds the laboratory on Valley Road, Orange. A young man appeared, who conducted me up the walk to the elegant office and library of the great laboratory. It is a place, this library, not to be passed through without thought, for with a further store of volumes in his home, it contains one of the most costly and well-equipped scientific libraries in the world; the collection of writings on patent laws and patents, for instance, is absolutely exhaustive. It gives, at a glance, an idea of the breadth of the thought and sympathy of this man who grew up with scarcely a common school education.

On the second floor, in one of the offices of the machine-shop, I was asked to wait, while a grimy youth disappeared with my card, which he said he would "slip under the door of Mr. Edison's office." "Curious," I thought; "what a lord this man must be if they dare not even knock at his door!"

Thinking of this and gazing out of the window, I waited until a working man, who had entered softly, came up beside me. He looked with a sort of "Well, what is it?" in his eyes, and quickly it began to come to me that the man in the sooty, oil-stained clothes was Edison himself. The working garb seemed rather incongruous, but there was no mistaking the broad forehead, with its shock of blackish hair streaked with gray. The gray eyes, too, were revelations in the way of alert comprehensiveness.

"Oh!" was all I could get out at the time.

"Want to see me?" he said, smiling in the most youthful and genial way.

"Why,—yes, certainly, to be sure," I stammered.

He looked at me blankly.

"You'll have to talk louder," said an assistant who worked in another portion of the room; "he don't hear well."

HIS GRANDFATHER WAS A BANKER.

This fact was new to me, but I raised my voice with celerity and piped thereafter in an exceedingly shrill key. After the usual humdrum opening remarks, in which he acknowledged with extreme good nature his age as fifty-five years, and that he was born in Erie county, O., of Dutch parentage, the family having emigrated to America in 1730, the particulars began to grow more interesting. His great-grandfather, I learned, was a banker of high standing in New York; and, when Thomas was but a child of seven years, the family fortune suffered reverses so serious as to make it necessary that he should become a wage-earner at an unusually early age, and that the family should move from his birth-place to Michigan.

"Did you enjoy mathematics as a boy?" I asked.

"Not much," he replied. "I tried to read Newton's 'Principia' at the age of eleven. That disgusted me with pure mathematics, and I don't wonder now. I should not have been allowed to take up such serious work."

"You were anxious to learn?"

"Yes, indeed. I attempted to read through the entire Free Library at Detroit, but other things interfered before I had done."

"Were you a book-worm and dreamer?" I questioned.

"Not at all," he answered, using a short, jerky method, as though he were unconsciously checking himself up. "I became a newsboy, and liked the work. Made my first *coup* as a newsboy."

"What was it?" I ventured.

"I bought up on 'futures' a thousand copies of the 'Detroit Free Press' containing important war news,—gained a little time on my rivals, and sold the entire batch like hot cakes. The price reached twenty-five cents a copy before the end of the route," and he laughed. "I ran the 'Grand Trunk Herald,' too, at that time—a little paper I issued from the train."

HIS FIRST EXPERIMENTS.

"When did you begin to be interested in inventions?" I questioned.

"Well," he said, "I began to dabble in chemistry at that time. I fitted up a small laboratory on the train."

In reference to this, Mr. Edison subsequently admitted

that, during the progress of some occult experiments in this workshop, certain complications ensued in which a jolted and broken bottle of sulphuric acid attracted the attention of the conductor. He, who had been long suffering in the matter of unearthly odors, promptly ejected the young devotee and all his works. This incident would have been only amusing but for its relation to and explanation of his deafness. A box on the ear, administered by the irate conductor, caused the lasting deafness.

"What was your first work in a practical line?" I went on.

"A telegraph line between my home and another boy's, I made with the help of an old river cable, some stove-pipe wire, and glass-bottle insulators. I had my laboratory in the cellar and studied telegraphy outside."

"What was the first really important thing you did?"

"I saved a boy's life."

"How?"

"The boy was playing on the track near the depot. I saw he was in danger and caught him, getting out of the way just in time. His father was station-master, and taught me telegraphy in return."

Dramatic situations appear at every turn of this man's life, though, temperamentally, it is evident that he would be the last to seek them. He seems to have been continually arriving on the scene at critical moments, and always with the good sense to take things in his own hands. The chance of learning telegraphy only gave him a chance to show how apt a pupil he was, and the railroad company soon gave him regular employment. He himself admits that, at seventeen, he had become one of the most expert operators on the road.

"Did you make much use of your inventive talent at this time?" I questioned.

"Yes," he answered. "I invented an automatic attachment for my telegraph instrument which would send in the signal to show I was awake at my post, when I was comfortably snoring in a corner. I didn't do much of that, though," he went on; "for some such boyish trick sent me in disgrace over the line into Canada."

A NOVEL METHOD OF TELEGRAPHING.

"Were you there long?"

"Only a winter. If it's incident you want, I can tell you one of that time. The place where I was and Sarnia, the American town, were cut off from telegraph and other means of communication by the storms until I got at a locomotive whistle and tooted a telegraphic message. I had to do it again and again, but eventually they understood it over the water and answered in the same way."

According to his own and various recorded accounts, Edison was successively in charge of important wires in Memphis, Cincinnati, New Orleans and Louisville. He lived in the free-and-easy atmosphere of the tramp operators—a boon companion with them, yet absolutely refusing to join in the dissipations to which they were addicted. So highly esteemed was he for his honesty that it was the custom of his colleagues, when a spree was on hand, to make him the custodian of those funds which they felt obliged to save. On a more than usually hilarious occasion, one of them returned rather the worse for wear, and knocked the treasurer down on his refusal to deliver the trust money; the other depositors, we are glad to note, gave the ungentlemanly tippler a sound thrashing.

"Were you good at saving your own money?" I asked.

"No," he said, smiling. "I never was much for saving money, as money. I devoted every cent, regardless of future needs, to scientific books and materials for experiments."

"You believe that an excellent way to succeed?"

"Well, it helped me greatly to future success."

"What was your next invention?" I inquired.

"An automatic telegraph recorder—a machine which enabled me to record dispatches at leisure, and send them off as fast as needed."

"How did you come to hit upon that?"

"Well, at the time, I was in such straits that I had to walk from Memphis to Louisville. At the Louisville station they offered me a place. I had perfected a style of handwriting which would allow me to take legibly from the wire, long hand, forty-seven and even fifty-four words a minute, but I was only a moderately rapid sender. I had to do something to help me on that side, and so I thought out that little device."

Later, he pointed out an article by one of his biographers, in which a paragraph, referring to this Louisville period, says:—

"True to his dominant instincts, he was not long in gathering around him a laboratory, printing office and machine shop. He took press reports during his whole stay, including, on one occasion, the Presidential message, by Andrew Johnson, and this at one sitting, from 3:30 P. M. to 4:30 A. M.

"He then paragraphed the matter he had received over the wires, so that printers had exactly three lines each, thus enabling them to set up a column in two or three minutes' time. For this, he was allowed all the exchanges he desired, and the Louisville press gave him a state dinner."

"How did you manage to attract public attention to your ability?" I questioned.

"I didn't manage," said the Wizard. "Some things I did created comment. A device that I invented which utilized one submarine cable for two circuits, caused considerable talk, and the Franklin telegraph office of Boston gave me a position."

It is related of this, Mr. Edison's first trip east, that he came with no ready money and in a rather dilapidated condition. His colleagues were tempted by his "hayseed" appearance to "salt" him, as professional slang terms the process of giving a receiver matter faster than he can record it. For this purpose, the new man was assigned to a wire manipulated by a New York operator famous for his speed. But there was no fun at all. Notwithstanding the fact that the New Yorker was in the game and was doing his most speedy clip, Edison wrote out the long message accurately, and, when he realized the situation, was soon firing taunts over the wire at the sender's slowness.

HIS FIRST PATENT.

"Had you patented many things up to the time of your coming east?" I queried.

"Nothing," said the inventor, ruminatively. "I received my first patent in 1869."

"For what?"

"A machine for recording votes and designed to be used in the State Legislature."

"I didn't know such machines were in use," I ventured.

"They ar'n't," he answered, with a merry twinkle. "The better it worked, the more impossible it was; the sacred right of the minority, you know,—couldn't filibuster if they used it,—didn't use it."

"Oh!"

"Yes, it was an ingenious thing. Votes were clearly pointed and shown on a roll of paper, by a small machine attached to the desk of each member. I was made to learn that such an innovation was out of the question, but it taught me something."

"And that was?"

"To be sure of the practical need of, and demand for, a machine, before expending time and energy on it."

"Is that one of your maxims of success?"

"It is."

In this same year, Edison came from Boston to New York, friendless and in debt on account of the expenses of his experiment. For several weeks he wandered about the town with actual hunger staring him in the face. It was a time of great financial excitement, and with that strange quality of Fortunism, which seems to be his chief characteristic, he entered the establishment of the Law Gold Reporting Company just as their entire plant had shut down on account of an accident in the machinery that could not be located. The heads of the firm were anxious and excited to the last degree, and a crowd of the Wall street fraternity waited about for the news which came not. The shabby stranger put his finger on the difficulty at once, and was given lucrative employment. In the rush of the metropolis, a man finds his true level without delay, especially when his talents are of so practical and brilliant a nature as were this young telegrapher's. It would be an absurdity to imagine an Edison hidden in New York. Within a short time, he was presented with a check for $40,000, as his share of a single invention—an improved stock printer. From this time, a national reputation was assured him. He was, too, now engaged upon the duplex and quadruplex systems—systems for sending two and four messages at the same time over a single wire,—which were to inaugurate almost a new era in telegraphy.

POVERTY AS AN INCENTIVE TO EFFORT.

Recalling the incident of the Law Gold Reporting Company, I inquired: "Do you believe want urges a man to greater efforts and so to greater success?"

"It certainly makes him keep a sharp lookout. I think it does push a man along."

"Do you believe that invention is a gift, or an acquired ability?"

"I think it's born in a man."

"And don't you believe that familiarity with certain mechanical conditions and defects naturally suggest improvements to any one?"

"No. Some people may be perfectly familiar with a machine all their days, knowing it inefficient, and never see a way to improve it."

"What do you think is the first requisite for success in your field, or any other?"

"The ability to apply your physical and mental energies to one problem incessantly without growing weary."

"Do you have regular hours, Mr. Edison?" I asked.

"Oh," he said, "I do not work hard now. I come to the laboratory about eight o'clock every day and go home to tea at six, and then I study or work on some problem until eleven, which is my hour for bed."

"Fourteen or fifteen hours a day can scarcely be called loafing," I suggested.

"Well," he replied, "for fifteen years I have worked on an average of twenty hours a day."

That astonishing brain has been known to puzzle itself for sixty consecutive hours over a refractory problem, its owner dropping quietly off into a long sleep when the job was done, to awake perfectly refreshed and ready for another siege. Mr. Dickson, a neighbor and familiar, gives an anecdote told by Edison which well illustrates his untiring energy and phenomenal endurance. In describing his Boston experience, Edison said he bought Faraday's works on electricity, commenced to read them at three o'clock in the morning and continued until his room-mate arose, when they started on their long walk to get breakfast. That object was entirely subordinated in Edison's mind to Faraday, and he suddenly remarked to his friend: "Adams, I have got so much to do, and life is so short, that I have got to hustle," and with that he started off on a dead run for his breakfast.

NEVER DID ANYTHING WORTH WHILE BY CHANCE.

"Are your discoveries often brilliant intuitions? Do they come to you while you are lying awake nights?" I asked him.

"I never did anything worth doing by accident," he replied, "nor did any of my inventions come indirectly through accident, except the phonograph. No, when I have fully decided that a result is worth getting, I go about it, and make trial after trial, until it comes.

"I have always kept," continued Mr. Edison, "strictly within the lines of commercially useful inventions. I have never had any time to put on electrical wonders, valuable only as novelties to catch the popular fancy."

"What makes you work?" I asked with real curiosity. "What impels you to this constant, tireless struggle? You have shown that you care comparatively nothing for the money it makes you, and you have no particular enthusiasm for the attending fame. What is it?"

"I like it," he answered, after a moment of puzzled expression. "I don't know any other reason. Anything I have begun is always on my mind, and I am not easy while away from it, until it is finished; and then I hate it."

"Hate it?" I said.

"Yes," he affirmed, "when it is all done and is a success, I can't bear the sight of it. I haven't used a telephone in ten years, and I would go out of my way any day to miss an incandescent light."

"You lay down rather severe rules for one who wishes to succeed in life," I ventured, "working eighteen hours a day."

"Not at all," he said. "You do something all day long, don't you? Every one does. If you get up at seven o'clock and go to bed at eleven, you have put in sixteen good hours, and it is certain with most men that they have been doing something all the time. They have been either walking, or reading, or writing, or thinking. The only trouble is that they do it about a great many things and I do it about one. If they took the time in question and applied it in one direction, to one object, they would succeed. Success is sure to follow such application. The trouble lies in the fact that people do not have an object—one thing to which they stick, letting all else go."

OPPORTUNITIES FOR FUTURE INVENTORS.

"You believe, of course," I suggested, "that much remains to be discovered in the realm of electricity?"

"It is the field of fields," he answered. "We can't talk of that, but it holds the secret which will reorganize the life of the world."

"You have discovered much about it," I said, smiling.

"Yes," he said, "and yet very little in comparison with the possibilities that appear."

"How many inventions have you patented?"

"Only six hundred," he answered, "but I have made application for some three hundred more."

"And do you expect to retire soon, after all this?"

"I hope not," he said, almost pathetically. "I hope I will be able to work right on to the close. I shouldn't care to loaf."

Shouldn't care to loaf! What a thought after fifty-two years of such magnificent achievement.

THE WIZARD AT HOME.

While the inventions of Thomas A. Edison keep him constantly in the public eye, as a man in private life he is comparatively unknown. If you should see him in his laboratory, buried deep in work, surrounded by battalions of machines and hosts of experimental appliances, dressed in his "shop clothes" spotted with chemicals, you would never suspect that, just seven hundred feet away, a palatial home awaits him.

Ten years ago he was an undomesticated man. His workshop and his chemical laboratory held such powerful sway over his mind that he was only supremely happy when "up to his eyes" in work. Gradually, almost insidiously, the "wizard" has been weaned away from the weaving of his spells, and now a new and more potent power than ever before controlled him has gained its mastery over him.

This is the power of love. Though the great inventor even now works as few men of his age and accomplishments are in the habit of doing, the last few years have seen a steady relaxation of his toil.

The time has passed when he was wont to lock himself in a room and work sixty hours at a stretch without taking more than an hour's sleep at various intervals in that time.

MRS. EDISON IS ALSO AN INVENTOR OF GOOD ABILITY.

When Mr. Edison toils now, there is one who shares his labors with him. It is Mrs. Edison, his second wife. She is the daughter of John Miller, who invented the famous Miller mowing machine, and inherits a great deal of inventive ability. It is through this additional bond of genius that they are united. She is a helpmeet in the true sense of the word. It is said that they are now working on an invention which they will patent jointly.

Whether Mrs. Edison intends to participate in one of her husband's inventions or not, she takes more than passing interest in all of his affairs, and has acquired, through her association with him, a vast amount of electrical and mechanical knowledge. When Mr. Edison met Miss Miller, twelve years ago, he was at the beginning of his fame. It was one of the most intensely busy periods of his career, his work engaging nearly every moment of his time.

The days of complete absorption in work have passed for him. His home-life has become necessary to him. Though he has had one or two relapses of "working fever,"—when he steadfastly refused to be moved from the laboratory by Mrs. Edison's persuasions,—he has reached the period when he is glad to go to his home. Much honor is due to the woman who has wrought so marvelous a change in her husband. Those who knew Mr. Edison best predicted that his present wife would soon become a secondary consideration in his life. They are, from all accounts, mistaken.

The Edison home is one of the finest residences in New Jersey, and is furnished with all the conveniences and luxuries of a modern palace. It bears evidence of Mrs. Edison's true taste and skillful management. The lower floor of the house is laid out in parlors, conservatories, and a magnificent dining room. Ponderous chandeliers bristling with electric-light bulbs hang from ceilings finished in open-work beams, exhibiting the best art of the builder. Mr. Edison has a fine library in his residence, though it does not contain so many scientific works as the library at his laboratory.

The upper floors are given up to sleeping rooms, and a special "den" for Mr. Edison. There he works out his plans, and has at hand the reference books he desires in chemistry, physics, heat, light, and electricity.

RISES EARLY AND WORKS LONG.

He is an early riser, and is ready for work at half-past six o'clock. His first daily occupation is to read the newspapers. He is anxious to know if the reporters who interviewed him wrote just what he said, for he dislikes, above all else, newspaper interviews that are not correct. He does not like to be misquoted, and is willing to go to any amount of trouble in order that his statements shall be reported without error. No matter how busily he may be engaged at the laboratory he will stop to look over an interview, and no one is more willing than he is to set a reporter right.

At half-past seven in the morning Mr. Edison starts for the laboratory. He usually walks, as the distance is short, and his physicians have ordered that he must take a certain amount of physical exercise every day. When he reaches the laboratory, he begins with a great rush, and starts men on certain phases of work which he planned the previous day. He usually has from fifty to seventy-five subjects on which he puts men to work. These subjects he prepares at home, between the time when he leaves the laboratory, half-past six, and midnight.

Every afternoon Mrs. Edison calls for her husband at the laboratory, and takes him away in her carriage, and they drive about the beautiful district of the Oranges.

Mrs. Edison has undertaken the task of keeping the inventor healthy. She will not permit him to neglect his meals, or to work more than she thinks is good for him. She insists that he shall leave the laboratory at a certain hour each night, and she undertakes to personally see that he does so. At times, Mr. Edison objects, but in a very mild way, to this *régime*. Not long ago, he was deeply engaged in a certain experiment, when Mrs. Edison called for him and insisted upon taking him home. After some resistance, he at last consented, saying, however, by way of a final protest, as he stepped into the carriage:—

"Billy" (his pet name for Mrs. Edison), "you're a nuisance."

Were it not, however, for the saving influence which Mrs. Edison exercises over her husband, it is doubtful if he would accomplish so much.

II

A "DOWN-EAST" YANKEE WHO DICTATES PEACE TO THE NATIONS.

HIRAM STEVENS MAXIM is a gunmaker and peacemaker, and to-day the terms are synonymous.

Two armed men, although hostile, will hesitate to attack one another; each will be careful to make no false move, lest the other's hand fly to his pistol pocket. Neither knows the other's equipment for aggression or defense. So both will smile and smile, and continue to hate.

It is often thus with nations.

When I asked Mr. Maxim how one feels to be in the business of making machines of war,—machines for killing men by the brigade, so to speak, he replied:—

"Men of my profession do more to keep peace on earth than all the churches of Christendom. They beg for peace,—we compel it."

Almost all famous men have two sides; the one is seen by the world, which never really sees the man at all, and is cold and glazed and more or less characterless,—being wholly intellectual. The other is the warm human side, full of points of strength and lovable weaknesses.

THE MAN WHOSE GUNS WILL CLEAR A JUNGLE.

Hiram S. Maxim is of this type. Mention his name to your neighbor, and he will say: "Oh, yes! Maxim,—he's the inventor of the rapid-fire gun, the flying machine, and smokeless powder, and a lot of other things." That's all he knows about him, and, very likely, it's all he cares. But the name Maxim is of tremendous import to every nation in the world; it is liable to have a potential influence in changing some of their boundaries, too. China had a good supply of rapid-fire guns when the war broke out between her and Japan, but the brass parts had all been stolen by traitorous Celestials, and the instruments left unfit for use. Otherwise, the results might have been different,—who can tell?

Ask the British Government how many British lives and how much British money was saved by the rapid-fire guns in South Africa. Also ask the "blacks" what they think of one of them. They call it "Johnny pop,—pop,—pop." But these guns were small affairs. Remember what their big brothers did for us at Santiago and Manila. I am told that they lashed the surface of the ocean into foam.

But let us look at the man as the public sees him.

Weigh the significance of his list of titles: Chevalier of the Legion of Honor, member of the American Society of Civil Engineers, honorary member of the Bridgeport Scientific Society, member of the Royal Society of Arts, of the English Society of Mechanical Engineers, of the English Society of Electrical Engineers, of the English Society of Junior Engineers, of the British Association for the Advancement of Science, of the British Empire League, of the Decimal Society, of the British Æronautical Society, of the London Chamber of Commerce, and also recipient of decorations from the Emperor of China and several European sovereigns.

HIS BRAIN IS BUILT UP OF INVENTIVE CELLS.

Mr. Maxim was the first man in the world to make an automatic gun; that is, a gun that loads and fires itself by its own reactionary force. He was also the first to combine gun-cotton and nitro-glycerine in a smokeless powder. The practicability of his flying machine is yet to be proved.

Such is Maxim, the ghost of whose presence appears to bellicose rulers and bids them halt,—and they do halt. It is said that the British Government and Hiram S. Maxim are two of the world's most powerful influences for peace.

Next consider the human being,—the big, brown-eyed, white-bearded man, over sixty years young,—for he was born in Maine, in 1840.

He seems to me to be a man with two ambitions: primarily, to keep on inventing, and, secondarily, to be the most famous inventor of all ages. His intellect and energy demand progress, his vanity demands fame. He doesn't appear to care for money, save as a means to a desired end. His personality might be considered unbalanced. His sense of self-suppression does not correspond with his fairly colossal intellect. The character of his intellectuality is uniform. The philosophical rather than the scholarly instinct dominates it. Another evidence of his quality of humanity is his sensitiveness to unfair censure. "I don't fear truthful criticism," he once said; "misrepresentation is what hurts."

It is difficult for one who knows him to imagine anything which he could not master. I once asked him the question, and he said he believed he would have succeeded at anything, except as a clergyman or a physician; that his religious views would preclude the former, and that he had a distaste for the latter.

BITING OFF THE DOG'S TAIL.

At the age of fourteen young Maxim left school, and became apprenticed to a carriage-builder, although he had previously learned the use of tools in his father's mill. He was a stockily built lad, and was noted for his physical strength and daring. His father was not an ardent advocate of "turn the other cheek" policy. On the contrary, he used to say: "If any one assails you, sail into him." Once Hiram's father promised to bring him a present if he would be good. The little fellow, then six years old, looked forward to the fulfilment with impatience. At length, the elder Maxim, returning from the village, brought a puppy as a playmate for his little son. Hiram regarded the animal with amazement for a few moments; then, bursting into tears, he rushed to hide his face in his mother's lap, exclaiming: "I am afraid of it, it looks so much like a dog." The two finally became great friends. One day the dog bit Hiram, and the lad asked his father what he ought to do under the circumstances. "Bite him back," was the verdict. In pursuit of this suggestion, the lad examined the dog and concluded that the end of his tail was about the most vulnerable point. Accordingly, he took that member between his teeth and began to put on pressure, raising the dog from the ground, in order to swing him once or twice. All the while the lad had tears in his eyes, for he loved his little play-fellow; but, with true Puritanical instinct, he deemed the chastisement just and necessary. The dog, however, did not join him in this view of the matter, and, in an attempt to escape, carried away one of his young master's upper front teeth. It is also said that one of Hiram's young brothers, in pursuit of this policy of retaliation, almost decapitated the family goose, which they were saving up for Christmas, which had savagely attacked the calf of the youngster's leg.

It is easier to give Mr. Maxim's manner of speech than his manner of speaking. He has wonderful brown eyes,—very honest eyes,—that stare at you inquiringly as he talks, and an extremely gentle voice of an almost hypnotic quality,—very attractive and soothing. Marvelously quick-witted himself, he has little patience with dullness in others. His power of explanation, too, is very great. He always uses language and methods according to the understanding of the listener. With a scientific man, he employs forms of speech that convey much in little, while to the ordinary layman he expresses himself in popular English.

"To what do you attribute your early success?" Mr. Maxim was asked.

"In the first place, I was a very large and strong boy, and, no matter where I worked, I always succeeded in doing more than any other man or boy in the shop. I was never absent from work or school."

PAT'S ANXIETY TO TRY "THE BOSS," AND ITS RESULT.

The development of his physical strength kept pace with that of his intellect. When he was thirty-five, he was manager of a large manufactory in Brooklyn. One day a herculean Irishman, who had long been ambitious to have a trial of strength with "the boss," asked the latter how it was that the Irish were so much stronger than the Americans.

"How much can you lift?" asked Mr. Maxim, quietly.

"Six hundred pounds," replied Pat.

"And how much do you weigh?"

"Two hundred pounds."

"Well," said Maxim, "I will lift you and your load together," and he did it.

HOW THE MAINE "BACKWOODSMAN" CAPTURED A ROBBER.

On another occasion, while taking lunch at a railroad station in France, Mr. Maxim recognized a notorious confidence man who had, years before, robbed him in Paris. The fellow, seeing that he was detected, tried to escape by leaping upon a moving train. Maxim followed and a fierce struggle ensued on the footboard of the coach, while the train was running at a high speed. Maxim had to fight both the fellow and his comrades, but he subjugated his man. The train was brought to a standstill, and the victor marched his prisoner back over the ties to the station, delivering him to the authorities, and subsequently had the satisfaction of seeing him sentenced to several years at hard labor. This was one result of the backwoods training in Maine.

"Whatever job I was at," Mr. Maxim told me, "I used to work at and think of day and night. I talked shop in season and out. If I was given work that was not good enough for me, I would do it so well and so quickly that they thought I was worthy of something better. No matter where I was, I managed, somehow, to get to the top. I noticed, the first thing, that the majority of the men around me were poor and the few rich; and I knew, of course, that the methods of the former were wrong, and that, consequently, the way to succeed was to follow the latter."

"When did you first begin to invent?"

"Almost before I learned to walk. When I went to work, I began to study out ways of improving tools and appliances."

FROM GAS MACHINES TO INCANDESCENT LAMPS.

"What were your first practical inventions?"

"In 1862-63 I was at work at Fitchburg, Massachusetts, making gas machines. I made various improvements at that time, which afterward came into general use. From Fitchburg I went to Boston, where I entered the service of Oliver P. Drake, who was not only a gas-machine maker, but also a philosophical-instrument maker. I first worked as a draughtsman, and then became his foreman. I learned from Mr. Drake many things that were useful to me in after life. From Boston I came to New York, where I obtained a situation as draughtsman at the Novelty Iron Works, East Twelfth street. At that time they were building the Pacific Mail steamers. Shortly after this, I thought of a new system of making gas from gasoline. All the machines that had existed would maintain only one hundred lights or less, and the density and illuminating power of the gas varied so much as to make the lights very unsatisfactory. I decided to make a machine that would make the gas, from first to last, of an equal density. I made this machine and patented it. It was intended for large consumers, and several were purchased by A. T. Stewart & Company. One of them was in the Park Avenue Hotel, and, for a time, another was used in the Post Office in New York City. I also made a very large machine, the biggest ever made, for the Grand Union and several other hotels at Saratoga which belonged to A. T. Stewart. From gas machines I turned my attention to small steam motors, and had a place in Centre street, which is still in existence, my successors being Messrs. Welch and Lawson, 205 Centre street. I soon began to experiment with electricity, and was the first man to file at the Patent Office an invention for building up and preserving the carbons of incandescent lamps, by the action of hydro-carbon vapors. I lost this patent, however, by a system of fraud, which I will not describe to-day. I was the first man to make an electrical regulator, and exhibited it at the Paris Exposition in 1881, and was made a Chevalier of the French Legion of Honor. I secured many patents on electrical inventions from 1880 to 1885. I next experimented with automatic firearms."

THE GENESIS OF THE AUTOMATIC GUN.

"How did you come to invent the automatic gun?"

"Many years ago, while firing at a target with a military musket, I was much surprised at the force of the recoil. It appeared to me that this waste of energy might be profitably employed in loading and firing the weapon, but it was not until I went to Europe and found myself in Paris with insufficient work to keep me fully employed, that I tried to make an automatic gun. I first made a drawing, which I afterward took to London; and, having obtained and equipped a small factory there, I commenced experiments with the view of evolving a gun which would load and fire itself. There were no data to refer to. No one had ever before spent a single cent in experimenting with automatic guns. I first thought of employing the recoil to working existing forms of mechanism, but found that impracticable. I then designed and constructed a totally new machine and a totally new system of feeding.

"In the spring of 1884, I constructed the first apparatus ever made in which the recoil of one cartridge would load another cartridge into the barrel and fire it. This is now in the South Kensington Museum, in London, labeled: 'This apparatus loads and fires itself, by force of its own recoil, and is the first machine ever made in which energy from the burning powder is employed for loading and firing the arm.'

"When I made my first gun and found that it would really load and fire itself, I knew it would have a great future. A few friends came in to see it. They told others, and very soon a great number of people came to see the new wonder. In fact, everybody, from the Prince of Wales down, came to see the gun and fire it. No less than two hundred thousand rounds of ammunition were used in explaining the gun and showing it to visitors. At first, no one would believe that an automatic gun had really been made. No one was prepared to believe, without seeing it. In fact, I may say that they were unable to understand that the gun actually loaded and fired itself. It was considered a nine days' wonder. The English Government was the first to give an order. It asked for a gun which would not weigh over one hundred pounds, and would fire four hundred rounds per minute. I made one that weighed forty pounds and fired two thousand rounds in three minutes, with one pull of the trigger. This is a result that no one else has ever attained. I showed my gun to Lord Wolseley at Hythe, where I fired at a target. That leader and Colonel Tongue were standing by the gun while I was firing it. I heard the latter say that it was the best firing that had ever been seen; that the accuracy was much better than had ever been known before; and that the rapidity of fire was without parallel. Everyone seemed astonished, and it was then that Lord Wolseley approached me and said: 'Mr. Maxim, I have seen your gun. It is simply wonderful. It is the most remarkable invention I ever saw in my life, and I congratulate you heartily upon your success; but,' he continued, 'it is of no good, as you will observe that the cloud of smoke is very large indeed. Unless you can get smokeless powder, I am afraid your gun will be of little use.' It was then that I began to think in earnest about smokeless powder, one of the directors having said that I was just the man to invent it. When I told him that I was not a chemist at all, as compared with Professors Fred. Adel and Dewar, his reply was: 'You know all the chemistry that is necessary in the matter, and, moreover, you have an imagination, and the others have not. If you take the matter up, I am sure you will go ahead of them.'"

AUTOMATIC GUNS MADE SMOKELESS POWDER INDISPENSABLE.

"Such was really the case, because I find that my application for a patent for a smokeless powder, consisting of nitro-glycerine and gun cotton, was filed at the patent office about fourteen days ahead of any other, and Sir Richard Webster, in speaking for the government in the celebrated case of Nobel against the Government on smokeless powder, said: 'H. S. Maxim is the first man to make a smokeless powder with nitro-glycerine and gun cotton. This powder was taken out to the States as much as eight or nine years ago, shown at Springfield, and put into competition with all other forms; and, according to the printed reports of the time, it was said to be superior to all others at all points, and I may say that the powder has not been improved on to any extent, as all the leading powders of to-day are practically the same as that invented by him at that time.'

"I was the first man to show a thoroughly good smokeless powder in the United States. Having succeeded in England, I took my guns abroad. Switzerland was the first country where I had a competitive trial with other makers. I was asked to fire at a dummy battery of artillery, at thirteen hundred yards, for one minute; but, as a matter of fact, I was only engaged half a minute in actual firing, when it was telephoned that I had technically killed three-fourths of the men and horses. I thought, perhaps, that I ought to have killed the whole of them, but the general said with great enthusiasm: 'No gun ever made has ever done anything like that. It is the most marvelous thing that has ever been done. It is simply amazing. A little gun weighing only fifty pounds puts a battery of artillery out of action in half a minute, at thirteen hundred yards.'

"I next took the gun to Italy, where I won another victory, and then returned to England. I received very large orders from all these countries, and the gun is now in use, I may say, nearly all over the world. These guns are being made not only by our own company, which has many factories in England, but by the British Government, by Ludwig Loewe, of Berlin; by Krupp, by Armstrong and by the United States Government at Washington. The company with which I am connected is a very large one, and we make about sixty varieties of rapid-firing and automatic guns. We are also makers of very large guns, builders of battleships, etc. I have also made guns for flying aerial torpedoes, by the use of compressed air and gas. About ten years ago I conducted a series of experiments at Baldwin Park, Bexley, England, with a view of ascertaining how much power is required to perform artificial flight. These experiments were on a much larger scale than had ever been attempted before, and excited a great deal of interest in the scientific world. Lord Kelvin, at the Oxford meeting of the British Association for the Advancement of Science, Lord Salisbury in the chair, spoke in the highest terms of these experiments. He was very enthusiastic at what he had seen at Baldwin's Park. He said that the work was all exceedingly well done, that the experiments were conducted with great care, and that they were very creditable to me."

HOW LI HUNG CHANG BECAME INTERESTED IN MAXIM.

"I have been decorated by the President of France, by the Sultan of Turkey, by the Queen of Spain, and by the King of Portugal, etc."

"How did you come to be decorated by the Emperor of China, Mr. Maxim?"

"On one occasion, when there was great excitement in London about a terrible massacre of missionaries in China, I attended a meeting which, at the beginning, was very much in favor of the missionaries and against the Chinese, but I made a speech from the Chinese standpoint and succeeded in getting a resolution passed about as follows: 'This meeting regrets exceedingly that the American and English Missionary Societies will persist in sending missionaries to China to attack the ancient faith of the Chinese, and we are very sorry that the missionaries will not remain in their own countries, and allow the Chinese to enjoy their own religion in their own way in their own country.' My speech was taken down in shorthand and sent to the Chinese Ambassador. He had it nicely written out in Chinese, beautifully bound, and sent it to Li Hung Chang. The latter sent it to the Emperor, and the Emperor gave me a decoration."

HOW A FIRST-CLASS FRAUD WAS EXPOSED.

"Tell about the exposure of the Dowe scheme."

"Some years ago a Hoboken barkeeper and a German tailor went to England to exploit the soundness of the alleged bullet-proof cloth. A whole town was placarded, to advertise Dowe's wonderful bullet-proof cloth, etc. The invention was shown at the El Cambria Theatre, and a great many of the old military men of England went to see this wonderful invention, for the secret of which the supposed inventors demanded two hundred thousand pounds. The thing actually shown, however, was not bullet-proof cloth, neither was it a bullet-proof coat, but a little shield about the size and thickness of a railway cushion, which was apparently of fibrous material, and would stop a bullet. A target was marked on a piece of paper, and a piece of paper folded over the gun. One of these pieces of paper fell into my hands. I saw where the bullet had entered, and where the flash came out. This was a complete 'give away,' as it showed exactly what was in the plan, viz., that it was a piece of sharp deception. I then put a notice in the paper that I had discovered a shield, steel, better than that of Herr Dowe; that his weighed twelve and one-half pounds to the square foot, and mine only ten; that he asked two hundred thousand pounds for his secret, whereas I would sell mine for seven shillings, sixpence. A great crowd of people came to see my supposed invention, and I showed the exact thing that Herr Dowe had, except that mine was thinner and lighter. I had used nickel steel where he had used chrome steel. Many people were very much disappointed, and many of them blackguarded me in the papers, but there was truth in all I said. I did exactly what I said I would, and beat Herr Dowe in the point of weight. This exposed the whole thing, and, at the end of three days, everybody in London knew that Herr Dowe and the Hoboken barkeeper had been deceiving the public. In fact, one of their own men revealed the secret, confessing that it was nothing more nor less than a piece of steel with a cushion around it. Then the newspaper men who had been abusing me roundly, because they did not understand, in the first place, invited me to London to a dinner, and Herr Dowe and the Hoboken barkeeper disappeared."

"To what do you attribute your success?"

"I never tried to exploit an invention till I had one to exploit.

That is, I never asked anyone to invest in a theory; and I never allowed my name to be used to promote worthless properties or projects."

MANUFACTURE

III

A POOR BOY ONCE BORROWED BOOKS NOW GIVES AWAY LIBRARIES.

SELFISH wealth stands surprised, amazed, almost indignant, at the announcement that Andrew Carnegie, instead of resting in Olympian luxury on the millions he has earned, and going to the grave with his gold tightly clutched in his stiffening fingers, proposes to expend the bulk of his riches, during his lifetime, for the benefit of his fellowmen. Great financiers, who, if they lived to be as old as Methuselah, could not use a tithe of their vast fortunes on their own ordinary maintenance, protest against Mr. Carnegie's plan of action, and declare that he ought to go on accumulating to the last. Others mildly suggest that his charity will be wasted on unworthy objects, and others frankly avow that they doubt the sincerity of his intentions. Altogether it may be said that Mr. Carnegie has stirred the very heart of Mammon as it has not been stirred since the Savior told the rich man to sell what he had and give to the poor.

IT IS HARDER NOW TO GET A START.

"There is no doubt," said Mr. Carnegie, in reply to a question from me, "that it is becoming harder and harder, as business gravitates more and more to immense concerns, for a young man without capital to get a start for himself, and in large cities it is especially so, where large capital is essential. Still it can be honestly said that there is no other country in the world, where able and energetic young men and women can so readily rise as in this. A president of a business college informed me, recently, that he has never been able to supply the demand for capable, first-class [Mark the adjective] bookkeepers, and his college has over nine hundred students. In America, young men of ability rise with most astonishing rapidity."

"As quickly as when you were a boy?"

"Much more so. When I was a boy, there were but very few important positions that a boy could aspire to. Everything had to be made. Now a boy doesn't need to make the place,—all he has to do is to fit himself to take it."

"Did you make your high places as you went along?"

"I shouldn't call them high, and I did not make the earliest ones. In starting new enterprises, of course, I made my place at the head of them. The earliest ones were the poorest kinds of positions, however."

"Where did you begin life?"

"In Dunfermline, Scotland. That was only my home during my earliest years. The service of my life has all been in this country."

"In Pittsburg?"

"Largely so. My father settled in Allegheny City, when I was only ten years old, and I began to earn my way in Pittsburg."

"Do you mind telling me what your first service was?"

"Not at all. I was a bobbin boy in a cotton factory, then an engine-man or boy in the same place, and later still I was a messenger boy for a telegraph company."

MR. CARNEGIE'S FIRST WAGES.

"At small wages, I suppose."
"One dollar and twenty cents a week was what I received as a bobbin boy, and I can tell you that I considered it pretty good, at that. When I was thirteen, I had learned to run a steam engine, and for that I received a dollar and eighty cents a week."
"You had no early schooling, then?"
"None, except such as I gave myself. There were no fine libraries then, but in Allegheny City, where I lived, there was a certain Colonel Anderson, who was well to do and of a philanthropic turn. He announced about the time I first began to work, that he would be in his library at his home, every Saturday, ready to lend books to working boys and men. He only had about four hundred volumes, but I doubt if ever so few books were put to better use. Only he who has longed, as I did, for Saturday to come, that the spring of knowledge might be opened anew to him, can understand what Colonel Anderson did for me and others of the boys of Allegheny. Quite a number of them have risen to eminence, and I think their rise can be easily traced to this splendid opportunity."
"How long did you remain an engine boy?"
"Not very long," Mr. Carnegie replied, "perhaps a year."
"And then?"
"I entered a telegraph office as a messenger boy."
Although Mr. Carnegie would not dwell much on this period, he once described it at a dinner given in honor of the American Consul at Dunfermline, Scotland, when he said—
"I awake from a dream that has carried me away back in the days of my boyhood, the day when the little white-haired Scottish laddie, dressed in a blue jacket, walked with his father into the telegraph office in Pittsburg to undergo examination as

an applicant for a position as messenger boy.

HIS FIRST GLIMPSE OF PARADISE.

"Well I remember when my uncle spoke to my parents about it, and my father objected, because I was then getting one dollar and eighty cents per week for running a small engine in a cellar in Allegheny City, but my uncle said a messenger's wages would be two dollars and fifty cents.... If you want an idea as to heaven on earth, imagine what it is to be taken from a dark cellar, where I fired the boiler from morning until night, and dropped into an office, where light shone from all sides, and around me books, papers, and pencils in profusion, and oh! the tick of those mysterious brass instruments on the desk, annihilating space and standing with throbbing spirits ready to convey any intelligence to the world! This was my first glimpse of paradise, and I walked on air."

"How did you manage to rise from this position?"

"Well, I learned how to operate a telegraph instrument, and then waited my opportunity to show that I was fit to be an operator. Eventually my chance came, as everyone's does."

The truth is that the boy had the appearance of one anxious to learn and quick to understand. James D. Reid, the superintendent of the office, and himself a Scotchman, favored the ambitious lad, and helped him. In his "History of the Telegraph," he says of him:—

"I liked the boy's looks, and it was easy to see that, though he was little, he was full of spirit. He had not been with me a month when he began to ask whether I would teach him to telegraph. I began to instruct him and found him an apt pupil. He spent all his spare time in practice, sending and receiving by sound and not by tape, as was largely the custom in those days. Pretty soon he could do as well as I could at the key, and then his ambition carried him away beyond doing the drudgery of messenger work."

"As you look back upon it," I said to Mr. Carnegie, "do you consider that so lowly a beginning is better than one a little less trying?"

IT IS BEST TO BEGIN AT THE BOTTOM.

"For young men starting upon their lifework, it is much the best to begin as I did, at the beginning, and occupy the most subordinate positions. Many of the present-day leading men of Pittsburg, who rose with me, had a serious responsibility thrust upon them at the very threshold of their careers. They were introduced to the broom, and spent the first hours of their business life sweeping out the office. I notice we have janitors and janitresses now in offices, and our young men, unfortunately, miss that salutary branch of early education. Still I would say to the boy who has the genius of the future partner in him, that if by chance the professional sweeper is absent any morning, do not hesitate to try your hand at the broom. It does not hurt the newest comer to sweep out the office if necessary."

"Did you?"

"Many's the time. And who do you suppose were my fellow sweepers? David McBargo, afterward superintendent of the Allegheny Valley Railroad; Robert Pitcairn, afterward superintendent of the Pennsylvania Railroad, and Mr. Moreland, subsequently City Attorney of Pittsburg. We all took turns, two each morning doing the sweeping; and now I remember Davie was so proud of his clean shirt bosom that he used to spread over it an old silk bandana handkerchief which he kept for the purpose, and we other boys thought he was putting on airs. So he was. None of us had a silk handkerchief."

"After you had learned to telegraph, did you consider that you had reached high enough?"

"Not in the least. My father died just at that time, and the burden of the support of the family fell upon me. I became an operator at twenty-five dollars a month, a sum which seemed to me almost a fortune. I earned a little additional money by copying telegraphic messages for the newspapers, and managed to keep the family independent."

HE WAS AN EXPERT TELEGRAPH OPERATOR.

More light on this period of Mr. Carnegie's career is given by the "Electric Age," which says: "He was a telegraph operator abreast of older and experienced men; and, although receiving messages by sound was, at that time, forbidden by authority as being unsafe, young Carnegie quickly acquired the art, and he can still stand behind the ticker and understand its language. As an operator, he delighted in full employment and the prompt discharge of business, and a big day's work was his chief pleasure."

"How long did you remain with the telegraph company?"

"Until I was given a place by the Pennsylvania Railroad Company."

"As an operator?"

"At first, until I showed how the telegraph could minister to railroad safety and success. Then I was made secretary to Thomas A. Scott, then superintendent, and not long afterward, when Colonel Scott became vice-president, I was made superintendent of the western division of the Pennsylvania Railroad."

Thinking of this period of his life, I asked Mr. Carnegie if his promotion was not a matter of chance, and whether he did not, at the time, feel it to be so. His answer was emphatic.

"Never. Young men give all kinds of reasons why, in their cases, failure is attributable to exceptional circumstances, which rendered success impossible. Some never had a chance, according to their own story. This is simply nonsense. No young man ever lived who had not a chance, and a splendid chance, too, if he was ever employed at all. He is assayed in the mind of his immediate superior, from the day he begins work, and, after a time, if he has merit, he is assayed in the council chambers of the firm. His ability, honesty, habits, associations, temper, disposition—all these are weighed and analyzed. The young man who never had a chance is the same young man who has been canvassed over and over again by his superiors, and found destitute of necessary qualifications, or is deemed unworthy of closer relations with the firm, owing to some objectionable act, habit or association, of which he thought his employers ignorant."

"It sounds true."

THE RIGHT MEN IN DEMAND.

"It is. Another class of young men attribute failure to rise to employers having near relatives or favorites whom they advance unfairly. They also insist that their employers dislike brighter intelligence than their own, and are disposed to discourage aspiring genius, and delighted in keeping young men down. There is nothing in this. On the contrary, there is no one suffering more for lack of the right man in the right place than the average employer, nor anyone more anxious to find him."

"Was this your theory on the subject when you began working for the railroad company?"

"I had no theory then, although I have formulated one since. It lies mainly in this: Instead of the question, 'What must I do for my employer?' substitute, 'What can I do?' Faithful and conscientious discharge of duties assigned you is all very well, but the verdict in such cases generally is that you perform your present duties so well, that you would better continue performing them. Now, this will not do. It will not do for the coming partners. There must be something beyond this. We make clerks, bookkeepers, treasurers, bank tellers of this class, and there they remain to the end of the chapter. The rising man must do something exceptional, and beyond the range of his special department. He must attract attention."

HOW TO ATTRACT ATTENTION.

"How can he do that?"

"Well, if he is a shipping clerk, he may do so by discovering in an invoice an error with which he has nothing to do and which has escaped the attention of the proper party. If a weighing clerk, he may save the firm by doubting the adjustment of the scales, and having them corrected, even if this be the province of the master mechanic. If a messenger boy, he can lay the seed of promotion by going beyond the letter of his instructions in order to secure the desired reply. There is no service so low and simple, neither any so high, in which the young man of ability and willing disposition cannot readily and almost daily prove himself capable of greater trust and usefulness, and, what is equally important, show his invincible determination to rise."

"In what manner did you reach out to establish your present great fortune?" I asked.

"By saving my money. I put a little money aside, and it served me later as a matter of credit. Also, I invested in a sleeping-car industry, which paid me well."

CARNEGIE AND THE SLEEPING-CAR.

Although I tried earnestly to get the great iron-king to talk of this, he said little, because the matter has been fully dealt with by him in his "Triumphant Democracy." From his own story there, it appears that, one day at this time, when Mr. Carnegie still had his fortune to make, he was on a train examining the line from a rear window of a car, when a tall, spare man, accosted him and asked him to look at an invention he had made. He drew from a green bag a small model of a sleeping-berth for railway cars, and proceeded to point out its advantages. It was Mr. T. T. Woodruff, the inventor of the sleeping-car. Mr. Carnegie tells the story himself in "Triumphant Democracy:"—

"He had not spoken a moment, before, like a flash, the whole range of the discovery burst upon me. 'Yes,' I said, 'that is something which this continent must have.'

"Upon my return, I laid it before Mr. Scott, declaring that it was one of the inventions of the age. He remarked: 'You are enthusiastic, young man, but you may ask the inventor to come and let me see it.' I did so, and arrangements were made to build two trial cars, and run them on the Pennsylvania Railroad. I was offered an interest in the venture, which, of course, I gladly accepted.

"The notice came that my share of the first payment was $217.50. How well I remember the exact sum! But two hundred and seventeen dollars and a half were as far beyond my means as if it had been millions. I was earning fifty dollars per month, however, and had prospects, or at least I always felt that I had. I decided to call on the local banker and boldly ask him to advance the sum upon my interest in the affair. He put his hand on my shoulder and said: 'Why, of course, Andie; you are all right. Go ahead! Here is the money.'

"It is a proud day for a man when he pays his last note, but not to be named in comparison with the day in which he makes his first one, and gets a banker to take it. I have tried both, and I know. The cars paid the subsequent payments from their earnings. I paid my first note from my savings, so much per month, and thus did I get my foot upon fortune's ladder. It was easy to climb after that."

"I would like some expression from you," I said to Mr. Carnegie, "in reference to the importance of laying aside money from one's earnings, as a young man."

THE MARK OF A MILLIONAIRE.

"You can have it. There is one sure mark of the coming partner, the future millionaire; his revenues always exceed his expenditures. He begins to save early, almost as soon as he begins to earn. I should say to young men, no matter how little it may be possible to save, save that little. Invest it securely, not necessarily in bonds, but in anything which you have good reason to believe will be profitable; but no gambling with it, remember. A rare chance will soon present itself for investment. The little you have saved will prove the basis for an amount of credit utterly surprising to you. Capitalists trust the saving young man: For, every hundred dollars you can produce as the result of hard-won savings, Midas, in search of a partner, will lend or credit a thousand; for every thousand, fifty thousand. It is not capital that your seniors require, it is the man who has proved that he has the business habits which create capital. So it is the first hundred dollars saved that tells."

"What," I asked Mr. Carnegie, "was the next enterprise with which you identified yourself?"

A FORTUNATE LAND PURCHASE.

"In company with several others, I purchased the now famous Storey farm, on Oil Creek, Pennsylvania, where a well had been bored and natural oil struck the year before. This proved a very profitable investment."

"Were you satisfied to rest with these enterprises in your hands?" I asked.

"No; railway bridges were then built almost exclusively of wood, but the Pennsylvania Railroad had begun to experiment with cast iron for bridge building. It struck me that the railway bridge of the future must be of iron, and I organized, in Pittsburg, a company for the construction of iron bridges. That was the Keystone Bridge Works. We built the first iron bridge across the Ohio."

His entrance to the realm of steel was much too long for Mr. Carnegie to discuss, although he was not unwilling to give information relating to the great subject. It appears that he realized the immensity of the steel manufacturing business at once. The Union Iron Mills soon followed as one of his enterprises, and, later the famous Edgar Thompson Steel Rail Mill. The last was the outcome of a visit to England, in 1868, when Carnegie noticed that English railways were discarding iron for steel rails. The Bessemer process had been then perfected, and was making its way in all the iron-producing countries. Carnegie, recognizing that it was destined to revolutionize the iron business, introduced it into his mills and made steel rails with which he was enabled to compete with English manufacturers.

THE HOMESTEAD STEEL WORKS.

His next enterprise was the purchase of the Homestead Steel Works,—his great rival of Pittsburg. By 1888, he had built or acquired seven distinct iron and steel works. All the plants of this great firm are within a radius of five miles of Pittsburg. In no other part of the world can be found such an aggregation of splendidly equipped steel works as those controlled by Carnegie and his associates. It now comprises the Homestead Steel Works, the Edgar Thompson Steel Works and Furnaces, the Duquesne Steel Works and Furnaces, all within two miles of one another; the Lucy Furnaces, the Keystone Bridge Works, the Upper Union Rolling Mills, and the Lower Union Rolling Mills.

In all branches, including the great coke works, mines, etc., there are employed twenty-five thousand men. The monthly pay roll exceeds one million, one hundred and twenty-five thousand dollars, or nearly fifty thousand dollars for each working day.

"You believe in taking active measures," I said, "to make men successful."

"Yes, I believe in anything which will help men to help themselves. To induce them to save, every workman, in our company, is allowed to deposit part of his earnings, not exceeding two thousand dollars, with the firm, on which the high interest rate of six per cent. is allowed. The firm also lends to any of its workmen to buy a lot, or to build a house, taking its pay by installments."

"Has this contributed any to the success of your company?"

INFANCY

A STRENGTHENING POLICY.

"I think so. The policy of giving a personal interest to the men who render exceptional service is strengthening. With us there are many such, and every year several more are added as partners. It is the policy of the concern to interest every superintendent in the works, every head of a department, every exceptional young man. Promotion follows exceptional service, and there is no favoritism."

"All you have said so far merely gives the idea of getting money, without any suggestion as to the proper use of great wealth. Will you say something on that score?"

"My views are rather well known, I think. What a man owns is already subordinate, in America, to what he knows; but, in the final aristocracy, the question will not be either of these, but what has he done for his fellows? Where has he shown generosity and self-abnegation? Where has he been a father to the fatherless? And the cause of the poor; where has he searched that out? How he has worshipped God will not be asked in that day, but how he has served man."

MR. CARNEGIE'S PHILANTHROPY.

That Mr. Carnegie has lived up, in the past, and is still living up to this radical declaration of independence from the practice of men who have amassed fortunes around him, will be best shown by a brief enumeration of some of his almost unexampled philanthropies. His largest gift has been to the city of Pittsburg, the scene of his early trials and later triumphs. There he has built, at a cost of more than a million dollars, a magnificent library, museum, concert hall and picture gallery, all under one roof, and endowed it with a fund of another million, the interest of which (fifty thousand dollars per annum), is being devoted to the purchase of the best works of American art. Other libraries, to be connected with this largest as a center, are now being constructed, which will make the city of Pittsburg and its environs a beneficiary of his generosity to the extent of five million dollars.

In his native land, Scotland, thrift is a virtue that is taught with the alphabet; and, when the twelve-year-old "Andy" Carnegie came to America with his father and mother, he was full of the notion of thrift and its twin brother, hard work.

CARNEGIE'S VIEWS ON THRIFT.

Once he wrote on the subject of thrift for a Scottish journal. He said:—

"The accumulation of millions is usually the result of enterprise and judgment, and some exceptional ability or organization. It does not come from savings, in the ordinary sense of the word. Men who, in old age, strive only to increase their already too great hoards, are usually slaves of the habit of hoarding, formed in their youth. At first they own the money they have made and saved. Later in life the money owns them, and they cannot help themselves, so overpowering is the force of habit, either for good or evil. It is the abuse of the civilized saving instinct, and not its use, that produces this class of men. No one needs to be afraid of falling a victim to this abuse of the habit, if he always bears in mind that whatever surplus wealth may come to him is to be regarded as a sacred trust, which he is bound to administer for the good of his fellows. The man should always be master. He should keep money in the position of a useful servant; he must never let it be his master and make a miser of him. A man's first duty is to acquire a competence and be independent, then to do something for his needy neighbors who are less favored than himself."

Mr. Carnegie has always lived up to this doctrine. He has made philanthropy a factor of existence. Already he has endowed over ninety libraries in different cities of the United States, having spent about $4,500,000 in this manner alone. He believes that a man can learn the science of true life and success in good books. In Scotland, where many of the residents of a poor hamlet have been benefited by his generosity, he is called "the good angel." Whenever he visits any of these places, he is a greater man than the King of Great Britain.

While thus endowing the city where his fortune was made, he has not forgotten other places endeared to him by association or by interest. To the Allegheny Free Library he has given $375,000; to the Braddock Free Library, $250,000; to the Johnstown Free Library, $50,000, and to the Fairfield (Iowa) Library, $40,000. To his native land he has been scarcely less generous. To the Edinburgh Free Library he has given $250,000, and to his native town of Dunfermline, $90,000. Other Scottish towns to the number of ten have received helpful donations of amounts not quite so large.

"I should like you to say some other important things for the young man to learn and benefit by."

"Our young partners in the Carnegie company have all won their spurs by showing that we did not know half as well what was wanted as they did. Some of them have acted upon occasions with me as if they owned the firm and I was but some airy New Yorker, presuming to advise upon what I knew very little about. Well, they are not now interfered with. They were the true bosses,—the very men we were looking for."

"THE MISFORTUNE OF BEING RICH MEN'S SONS."

"Is this all for the poor boy?"

"Every word. I trust that few, if any, of your readers have the misfortune to be rich men's sons. They are heavily weighted in the race. A basketful of bonds is the heaviest basket a young man ever had to carry. He generally gets to staggering under it. The vast majority of rich men's sons are unable to resist the temptations to which wealth subjects them, and they sink to unworthy lives. It is not from this class that the poor beginner has rivalry to fear. The partner's sons will never trouble you much, but look out that some boys poorer, much poorer, than yourselves, whose parents cannot afford to give them any schooling, do not challenge you at the post and pass you at the grand stand. Look out for the boy who has to plunge into work direct from the common school, and begins by sweeping out the office. He is the probable dark horse that will take all the money and win all the applause.

"The first thing that a man should learn to do is to save his money. By saving his money he promotes thrift,—the most valued of all habits. Thrift is the great fortune-maker. It draws the line between the savage and the civilized man. Thrift not only develops the fortune, but it develops, also, the man's character."

IV

A GOOD SHOEMAKER BECOMES DETROIT'S BEST MAYOR AND MICHIGAN'S GREATEST GOVERNOR.

AN interview with Hon. Hazen S. Pingree, Governor of Michigan, was not an easy thing to obtain. "Approachable?" Very. He was a great favorite with newspaper men, but the most-sought-after man in Michigan. When he arrived at the simply furnished room that served as his official headquarters in Detroit, it was to find it bordered with a human wainscoting, each anxious member of which was waiting patiently, or otherwise, to ask some favor of the chief executive. As he entered the room suddenly became quiet; for there was something about the Governor's powerful personality that compelled attention. But soon each want, no matter how small, was attended to in his kindly but straight-forward way.

An interesting medley of petitioners was present on the day of my interview. The first was a widowed mother requesting a favor for her son—a wreck of the Spanish-American war.

"I'll do the best I can for you," said the governor heartily as she left the room—and everyone knew what that meant.

Next came a gayly-dressed young woman, with a bill from the mint of her own imagination, which she asked the Governor to please push through the legislature. She was patiently referred to the representative from her district. Then a soldier stood before him with a transportation snarl to untangle; a book agent; a broadcloth-coated dandy, and a street laborer, each seeking help; and then a gaunt, ill-clad old woman, who in broken English, with harrowing tears and gestures of despair, laid her humble burdens in supplication before him. It was a touching picture.

Hers was not a case to lay before the Governor of the State, but she will never know it, poor woman, for the generous hand of the great-hearted man slid quickly down to the nest of the golden eagle that sent her gratefully away.

"You are not a native of the State you govern," said I, as the Governor leisurely seated himself for the interview.

"No; I was born in Denmark, Maine. My father owned a forty-acre farm, and I was brought up there until I was about seventeen years old."

"And you did——"

"Just what any one would do on a small farm; worked in summer and went to school in the winter. Then I started out to make my own way in the world, and the first work I found was in a cotton mill at Saco, Maine. In 1860, I went to Hopkinton, Massachusetts, and learned the trade of a cutter in a shoe factory. Soon after that the war broke out."

"And you enlisted?"

"Yes, I have two honorable discharges as a private. I value them more than my position as governor."

"How long were you in the war?"

"From 1862 until its close. I first enlisted in Company F, First Massachusetts Heavy Artillery, and, with that regiment, took part in the battles of Bull Run, Fredericksburg Road, Harris Farm, Cold Harbor, Spottsylvania Court House, North Anna and South Anna."

"Then you know something of the horrors of war from your own experience?"

"Yes; that is the reason I am an advocate of the universal peace project."

"You believe in that?"

"Decidedly; and, moreover, I believe that ten years from now every man who calls himself a Christian will be ready to stand by the side of the Emperor of Russia in his plea for peace."

"Let us return to your experience in the war. Were you ever a prisoner?"

"Several others and myself were captured on May 25, 1864, by a squad of Mosby's men. We were confined five months at Andersonville; and from there were taken to Salisbury prison in North Carolina, then to Millen, Georgia, where we were exchanged in November, 1864. I rejoined my regiment in front of Petersburg, and was in the expedition to Weldon Railroad, the battles of Boynton Road, Petersburg, Sailors' Creek, Farmsville, and Appomattox."

"And after the war?"

"I came to Detroit and obtained employment in a shoe factory. Soon after that my partner and myself started one of our own. He had a little less than a thousand dollars, and I had $460—left from my army pay."

"That seemed a large sum, I suppose?"

"Yes, and I thought if I could ever get to making fifty pairs of shoes a day I would be perfectly happy."

The number is amusingly small, when it is remembered that this factory, the embryo of which he spoke, grew up under the Governor's personal supervision, until it is now one of the largest in the United States.

"But tell me, Governor, when you were starting out in life, did you ever look forward to the career you have carved out for yourself?"

"No," said he, with the promptness that characterizes all of his speech; "I never had anything mapped out in my life. I did whatever there happened to be for me to do, and let the result take care of itself."

"Is it the same with your political success, or is that the outgrowth of youthful ambition?"

HOW HE BECAME MAYOR OF DETROIT.

"No, I was pushed into that by accident. I had never been in the common council chamber before I was elected Mayor of Detroit. The thing that caught me was that my friends began to say I was afraid of the position, so, of course, I had to accept the nomination to prove that I wasn't."

This was clever of his friends. The fact is that, at that time, the city needed the Governor's brains to manage its affairs. He was elected Mayor of Detroit four consecutive terms and was in his eighth year as mayor when he resigned. Even his most earnest political opponents admit that he was the best mayor the city ever had.

"But, during the formative years of your career, did you ever worry over the possibility of failure?"

"No," said the Governor serenely, "I never did, and don't now. I was never given to worrying."

In this as in other ways, Mr. Pingree was remarkable. During the stormiest of his political times he was never in the least disturbed when he reached home, and he would sleep as peacefully as a child.

"What would you suggest, Governor, as the best route by which the young man of to-day may obtain success?"

"He can do one of two things: go to work for somebody else; or, if he cannot stand that, he can buy a small farm."

"Then you think there is not the chance in the United States now that there was thirty years ago?"

"There isn't a doubt about it. The young men of to-day are to be pitied—there isn't anything for them to do. The subject is a serious one," said the Governor, speaking rapidly. "Why, if I had nothing, I wouldn't know how to advise my own son to start. I don't claim to know much, but I do understand a little about the shoe business, and I can tell you honestly that, with the knowledge I have gained in many years of experience, and with the influence of my friends, I could not start in the shoe business to-day with the chance of success that I had then."

"And the causes of this?"

"Are trusts and monopolies."

"And the result?"

A GREAT CHANGE PROPHESIED.

"There will be a great change in this country before many years. Free schools have so educated the people that they will not submit to this injustice forever, even though it is organized against them."

"But how will this change be effected?"

"Through the splitting up of political parties—but it is sure to come."

"Recognizing the conditions that the young man of to-day has to contend with, what guide-posts would you point out to him?"

"In the first place, I would advise every young man to be honest and outspoken at all times. What people want is open, frank talk. There is too much catering and palavering and roundabout talking nowadays. It is a great mistake. Then, of course, in order to accomplish anything, the young man must have plenty of energy and perseverance."

By inheritance, Governor Pingree was a patriot and fighter. In his possession were three historic muskets, one of which was used by his great-grandfather in the Revolutionary War; another by his grandfather in the War of 1812, and one by himself in the Civil War. His first American forefather was Moses Pingree, who emigrated to this country in 1640. Many of his descendants have figured with distinction in American history, among them being Samuel Everett Pingree, Governor of Vermont from 1884 to 1886.

Governor Pingree was a strikingly interesting example of self-earned success. His indomitable will, tireless energy and unyielding perseverance were the machinery with which he manufactured the fabric of his career. But the pattern was stamped by his own individuality, and was like no other ever seen—it was *sui generis*.

On the battlefield of public life, Governor Pingree was a general who said, "Come on!" not "Go on!" He acted with the bold, unfettered authority that springs from an honest belief in the justice of his opinions, and never put his plans out of focus by shifting his ground. When once resolved, he was as immovable as a fixed star. He was absolutely fearless because he was absolutely honest, and was not afraid to fight, single-handed, the greatest financial power the world has ever known.

The political spider was never able to bind his arms with the thread of party combination—scheme or intrigue. He was at all times a free lance, fearless and ceaseless in his efforts to chip the veneer from gilded fraud, to pierce the heart of injustice and to befriend those not able to shield themselves. He was a champion of the people and a believer in them.

HE WAS NOT A DEMAGOGUE.

"But they call you a demagogue. How does that accusation affect you?"

The Governor smiled, as if he considered it a good joke.

"Well, that amuses me," said he. "They don't do that around here any more. They've worn it out, I guess. No, it doesn't disturb me a particle. I always go on the principle that lies never hurt anybody."

Governor Pingree was a man of powerful physique and dignity of bearing. But he was delightfully oblivious to his own importance, and was entirely devoid of ostentation in everything that he did or said. His disposition was buoyant, his manner that of frank simplicity, and he was prodigal in his generosity and sympathy for those in need. In his private business, the welfare of his employees was always balanced in the scale with his own.

In the camps of war he was known as "Father Pingree," and when the boys returned to Detroit he was the first to greet them. But no one ever saw him in an open carriage behind the band; he was always away off in a corner of the station, where the ambulances were waiting, giving a word of encouragement to this poor fellow and patting that one on the back. He worked for forty hours at a time, without a thought of sleep, to keep up a cheerful welcome, though many a time he was seen to turn away just long enough to brush the tears from his eyes.

GOVERNOR PINGREE'S LUXURIOUS HOME.

The home life of Governor Pingree was as beautiful as his life in public was successful. His residence, a three-story gray stone house, was a model of quiet elegance and refinement, and there his greatest happiness was found.

The accusation was often made that the people of Michigan did not appreciate the Governor. However, during his last election, he was not a prophet without honor in his own country, for the long-continued climbing up of his majority caused one of the local newspapers to suggest that the State set aside special holidays to satisfy the appetite for voting for Pingree.

COMMERCE

V

DETERMINED NOT TO REMAIN POOR,
A FARMER BOY BECOMES A MERCHANT PRINCE

MARSHALL FIELD, one of the greatest merchants of the United States, and that means of the world, is not readily accessible to interviewers. He probably feels, like most men of real prominence, that his place in the history of his time is established, and he is not seeking for the fame that is certain to attend his name and his business achievements. No more significant story, none more full of stimulus, of encouragement, of brain-inspiring and pulse-thrilling potency has been told in any romance. It is grand in its very simplicity, in its very lack of assumption of special gifts or extraordinary foresight. The Phœnix-like revival from the ashes of ruined Chicago is spoken of by Mr. Field as an incident in the natural and to be expected in the order of events. In Marshall Field it was no doubt natural and to be expected, and it touches the very keynote of the character of the celebrated western merchant, sprung from rugged eastern soil, whose career is an example to be studied with profit by every farmer boy, by every office boy, by every clerk and artisan,—yes, and by every middle-aged business man, whether going along smoothly or confronted by apparently ruinous circumstances, throughout our broad land.

I was introduced to Mr. Field in the private office of Mr. Harry G. Selfridge, his most trusted lieutenant, and this first of interviews with the head of Chicago's greatest mercantile house followed.

"My object," I said to Mr. Field, "is to obtain your opinion as to what makes for and constitutes success in life."

"That can be quickly given," said Mr. Field; "what would you like to know?"

"I wish to know something of your early life, and under what conditions you began it."

"I was born in Conway, Massachusetts, in 1835. My father's farm was among the rocks and hills of that section, and not very fertile."

"And the conditions were?"

"Hard."

"You mean that you were poor?"

"Yes, as all people were in those days, more or less. My father was a farmer. I was brought up under farming conditions, such as they were at that time."

HIS PARENTS HELPED HIM.

"Did the character and condition of your parents tend in any way to form your ambition for commercial distinction?"

"Yes, somewhat. My father was a man who, I consider, had good judgment. He made a success out of the farming business. My mother was more intellectually bent, if anything, and, naturally, both my parents were anxious that their boys should amount to something in life. Their interest and care helped me."

"Had you early access to books?"

"No; I had but few books, scarcely any to speak of. There was not much time for literature. Such books as we had, though, I made use of."

"Were you so placed that your commercial instincts could be nourished by contact with that side of life?" I asked.

"Yes, in a measure. Not any more so than any other boy raised in that neighborhood. I had a leaning toward business, and took up with it as early as possible."

"Were you naturally of a saving disposition?"

"Oh, yes. I had to be. Those were saving times. A dollar looked very big to us boys in those days, and as we had difficult labor earning it, it was not quickly spent. I may say I was naturally saving, however, and was determined not to remain poor."

"Did you attend both school and college?"

"Only the common and high schools at home, but not for long. I had no college training. Indeed, I cannot say that I had much of any public school education. I left home when I was seventeen years of age, and, of course, had not time to study closely."

"What was the nature of your first venture in trade, Mr. Field?"

"My first venture was made as a clerk in a country store at Pittsfield, Massachusetts, where all things were sold, including dry goods, and there I remained for four years. There I picked up my first knowledge of that business."

"Do you consider those years well spent?"

"I think my employer did, anyway." He laughed.

"I saved my earnings and attended strictly to business, and so made them valuable years to me."

"Was there no inducement to remain there as you were?"

"Yes; before I went west, my employer offered me a quarter interest in his business if I would remain with him. Even after I had been here several years, he wrote and offered me a third interest if I would go back. But I was already too well placed."

"Did you fancy that you were destined for some other field than that in which you have since distinguished yourself?"

ALWAYS INTERESTED IN COMMERCE.

"No, I think not. I was always interested in the commercial side of life, and always thought I would be a merchant. To this end, I bent my energies, and soon realized that, successful or not, my labor would always be of a commercial nature."

"When did you come to Chicago?" I inquired.

"I caught what was then the prevalent fever to come west, and grow up with the country, and west I came. I entered as a clerk in the dry goods house of Cooley, Woodsworth & Co., in South Water street."

"Did you foresee Chicago's growth in any way?"

"No, there was no guarantee at that time that the place would ever become the western metropolis. The town had plenty of ambition and pluck; but the possibilities of greatness were hardly visible."

It is interesting to note in this connection that the story of Mr. Field's progress is a wonderfully close index of Chicago's marvelous growth. An almost exact parallel may be drawn between the career of the individual and the growth of the town. Chicago was organized in 1837, two years after Mr. Field was born on the far-off farm in New England, and the place then had a population of a little more than four thousand. In 1856, when Mr. Field, fully equipped for a successful mercantile career, became a resident of the future metropolis of the west, the population had grown to little more than eighty-four thousand. Mr. Field's prosperity advanced in strides parallel to those of the city; with Chicago he was stricken but not crushed by the great fire of 1871, and with Chicago he advanced again to higher achievement and far greater prosperity than before the calamity.

"What were your equipments for success when you started as a clerk here in Chicago, in 1856?"

"Health, sound principles, I hope, and ambition,"

answered Mr. Field.

"And brains," I suggested; but he only smiled.

"What were the conditions here?"

"Well, merit did not have to wait for dead men's shoes in a growing town, of course. Good qualities were usually promptly discovered, and men were pushed forward rapidly."

"How long did you remain a clerk?"

"Only four years. In 1860, I was made a partner, and in 1865, there was a partial reorganization, and the firm consisted after that of Mr. Leiter, Mr. Palmer and myself (Field, Palmer & Leiter). Two years later Mr. Palmer withdrew, and until 1881 the style of the firm was Field, Leiter & Co. Mr. Leiter retired in that year, and since then it has been as at present: (Marshall Field & Co.)

"What contributed most to the great growth of your business?" I asked.

"To answer that question," said Mr. Field, "would be to review the condition of the west from the time Chicago began until the fire in 1871. Everything was coming this way: immigration, railways and water traffic, and Chicago was enjoying what was called 'flush times.' There were things to learn about the country, and the man who learned the quickest fared the best. For instance, the comparative newness of rural communities and settlements made a knowledge of local solvency impossible. The old state banking system prevailed, and speculation of every kind was rampant. The panic of 1857 swept almost everything away except the house I worked for, and I learned that the reason they survived was because they understood the nature of the new country, and did a cash business. That is, they bought for cash, and sold on thirty and sixty days, instead of giving the customers, whose financial condition you could hardly tell anything about, all the time they wanted. When the panic came, they had no debts, and little owing to them, and so they weathered it all right. I learned what I consider my best lesson, and that was to do a cash business."

HIS PRINCIPLES OF BUSINESS.

"What were some of the principles you applied to your business?" I questioned.

"Well, I made it a point that all goods should be exactly what they were represented to be. It was a rule of the house that an exact scrutiny of the quality of all goods purchased should be maintained, and that nothing was to induce the house to place upon the market any line of goods at a shade of variation from their real value. Every article sold must be regarded as warranted, and every purchaser must be enabled to feel secure."

"Did you suffer any losses or reverses during your career?"

"No loss except by the fire of 1871. It swept away everything,—about three and a half millions. We were, of course, protected by insurance, which would have been sufficient against any ordinary calamity of the kind. But the disaster was so sweeping that some of the companies which had insured our property were blotted out, and a long time passed before our claims against others were settled. We managed, however, to start again. There were no buildings of brick or stone left standing, but there were some great shells of horse-car barns at State and Twentieth streets which were not burned, and I hired those. We put up signs announcing that we would continue business uninterruptedly, and then rushed the work of fitting things up and getting in the stock."

"Did the panic of 1873 effect your business?"

"Not at all. We didn't have any debts."

"May I ask what you consider to have been the turning-point in your career,—the point after which there was no more danger of poverty?"

"Saving the first five thousand dollars I ever had, when I might just as well have spent the moderate salary I made. Possession of that sum, once I had it, gave me the ability to meet opportunities.

That I consider the turning-point."

PERSEVERANCE, MR. FIELD'S ESSENTIAL TRAIT.

"What one trait of your character do you look upon as having been the most essential to your successful career?"

"Perseverance," said Mr. Field; but another at hand insisted upon the addition of "good judgment" to this, which Mr. Field indifferently acknowledged. "If I am compelled to lay claim to these traits," he went on, "it is simply because I have tried to practice them, and because the trying has availed me much, I suppose. I have always tried to make all my acts and commercial moves the result of definite consideration and sound judgment. There were never any great ventures or risks,—nothing exciting whatever. I simply practiced honest, slow-growing business methods, and tried to back them with energy and good system."

"Have you always been a hard-worker?"

"No," Mr. Field said, with the shadow of a smile. "I have never believed in overworking, either as applied to myself or others. It is always paid for with a short life, and I do not believe in it."

"Has there ever been a time in your life when you gave as much as eighteen hours a day to your work?"

"Never. That is, never as a steady practice. During the time of the fire in 1871, there was a short period in which I worked very hard. For several weeks then I worked the greater part of night and day, as almost anyone would have done in my place. My fortune, however, has not been made in that manner, and, as I have said, I believe in reasonable hours for everyone, but close attention during those hours."

"Do you work as much as you once did?"

"I never worked very many hours a day. Besides, people do not work as many hours a day now as they once did. The day's labor has shortened in the last twenty years for everyone. Still, granting that, I cannot say that I work as much as I once did, and

I frankly admit that I do not feel the need of it."

"Do you believe," I went on, "that a man should cease laboring before his period of usefulness is over, so that he may enjoy some of the results of his labor before death, or do you believe in retaining constant interest in affairs while strength lasts?"

"As to that, I hold the French idea, that a man ought to retire when he has gained a competence wherewith to do so. I think that is a very good idea. But I do not believe that when a man retires, or no longer attends to his private business in person every day, he has given up interest in the affairs of the world. He may be, in fact should be, doing wider and greater work when he has abandoned his private business, so far as personal attention is concerned."

QUALITIES THAT MAKE FOR SUCCESS.

"What, Mr. Field," I said, "do you consider to be the first requisite for success in life, so far as the young beginner is concerned?"

"The qualities of honesty, energy, frugality, integrity, are more necessary than ever to-day, and there is no success without them. They are so often urged that they have become commonplace, but they are really more prized than ever."

"I should like to know what you believe should be the aim of the young man of to-day?"

"He should aim," said Mr. Field, "to possess the qualities I have mentioned."

"By some, however," I suggested, "these are looked upon as a means to an aim only. Would you say to the young man, 'get wealth?'"

"Not," Mr. Field answered, "without practicing unflinchingly these virtues."

"Would you say to him, 'acquire distinction?'"

"Not at any expense to his moral character. I can only say,

'practice these virtues and do the best you can.' Any good fortune that comes by such methods is deserved and admirable."

"Do you believe a college education for the young man to be a necessity in the future?"

"Not for business purposes. Better training will become more and more a necessity. The truth is, with most young men, a college education means that just at the time when they should be having business principles instilled into them, and be getting themselves energetically pulled together for their life's work, they are sent to college. Then intervenes what many a young man looks back on as the jolliest time of his life,—four years of college. Often when he comes out of college the young man is unfitted by this good time to buckle down to hard work, and the result is a failure to grasp opportunities that would have opened the way for a successful career."

"Would you say that happiness consists in labor, or in contemplation of labor well done, or in increased possibility of doing more labor?"

"I should say," said Mr. Field, "that a man finds happiness in all three. There certainly is no pleasure in idleness. I believe, as I have said, that a man, upon giving up business, does not necessarily cease laboring, but really does, or should do, more in a larger sense. He should interest himself in public affairs. There is no happiness in mere dollars. After they are had one cannot use but a moderate amount of them. It is given a man to eat so much, to wear so much, and to have so much shelter, and more he cannot use. When money has supplied these, its mission, so far as the individual is concerned, is fulfilled, and man must look further and higher. It is only in the wider public affairs, where money is a moving force toward the general welfare, that the possessor of it can possibly find pleasure, and that only in doing constantly more."

"What," I said, "in your estimation, is the greatest good a man can do?"

"The greatest good he can do is to cultivate himself in order that he may be of greater use to humanity."

"What one suggestion," I said, in conclusion, "can you give to the young men of to-day, that will be most useful to them, if observed?"

"Regardless," said Mr. Field, "of any opinion of mine, or any wish on the part of the young men for wealth, distinction or praise, we know that to be honest is best. There is nothing better, and we also know that nothing can be more helpful than this when combined with other essential qualities."

VI

HONESTY, THE FOUNDATION OF A GREAT MERCHANT'S CAREER

THE men who manipulate the levers that move the world, with few exceptions, were once poor boys. One of the largest retail stores in the world, in Philadelphia, and one of the handsomest stores in America, in New York, are monuments of the genius, industry and integrity of a "boy with no chance" who has become the peer of any of the merchant kings of our century. He is also one of the very foremost in many other enterprises.

To accomplish all these various things, it would be supposed that Mr. Wanamaker must have been a pet of fortune from the first. But that is not so. He began with nothing, as money goes, and has pushed his way to the top by sheer force of character, and by unwearying work.

I know of no career in this country that offers more encouragement to young people. It shows what persistency can do; it shows what intelligent, well-directed, tireless effort can do; and it proves that a man may devote himself to helping others, to the Sunday school, to the church, to broad philanthropy, and still be wonderfully successful in a business way.

A STANCH INHERITANCE.

John Wanamaker, the boy, had no single thing in all his surroundings to give him an advantage over any one of hundreds of other boys in the city of Philadelphia. Indeed, there were hundreds of other boys of his own age for whom anyone would have felt safe in prophesying a more notable career. But young Wanamaker had an inheritance beyond that of almost any of the others. It was not money; very few boys in all that great city had less money than John Wanamaker, and comparatively few families of average position but were better off in the way of worldly goods. John Wanamaker's inheritance, that stood him in such good stead in after life, was good health, good habits, a clean mind, thrift in money matters, and tireless devotion to whatever he thought to be duty.

He went to school some, not very much; he assisted his mother in the house a great deal, and around his father's brickyard he was very helpful so far as a boy could be helpful in such hard work. But he had ambition beyond such things, and in 1852, when in his fifteenth year, he found work with a publishing house at $1.50 a week.

I know a number of people who were well acquainted with John Wanamaker when he was a book publisher's boy. Most of them say that he was an exceptionally promising boy; that he was studious as well as attentive to business. Some of them declare that he used to buy a book or some such gift for his mother regularly with part of his savings. This may be partly romance,— the exaggerated remembrance that most people have of a boy who, as a man, cuts a notable figure in the world. Very likely he did buy some books, but the best that I can get is that, after all, he was very much like other boys, except that he did not take kindly to rough play, or do much playing of any kind, and that he was saving of his money. He was earnest in his work, unusually earnest for a boy, and so when, a little later, he went to a Market street clothing house and asked for a place, he had no difficulty in getting it, nor had he any trouble in holding it.

HE WAS ALWAYS PROMPT.

His effort was to be first at the store in the morning, and he was very likely to be one of the last, if not the last at the store in the evening. But he did not expect credit for this. Men who worked with him in the Tower Hall clothing store say that he was always bright, willing, accommodating, and very seldom out of temper. If there was an errand, "John" was always prompt and glad to do it. And so the store people liked him, and the proprietor liked him, and, when he began to sell clothing, the customers liked him. He was considerate of their interests. He did not try to force undesirable goods upon them. He treated them so that when they came again they would be apt to ask, "Where is John?" There was nothing in all this that any boy could not have done; it is simply the spirit that any boy or young man should show now,—must show if he expects to succeed wonderfully. Of course this could only lead to something higher. An ambitious young man, such as John Wanamaker, was not to be contented to sell goods all his days for other people. It was not long before he became secretary of the Young Men's Christian Association at $1,000 a year. In the course of a few years he had saved $2,000, when, joining with a friend who had $2,000, they decided to open a clothing store of their own.

Now here was successful growth without one single outside influence to help the young man along. He got his first situation without influence. He got into Tower Hall without influence. His earnestness, activity and ability got him the secretaryship. He saved $2,000 while other young men, who perhaps had earned many times more than he, had saved nothing. He had made friends among the customers of the old store, and he had not only made friends of many of the employees there, but he had impressed them all with the feeling that here was a young man whom it was safe to tie to. He had also made friends among church people and helpful folk generally. All of this was great capital.

STEP BY STEP UPWARD.

At the very outset of his storekeeping, John Wanamaker did what almost any other business man would have stood aghast at. He chose the best man he knew as a salesman in the clothing business in Philadelphia, and agreed to pay him $1,350 a year,—one-third of the entire capital of the new concern. It seemed reckless extravagance. And there were other employees, too. What could Mr. Wanamaker be thinking of to make the promise of this great sum just for one assistant! This move that seemed so audacious was really a very wise one; for, when the new employee went with Mr. Wanamaker to New York to buy goods, the fact of his association added credit to the young house and so a little money was eked out with a good deal more of credit, and a very fair stock of goods was laid in. This was just as the war began. Oak Hall was a success from the start. Possibly, under the circumstances, any sort of a clothing venture that had fair backing would have been a success. But no ordinary concern could have grown so rapidly and so healthfully as Oak Hall grew.

And right here another characteristic of Mr. Wanamaker's makeup strikingly manifested itself; *he was not bound by precedent.* No matter how time-honored a business method might be if it did not strike him as the wisest, he put it aside at once. And from the first he fully appreciated the importance of attracting public attention. As a boy he had published "Everybody's Journal,"—a hodge-podge of odd bits with dabs of original matter; notable then and now mainly because it indicated the bent of the young mind. At Oak Hall the same spirit of innovation was continually shown. It has often been told how Mr. Wanamaker delivered his first order in a wheelbarrow, and put the money ($38) into an advertisement in "The Inquirer." But this was only one instance significant of the man.

"WAKING UP" A TOWN.

Philadelphia awoke one morning to find "W. & B." in the form of six-inch square posters stuck up all over the town. There was not another letter, no hint, just "W. & B." Such things are common enough now, but then the whole city was soon talking and wondering what this sign meant. After a few days, a second poster modestly stated that Wanamaker & Brown had begun to sell clothing at Oak Hall.

Of course the young firm got business rapidly. When any man gets out of a rut and in the direction of more enterprise, it helps him. Before long there were great signs, each 100 feet in length, painted on special fences built in a dozen places about the city, particularly near the railroad stations. These told of the new firm and were the first of a class that are now seen all over the country. New ideas in advertising were cropping out. In time balloons more than twenty feet high were sent up, and a suit of clothes was given to each person who brought one of them back. Whole counties were stirred up by the balloons. It was grand advertising, imitated since by all sorts of people. When the balloon idea struck the Oak Hall management it was quickly found that the only way to get these air-ships was to make them, and so, on the roof of the store, the cotton cloth was cut and oiled and put together. Being well built, and tied very tightly at the neck, they made long flights and some of them were used over and over again. In one instance, a balloon remained for more than six months in a cranberry swamp, and when the great bag was discovered, slowly swaying in the breeze, among the bushes, the frightened Jerseymen thought they had come upon an elephant, or, maybe, a survivor of the mastodons. This made more advertising of the very best kind for the clothing store,— the kind that excites interested, complimentary talk.

SEIZING OPPORTUNITIES.

Genius consists in taking advantage of opportunities quite as much as in making them. Here was a young man doing things in an advertising way regardless of the custom of the business world, and with a wonderful knowledge of human nature. He took common-sense advantage of opportunities that were open to everybody.

Soon after the balloon experience, tally-ho coaching began to be a Philadelphia fad of the very exclusives. Immediately afterward a crack coach was secured, and six large and spirited horses were used instead of four, and Oak Hall employees, dressed in the style of the most ultra coaching set, traversed the country in every direction, scattering advertising matter to the music of the horn. Sometimes they would be a week on a trip. No wonder Oak Hall flourished. It was kept in the very front of the procession all the time.

A little later, in the yachting season, the whole town was attracted and amused by processions and scatterings of men, each wearing a wire body frame that supported a thin staff from which waved a wooden burgee, or pointed flag, reminding them of Oak Hall. Nearly two hundred of these prototypes of the "Sandwich man" were often out at one time.

But it was not only in the quick catching of a novel advertising thought that the new house was making history; in newspaper advertising, it was even further in advance. The statements of store news were crisp and unhackneyed, and the first artistic illustrations ever put into advertisements were used there. So high was the grade of this picture-work that art schools regularly clipped the illustrations as models; and the world-famous Shakespearean scholar, Dr. Horace Howard Furness, treasured the original sketches of "The Seven Ages" as among the most interesting in his unique collection.

As a storekeeper he was just as original. It was the universal rule in those days, in the clothing trade, not to mark the prices plainly on the goods that were for sale. Within rather liberal bounds, the salesman got what he could from the customer. Mr. Wanamaker, after a time, instituted at Oak Hall the plan of "but one price and that plainly marked,"—the beginning of still another revolution in business methods. He saw to it that customers had prompt and careful attention. If a sale was missed, he required a written reason for it from the salesman. There was no haphazard business in that store,—nothing of the happy-go-lucky style. Each man must be alert, wide-awake, attentive, or there was no place for him at Oak Hall.

ECONOMICAL WAYS.

And Mr. Wanamaker's habits of economy were never relaxed. It is told of him that, in the earlier days of Oak Hall, he used to gather up the short pieces of string that came in on parcels, make them into a bunch, and see that they were used when bundles were to be tied. He also had a habit of smoothing out old newspapers, and seeing that they were used as wrappers for such things as did not require a better grade of paper.

A considerable portion of the trade of the new store came from people in the country districts. Mr. Wanamaker had a way of getting close to them and gaining their good will. An old employee of the firm says: "John used to put a lot of chestnuts in his pocket along in the fall and winter, and, when he had one of these countrymen in tow, he'd slip a few of the nuts into the visitor's hand and both would go munching about the store." Another salesman of the old house says: "If we saw a man come in chewing gum, we knew it was of no use trying to sell him anything. You see, he was sure to be as green as grass and fully convinced that we were all watching for a chance to cheat him. John said it was all nonsense; that such people came on purpose to buy, and were the easiest people in the world to sell to. And he would prove it. He would chew gum with them, and talk farm or crops or cattle with them. They'd buy of him every time. But none of us could ever get his knack of dealing with countrymen."

There it is. This young merchant understood human nature. He put his customer at ease. He showed interest in the things that interested the farmer. He was frank and open with him, and just familiar enough not to lose a bit of the respect and deference that superiority commands.

CHRISTIAN PHILANTHROPIST.

Meantime Mr. Wanamaker was interesting himself in Sunday school work, as well as in Christian Association matters. He established a Sunday school in one of the most unpromising of the down-town sections, and there built up the largest school of the kind in the world,—with a membership of something like three thousand. This school proved a powerful factor for good.

He was also active in general philanthropic work. He was making his mark on almost every phase of the city's life. Such activity and forceful good sense are always sure to make their mark.

When the great store was started in 1877 at Thirteenth and Market streets, Mr. Wanamaker announced certain fundamental principles that should mark the course of the enterprise. The one-price thought was continued, of course. But he went far beyond that. He announced that *those who bought goods of him were to be satisfied with what they bought, or have their money back.*

To the old mercantile houses of the city this seemed like committing business suicide. It was also unheard of that special effort should be made to add to the comfort of visitors, to make them welcome whether they cared to buy or not, to induce them to look upon the store as a meeting-place, a rendezvous, a resting-place,—a sort of city home, almost. Yet these things that were thought to forebode so much of disaster to the old generation of merchants, have completely overturned the methods of retailing throughout the United States. That "Wanamaker way" is now almost the universal way.

When asked what he attributed his great success to, Mr. Wanamaker said: "To thinking, toiling, trying and trusting in God." Surely, his life has been crowded with work. Even now, when wealth and honor have been heaped upon him, he is likely to be the earliest man at the store, and the last to leave at night,— just as when a boy at Tower Hall.

HIS ADVICE TO YOUNG MERCHANTS.

He cares little for money, and even less for fame. When I asked him to name the essentials of success, he replied, curtly: "I might write a volume trying to tell you how to succeed. One way is to not be above taking a hint from a master. I don't care to tell why I succeeded, because I object to talking about myself. It isn't modest."

Mr. Wanamaker is epigrammatical at times. I asked him if a man with means but no experience would be safe in embarking in a mercantile business, and he replied, quickly:—

"A man can't drive a horse who has never seen one. No; a man must have training, must know how to buy and sell; only experience teaches that."

When I asked him whether the small tradesmen has any "show" to-day against the great department stores, he said:—

"All of the great stores were small at one time. Small stores will keep on developing into big ones. You wouldn't expect a man to put an iron band around his business in order to prevent expansion, would you? There are, according to statistics, a greater number of prosperous small stores in the city than ever before. What better proof do you want?

"The department store is a natural product, evolved from

conditions that exist as a result of fixed trade laws. Executive capacity, combined with command of capital, finds opportunity in these conditions, which are harmonious with the irresistible determination of the producer to meet the consumer directly, and of merchandise to find distribution along the lines of least resistance. Reduced prices stimulate consumption and increased employment, and it is sound opinion that the increased employment created by the department stores goes to women without curtailing that of men. In general it may be stated that large retail stores have shortened the hours of labor, and by systematic discipline have made it lighter. The small store is harder upon the sales-person and clerk. The effects upon the character and capacity of the employees are good. A well-ordered, modern retail store is a means of education in spelling, writing, English language, system and method. Thus it becomes to the ambitious and serious employees, in a small way, a university, in which character is broadened by intelligent instruction practically applied."

A feature of his make-up that has contributed largely to the many-sidedness of his success is his ability to concentrate his thoughts. No matter how trivial the subject that is brought before him, he takes it up with the seeming of one who has nothing else on his mind. While under the cares of his stores,—retail and wholesale,—of the Sunday school, of the postmaster-generalship, of vast railroad interests, of extensive real estate transactions, and while he was weighing the demands of leading citizens that he accept a nomination for mayor of Philadelphia, I have seen him take up the case of a struggling church society, or the troubles of an individual, with the interest and patience that would be expected of a pastor or a professional adviser. He is phenomenal in this respect. Probably not one young man in a thousand *could* develop this trait so remarkably, but any young man can try for it, and he will be all the better and stronger for so trying.

In one physical particular Mr. Wanamaker is now very remarkable; he can work continually for a long time without sleep and without evidence of strain, and make up for it by good rest afterward. This, perhaps, is because of his lack of nervousness. He is always calm. Under the greatest stress he never loses his head. I fancy that this comes from training, as well as from inheritance. It adds amazingly to the power that any man can assert. It is certainly a tendency that can be cultivated.

CONDITIONS THEN AND NOW.

I have heard it said a hundred times that Mr. Wanamaker started when success was easy. Here is what he says himself about it:—

"I think I could succeed as well now as in the past. It seems to me that the conditions of to-day are even more favorable to success than when I was a boy. There are better facilities for doing business, and more business to be done. Information in the shape of books and newspapers is now in the reach of all, and the young man has two opportunities where he formerly had one.

"We are much more afraid of combinations of capital than we have any reason for being. Competition regulates everything of that kind. No organization can make immense profits for any length of time without its field soon swarming with competitors. It requires brain and muscle to manage any kind of business, and the same elements which have produced business success in the past will produce it now, and will always produce it."

I have heard others marvel at the unbroken upward course of Mr. Wanamaker's career, and lament that they so often make mistakes. But hear him:—

"Who does not make mistakes? Why, if I were to think only of the mistakes I have made, I should be miserable indeed."

THE VALUE OF "PUSH."

He has exceptional skill in getting the best that is possible out of his helpers. On one occasion he said:—

"We are very foolish people if we shut our ears and eyes to what other people are doing. I often pick up things from strangers. As you go along, pick up suggestions here and there, jot them down and send them along. Even writing them down helps to concentrate your mind on that part of the work. You need not be afraid of overstepping the mark and stepping on somebody's heels. The more we push each other, the better."

This is another Wanamaker characteristic: he wants everyone associated with him to "push." Stagnation and death are very nearly synonymous words in his vocabulary.

Out of it all stands a man who has been monumentally successful as a merchant and in general business; a man who has helped his fellow-man while helping himself.

The lesson of such a life should be precious to every young man. It teaches the value of untiring effort, of economy, of common sense applied to common business. It gives one more proof that no height of success is, in this country, beyond the reasonable ambition of any youth who desires to succeed.

I have no doubt that thousands on thousands of young men in the United States are to-day better equipped in almost every way than was John Wanamaker when he began business for himself in 1861. Very likely, not one in a hundred of them will make a mark of any significance. The fault will be their own,—they will not have the compelling force that comes from "thinking, toiling, trying," and the serene confidence that *then* comes from "trusting" a guiding power through every change of circumstances.

VII

A BRITISH BOY WINS FORTUNE AND TITLE BY AMERICAN BUSINESS METHODS.

THE lower bay was charged with subdued excitement everywhere as the "Water Witch" hove to alongside Sir Thomas J. Lipton's "Erin," and I stepped aboard. The hum of preparation for the great race was heard above the lapping waves. Fresh and keen came the breezes from the snowy ridges of the ocean's breast. A thousand spreads of sail studded the bay, the great ships standing up in fixed majesty, the smaller vessels darting here and there in the wind, while right in the path of the sun's glare lay the green hull of the "Shamrock." Along the whitened shores beyond were hundreds of fishing craft dancing at their work, and in the offing were the smoke-stacks of the Atlantic liners.

"Good morning!" came a cheery sailor's voice from the promenade deck. "Step right up here and you will get a better view of our little beauty."

The voice belonged to Sir Thomas Lipton, and the "little beauty" was the dainty craft to which he had pinned his faith. The Scotch-Irish knight was as enthusiastic as a boy. With a cordial handshake, he led the way to the rail and pointed to the emerald swan below.

"There she is," he tenderly exclaimed; "the pride of a nation; isn't she a picture!" His tone fairly caressed the graceful thing. I fully expected to see him clamber down the rope-way and go out to pet her, as the Arab is said to pet his steed, but he satisfied himself by gazing at her and talking about her.

Confessedly, I was more interested in her owner than in the

"Shamrock," but I was too diplomatic to show it, so I quite won my way into his heart by praising her.

SIR THOMAS WAS WON.

"Sir Thomas," I said, "I can't say I hope she will win, but I hope she will come so close to it that she will turn us all green with envy!"

"Ah, my boy, that's the spirit," he said; "that's why it's a pleasure to race against you Americans. You meet a fellow more than half way."

The "Erin" is no less beautiful than the racer. With the "Shamrock's" pennant at the foremast and the Stars and Stripes flying from the after-pole, she is a model. Commodore Morgan says she is one of the three finest ocean-going yachts in the world. The Prince and Princess of Wales visited her often, and gave signed photographs of themselves to hang in the elegant cabin. Admiral Dewey's likeness hangs near the "Columbia's." The appointments of the yacht are worthy of the Waldorf-Astoria. Sir Thomas never leaves her, he told me, except to go aboard the "Shamrock." I could not blame him. Finding a pair of upholstered steamer chairs forward, we dropped into them.

The conversation drifted into the early struggles of the baronet, to the days when he did not own a floating palace or an international cup challenger.

WHEN HE BORROWED FIVE CENTS.

"I remember, as if it were yesterday," said Sir Thomas, "how utterly hopeless my financial condition seemed to be when I was a boy of fifteen in New York. I had run away from home to see the world. My experiences were anything but pleasant, without work as I was, a stranger in a great city. I got used to living on a few cents a day, but when it came to such a pinch that I couldn't buy a five-cent stamp to carry a letter to the old folks in Glasgow, I very nearly gave up. I really think that decided me to go back. It accentuated my homesickness. I thought of the prodigal son. I borrowed five cents for that letter, and resolved to get back as soon as a chance offered. I can tell you I was glad when I once more set foot on the other side. I had refrained from telling my people how hard up I had been. This was largely a matter of pride with me, but another consideration was their feelings. I would do anything rather than distress them. So I stepped up, on my arrival, as jauntily as you ever saw a lad, and when a proposition was made to me by my father, soon after my home-coming, to set me up in a small grocery, I jumped at the chance."

"Was that the beginning of your fortune?"

"Yes. I made money from the start. I put in practice what I had seen abroad,—such as displaying goods attractively in windows, keeping the place as neat as a pin, and waiting personally on my customers. Every dollar that I earned I saved,—not that I really loved money myself. That was not my inspiration,—it was my father and mother."

AMERICAN BUSINESS METHODS GAVE HIM HIS START.

"I am willing to admit that it was my admiration for American methods that gave me my start," said Sir Thomas, as he leaned against the taffrail. "It was the application of proper methods to conditions that needed them. These applications and conditions are always with us. The world is full of them. A man only needs to know both when he sees them.

"We have all marveled at the prosperity of America, but, years ago, I felt that it would come. But your country is still young, and has many more victories to win. I may say the same thing of all the world. Every country has a future still. Honest competition will still give all the nations a chance for supremacy. It only remains for the people to catch those chances, and not let them pass by. If I were a poor man to-day, I would be just as happy; I know that I could start anew and win.

"Honest application is the stimulus of all effort. That, to me, is the science of achievement. Whenever you find an opportunity to do something that will benefit you, do not fail to take advantage of it. Often, the most trying periods will produce the best results. For instance, fifteen years ago, while sailing down the African coast in a steamer which carried, as the bulk of its cargo, my teas, we encountered a terrific storm. The steamer had to be lightened. At one time it even looked as if we were going to be wrecked; but, really, I thought more of the loss of that tea than of anything else. I had it brought on deck, with the idea of using it for advertising purposes, if for nothing else. On each case I had painted, in large black letters, 'Lipton's Tea,' and then cast it overboard, dreaming that it would float to the African coast, and be picked up by someone who had not heard of the product before. Sure enough, it was."

HE OWNS NEARLY FIVE HUNDRED STORES.

"Your business must be an enormous one now, Sir Thomas, from the stories in the English papers about the organization of your enterprises into a limited company."

"Yes, I have a good deal to attend to," he said, smiling. "I have sixty stores in London alone, and four hundred and twenty the world over, most of them being in the British Isles. I sell all food products except beef, which I have never handled. I own thousands of acres on the island of Ceylon, where I am the largest individual land-owner. On this land I grow tea, coffee and cocoa, and employ several thousand natives to cultivate and ship it. I have warehouses all over Asia, and branch stores in Hamburg and Berlin. In Chicago I have a packing-house where

I sometimes kill three thousand hogs in a day. So, you see, my enterprises are pretty well scattered over the earth.

"How many employees have I? Well, all in all, I have somewhat over ten thousand, and a nicer lot of employees you never saw. I have never had a strike, and never expect to have one, for I make it my personal duty to see that my men are all comfortably fixed. We live together in perfect harmony."

"And what advice would you give young men who are about to start out for themselves, Sir Thomas?"

"That's a broad question," laughed the great man. "It would take me some time to answer it properly. But, to begin with, I say that hard work is the cardinal requisite for success. I always feel that I cannot impress that fact too strongly upon young men. And then a person's heart and soul must be in his work. He must be earnest, above all, and willing to give his whole time to his work, if necessary. Honesty, it goes without saying, is necessary, and if you want to be wholly successful, you must do unto others as you would have them do unto you. If you don't, they will be sure to retaliate, when you least expect it. If young men would follow these rules, they would get along very well; but few of them will. If your article can inspire any of them to harder work, its mission will be blessed."

CHANCES FOR YOUNG MEN TO-DAY.

I inquired whether the chances for young men in Great Britain are equal to those in America.

"That is a difficult question to answer," said Sir Thomas. "Being a merchant, I can speak of trade opportunities, but in the professions I really do not know which side of the Atlantic is the better. Literature, of course, knows no country; neither does art. In the legal profession, the chances are two to one in favor of the United States. You make more of your lawyers there; you utilize them in legislation, in places of trust, while abroad their duties are limited. A good physician in England will probably make as much money as your leading ones here. Taking it altogether, there seems to be as good a chance for professional men on one side as on the other. The British isles are small compared with the states, but young men are going out every day into new British fields, just as your young men are pushing out into every part of your magnificent stretch of country.

"THRIFT IS THE TRUE SECRET OF SUCCESS."

"When men tell you," continued the baronet, "that there are no more chances in this world, tell them that they are mistaken. Your country abounds in so many that I marvel why any American cares to leave its shores. There are thousands of manufactures that are still in an imperfect state; there are millions of acres that are still to be made productive; there are, seemingly, countless achievements yet to be undertaken. What I say is best proven by the international yacht races. Every year we race we believe that we have produced the best possible boat, but we find, after the race is over, that we can improve it in some respect. If all men would use their minds in the same way that the builders of these big yachts use theirs, what a world of improvement would be made! After every race, we produce something better, something finer,—the result of brains and workmanship,—and we are not satisfied yet.

"I have often been asked to define the true secret of success. It is thrift in all its phases, and, principally, thrift as applied to saving. A young man may have many friends, but he will find none so steadfast, so constant, so ready to respond to his wants, so capable of pushing him ahead, as a little leather-covered book, with the name of a bank on its cover. Saving is the first great principle of all success. It creates independence, it gives a young man standing, it fills him with vigor, it stimulates him with the proper energy; in fact, it brings to him the best part of any success,—happiness and contentment. If it were possible to inject the quality of saving into every boy, we would have a great many more real men.

"Success depends also on character to carry it through life.

"Knowledge should be a compound of what we derive from books, and what we extract, by our observation, from the living world around us. Both of these are necessary to the well-informed man; and, of the two, the last is, by far, the most useful for the practical purposes of life. The man who can combine the teachings of books with strong and close observation of life, deserves the name of a well-informed man, and presents a model worthy of imitation."

The great passion of Sir Thomas's life, yachting, has been a costly indulgence for him, yet he has inadvertently secured more popularity through his efforts to win the "America's" Cup than would have been possible in any other way. The three "Shamrocks" have cost him, all told, reckoning the expenses of sailing the races as part of the grand total, more than one million dollars.

FINANCE

VIII

A SELF-MADE MAN WHO STRIVES TO GIVE OTHERS A CHANCE

"IF a bootblack does all the good he possibly can for his fellowmen, his life has been just as successful as that of the millionaire who helps thousands."

That was what Darius Ogden Mills said when I asked him to give me his idea of a successful life. His next reply was quite as epigrammatic.

"What, Mr. Mills, do you consider the keynote of success?"

"Work," he replied, quickly and emphatically. "Work develops all the good there is in a man; idleness all the evil. Work sharpens all his faculties and makes him thrifty; idleness makes him lazy and a spendthrift. Work surrounds a man with those whose habits are industrious and honest; in such society a weak man develops strength, and a strong man is made stronger. Idleness, on the other hand, is apt to throw a man into the company of men whose only object in life usually is the pursuit of unwholesome and demoralizing diversions."

Mr. Mills is quite averse to being interviewed, but when I told him that his words would be carried to many thousands of young men, and probably do considerable good in the way of encouragement and inspiration, he consented to a brief talk.

AN AGE OF OPPORTUNITIES.

I asked Mr. Mills when he would be ready for me, and he replied:—

"I am just as ready now as I ever will be. There is no time like the present."

Like an oasis in the desert is the experience of a man, the accumulation of whose wealth has been on lines parallel with the conducive rather than counter to the welfare of mankind. This is what Mr. Mills says on the subject:—

"A man can, in the accumulation of a fortune, be just as great a benefactor of mankind as in the distribution of it. In organizing a great industry, one opens up fields of employment for a multitude of people who might otherwise be practically helpless, giving them not only a chance to earn a living for themselves and their families, but also to lay by a competency for old age. All honest, sober men, if they have half a chance, can do that; but only a small percentage can ever become rich. Now the rich man, having acquired his wealth, knows better how to manage it than those under him would, and having actual possession, he has the power to hold the community of his employees and their interests together, and prevent disintegration, which means disaster so much oftener to the employee than to the employer."

Volumes of fascinating matter could be written of the career of Mr. Mills, but the purpose of this article is a talk with, rather than a talk about him.

"To what formative influence do you attribute your material success, Mr. Mills?" I asked.

"I was taught very early that I would have to depend entirely upon myself; that my future lay in my own hands. I had that for a start, and it was a good one. I didn't waste any time bothering about succession to wealth, which so often acts as a drag upon young men. Many persons waste the best years of their lives waiting for dead men's shoes; and, when they get them, find them entirely too big to wear gracefully, simply because they have not developed themselves to wear them. I have never accepted an inheritance or anything but goodwill from my family or relatives."

THE FIRST HUNDRED DOLLARS.

"As a rule, the small inheritance, which, to a boy, would seem large, has a tendency to lessen his efforts, and is a great damage to him in the way of acquiring habits necessary to success. Above all, no one can acquire a fortune unless he makes a start; and the habit of thrift, which he learns in saving his first hundred dollars, is of inestimable value later on. It is not the money, but the habit which counts. There is no one so helpless as a man who is 'broke,' no matter howcapable he may be, and there is no habit so detrimental to his reputation among business men as that of borrowing small sums of money. This cannot be too emphatically impressed upon young men. Another thing is that none but the wealthy, and very few of them, can afford the indulgence of expensive habits; how much less then can a man with only a few dollars in his pockets? More young men are ruined by the expense of smoking than in any other way. The money thus laid out would make them independent, in many cases, or at least would give them a good start. A young man should be warned by the melancholy example of those who have been ruined by smoking, and avoid it."

TRAITS OF INFLUENTIAL MEN.

"What marked traits have the influential men, with whom you have been associated, possessed, which most impressed you?"

"A habit of thinking and acting for themselves. No end of people are ruined by taking the advice of others. This may answer temporarily, but in the long run it is sure to be disastrous. Any man who hasn't ability to judge for himself would better get a comfortable clerkship somewhere, letting some one of more ambition and ability do the thinking necessary to run the business."

"Are the opportunities for making money as numerous to-day as they were when you started in business?"

"Yes, the progress of science and invention has increased the opportunities a thousandfold, and a man can find them wherever he seeks them, in the United States in particular. It has caused the field of employment of labor of all kinds to expand enormously, thus creating opportunities which never existed before. It is no longer necessary for a man to go to foreign countries or distant parts of his own country to make money. Opportunities come to him in every quarter. There is hardly a point in the country so obscure that it has not felt the revolutionizing influence of commercial enterprise. Probably railroads and electricity are the chief instruments in this respect. Other industries follow closely in their wake."

SOME SECRETS OF SUCCESS.

"In what part of the country do you think the best chances for young men may be found?"

"The best place for a young man to make money is the town in which he was born and educated. There he learns all about everybody, and everybody learns about him. This is to his advantage if he bears a good character, and to the advantage of his townspeople if he bears a bad one. While a young man is growing up, he unconsciously absorbs a vast deal of knowledge of people and affairs, which would be equal to money if he only has the judgment to avail himself of it. A knowledge of men is the prime secret of business success. Upon reflection, how absurd it is for a man to leave a town where he knows everything and everybody, and go to some distant point where he doesn't know anything about anybody, or anything, and expect to begin on an equal footing with the people there who are thoroughly acquainted."

"What lesson do you consider best for young men to learn?"

"The lesson of humility;—not in the sense of being servile or undignified, but in that of paying due respect to men who are their superiors in the way of experience, knowledge and position. Such a lesson is akin to that of discipline. Members of the royal families of Europe are put in subordinate positions in the navies or armies of their respective countries, in order that they may receive the training necessary to qualify them to take command. They must first know how to obey, if they would control others."

THE BOTTOM OF THE LADDER.

"In this country, it is customary for the sons of the presidents of great railroads, or other companies, to begin at the bottom of the ladder and work their way up step by step, just the same as any other boy in the employ of the corporation. This course has become imperatively necessary in the United States, where each great business has become a profession in itself. Most of the big machine shops number among their employees, scions of old families who carry dinner pails, and work with files or lathes, the same as anyone else. Such shoulder-to-shoulder experience is invaluable to a man who is destined to command, because he not only masters the trade technically, but learns all about the men he works with and qualifies himself to grapple with labor questions which may arise.

"There is no end of conspicuous examples of the wisdom of this system in America. There are also many instances of disaster to great industrial concerns due to the inexperience or the lack of tact of men placed suddenly in control."

"What is the responsibility of wealth, Mr. Mills?"

"A man must learn not to think too much of money. It should be considered as a means and not an end, and the love for it should never be permitted to so warp a man's mind as to destroy his interest in progressive ideas. Making money is an education, and the wide experience thus acquired teaches a man discrimination in both men and projects, where money is under consideration. Very few men who make their own money use it carelessly. Most good projects that fail owe their failure to bad business management, rather than to lack of intrinsic merit. An inventor may have a very good thing, and plenty of capital may be enlisted, but if a man not acquainted with the peculiar line, or one who is not a good salesman or financier be employed as manager, the result is disastrous. A man should spend his money in a way that tends to advance the best interests of society in the country he lives in, or in his own neighborhood at least. There is only one thing that is a greater harm to the community than a rich spendthrift, and that is a miser."

A WORD ABOUT CHEAP HOTELS.

"How did you happen to establish the system of hotels which bear your name, Mr. Mills?"

"I had been looking around for several years to find something to do that would be for the good of the community. My mind was largely on other matters, but it occurred to me that the hotel project was the best, and I immediately went to work at it. My purpose was to do the work on so large a scale that it would be appreciated and spread all over the country, for as the sources of education extend, we find more and more need of assisting men who have a disposition for decency and good citizenship. The mechanic is well paid, and the man who has learned to labor is much more independent than he who is prepared for a profession, science or other objects in life that call for higher education. Clerks commencing at small salaries need good surroundings and economy to give themselves a start. Such are the men for whom the hotels were established."

IX

THRIFT,
THE SECRET OF A FORTUNE
BUILT IN A SINGLE LIFETIME.

VERY few great fortunes have been acquired by one man, or within the limits of a single lifetime. The vast wealth of the Vanderbilts, the Astors, and many others, has accumulated through several generations. It is seldom, indeed, that a fortune like that of Russell Sage is amassed by one man. For years, the newspapers of the country have been filled with stories of his eccentricities.

When I called at the great banker's office, I found it very hard to obtain an audience with Mr. Sage, even though I had an introduction to him. He has so often been the victim of cranks, and has so many callers at his office, that he has been obliged to deny himself to all alike. He finally decided to see me. I found him seated at an old flat-topped desk, looking over the stock reports of the day, and I was surprised at the extreme simplicity of all his surroundings. The furnishings of the room looked as if they might have seen service before the Civil War, and, upon later inquiry, I learned that most of the chairs and the desk itself have been in use by Mr. Sage for more than twenty-five years. He has become so attached to them that he cannot think of discarding them for more modern inventions. Mr. Sage is smooth-faced, and his hair is thin and gray. His clothes are fashioned in the style of thirty years ago, but of good material, and well kept. His shoulders are bent with care and age, but his face has a good color, and a happy smile that betokens health and a peaceful mind.

"I have come to ask you to tell me the story of your life," I said, "for I am sure it must be of great interest."

HE BEGAN AS A GROCERY CLERK.

Mr. Sage smiled. "I don't know about its being of interest. It is very simple and commonplace to me. You know I began as a grocery clerk, in a country town. That is a very humble beginning, I'm sure."

"Yes, but it's the beginning that counts," I said; "not the end."

"You are right," replied the financier. "Well, when I was even younger than you are, I received a dollar a week for working from early morning until late at night, but I was well satisfied with my lot, because I knew that it was bound to lead to better things. So I worked my very best, and saved my wages, which were slowly increased as I went along, and finally I had enough money to start a little store for myself. When I was twenty-one years old, I had a store of my own, and I made a success of it, too." He smiled, as he remembered those early days.

"But how did you happen to come to New York?" I asked.

"Oh, I was ambitious," laughed Mr. Sage. "Like most boys, I thought there was no other place like a city for success, and I finally sold my country store when I was still very young, and came to New York. I started in as an office-boy, at very low wages, and, from that day on, I worked myself up and up, until I finally became a financier on my own account. It took a long time, though. It wasn't all accomplished in a day; though, when I came to New York, I expected to be rich in two or three years. I was very much like other boys, you see. They all expect to get rich in a day."

"But some of them never get rich," I said.

"Well, it's their own fault if they don't succeed," said the financier. "Surely, everyone has as good a chance as I had. I don't think there could be a poorer opportunity for a boy to rise. The trouble is that most of them are not very anxious to rise. If they find themselves wealthy some morning they are glad, of course; but they are not willing to work and make themselves rich."

NO LUCK IN HIS ACHIEVEMENT.

"Some say that it is all luck," I ventured to suggest.

"Oh, pshaw!" said Mr. Sage, with great disgust. "There's no such thing as luck. I'm sure there was none of it about my career. I know just how I earned every penny, and the reason for it, and I never got anything I didn't work for. I never knew anyone to obtain lasting wealth without lots of hard work."

"Do you think there are as good opportunities for getting rich to-day as there were thirty years ago, or when you made your start, Mr. Sage?"

"Undoubtedly. I think there are even greater opportunities, for new industries are being established all the time, and there are broader fields to work in. But then, the old fields of business are not overworked, by any means. I always say that there is room for good men anywhere and at any time. I don't think there can be ever too many of them. It is true that there are many applicants for every place in New York, but if I were unable to get a place in an eastern city, I should go west, for there are great opportunities there for everyone."

"People say, though, that the west is not what it is supposed to be," I remarked.

"Yes, there are always pessimists," said Mr. Sage. "The people who say the west has no opportunities are the same persons who used to call it foolish for any young man to come to New York. When I decided to come here, I was told on every side that I would regret my action; but I never have. Some people never see opportunities in anything, and they never get along. I didn't see any very great opportunity ahead of me when I came to New

York, but I knew that, if I had a chance, I could make one. I knew that there are always openings for energetic, hard-working fellows, and I was right."

CHILDHOOD

STRICT HONESTY IS NECESSARY.

"Of course, you believe that strict honesty is essential to success, Mr Sage? I've heard many people say that honesty doesn't pay, especially in Wall street."

"That is a foolish question," said the financier. "It is absurd to imagine that it pays to be dishonest, whatever your business or profession. Do you suppose, if I had been dishonest in any dealings when I started out, that I would be worth anything to-day?"

"What do you think of the chances for country boys in a great city like New York to-day, Mr. Sage?"

"I think they are as great as ever. Employers are on the lookout for bright young men, and I believe that they would prefer that they come from the country, provided there is no danger of their becoming dissipated. I think that is the only thing men have against country fellows, and there are many things in their favor. I think an earnest, ambitious, hard-working boy from the country has a splendid chance of becoming somebody. There are much greater opportunities for him to exercise his good qualities, and the reward of his enterprise is much larger. The same energetic labor that would make a man worth twenty-five thousand dollars in a small town would be very likely to make him worth a hundred thousand or so in a great city, and all on account of the wider field."

"To what do you owe your wonderful vitality?" I asked. Mr. Sage smiled before answering me.

"I never smoke, I never drink any liquors, I retire early, and get up early, and take care of myself in every possible way," he said. "Don't you think I ought to be healthy? I have always taken care of myself, and I think I've proved that hard work is not bad for one's health. In fact, I think that work is the best thing I know of for improving a man's constitution, for it makes a good appetite, and encourages digestion. It isn't work that ruins so many men.

It's the wine they drink, and the late hours they keep, and their general dissipation. I expect to be at my desk for many years to come, and just because I've taken good care of myself."

X

CUT OUT FOR A BANKER, HE ROSE FROM ERRAND BOY TO SECRETARY OF THE U. S. TREASURY.

"IN my own career, I have learned that varied experience in early youth is often of great value in after life. My schooldays ended when I was fourteen years old, and I began work as a mail agent on the Rome, Watertown and Ogdensburg Railroad. I do not mean to say that, when I stopped school, my education ceased, for it was after 1850 that my character received its greatest development. I was but poorly satisfied with my work as mail agent, although it taught me much that I didn't know before, and I kept my eyes open for something better. In a short time, the death of the president of the United States resulted in the loss of my first position. The village postmaster was removed from office, and, of course, my dismissal followed. This was discouraging, but I re-entered the village academy to pursue, for a time, my studies. There was in our town a small bank, and this institution had always possessed a fascination for my youthful mind. I used to watch the merchants going in with bags of gold and bundles of greenbacks, and coming out again with only account books in their hands. I knew that the bank had some connection with the government, and, being greatly impressed with its dignified appearance and the actions of its officers, I was seized with a desire to work within its walls. When I applied for a position, I learned that there was no likelihood of a vacancy occurring in the near future; so, when I was offered a place in a local stationery shop at a salary of a hundred dollars a year, I accepted with alacrity. The wages were small, indeed, but in this shop I was privileged to become acquainted with general literature, and spent many hours with the great authors. So the months with the stationer were not without profit.

"After a time there was a rival bank established in the town, and I was offered the position of 'messenger and general assistant,' at the same old salary of a hundred dollars a year. I didn't hesitate, but left the store to enter the bank, and so began my career in the financial world. My duties as 'general assistant' were many and varied. I was janitor, first of all, and attended to the heating of the building. I made many trips every day to the cellar for coal, and I used to think the officials most extravagant when they insisted on a fire when the days were comparatively warm. I was obliged to keep the front sidewalk clear of dirt in the summer and of snow in the winter, and had to sweep the floor of the banking room daily, and dust the desks and furniture frequently.

WHEN YOU START IN LIFE IN A STRANGE CITY, DO NOT EXPECT "SOFT SNAPS."

"As the 'messenger' of the bank, I was sent around town with notices of notes which had fallen due, and with drafts which had been sent to the bank for collection from other cities. All these duties kept me fairly busy, but I still had time to learn something of banking as a business, and of the transactions which took place behind the counters. As the business of the bank increased, the teller and the bookkeeper welcomed my assistance in their departments; and, when summer came, and there were no fires to make and no snow to shovel, I had opportunity to learn most of the details of the business. After a while I was intrusted with the work of the teller or of the bookkeeper when either was kept at home by illness, and at the end of my first year I felt that I was indeed 'cut out for a banker.'

"I had so good an opinion of my accomplishments that I demanded of my employers an increase of salary for my second year. They replied that I was receiving all they could afford to pay, and I immediately resigned. At this time, nearly every boy in Central New York had the 'Western Fever,' and, after I left the bank, I developed a very bad case. I determined to start for Chicago to make my fortune, and arrived there one day in 1855, with few dollars and no friends. I had my mind made up to be a banker, and supposed that it would be easier to find an opening in the western city than it had been in my native village. But when I made the rounds, I found that no embryo banker was needed. I could not afford to be idle, so I determined to accept the first position which should offer, whether or not it was to my liking. It does not pay for a young man starting in life in a strange city to be too particular about what he does for a living. I soon found a place as bookkeeper for a lumber company. The panic of 1857 effected even bookkeepers, however; and, when the firm found it necessary to reduce expenses, I gladly accepted appointment as night watchman.

"I had been in Chicago three years before good fortune seemed to come my way. I had visited every banking house several times in search of a position, for I was convinced that banking ought to be my career, and I was a familiar applicant to all the officials. On the third of August, 1858, a date I shall always remember, I was summoned to the office of the Merchants' Loan and Trust Company, where my name was on file as a candidate for any position, however humble. 'Can you keep a set of books?' asked Mr. Holt, the cashier. 'I can try,' was my answer. 'That isn't what we want,' said Mr. Holt; 'can you do it?' 'I can, if it can be done in twenty-three hours out of twenty-four,' I replied, and I was thereupon engaged at an annual salary of five hundred dollars. After working for so long at uncongenial employment with low wages, this opening made me very happy. I felt that my future was assured, for I had obtained, at length, the long-desired standing-room in a Chicago bank.

THE PUBLIC WOULD RATHER INVEST ITS MONEY IN MEN THAN IN FINE BUILDINGS.

"The story of my further progress can be of little interest to those who are beginning life in the financial world. My early preparation in the New York village was most useful, and, since I had also benefited from my experience with the world, my position was secure. If a young man has some preparation for his work, if he secures a proper opening, and if he behaves himself, there can be no question of his future. In two years after I entered the service of the Merchants' Loan and Trust Company, I was given the position of cashier, at an annual salary of two thousand dollars, and naturally I was encouraged to find that my efforts were appreciated. I enjoyed my work, and was more convinced than ever before that banking was the career for which I was best fitted by nature.

"Every successful man started in a different way from that adopted by any other, and there is no rule which can be laid down as certain to win in the end. Some have received the benefit of a college training, and others have been self-educated. Some began life in other business and drifted into banking, and some were employed in financial houses from the very beginning. It often happens that those who make the most earnest efforts to succeed accomplish less than others who have had less preparation for the work. The prizes of life do not always come to the most deserving. Many things must co-operate to bring great results. Innate ability, which schools cannot furnish, must find conjunction with conditions, circumstances, and opportunities which lie outside of individual control. If you find a man great, distinguished, a business Saul among his brethren, do not worship him overmuch. Perhaps among the humble and unrecognized are a score or a hundred as worthy as he, to whom circumstances were unfavorable or opportunity did not come.

"The public appreciates more and more the importance of investing money in men, not in buildings. When I hear of large gifts to erect magnificent halls at our colleges, I think what greater good would be accomplished if that money were used to help a number of deserving young men and women through their college courses. When these young people have finished their work in the world, they may each and all be able to erect fifty-thousand-dollar buildings for their *alma maters*. A certain generous-minded man once said to me, 'I have given money quite freely to help the distressed, to soften the bitterness of helpless age, and to alleviate the condition of the unfortunate; but there was little or no inspiration in it. When, on the other hand, I have helped a bright boy to secure for himself a good education, my imagination has become effected. I have seen my dollars— won by hard application, in sordid ways,—transmitted into intellectual agencies powerful to effect the thoughts and feelings of generations which will live when I am dead.' This sentiment is becoming prevalent among the thoughtful men of America."

XI

A YOUNG MILLIONAIRE NOT AFRAID TO WORK IN OVERALLS.

A TALL, slender young man walked into the office of the master of motive power and construction, in the Grand Central Station, New York. He was dressed in clothes that showed marks of travel, and his face had a tired look. This was young Cornelius Vanderbilt, son of the head of the house of Vanderbilt, and great-grandson of his namesake, the founder of the Vanderbilt fortune. Cornelius had come to the office to report to the man under whom he is working, for the heir to the Vanderbilt millions was then serving his apprenticeship in the railroad business, and had to report the work he had accomplished, just like any other young mechanic on the road. Every clerk in the office stared at him, but the stare was affectionate, for every employee of the road has learned to like him. They have seen him with jacket and overalls, working in the yards and in the round-houses and machine-shops all along the system.

"It was not a sudden determination which led me to go out on the road and study the practical side of the railroad business," said young Cornelius Vanderbilt, in answer to my question as to his motive; "I had long intended to do it, because I know that the best way to learn a business is to begin at the bottom and work up. So when Mr. Depew arranged for me to begin in this department, I gladly accepted the place. I have been out on the road, off and on, for several months, and feel that I have learned a great deal that I could never have learned in any other way."

FROM THE FOUNDATION UP.

"I have enjoyed the experience, too. I think I have had a natural inclination for mechanics all my life, and I enjoyed having to do with engines and the construction of the road-bed. I am learning, gradually, of course, to build an engine, and to run one successfully. It won't be long before I can do that."

"And what will you undertake when you have finished with the construction and motive-power departments?" I asked.

"Well, I haven't planned that far ahead yet, but I hope, eventually, to know as much about the finances of the road as I do about the mechanics, and I also want to know something of the way in which the road is managed. All this will take time, but I am determined to give it all the time it needs. I think the advantages to be derived from such a training are worth a great deal of time and work."

"Does it seem like very hard work to you?"

"No; you know, I'm very much interested in such things, and so I don't mind the work. I would much prefer working in the yards and round-houses to working in the offices. It is much more to my taste."

I asked Mr. Vanderbilt whether he ever expected to run an engine attached to a train, and he said he had no idea of doing so, but he could, if necessary. "I'm glad to know how," he said.

And then Mr. Vanderbilt went to attend to some work awaiting him outside, and I entered Mr. Depew's office. When I asked Mr. Depew to tell me something more of the young man whom he has so nobly befriended in all his trials, he spoke with great animation.

WISE DEVELOPMENT OF INHERITED TENDENCIES.

"Cornelius," said he, "is a remarkable youth. From his early boyhood, I have seen in him signs of a peculiar ability. He has always been passionately fond of mechanics, and once, when a boy, was found trying to construct a steam engine out of an old saucepan. I have always hoped that he would enter actively into the work of the road, and I believe he has now begun a career that will prove both remarkable and glorious. I believe that, by pursuing this course, he will be the greatest railroad man of the age."

"Where did he get this natural taste for the work, Mr. Depew?" I asked.

"From his father, who did much the same work, when he was young, that Cornelius Jr., is doing now. But I believe Cornelius, Jr., takes an even greater interest in the work. It is not a new duty with him, but a natural ambition, and I believe that he would have become a railroad man even if he were the son of the poorest parents in the land. He is fitted by nature for such a career.

"His progress has so far been very satisfactory in every way. He has a genius for mastering details, and has already learned the construction of a locomotive. He has an inventive faculty, too, and has prepared plans for a locomotive that will achieve greater speed with smaller expenditure of coal. He expects to devote the next few years to mastering every department of railroad business, and he will eventually be competent to fill almost any position on the road. He will shovel coal and dig in the trenches, and polish engines. He will lay rails and take them up, and learn how to mend a cracked one. He will learn to detect uncertain ground, too, and how to make it solid again. He agrees with me that the way to make a workman respect you is to work with him."

HE WILL MASTER EVERY DETAIL.

"When he has finished his work on the road, he will take his place in the offices here, and learn how the system is administered. He will study the financial department especially, which deals with expenditures and receipts. This is, perhaps, the most important department of all for him, but he will also study the freight and passenger departments, and learn why the business increases and decreases, and the remedy for a falling off. There are a hundred and one things to learn, and he couldn't learn them in any other way. It will, of course, take a long time, perhaps fourteen or fifteen years, but he has a great deal of grit and perseverance, and I believe he will stick to it until he has thoroughly mastered the business.

"He will, in all likelihood, be the next member of the family to enter into the active management of the road. His brothers and cousins may eventually go through the same training, but Cornelius, Jr., is destined to be the most active in the management. I may not live to see it, but if his health holds out, and he is allowed to pursue his own course, he will perpetuate the name and fame of the Vanderbilts for another century."

"He is a chip of the old block, indeed," said another friend of the Vanderbilt family, "and his industry brings to mind the push and energy of the first Cornelius Vanderbilt in the early part of his career. The Commodore was never ashamed of any kind of honest work, and Cornelius is not. He will always be a worker, and his success in life is therefore assured, whether his father disinherits him or not. It is not believed, however, that Cornelius Vanderbilt will deprive his son of his fair share in the estate. On the contrary, however strong the feeling of displeasure the father may have entertained toward Cornelius, it is thought by friends of the family that he will treat his son and namesake fairly and even liberally."

WORKING AS A MACHINIST.

Young Cornelius, in his work as a machinist and office clerk, presents an example which other sons of millionaires could follow with profit. He is not alone, however, among young men of his class in training for a useful life. One of New York's richest young men is said to be not only a worker, but an authority on mechanics, and is able both to roll up his shirt-sleeves and go to the bench, and to describe in the minutest detail the work on which he is engaged. His ability in the mechanical line would probably have won wealth and success for him, even had he not been born to a vast fortune. At the same time, the course of the next in succession to the control of the Vanderbilt millions, in entering upon an education in skilled labor as a common workingman, is an excellent assurance that the family stock is not degenerating, and that its interests are in trustworthy hands.

The ambition of Commodore Vanderbilt to establish and perpetuate a great railway empire seems likely to be fulfilled, so far as the present and the rising generation of the Vanderbilts are concerned. It is the most remarkable experiment of the kind since the beginning of the American republic.

TRANSPORTATION

XII

A MESSENGER BOY'S ZEAL LIFTS HIM TO THE HEAD OF THE WORLD'S GREATEST TELEGRAPH SYSTEM.

WHEN romance can be added to hard facts in telling the life-story of a man, such a narrative becomes more pointed and interesting than the rarest dreams of a fictionist; therefore, the true story of a man who has made himself cannot fail to be instructive as well as interesting. No other man in the United States, to-day, can look back on a more remarkable career than that of Colonel Robert C. Clowry, president of the Western Union Telegraph Company. Mr. Clowry was delivering messages for that company in 1852, with but one object in view,—to hold his position. He is the busiest man, perhaps, in America to-day, and has little time to spend with an interviewer. He dislikes the notoriety that the world gives to men who fight and win, but the story of such a man is of more than passing interest. It is an important, valuable, uplifting factor in the great compound that makes America. It belongs to the people. It is for their use to profit by, and, with this one condition impressed on Mr. Clowry, he agreed to tell what he knows about himself.

"I began my telegraph career on April 4, 1852," he said. "I shall never forget the day. I walked into the office of Judge Caton's old Illinois and Mississippi Telegraph Company, at Joliet, Illinois, and told the operator that I had come to learn the business. I can see the rickety building now, and the surprised expression on the operator's face when he looked at me.

HE WAS SO POOR HE HAD TO DO HIS OWN COOKING.

"I had been living with my mother on a farm in Will county, not far from Joliet, and, having reached the age of fifteen, I thought it time to start out in the world for myself. Ever since I first heard of the telegraph, I was fascinated with its workings, and at that time my chief ambition was to be able to send a message over the wires.

"'What kind of work do you want to do?' the operator asked me. I replied that I didn't suppose I was capable of doing anything but carry messages. 'Well,' he said, 'we don't pay boys anything the first six months; but, if you want to work, you will have a chance to learn the business. When you're in the office you can easily pick up the knack of operating the keys, and, eventually, you'll get an office of your own.'

"I hadn't expected to earn any money at first, so I told him I was ready to begin at once. That was the beginning of my experience in the telegraph business."

"But, if you received no money for six months, how did you live in Joliet during that time?" I asked Colonel Clowry.

"I was able to earn money by doing various odd jobs around town, and of course my expenses were very low. For a while I used to get my own meals. I had learned to do plain cooking at home, and it was no hardship for me to fry an egg or broil a piece of steak. Joliet was a very small town in 1853, and I had never been accustomed to luxuries living at home. I had to work long hours at the office. I was the only messenger, and had all the work to do, so I hardly had time to be homesick. After my life on the farm, Joliet was a regular metropolis in my eyes and I found much to interest me. Of course, I was discouraged at times. I was very young to be away from home and dependent on my own resources, and it was only natural that I should occasionally get the blues. But for the most part I was wrapped up in my work and occupied with ambitious plans for the future."

"Were you able to learn telegraphy in a short time?"

"Yes, it seemed to come natural to me. I always liked mechanics and didn't rest until I knew the function of every key and lever connected with the instruments in the office. Within two months, I was able to send and receive a message, and in four months I was quite as expert as the regular operator. He was surprised at the readiness with which I learned, and remarked one day that I wouldn't remain a messenger long. This encouraged me, of course, but I had no idea how soon I should be given an office of my own.

"I had various unpleasant experiences as a messenger. I learned that, no matter how zealous I was in my work, it was impossible to please everybody, and I was frequently accused of loitering when in reality I had hurried as much as possible. The telegraph was a new institution in those days, and people were always doubtful of its success. They seemed actually surprised when a message was delivered without delay."

IT IS WELL TO KNOW WHAT MEN HAVE ACCOMPLISHED.

"In the beginning I was discouraged every time a man scolded me and found fault, but after a time I realized that it was foolish to be worried over trifles. I was doing my very best and knew that my services were appreciated by the officials over me. When I had been working six months as a messenger, I was delighted, one day, by the information that the office at Lockport, Illinois, was vacant, and that I was to be placed in charge. I was not yet sixteen years old, but most people took me to be nineteen or twenty, and the superintendent said that age shouldn't count against ability. Lockport is in the same county as Joliet, so I was stationed near home, and my mother was delighted at the progress I had made."

"At such an age you must have felt the responsibility of having the entire office in your charge."

"Yes," said Colonel Clowry, "I think I did. It was my constant endeavor to appear older than sixteen, because I felt that business men might not have confidence in my ability if they knew I was so very young. I was fortunate in my work. Everything progressed favorably under my management, and, as the business rapidly increased, the superintendent was pleased with my work."

"Do you think the company would nowadays employ a boy of sixteen as manager?"

"That's a difficult question to answer," said Colonel Clowry. "I think, if the boy were capable and earnest, he would be given such a position. Merit is as quickly rewarded to-day as ever."

"I suppose you did not stay long at Lockport?"

"I wouldn't have been satisfied to stay there long. It was my ambition to be manager of a more important office, and I tried to prove myself worthy of a better position. I took advantage of every opportunity to improve my education. I read every book which could give me any knowledge of telegraphy and electricity, and was especially interested in biography, travel, history, and geography. I was obliged to remain at the office until late in the evening, but often I sat up until after midnight, reading and studying. I think it is helpful for every boy to know what great and successful men have really accomplished. Among my favorite books were the journals of Lewis and Clark on their expedition across the continent in 1804, and, when I was discouraged or disheartened, it cheered me to remember the vicissitudes encountered by them."

HE TRIED TO DO MORE THAN HE WAS PAID TO DO.

"I always endeavored, while at Lockport, and in every other position I have filled, to perform more service than that which was allotted to me and to watch my employer's interests at all times, regardless of stipulated hours. It is a great mistake for a young man to think that his efforts to be efficient and to perform more work than is set apart for him will not be noticed by his employers or superior officers. The appreciation of such services may seem tardy, but it is almost sure to come, and, in my case, it came very soon. After I had served at Lockport for a few months, I was transferred to Springfield, Illinois, which is a more important station. I was not seventeen when I began my work there, but I felt myself to be quite an experienced person in the business, and capable of caring for almost any office. On account of my night study I had a thorough knowledge of the principles of telegraphy, and my practice as an operator had given me the necessary technical qualifications.

"Operators didn't receive as much then as they do now, but living expenses were low. When I went to Lockport, I believe that I was paid about a dollar a day, and at Springfield my wages were somewhat higher. In 1854, two years after I first began to carry messages, I was sent to St. Louis, as the company's chief operator, and of course that was a considerable promotion. I remained in that position until 1858, when I became superintendent of the St. Louis and Missouri River Telegraph Company, which was constructing many new lines in the border region. The company was not very rich, but it was very necessary that its system should be extended. It occurred to me that the citizens of the border towns ought to be willing to pay something to have the convenience of the telegraph; so, when the line was constructed to Kansas City, I raised three thousand dollars in Leavenworth to extend it to that place, and two thousand dollars in Atchinson to have it built to that city from Leavenworth. In this way we accomplished what the company was financially unable to do.

THERE ARE AS GOOD CHANCES IN THE WORLD TO-DAY.

"When the Civil War began, I offered my services to the government, and was placed in charge of the military telegraph in the Department of Arkansas. Missouri and Kansas were subsequently added to my territory. I served through the war, and, at its close, when I was twenty-seven years old, I became a district superintendent for the Western Union Telegraph Company in the southwest. I have been with this company ever since, having served in various capacities in St. Louis and Chicago. This is my fiftieth year in the telegraph business, and I became president of the Western Union just fifty years to a month after I first entered the Joliet office and asked for work."

"Do you think that a young man starting in commercial life to-day has as good a chance to rise as one had fifty years ago?" Colonel Clowry was asked.

"Yes, indeed; in my opinion the chances of success in commercial business, for the right sort of young men, have never before been so good as they are at the present time, provided that the young men are well educated, honest, industrious, and faithful, and not handicapped by mental or physical defects."

"But you had only a common-school education, Colonel Clowry."

"Yes, and that is quite sufficient in business if it is supplemented by some technical training. I have always thought that a full university course has a tendency to unfit young men for the rough struggles incident to the small beginnings of a commercial business career. It is advisable for boys to enter business early in life, so that they may be moulded to their work, and be in line for promotion when opportunities present themselves. Boys have an idea nowadays that they can leave college and immediately fill important positions in business life. There was never a greater mistake. Although I was in charge of an office six months after beginning work, it has taken fifty years to reach my present position."

XIII

ENTHUSIASM FOR RAILROADING MAKES A SECTION HAND HEAD OF THE METROPOLITAN SYSTEM.

SOME time ago New York learned with interest and some astonishment that the head of its greatest transportation system, Herbert H. Vreeland, had received from several of his associates, as individuals, a "valentine" present of $100,000, in recognition of his superb management of their properties. Many New Yorkers then learned, for the first time, what railroad experts throughout the country had long known, that the transportation of a million people a day in New York's busy streets, without serious friction or public annoyance, is not a matter of chance, but is the result of perhaps the most perfect traffic organization ever created, at the head of which is a man, quiet, forceful, able, with the ability of a great general,—a master, and, at the same time a friend of men,—himself one for whom, in the judgment of his associates, almost any career is possible.

Thirty years ago Mr. Vreeland, then a lad thirteen years old, was, to use his own humorous, reminiscent phrase, "h'isting ice" on the Hudson River, one of a gang of eighteen or twenty men and boys filling the ice carts for retail city delivery. A picture just brought to light shows him among the force lined up to be photographed, as a tall, loosely built, hatchet-faced lad in working garb, with a fragment of a smile on his face, as if he could appreciate the contrast of the boy of that day with the man of the future.

How do these things happen? What was the divine spark in

this boy's brain and heart that should lift him out of the crowd of the commonplace to the position of responsibility and influence in the world which he now occupies? If my readers could have been present at the interview kindly granted by Mr. Vreeland and could have heard him recalling his early life and its many struggles and disappointments with a smile that was often near a tear, they would have gone away feeling that nothing is impossible to him who dares, and, above all else, who *works*, and they would have derived inspiration far greater than can possibly be given in these written words.

HE INHERITED A TASTE FOR HARD WORK.

The desire to work was hereditary with Mr. Vreeland. His father incurred the displeasure of his own father and family, who were people of large means, by refusing to lead a life of gentlemanly idleness, and deciding, instead, to enter the ministry. The boy Herbert was the youngest son in a family of several children, each of whom in turn helped to support the mother and younger members after the death of the father. At ten years of age, in his passionate desire to do *something*, he drove a grocery wagon in Jersey City, to which his family had moved from his birth-place in Glen, New York, and, as before said, at thirteen years of age, he was hard at work in an ice business, of which an elder brother was superintendent.

"I first entered the railroad business in 1875," said Mr. Vreeland, "shoveling gravel on one of the Long Island Railroad Company's night construction trains. Though this position was certainly humble enough, it was a great thing to me then to feel myself a railroad man, with all that that term implied; and, when, after a few months' trial, I was given the job of inspecting ties and roadbed at a dollar a day, I felt that I was well on the road to the presidency.

"One day the superintendent asked the boss if he could give

him a reliable man to replace a switchman who had just made a blunder leading to a collision, and had been discharged. The reply was: 'Well, I've got a man here named Vreeland, who will do exactly what you tell him to.' They called me up, and, after a few short, sharp questions from the train-master, I went down to the dreary and desolate marsh near Bushwick, Long Island, and took charge of a switch. For a few days I had to camp out near that switch, in any way that might happen, but finally the officers made up their minds that they could afford me the luxury of a two-by-four flag house with a stove in it, and I settled down for more railroading."

HE LOVED HIS WORK.

"The Bushwick station was not far away, and one of the company's division headquarters was there. I soon made the acquaintance of all the officials around that station, and got into their good graces by offering to help them out in their clerical work at any and all times when I was off duty. It was a godsend to them, and exactly what I wanted, for I had determined to get into the inside of the railroad business from bottom to top. Many's the time I have worked till eleven or twelve o'clock at night in that little station, figuring out train receipts and expenses, engine cost and duty, and freight and passenger statistics of all kinds; and, as a result of this work, I quickly acquired a grasp of railroad details in all stages, which few managers possess, for, in one way and another, I got into and through every branch of the business.

"My Bushwick switch was a temporary one, put in for construction purposes only, and, after some months' use, was discontinued, and I was discharged. This did not suit me at all, and I went to one of the officials of the road and told him that I wanted to remain with the Long Island Railroad Company in any capacity whatsoever, and would be obliged to him if he would give me a job. He said, at first, that he hadn't a thing for me to do, but finally added, as if he was ashamed to suggest it, that, if I had a mind to go down on another division and sweep out and dust cars, I might do it. I instantly accepted, and thereby learned the details of another important railroad department.

"Pretty soon they made me brakeman on an early morning train to Hempstead, and then I found that I was worth to the world, after two years of railroad training, just forty dollars a month, plus a perquisite or two obtained from running a card-table department in the smoking-cars. I remember that I paid eighteen dollars of my munificent salary for board and lodging, sent twenty dollars home for the support of my mother and sister, and had two dollars a month and the aforesaid perquisites left for 'luxuries.'"

A NICKNAME THAT BECAME A REAL TITLE.

"It was at about this time, thus early in my career, that I first came to be known as 'President Vreeland.' An old codger upon the railroad, in talking to me one day, said, in a bantering way: 'Well, I suppose you think your fortune is made, now you have become a brakeman, but let me tell you what will happen. You will be a brakeman about four or five years, and then they will make you a conductor, at about one hundred dollars a month, and there you will stick all your life, if you don't get discharged.' I responded, rather angrily, 'Do you suppose I am going to be satisfied with remaining a conductor? I mean to be president of a railroad,' 'Ho, ho, ho!' laughed the man. He told the story around, and many a time thereafter the boys slyly placed the word 'President' before my name on official instructions and packages sent to me.

"A conductor on one of the regular trains quarreled one morning with the superintendent, and was discharged. I was sent for and told to take out that train. This was jumping me over the heads of many of the older brakemen, and, as a consequence, all the brakemen on that train quit. Others were secured, however, and I ran the train regularly for a good many months.

"Then came an accident one day, for which the engineer and I were jointly responsible. We admitted our responsibility, and were discharged. I went again to the superintendent, however, and, upon a strong plea to be retained in the service, he sent me back to the ranks among the brakemen. I had no complaint to make, but accepted the consequence of my mistake.

"Soon after this, the control of the road passed into other hands. Many were discharged, and I was daily expecting my own 'blue envelope.' One day I was detailed to act as brakeman on a special which was to convey the president and directors of the road, with invited guests, on a trip over the lines. By that time I had learned the Long Island Railroad in all its branches pretty well, and, in the course of the trip, was called upon to answer a great many questions. The next day I received word that the superintendent wanted to see me. My heart sank within me, for summons of this kind were ominous in those days, but I duly presented myself at the office and was asked, 'Are you the good-looking brakeman who was on the special yesterday who shows his teeth when he smiles?' I modestly replied that I was certainly on the special yesterday, and I may possibly have partly confirmed the rest of the identification by a smile, for the superintendent, without further questioning, said: 'The president wants to see you upstairs.'

"I went up, and in due time was shown into the presence of the great man, who eyed me closely for a minute or two, and then asked me abruptly what I was doing. I told him I was braking Number Seventeen. He said: 'Take this letter to your superintendent. It contains a request that he relieve you from duty, and put somebody else in your place. After he has done so, come back here.'"

AN IMPORTANT MISSION WELL PERFORMED.

"All this I did, and, on my return to the president, he said, 'Take this letter at once to Admiral Peyron, of the French fleet (then lying in the harbor on a visit of courtesy to this country), and this to General Hancock, on Governor's Island. They contain invitations to each to dine with me to-morrow night at home in Garden City with their staffs. Get their answers, and, if they are "yes," return at once to New York, charter a steamer, call for them to-morrow afternoon, land them at Long Island City, arrange for a special train from Long Island City to Garden City, take them there, and return them after the banquet. I leave everything in your hands. Good day.'

"I suppose this might be considered a rather large job for a common brakeman, but I managed to get through with it without disgracing myself, and apparently to the satisfaction of all concerned. For some time thereafter, I was the president's special emissary on similar matters connected with the general conduct of the business, and while I did not, perhaps, learn so very much about railroading proper, was put in positions where I learned to take responsibility and came to have confidence in myself.

"The control of the Long Island Railroad again changed hands, and I was again 'let out,' this time for good, so far as that particular road was concerned,—except that, within the last two or three years, I have renewed my acquaintance with it through being commissioned by a banking syndicate in New York City to make an expert examination of its plant and equipment as a preliminary to reorganization.

"This was in 1881, or about that time, and I soon secured a position as conductor on the New York and Northern Railroad, a little line running from One Hundred and Fifty-fifth Street, New York City, to Yonkers. Not to go into tedious detail regarding my experience there, I may say in brief that in course of time,

I practically 'ran the road.' After some years, it changed hands (a thing which railways, particularly small ones, often do, and always to the great discomposure of the employees), and the new owners, including William C. Whitney, Daniel S. Lamont, Captain R. Somers Hayes and others, went over the road one day on a special train to visit the property. As I have said, I was then practically running the road, owing to the fact that the man who held the position as general manager was not a railroad man and relied upon me to handle all details, but my actual position was only that of train-master. I accompanied the party, and knowing the road thoroughly, not only physically but also statistically, was able to answer all the questions which they raised. This was the first time I had met Mr. Whitney, and I judge that I made a somewhat favorable impression upon him, for not long after that I was created general manager of the road."

HOW HE WAS ELECTED TO THE PRESIDENCY OF HIS COMPANY.

"A few months later, I received this telegram:—

"'H. H. Vreeland.

"'Meet me at Broadway and Seventh Avenue office at two o'clock to-day.

"William C. Whitney.'

"I had to take a special engine to do this, but arrived at two o'clock at the office of the Houston Street, West Street and Pavonia Ferry Railroad Company, which I then knew, in an indistinct sort of way, owned a small horse railway in the heart of New York. After finding that Mr. Whitney was out at lunch, I kicked my heels for a few minutes outside the gate, and then inquired of a man who was seated inside in an exceedingly comfortable chair, when Mr. Whitney and his party were expected, saying, also, that my name was Vreeland, and I had an appointment at two. He replied: 'Oh, are you Mr. Vreeland? Well, here is a letter for you. Mr. Whitney expected to be here at two o'clock, but is a little late.' I took my letter and sat down again outside, thinking that it might possibly contain an appointment for another hour. It was, however, an appointment of quite a different character. It read as follows:

"'Mr. H. H. Vreeland.

"'Dear Sir:—At a meeting of the stockholders of the Houston Street, West Street and Pavonia Ferry Railroad Company, held this day, you were unanimously elected a director of the company.

"'At a subsequent meeting of the directors, you were unanimously elected president and general manager, your duties to commence immediately.

"'Yours truly,

"C. E. Warren, Secretary.'

"By the time I had recovered from my surprise at learning that I was no longer a steam-railroad, but a street-railroad man, Mr. Whitney and other directors came in, and, after spending about five minutes in introductions, they took up their hats and left, saying, simply, 'Well, Vreeland, you are president; now run the road.' I then set out to learn what kind of a toy railway it was that had come into my charge."

HIGH-PRICED MEN ARE IN DEMAND.

Mr. Vreeland was asked the secret of successfully managing a street-railway system of this sort.

"High-priced men," he unhesitatingly replied. "High-priced men, and one-man power in all departments. Ten-thousand-dollar-a-year men are what I want,—one of these rather than five two-thousand-dollar-a-year men."

"I began at the bottom and worked up. I think that is always the way for a young man to do, as soon as he has decided upon his career. I was fitted for the railroad business, and it didn't take me long to decide just what I wanted to be. I think much of my progress was due to my early beginning. I think an early beginning means a great deal in after life.

"I have always been glad that I chose the business I did. I have never had any reason to regret having done so. Of course, when I was very young, I had discontented moments, like almost every other youth, but I overcame them, and stayed with the railroad. I believe that everyone should overcome those passing fancies, instead of yielding to them. Too many young fellows, just starting out, go from one thing to another, never satisfied, and consequently never making any progress. I think the faculty for 'sticking' is one of the most valuable a young man can have. When an employer hires a man, he likes to feel that he won't be wasting his time in teaching him the business. He likes to feel that the man will remain with him, and be a real help, instead of leaving at the first opportunity."

The rest of the history is well known to the people of New York, and to experts in street railroading throughout the country. The "Whitney syndicate," so-called, was then in possession of a few only out of some twenty or more street railway properties in New York City, the Broadway line, however, being one of these, and by far the most valuable. With the immense financial resources of

Messrs. Whitney, Widener, Elkins, and their associates, nearly all the other properties were added to the original lines owned by the syndicate, and with the magnificent organizing and executive ability of Mr. Vreeland, there has been built up in New York a street railway system which, while including less than two hundred and fifty miles of track, is actually carrying more than one-half as many passengers each year as are being carried by all the steam railroads of the United States together.

LABOR

XIV

A FACTORY BOY'S PURPOSE TO IMPROVE LABOR MAKES HIM A GREAT LEADER.

"TO reduce the burdens of the overworked and find employment for the workless workers," as expressed in his own words, is the life-work of Samuel Gompers. This single aim has been the wellspring of the manifold activities, excitements, vicissitudes, and achievements of a remarkable career. Nearly forty years ago, when Samuel Gompers, a boy of ten, worked fourteen hours a day in a shop in London, the hardships of the workingman made an impression on his childish mind, and this impression, and vague ideas that followed it, were the beginnings of his life purpose,—a purpose that kept growing and strengthening during twenty-six years at the cigarmaker's bench, and finally raised him to the position of foremost representative in America of the interests of labor.

Being president of the American Federation of Labor, whose headquarters are in Washington, Mr. Gompers now lives in that city, but not long ago he was in New York as one of the distinguished speakers before a great mass meeting. The following night, in an obscure hall on the "eastside" where a number of his old friends and fellow-workers in the cigarmaker's trade had gathered to discuss their common interests, I had my interview with him.

LOOKS LIKE EDWIN FORREST.

"He's not here yet," I was informed on my arrival; "but come in and wait. When he comes, anybody will point out Sam to you." The room filled rapidly, and at length there appeared in the doorway a small man with a great head, covered with a luxuriant growth of very black hair. His short, robust figure, his high forehead, deep-set eyes, heavy mustache and short imperial made him look strikingly like some of the portraits of Edwin Forrest. He came in alone and attracted no special attention, but I knew intuitively that it was Samuel Gompers. With such easy and cordial salutations as "Hello, Jack!" "How are you, Herman?" and "Glad to see you, Mac!" he began to greet his old friends, and they responded in the same spirit, almost invariably addressing him as "Sam." This did not imply a lack of dignity on his part, for these were his old shopmates,—men who had for years worked with him at the same benches. They recognized each other as fellow-workmen, with no difference between them, and, indeed, the only difference was that Sam Gompers had thought much and seen much in his mental vision as he sat at the mechanical work of cutting and rolling tobacco leaves, while the others had seen only their own environment and machine-like toil. But this difference has made one a leading citizen of the Republic, while his mates have remained humble cigarmakers, looking to Mr. Gompers as their champion and friend.

"It was just at such meetings as you see here to-night," Mr. Gompers said to me later in the evening, "that I began to try to do something in behalf of the workingmen. Even when a small boy in London, and working pretty hard for the child I was, I used to attend some of the gatherings of workingmen, and I remember how I was stirred by the excitement and enthusiasm when the question of recognizing the Confederate States was before the government and there were great meetings of the working classes to show the feeling of British workmen against slavery of any sort. I had already vaguely begun to feel that there was more than one kind of slavery, and that the workingmen who had protested so vigorously against slaves in America could hardly call themselves free men. I knew little of the matter; I only knew that my own life was hard, while that of many other children was easy."

HE WORKED IN A FACTORY AT TEN.

"When I was ten, I had been put in a factory to learn shoemaking, but a few months afterward was apprenticed to a man in my father's trade,—that of a cigarmaker. I went to school at night, but it was a very meagre foundation for an education that I got this way, and I have been trying ever since to make up for it by reading and study. My lack of early opportunity to learn and develop normally, with schooling and much recreation, as a boy should, has always been a great drawback to me, but it has made me zealous in the cause of keeping the children of the workers out of the workshops and giving them a fair education. College training is not necessary for success in any but scholastic pursuits, but boys must certainly know the rudiments."

THE LATER ARISTOCRACY.

"Times were bad in London when I was a child there. Gangs of workmen used to parade the streets, singing mournfully, 'We have no work to do!' This condition led my father to immigrate to this country, in 1863, when I was thirteen. I continued my trade of cigarmaker in New York, and joined the 'Cigarmakers'

International Union' when it was organized, in 1864. It now has thirty thousand members, but mine is the longest continued membership; my due card is No. 1. This was the first labor organization I belonged to. I attended its meetings and got into the habit of studying and thinking about labor matters and the many changes in the workingman's condition that would be beneficial to himself and to the commonwealth.

"I began to realize that, in the struggles of the ages, lords and nobles have lost their gold lace and velvet, but that they survive as the economic lords of the means of life, and that their aggressions must be opposed by combinations of labor—by trade unions. I began to appreciate the true dignity of labor and the importance to the state of fair conditions for workingmen. The older I grew, the more essential seemed the strong organization of labor. I felt what Wendell Phillips expressed in these words: 'I rejoice at every effort workingmen make to organize. I hail the labor movement. It is my only hope for democracy. Organize and stand together. Let the nation hear a united demand from the laboring voice.'

THE NEED OF ORGANIZED LABOR.

"Of course the idea of organized labor is a very old one. Trade unions have been in existence since the Middle Ages, but what they needed in this country was more cohesive strength. There were a great number of separate unions and some general organizations, but they were not strong enough. A new plan was needed, and we published a call which resulted in a convention at Pittsburg, in 1881, at which the American Federation of Labor was formed. Most of the delegates to that convention were strongly opposed to our project for an organization on broader lines than had been before attempted, but we carried the point, and at present the Federation has six hundred and fifty thousand members."

It is a matter of history that Samuel Gompers was the founder of the American Federation of Labor. The first impulse came from him. While sitting at his bench in New York rolling cigars, he conceived the plan that has made the Federation the largest and most important and useful labor organization that has ever existed.

HE WAS ELECTED PRESIDENT OF THE FEDERATION.

Mr. Gompers declined the presidency at the first convention, but he was obliged to accept it at the second great gathering, held in Cleveland, in 1882. For some time after his election he remained at work at his trade, but the growing number and importance of his duties at length made it necessary for him to devote all his time to the Federation, which he does for a salary that many clerks would scoff at. Mr. Gompers has received offers for nominations to congress from both the Republican and Democratic parties in his New York district, and has been asked by several presidents of the United States to accept important and highly salaried offices, but he has declined them all, feeling that his present position gives him greater opportunities of usefulness to the workingman.

The laws whose place on the statute books are due to the efforts of Mr. Gompers make a long list. They include sanitary inspection for factories, mills, mines, etc., the age limit law, employers' liabilities for damages to life and limb, wage-lien laws, uniform car-coupling laws, anti-sweatshop legislation, the anti-conspiracy law, the state-board-of-arbitration law, laws restricting the hours of labor, and the enactment making the first Monday in September a holiday.

FOR THE EIGHT-HOUR WORKDAY.

"At present," said Mr. Gompers, "one of our chief slogans is,—'An Eight-Hour Workday!' There is more in this than one might think at a first glance. With a little leisure, the workingman has an opportunity to read and cultivate his mind and devote himself to his home and family. It makes him expand intellectually and think more, and with this new life come new desires. He wants to have his home more comfortable than it has been. He wants a few books, a few pictures, a little recreation for himself and family, and for these things he makes outlays of money which are very modest in individual cases, but which, in the aggregate, amount to vast sums and have a stimulating effect on all trades. This makes an increased demand for labor. It has a tendency to raise wages and diminish the number of the unemployed. These important benefits to be derived from shorter hours of labor constitute the reason why I am making an issue of the eight-hour workday. We have already done much and expect to do more. Yet you have no idea how hard it sometimes is to procure the passage of a measure. When the uniform car-coupling bill was before the senate, the senators would run into the coat-room to avoid voting, and I stood at the door in a half frantic condition, sending my card to this senator and that senator, and telling each that he simply must support the measure. It was hard work, but we carried it through."

STRIKES AS A LAST RESORT.

Strikes are not favored by Mr. Gompers except under certain circumstances and as a last resort. During the great Chicago strike, the most intense pressure was brought to bear upon him to issue an order calling out all the workingmen in the country. It took high moral courage to resist the many strenuous appeals, but Samuel Gompers possessed this courage and the country was saved from an experience which might have proved most calamitous.

"I firmly believe in arbitration," said Mr. Gompers, "but to arbitrate, the power must be equal, or nearly so, on both sides; therefore labor must be strongly organized."

I asked him to what he attributed his success in his life-work.

"Well," he answered slowly, "I learned both to think and to act, and to feel strongly enough on these great questions of labor to be willing to sacrifice my personal convenience for my aims. I have felt great devotion to the common cause of the manual workers, and I can say nothing better to young men than,—'Be devoted to your work.'"

When I asked a very intelligent workingman why Samuel Gompers is so highly respected by the workers, he replied:—

"Why, because,—because he's Sam Gompers,—but that doesn't explain much, does it? Well, I will say because he has done more for labor than any other man in this country, because we can trust him down to the ground, and because he's in his work heart and soul."

PUBLIC LIFE

XV

A PUNY BOY, BY PHYSICAL CULTURE, BECOMES THE MOST VIGOROUS OF AMERICAN PRESIDENTS.

THE way to study a man, I find, is at close range, when he is not on the platform or under the limelight. Better than any other is his vacation time, when the armor has been laid aside and the man himself stands forth. My card of introduction proved a ready passport to the country seat of Theodore Roosevelt, near Oyster Bay, Long Island. As I drove up, one bright July morning, the shore of this sequestered inlet was framed in a background of heavy green. No painter could do justice to the mirrored loveliness of the water, or the graceful line of sailboats lazily floating over it. The beach was a silver mat in an emerald frame, and every tree on the opposite shore was inverted in the clear depths. The Roosevelt house stands on a hill overlooking a magnificent view of Long Island Sound. It is three miles away from the railway station, just the sort of place one would choose for complete rest. The dreamy beauty of the scene was conducive to indolence, and so, sure enough, I found Mr. Roosevelt in outing attire, surrounded by his children and entering with zest into their out-door sports.

Little Theodore was prancing up and down the road on his favorite black pony, a genuine rough rider in horsemanship, brown as a berry, and an unmistakable cadet of the Roosevelt house. The president's war-horse, "Texas," whose right ear was clipped by a Spanish "Mauser," was out for an airing. Over the veranda flared a pair of great antlers, a trophy of the chase, while in the big reception hall were other antlers. The sword worn by Colonel Roosevelt in Cuba has found a resting-place across the mantel mirror, its leathern strap all ready to be buckled on again should a military emergency arise. The overcoat is there, too, with the hat and boots.

I found him averse to politics as a topic for discussion, but I hinted that I would be pleased to quote his views on young men in politics,—their chances and their duties.

YOUNG MEN IN POLITICS.

"That opens up," said he, as he smiled graciously, "such a vista of human thought that I know you will excuse me from its contemplation this hot weather."

The shade of the veranda where we sat was deliciously somnolent, and I was beginning to regret my question when the president relented for a moment.

"You know I have always advocated an earnest, intelligent study of political subjects by young men. Our American politics offer a clean, wholesome field, after all is said and done, for the young man of character and ability; but never should one enter politics for a living."

"Now, we know that you approve of college education for boys, but want your own words about it."

"It depends somewhat on the boy. I don't believe in every boy going to college."

"But do you not think it makes them less practical than they would be if they grew up in business pursuits?"

"Not at all. The best kind of college graduates are the most practical, and they are becoming more numerous every year. Don't you think I'm practical?"

"Do you think the boys in towns like this have as good a chance for success in life as those who live in large cities?"

"Certainly, and often better chances. I have always been glad to have been raised in the country. Of course it is often a good thing for a boy to go to the city when he is grown. He sometimes does better there than in a small place; not always, though. It depends upon the boy."

OPPORTUNITIES AND TALENTS.

"Are you a believer in opportunity, Mr. Roosevelt?"

"To a certain extent. Many of the great changes in our lives can be traced to small things, a chance acquaintance, an accident, or some little happening. A time comes to every man when he must do a thing or miss a great benefit. If the man does it, all is well. If not, it isn't likely that he will have the chance again. You can call that opportunity if you wish, but it is foresight that leads a man to take advantage of the condition of things. Foresight is a most valuable thing to have."

"Some men," I remarked, after a time, "have a talent for working themselves, while others have a talent for setting others to work. Which is the more valuable?"

"I think a man ought to have both. If he can't, I think he ought to be able to work himself. The ability to work hard is, perhaps, the most valuable aid to success. One can't have much success without it."

"They say it isn't a good thing for a young man to have too many talents, Mr. Roosevelt. Is it true?"

"That's very hard to answer. I have managed to do many different things in a lifetime. I might have done better by doing only one. Still, that is another thing that depends very much upon the young man, and his capabilities."

"I know you must believe in recreation for people who are working, since you are yourself indulging in it now."

"Oh, yes, one must have some change. A man who has no outdoor exercise is likely to wear himself out in short order. I love to be out of doors. I always have, and that is one thing that has helped me to do some things that I have. I go out for a time every day when I am here at home. I enjoy being in the open air."

"I know you think that the young man of to-day has a better chance to make a success in life than those who lived twenty-five years ago."

"Certainly. The young man of to-day has greater opportunities for advancing himself and achieving a real success than any men have ever had before. Everything offers better chances, and all a boy needs is education enough to appreciate them when they are here. That is one of the chief values of a good education. It aids a young man in many things that would be invisible to the uneducated fellow. It helps him to weigh things in his mind before deciding what to do. It is mind-training that we need. The power to think is almost absolutely necessary to success. Without it, a man is sure to be unequal to the great struggle for supremacy that is going on constantly in certain professions and lines of business."

In a contributed article President Roosevelt gave his views of what constitutes good citizenship. An extract from this article is given herewith:

THE CITIZENSHIP THAT COUNTS.

"After honesty as the foundation of the citizenship that counts, in business or in politics, must come courage. You must have courage not only in battle, but also in civic life. We need physical and we need moral courage. Neither is enough by itself. You need moral courage. Many a man has been brave physically who has flinched morally. You must feel in you a fiery wrath against evil. When you see a wrong, instead of feeling shocked and hurt, and a desire to go home, and a wish that right prevailed, you should go out and fight until that wrong is overcome. You must feel ashamed if you do not stand up for the right as you see it; ashamed if you lead a soft and easy life and fail to do your duty. You must have courage. If you do not, the honesty is of no avail.

"But honesty and courage, while indispensable, are not enough for good citizenship. I do not care how brave and honest a man is; if he is a fool, he is not worth knocking on the head. In addition to courage and honesty, you must have the saving quality of common sense. One hundred and ten years ago, France started to form a republic, and one of her noted men—an exceedingly brilliant man, a scholar of exceptional thought, the Abbe Sieyés,—undertook to draw up a constitution. He drew up several constitutions, beautiful documents; but they would not work. The French national convention resolved in favor of liberty; and, in the name of liberty, they beheaded every man who did not think as they did. They resolved in favor of fraternity, and beheaded those who objected to such a brotherhood. They resolved in favor of equality, and cut off the heads of those who rose above the general level. They indulged in such hideous butcheries, in the name of liberty, equality, and fraternity, as to make tyranny seem mild in comparison;—and all because they lacked common sense, as well as morality.

"Two or three years before that, we, in America, had a body of men gathered in a constitutional convention to make a constitution. They assembled under the lead of Washington, with Alexander Hamilton, Madison, and many other eminent men. They did not draw up a constitution in a week, as the brilliant Sieyés did, but just one constitution, and that one worked. That was the great point!

"It worked, primarily, because it was drawn up by practical politicians,—by practical politicians who believed in decency, as well as in common sense. If they had been a set of excellent theorists, they would have drawn up a constitution which would have commended itself to other excellent theorists, but which would not have worked. If they had been base, corrupt men, mere opportunists, men who lacked elevating ideals, dishonest, cowardly, they would have drawn up a document that would not have worked at all. On the great scale, the only practical politics is honest politics. The makers of our constitution were practical politicians, who were also sincere reformers, and as brave and upright as they were sensible."

THE BOYHOOD OF ROOSEVELT.

Nobody thought of calling Theodore Roosevelt "Teddy," when he was a boy. He was always known as "Tedie,"—pronounced as if written "Teedie." But several years before he went to Harvard, when he was about fifteen years old, his mother thought that it was high time that the baby name was replaced by something more dignified, and so it was decided, in family council, that he should be addressed as Theodore.

Unfortunately, family decisions of this kind are not always respected at school or college, and, when young Roosevelt became a freshman at Harvard, he was promptly dubbed "Teddy" by his classmates. The nickname stuck; he has been "Teddy" ever since to his intimates, and to-day he is more generally known under that title by seventy-six millions of people than by any other. There is every reason to believe that he enjoys the little informality, justly regarding it as a tribute to his popularity.

When he was nine years of age, young Roosevelt was taken abroad by his parents, and he made another trip with them to Europe not long afterward, greatly enjoying a voyage up the Nile. At seventeen he entered Harvard, and promptly grew a pair of side-whiskers, of which it may reasonably be supposed that he was very proud. The side-whiskers resembled those of Pendennis, as pictured by Thackeray. It goes without saying that he soon became extremely popular at college, where he acquitted himself fairly well in his studies. Old classmates recall the fact that he had a passion for animals and that he collected many queer natural history specimens, which he kept in his room.

WHERE HE GAINED STRENUOSITY.

On the whole, it is rather surprising that Theodore Roosevelt ever lived to grow up and become the President of the United States. He was an exceedingly delicate child, suffering such tortures with asthma that on many occasions his father was obliged to harness his four-in-hand in the middle of the night, take the boy from his bed, and drive many miles, in order that he might get his breath.

To my thinking, his inherent manliness, his independence of thought and action, his firm determination to do his duty as he sees it, found early expression in the character of Theodore Roosevelt when, as a youth, in search of health and strength, he went to the great west. It is probable that, while yet a young man, he was ambitiously inspired to do something out of the ordinary, and was shrewd enough to know that, to win success in life's undertakings, vigorous health is a prime requisite. He elected the arid plains and mountains of our western country, as a likely locality wherein he might build up a constitution sturdy and strong.

HE DASHED INTO THE VORTEX OF THE CHASE.

It was in the summer of 1883 that he entered the then "wild and woolly" town of Little Missouri, situated on the Northern Pacific Railroad, in the very heart of the "bad lands" of Dakota. Little Missouri contained at that time some of the worst "bad men" and outlaws to be found outside the borders of civilization.

But it was not in the town that he expected to find the health and strength to carry him through the strenuous life he, perhaps, had already mapped out, but in the saddle, camp, and chase, by living close to nature and taking "pot luck" with the rough and rugged men who became his companions, and who understood him and whom he understood from the outset. During that summer, with one man and a pack-outfit, he hunted over the country, from Yellowstone Park to the Black Hills, from the Black Hills to the Big Horn Mountains, through the Big Horn Basin to Jackson Hole and in the majestic Rocky Mountains, back to Yellowstone Park, down Clark's Fork to the Yellowstone, the Big and Little Horn Rivers, through the Crow Indian Reservation where General George A. Custer, the gallant and lamented soldier, went to a heroic death. Back again to the "bad lands" of the Little Missouri, went Theodore Roosevelt, having hunted buffaloes, elk, deer, antelope, mountain sheep, bear, lion and the smaller game of that country. He fished in the numerous mountain streams, and lived the rough, hardy life of a frontiersman. For five months, the heavens were his only canopy. He caught and killed game for his own use, saddled his mounts, did his own cooking, was his own scout, and performed his half of the night-work. The capacity to do for himself and meet men upon an equal basis—self-reliance and personal courage,—came to him as the fruition of this and similar experiences in the Far West. I know that this democracy still influences him.

HE SHOWED PIONEERS HOW TO WINTER CATTLE.

Having studied the conditions of the wild animal life of mountain and plain, he found that the fattest and best wild game inhabited the "bad lands" of Little Missouri. Although without food or shelter, save what they could gather from the grasses that grew there, the wild game was in splendid condition. As a result of these conditions, the young hunter made up his mind to engage in the business of raising cattle. Old frontiersmen told him that cattle could not be wintered in the "bad lands." This he disputed, and he argued, as proof of his contention, the fact that the finest wild game was to be found there, and he could not understand why cattle would not thrive under the same conditions. The following spring, Theodore Roosevelt shipped to Little Missouri, by the Northern Pacific Railroad, several hundred head of cattle, hired *vaqueros*, purchased mess-wagons and provisions, and drove the cattle from the cars to his range in the very heart of the "bad lands." There he took up the life of a western ranchman, and asked of his men nothing that he would not undertake himself. He faced the most violent blizzards while rounding up the cattle for safety. I remember this intrepid son of fortune, participating in the stampedes, doing his share of the night-herding, breaking his own horses, sleeping at night with his saddle for a pillow, and, perhaps, the snow for a blanket, eating the same rough, substantial fare as his employees, and evidencing the indomitable will, courage and endurance which brought to him the affection and respect of his men.

HE CIVILIZED MANY "BAD MEN" BY HIS INFLUENCE.

The country at that time was the habitat of horse thieves, stage robbers, desperadoes, and criminals in general. Surely this "tenderfoot" from the east would prove an excellent subject for imposition! Other men had been made to feel that lawlessness and depredation were united as a common lot visited upon each newcomer, the only apparent, quick redress being in the power and ability of the offended party to protect himself and chastise the marauders. Mr. Roosevelt's salutatry to such persons came early, and was effective. His influence and example did much toward civilizing the "bad men" in his locality, who found him to be an absolutely just man, possessing nerve, and handy with gun and fists. No person ever stole a hoof of his cattle or horses but was captured and punished according to the laws then existing in that country.

Theodore Roosevelt early acquired the reputation of being abundantly able to protect himself and his interests, his aptitude along such lines being brought out in bold relief by what is remembered in the west as the Marquis De Mores incident. Marquis De Mores was a Frenchman by birth and a western ranchman through preference. He went west heralded as a duelist of great reputation, and located upon a ranch some miles distant from that of the subject of this article. Although thoroughly an honorable man, he believed in governing the country by force, and it was the popular impression that the cowboys in his employ were "killers" and ready to fight at the drop of the hat. Soon after De Mores had established his headquarters in a town called Medora, Roosevelt's cowboys and those in De Mores' employ became involved in a dispute over some cattle, which resulted in a pitched battle between the disputants. Victory, and a decisive one, perched upon the Roosevelt standard. De Mores' anger and chagrin were boundless when he learned of the outcome of the affair, and he informed his men that, if they could not whip Roosevelt's cowboys, he, personally, could whip their boss, and that some day he would go to Roosevelt's ranch and accomplish such a task. Roosevelt heard of this threat and sent immediate word to De Mores that he need not trouble to undertake the journey to his (Roosevelt's) ranch, but that he would meet him half way, at any designated point, when any differences could be speedily, if not peacefully, adjusted. Marquis De Mores did not choose to seriously consider our friend's message, and the impression became prevalent and widespread in that section of the country that the Frenchman's hand had been "called" and that he had been found bluffing.

"GAMENESS" WAS NEEDED; ROOSEVELT HAD PLENTY.

In those days, if there was one attribute of character and make-up more thoroughly acceptable than another, to the average westerner, it was the "gameness" a man possessed and displayed at an opportune time, such qualities always proving the open sesame to the regard and affections of the men of the camp. The De Mores episode gained for Roosevelt no little distinction. Contrary to predictions, his cattle industry proved to be a financial success. The cattle wintered well in the "bad lands," and, from there, he shipped some of the finest beeves ever placed in the Chicago market. He remained in the business for about three years, when he found himself the owner of several thousand head of cattle, splendid ranch houses, and corrals, and no doubt he could have remained in the business and become one of the cattle kings of the west. But by that time he had obtained what he went west for,—vigorous health and an iron constitution, the result of his labor and life on the plains, had come to him and he was ready for greater things. He gave to the people of the west an example of splendid integrity and forceful character, early winning their esteem and loyalty, the possession of which he has never forfeited but rather increased by the continued exercise of the sturdy independence which found such early expression among a people whose pluck and perseverance in the upbuilding of a great and new country has been immortalized in song and legend.

HIS FRONTIER LIFE WAS AMPLY WORTH THE WHILE.

As a legislator, police commissioner, governor and soldier, he has proved his capacity and worth, performing his work well and conscientiously. His fellow citizens, regardless of geographical distribution, believe that he will not be found wanting in the discharge of the exacting duties of his present exalted station, and his career may well be an inspiration to American youths. To all who have ever lived the untrammeled life of plain and mountain, the sweet memory of it abideth forever. To our president the freedom of it still strongly appeals, and we find him making occasional excursions into a country where the pleasures of the camp and the chase are still to be found, and where democracy prevails. To live as he did, and accomplish what he has, meeting the conditions of a new country, gaining health, strength, and a knowledge of men, was indeed worth while.

XVI

A BRAVE VOLUNTEER FIGHTS HIS WAY TO THE HEAD OF THE AMERICAN ARMY.

GENERAL MILES has had a remarkable military career.

He was not quite twenty-two when Fort Sumter was fired upon, and was, at the time, employed in a store near Boston. He spent his money in organizing a company, of which he was elected captain, but was commissioned only as a lieutenant, on account of his age. But he rapidly rose to be captain, colonel, brigadier-general and major-general. General Hancock quickly discovered his abilities. He was in charge of that commander's line at Chancellorsville, and held his own successfully against every attack by Lee's veterans. The second day, he was seriously wounded, and General Hancock, in a letter to Washington urging his promotion, said: "If Colonel Miles lives, he will be one of the most distinguished of our officers."

In February, 1865, this young man of twenty-six commanded the Second Army Corps. Never before had an American officer, at that age, had charge of so large a body of soldiers. When Lee surrendered at Appomattox, he had command of the First Division of the Second Army Corps.

SIX YEARS OF INDIAN FIGHTING.

General Miles is best known as an Indian fighter. His six years of work among the Indians covered a belt of country from the Rio Grande to Canada, and four hundred miles wide. In

1874, powerful Indian tribes roamed over this land. But Miles and his companions-in-arms, officers and soldiers, guarded the newly constructed railroads, and the towns which arose on the plains, until civilization prevailed. In 1876, he fought at Staked Plains, defeating the Cheyennes, Kiowas and Comanches. He subjugated the Sioux, and drove Sitting Bull, Crazy Horse and other braves across the Canada line. In September, he conquered the Nez Percés, with Chief Joseph; in 1878, the Bannocks. For five years,—(1880-1885),—he commanded the Columbia Department; in 1885, he was transferred to the Arizona Department, and subdued the Apaches under Geronimo and Natchez. He was made a major-general, United States Army, April 5, 1890; in 1891, he closed the war with the Sioux.

General Miles carries the honorable scars of four serious bullet-wounds. His wife was a Sherman, daughter of Judge Sherman, and niece of ex-Secretary Sherman and of General William Tecumseh Sherman. She is a "comrade" as well as a home-companion, and went with him to inspect fortifications and visit our southern camps during the late war.

HIS RECORD IN THE CIVIL WAR.

In the Civil War he was noted for his audacity and dash. He was a fighting commander. He never hesitated to obey an order to advance, and he never wanted to retreat. His courage was an inspiration to his troops, and undoubtedly prevented disaster on more than one occasion. Hancock had the utmost confidence in Miles, and put him to the front to bear the brunt of the enemy: the latter never failed his chief. When the break took place at Reams' Station,—that unfortunate battle, the name of which is said to have been printed on the heart of Hancock like Calais in the heart of Queen Mary,—Miles and his staff pushed to the very front to stay the backward rush of the troops, and the gallant defense which he offered to the victorious enemy saved the day from becoming one of the great catastrophes of the war.

While Miles is famous for his gallantry as a commander, he is equally noted for his coolness and good judgment. He always insisted upon the proper treatment of his men by the commissary department, and his division, the Second Corps, never had any reason to complain of want of attention on the part of their general to their comforts. "Good treatment and good fighting" was his rule.

A LOYAL, DAUNTLESS LEADER.

As commander of the army, General Miles is not different from the Miles of thirty years ago. Those who knew him then say that he has changed very little in appearance, and not at all in his devotion to duty and to the army. He was always above petty jealousy, and never withheld from a subordinate the credit due to him,—and this is a prominent trait in Miles to-day. The public wondered that Miles showed no impatience when he was not sent in command of the troops to Cuba, but those who knew the General felt that he was too firm a believer in discipline to object to any lawful act of his commander-in-chief. Miles is known to have been anxious to lead the fighting in the only war likely to offer him an opportunity to prove his ability as a general in command, but he obeyed without a murmur the orders which placed in other hands the leadership of the troops in the field. He maintained a vigilant supervision of all that was going on, and was especially watchful of the supplies which had been intended for the support of the army at the front. His criticism of those supplies has caused a widespread sensation and there were earnest demands that all the facts should be known, and the responsibility fixed.

A YOUNG MAN'S CHANCES IN THE ARMY.

General Miles is not willing to see callers when he is busy with his official duties. At other times, he is readily approached. He said to me that he did not care to talk about matters pending in connection with the army. I assured him at once that I had no intention of questioning him in regard to the matters to which he alluded, but would be glad to have his opinion about the chances of a young man in the army, and the proper qualifications for one seeking to enter the service.

YOUTH

General Miles replied that he would not object to answering questions on that point.

I asked the general if he thought an education necessary for a good soldier.

"Certainly," was the reply; "education is a good thing for a soldier, and he ought to be educated in more than reading, writing and arithmetic. He ought to have character, stability, energy and a willingness to obey. These qualities are largely brought out by the right kind of education. It can be set down as a rule, that a worthless civilian would be a worthless soldier. There are exceptions to the rule, of course, but the man who has the right kind of training to make him a good citizen is the best man for the army."

CHARACTER THE FOUNDATION OF TRUE COURAGE.

"And such a man will get along best in the army?" I suggested.

"Most assuredly," answered General Miles. "You can see that by looking over the list of heroes in the past. They have always been men of character. An officer should be a man of character, in order to command the respect of his men. Without their respect and esteem, he cannot succeed. With them, he can accomplish great things, if the opportunity offers. Look at the regard which the English soldiers had for the Duke of Wellington. It was chiefly based on his character, for he was not what might be called a lovable man. His men were ready to go anywhere that he sent them, for they knew their commander, and had confidence in him. Character is as important in a great general as in a great statesman or a great merchant. Character is just as necessary, also, in the private as in the officer. It will command recognition in time."

"Would you say, General, that the army really holds out very great chances for advancement?"

"I think it holds out as many chances as any profession or business does; for in the army, as in business, merit wins every time, and if a soldier has real merit, it is bound to be recognized, sooner or later."

"There is a chance, then, for every man who goes into the army as a private to become a general?"

"I don't know that I would make the statement as strong as that, but I believe that every soldier who deserves it will be promoted."

"Would you advise young men to select the army in preference to other professions?"

"That depends," the general replied, "on the young man. If he is fairly educated and properly trained, if his tastes are military, and he understands the importance and duty of discipline, if he is willing to learn and to obey, he will make no mistake in entering the army. There are, of course, other circumstances, such as family claims and associations which must have their bearing upon the choice of a career, but, speaking from the standpoint of the army, I would say that it is a good place for any young American with the right qualifications."

COURAGE NATURAL TO AMERICANS.

When asked about the conduct of our troops in the late war, General Miles answered: "Our soldiers fought bravely, but nothing else could be expected from American soldiers. They have no superiors in the field, and American history has shown that they can cope successfully with any foe. Courage is a natural virtue with all Americans, and the late war has shown that it has not been weakened any by years of peace. There is no better material in the world for an army than the young men who grow up in the cities and towns and on the farms of the United States. I have already said that a young man who enters the army should have education, and the intelligence of the average American soldier is one of his most valuable traits. He is not merely a machine; he is an intelligent machine. He is conscious of his duty and his responsibilities.

"What do you think of the future of the army, General?"

General Miles replied deliberately: "The American people will never have any occasion to be otherwise than proud of their army. It will be found equal to every call that can possibly be made upon it, and prepared to face any danger in defense of the nation."

LITTLE VISITS WITH GREAT AMERICANS

XVII

MAKING THE MOST OF HIS OPPORTUNITIES WINS A COVETED EMBASSY.

"YOU may say what you will," said a young lawyer in a conversation wherein Joseph H. Choate and his ability were the topics of conversation; "a man cannot hope to distinguish himself without special opportunities."

"Not even in law?" questioned one.

"There least of all," was the answer.

"Well," said another, "the period in which Mr. Choate began his career in New York is commonly referred to as the golden age of the metropolitan bar. James T. Brady was a conspicuous figure in the popular eye. Charles O'Connor had already made a lasting impression. Mr. Evarts was in the front rank in politics as well as in law. Mr. Hoffman was equally prominent on the Democratic side, and Mr. Stanford's brilliancy in cross-examination had given him an enviable reputation. The legal heavens were studded with stars of such lustre as to make any newcomer feel doubtful about his ability to compete. But Choate displayed no anxiety. He hung out his shingle and began to look for clients, and they came."

A YOUNG LAWYER'S CHANCES THEN AND NOW.

"That was before the war," resumed the original speaker. "Do you imagine he could have attained his position as the foremost American lawyer under conditions as they exist to-day without special advantages?"

"Possibly," I said, and added that it was probable that Mr. Choate, if approached, would kindly throw light on the subject.

In pursuance of this idea, I called one evening at the residence of Mr. Choate. Previous inquiry at the law office of Evarts, Choate and Beaman, on Wall Street, elicited the information that Mr. Choate's days were filled to overflowing with legal affairs of great importance. Consequently it was surprising to find him so ready to see a stranger at his home.

It was into a long room on the ground floor that I was introduced, three of its walls lined with tall, dark walnut book-laden cases, lighted by a bright grate fire and by a student's lamp on the table by night, and by two heavily-shaded windows by day. As I entered, the great lawyer was busy prodding the fire, and voiced a resonant "good-evening" without turning. In a moment or two he had evoked a blaze, and assumed a standing attitude before the fire, his hands behind him.

ARE SPECIAL ADVANTAGES NECESSARY?

"Well, sir," he began, "what do you wish?"

"A few minutes of your time," I answered.

"Why?" he questioned succinctly.

"I wish to discover whether you believe special advantages at the beginning of a youth's career are necessary to success?"

"Why my opinion?"

I was rather floored for an instant, but endeavored to make plain the natural interest of the public in the subject and his opinion, but he interrupted me with the query:—

"Why don't you ask a man who never had any advantages," at the same time fixing upon me one of his famous "what's in thy heart?" glances.

"Then you have had them?" I said, grasping wildly at the straw that might keep the interviewer afloat.

"A few, not many," he replied.

"Are advantages necessary to success to-day?"

"Define advantages and success," he said abruptly, evidently questioning whether it was worth while to talk. A distinguished looking figure he made, looking on, as I collected my defining ability. The room seemed full of his atmosphere. He is a tall man, oaken in strength, with broad, intelligent face, high forehead, alert, wide-set eyes, and firm, even lips expressive of great self-control. His fluency, his wit and humor, his sound knowledge, his strength and perfect self-possession, were all suggested by his face and expression, and by the firmness of his squarely set head and massive shoulders.

"Let us," I said, "say money, opportunity, friends, good advice, and personal popularity for early advantages."

"The first isn't necessary," said the jurist, leisurely adjusting his hands in his pockets. "Opportunity comes to everyone, but all have not a mind to see; friends you can do without for a time; good advice we take too late, and popularity usually comes too early or too tardy to be appreciated. Define success."

WHAT SUCCESS MEANS.

"I might mention fame, position, income, as examples of what the world deems success."

"Foolish world!" said Mr. Choate. "The most successful men sometimes have not one of all these. All I can say is that early advantages won't bring a man a knowledge of the law, nor enable him to convince a jury. What he needs is years of close application, the ability to stick until he has mastered the necessary knowledge."

"Where did you obtain your wide knowledge of the law?" I asked.

"Reading at home and fighting in the courts,—principally fighting in the courts."

"And was there any good luck about obtaining your first case? Was it secured by special effort?"

THE GOOD LUCK OF BEING PREPARED.

"None, unless it was the good luck of having a sign out, large enough for people to see. The rest of it was hard work, getting the evidence and the law fixed in my mind.

"You believe, of course," I ventured, "that advantageous opportunities do come to all?"

"Yes," said he, drawing up a chair and resignedly seating himself. "I believe that opportunities come to all,—not the same opportunities, nor the same kind of opportunities, nor opportunities half so valuable in some cases as in others, but they do come, and if seen and grasped will work a vast improvement in the life and character of an individual. Every boy cannot be president, but my word for it, if he is industrious, he can improve his position in the world."

TURNING OBSTACLES INTO AIDS.

"It has been said, Mr. Choate," I went on, "that you often ascribe both your success in particular cases, and your general success at the bar, to good luck and happy accidents."

"Just so, just so," he answered, smiling in a manner that is at once a question and a mark of approbation. "I hope I have always made the most of good luck and happy accidents. We all should. My friend, John E. Parsons, once denounced a defendant insurance company as a 'vampire,—one of those bloodless creatures that feed on the blood of the people.' It was a savage address of the old-fashioned style, and convincing, until I asked the judge and jury if they knew what a vampire really is. 'Look at the Quaker gentleman who is president of this company,' I said, pointing him out. 'Also look at that innocent young man, his attorney, who sits next to him with a smile on his face. You thought vampires were something out of the way when Brother Parsons described them, but these are regular, genuine vampires.' That brought a laugh and good feeling, and I suppose you might call the whole thing an opportunity to turn a bad assault into a helpful incident."

The great lawyer was a study as he spoke, his easy, unaffected attitude and bearing itself carrying weight. His manner of accepting the intrusion with mild acquiescence and attention, but with no intention of allowing himself to be bored, was interesting. It has become customary to say that he is a poor politician, and as the term is ordinarily employed and understood, he is, because he is ever ready to say what he really thinks. It is precisely this quality, this freedom from cowardice, this detestation of truckling to ignorance and brutality, this independence, that cause him to stand out so boldly in the legal profession.

DOES LACK OF OPPORTUNITY JUSTIFY.

"If equally valuable opportunities do not come to all," I went on, "hasn't an individual a right to complain and justify his failure?"

"We have passed the period when we believe that all men are equal," said Mr. Choate. "We know they're free, but some men are born less powerful than others. But if an individual does not admit to himself that he is deficient in strength or reasoning powers, if he claims all the rights and privileges given others because he is 'as good as they' then his success or failure is upon his own head. He should prove that he is what he thinks he is, and be what he aspires to be."

"You believe, of course, that an individual may overestimate his abilities?"

"Believe it," he answered, with a deprecatory wave of the

hand, "trust the law to teach that. But if a man does overestimate himself he still owes it to himself to endeavor to prove that his estimate of himself is correct. We all need to. If he fails, he will be learning his limitations, which is better than never finding them out. No man can justify inaction."

"What do you consider to be the genuine battle of a youth to-day?—the struggle to bear poverty while working to conquer?"

"Not at all," came the quick answer. "Poor clothes and poor food and a poor place to dwell in are disagreeable things and must be made to give place to better, of course, but one can be partially indifferent to them. The real struggle is to hang on to every advantage, and strengthen the mind at every step. There are persons who have learned to endure poverty so well that they don't mind it any longer. The struggle comes in maintaining a purpose through poverty to the end. It is just as difficult to maintain a purpose through riches."

"Money is not an end, then, in your estimation."

"Never, and need is only an incentive. Erskine made his greatest speech with his hungry children tugging at his coat-tail. That intense feeling that something has got to be done is the thing that works the doing. I never met a great man who was born rich."

MR. CHOATE'S ANTECEDENTS.

This remark seemed rather striking in a way, because of the fact that Mr. Choate's parents were not poor in the accepted sense. The family is rather distinguished in New England annals. His father was a cousin of the famous Rufus Choate, and the latter, at the date of Joseph's birth, January 24, 1832, was just entering his second term in congress to distinguish himself by a great speech on the tariff. Mr. Choate was the youngest of four brothers, and, after receiving a fair school education in Salem, was sent to Harvard, where he was graduated in 1852, and later from its law school in 1854. Influence procured him a position in a Boston law office. After a year of practical study, he was admitted to the bar of Massachusetts. In October of that year he made a tour of observation in the western states, in company with his brother William, and on his return determined to settle in New York.

"Isn't it possible, Mr. Choate," I ventured, "that your having had little or no worry over poverty in your youth might cause you to underestimate the effect of it on another, and overestimate the importance of sticking with determination to an idea through wealth or deprivation?"

"No," he replied, after a few moments' delay, in which he picked up one of the volumes near by as if to consult it; "no, the end to be attained makes important the need of hanging on. I am sure it is quite often more difficult to rise with money than without."

DOES SUCCESS BRING CONTENT AND HAPPINESS.

"You have had long years of distinction and comfort; do you find that success brings content and happiness?"

"Well," he answered, contracting his brows with legal severity, "constant labor is happiness, and success simply means ability to do more labor,—more deeds far-reaching in their power and effect. Such success brings about as much happiness as the world provides."

"I mean," I explained, "the fruits of that which is conventionally accepted as success; few hours of toil, a luxuriously furnished home, hosts of friends, the applause of the people, sumptuous repasts, and content in idleness, knowing that enough has been done."

"We never know that enough has been done," said the lawyer. "All this sounds pleasant, but the truth is that the men whose great efforts have made such things possible for themselves are the very last to desire them. You have described what appeals to the idler, the energyless dreamer, the fashionable dawdler, and the listless voluptuary. Enjoyment of such things would sap the strength and deaden the ambition of a Lincoln. The man who has attained to the position where these things are possible is the one whose life has been a constant refutation of the need of these things. He is the one who has abstained, who has conserved his mental and physical strength by living a simple and frugal life. He has not taken more than he needed, and never, if possible, less. His enjoyment has been in working, and I guarantee that you will find successful men ever to be plain-mannered persons of simple tastes, to whom sumptuous repasts are a bore, and luxury a thing apart. They may live surrounded by these things, but personally take little interest in them, knowing them to be mere trappings, which neither add to nor detract from character."

THE DELUSION OF LUXURY AND EASE.

"Is there no pleasure then in luxury and ease without toil?" I questioned.

"None," said the speaker emphatically. "There is pleasure in rest after labor. It is gratifying to relax when you really need relaxation, to be weary and be able to rest. But to enjoy anything you must first feel the need of it. But no more," he said, putting up his hand conclusively. "Surely you have enough to make clear what you wish to know."

Mr. Choate had talked for ten minutes. His ease of manner, quickness of reply, smoothness of expression, and incisive diction, were fascinating beyond description. As I was about to leave, I inquired if he would object to my making our conversation the subject of an article, to which he smiled his willingness, waiving objection with a slight movement of the hand.

MR. CHOATE'S SHARE OF NEW YORK'S LAW BUSINESS.

In court circles it is common report that Mr. Choate's contemporaries divide half of the business among them, and Mr. Choate has the other half to himself.

This is due to his wonderful simplicity and directness, which never falters for a moment for thought or word. He drives straight for the heart and head of client or officer, witness or counsel, judge or juryman. A distinguished barrister has said of him:

"Where other lawyers are solemn and portentous, or wild or unpleasant, he is humorous and human. He assumes no superior air; often he speaks with his hands in his pockets. He strives to stir up no dark passions. While he is always a little bit keener, a little finer and more witty than the man in the box or on the bench, yet he is always a brother man to him."

XVIII

A VILLAGE BOY'S GIFT OF ORATORY EARNS HIM WEALTH AND FAME.

OF the busy men of the world, there are none more so than Chauncey M. Depew, until recently president of the New York Central and Hudson River Railroad, and now president of the board which looks after all the Vanderbilt interests. One must have something worthy his attention to gain admittance to the busy man, and I need say no more for the present interview than that the distinguished orator and statesman saw fit to discuss the possibilities of young men and their future, and gave readily of his time and opinions. I stated to him the object of my interview,—that it was intended to obtain his views as to what qualities in young men best make for success, and to ask him, if possible, to point out the way, by the aid of example, to better work and greater success for them. He smiled approvingly, and, to my question, whether, in his opinion, the opportunities awaiting ambitious young men are less or more than they have been in the past, replied:—

"More, decidedly more. Our needs in every field were never greater. The country is larger, and, while the population is greater, the means to supply its increased wants require more and more talent, so that any young man may gain a foothold who makes his effort with industry and intelligence."

"Do you mean to say that there is an excellent position awaiting everyone?"

"I mean to say that, while positions are not so numerous that any kind of a young man will do, yet they are so plentiful that you can scarcely find a young man of real energy and intelligence who does not hold a responsible position of some kind. The chief affairs are in the hands of young men."

"Was it different in your day, when you were beginning?"

"Energy and industry told heavily in the balance then, as now, but the high places were not available for young men because the positions were not in existence. We had to make the places, in those days; and not only that, but we were obliged to call ourselves to the tasks. To-day, a man fits himself and is called. There are more things to do."

"How was it with boys, in your day, who wanted to get an education?"

HE HAD TO EARN HIS OWN WAY.

"With most of them, it was a thing to earn. Why, the thing that I knew more about than anything else, as I grew from year to year, was the fact that I had nothing to expect, and must look out for myself. I can't tell you how clear my parents made this point to me. It absolutely glittered, so plain was it."

"Your parents were Americans?"

"Yes. I was born at Peekskill, in 1834."

Although Mr. Depew modestly refrains from discussing his ancestry, he comes from the best New England stock. He descends, through remote paternal ancestors, from French Huguenots, who were among those who came to America in the early days of the country, and who founded the village of New Rochelle, in Westchester county. His mother, Martha Mitchell, was of illustrious and patriotic New England descent, being a member of the family to which belonged Roger Sherman, a signer of the Declaration of Independence; and he is a lineal descendant of the Rev. Josiah Sherman, chaplain of the Seventh Connecticut Continental infantry, and of Gabriel Ogden, of the New Jersey militia, both of whom served in the American Revolution.

"Had you any superior advantages in the way of money, books, or training?" I continued.

"If you want to call excellent training a superior advantage I had it. Training was a great point with us. We trained with the plow, the ax, and almost any other implement we could lay our hands on. I might even call the switch used at our house an early advantage, and, I might say, superior to any other in our vicinity. I had some books, but our family was not rich, even for those times. We were comfortably situated, nothing more."

"Do you owe more to your general reading than you do to your early school training?"

"Yes, I think so. I attended the school in our village regularly, until I went to college; but I was not distinguished for scholarship, except on the ballground."

"Do you attribute much of your success in life to physical strength?"

"It is almost indispensable."

HE ENTERED YALE AT EIGHTEEN.

"I was always strong. The conditions tended to make strong men, in those days. I went to college in my eighteenth year. I think I acquired a broader view there, and sound ideals which have been great helps. It was not a period of toil, however, as some would have made it."

His time at Yale was in no respect wasted. The vigorous, athletic, fun-loving boy was developing into a man with a strength and independence of character, very imperfectly understood at first by the already long list of men who liked him.

"What profession did you fix upon as the field for your life work?" I asked.

"That of the law. I always looked forward to that; and, after my graduation, in 1856, I went into a law office (that of Hon. William Nelson,) at Peekskill, and prepared for practice. That was a time of intense political excitement. There were factions in the Democratic party, and the Whig party seemed to be passing away. The Republican party, or People's party, as it had first been called, was organized in 1856, and men were changing from side to side. Naturally, I was mixed in the argument, and joined the Republican party.

"When I was graduated at Yale College, in 1856," he continued, "I came home to the village of Peekskill to meet my father, my grandfather, my uncles and my brothers, all old Hunker, state-rights, pro-slavery Democrats. But I had been through the fiery furnace of the Kansas-Nebraska excitement at New Haven, and had come out of it a free-soil Republican. Two days after my return, I stood, a trembling boy, upon a platform to give voice in the campaign which was then in progress, to that conversion which nearly broke my father's heart, and almost severed me from all family ties. It seemed then as if the end of the world had come for me in the necessity for this declaration of convictions and principles, but I expressed my full belief. In this sense, I believe a young man should be strong, and that such difficult action is good for him."

HIS BEGINNING AS AN ORATOR.

"Is that where you began your career as an orator?" I asked.

"You mean as a stump-speaker? Yes. I talked for Fremont and Dayton, our candidates, but they were defeated. We did not really expect success, though, and yet we carried eleven states. After that, I went back to my law books, and was admitted to the bar in 1858. That was another campaign year, and I spoke for the party then, as I did two years later, when I was a candidate for the state assembly, and won."

The real glory hidden by this modest statement is that Mr. Depew's oratory in the campaign of 1858 gained him such distinction that he was too prominent to be passed over in 1860.

During that campaign, he stumped the entire state, winning rare oratorical triumphs, and aiding the party almost more than anyone else. How deep an impression the young member from Peekskill really made in the state legislature by his admirable mastery of the complex public business brought before him, may be gathered from the fact that when, two years later, he was re-elected, he was speedily made chairman of the committee on ways and means. He was also elected speaker, *pro tem.*, and at the next election, when his party was practically defeated all along the line, he was returned.

After briefly referring to the active part he took in the Lincoln campaign, I asked:—

"When did you decide upon your career as a railroad official?"

"In 1866. I was retained by Commodore Vanderbilt as attorney for the New York and Harlem Road."

"To what do you attribute your rise as an official in that field?"

"Hard work. That was a period of railroad growth. There were many small roads and plenty of warring elements. Out of these many small roads, when once united, came the great systems which now make it possible to reach California in a few days. Anyone who entered upon the work at that time had to encounter those conditions, and if he continued at it, to change them. I was merely a counselor at first."

In 1869, Mr. Depew was made attorney for the New York Central and Hudson River Railroad, and afterward a director. This was the period of the development of the Vanderbilt system. Mr. Depew was a constant adviser of the Vanderbilts, and, by his good judgment and sagacious counsel, maintained their constant respect and friendship. In 1875, he was made general counsel for the entire system and a director in each one of the roads.

A SALARY OF .5,000 A YEAR.

It has often been urged by the sinister-minded, that it was something against him to have gained so much at the hands of the Vanderbilts. The truth is that this is his chief badge of honor. Many times he has won influence and votes for the Vanderbilt interests, but always by the use of wit, oratorical persuasion and legitimate, honorable argument,—never by the methods of the lobbyist. Commodore Vanderbilt engaged him as counsel for the New York Central Railroad, at a salary of $25,000 a year,—then equal to the salary of the president of the United States,—and he always acknowledged that Mr. Depew earned the money.

He is now the head of the entire Vanderbilt system, or the controlling spirit of thirty distinct railroads, besides being a director in the Wagner Palace Car Company, the Union Trust Company, the Western Union Telegraph Company, the Equitable Life Insurance Society, the Western Transit Company, the West Shore and International Bridge Company, the Morris Run Coal Mining Company, the Clearfield Bituminous Coal Corporation, the Hudson River Bridge Company, the Canada Southern Bridge Company, the Niagara River Bridge Company, the Niagara Grand Island Bridge Company, the Tonawanda Island Bridge Company, the American Safe Deposit Company, the Mutual Gas Light Company, and the Brooklyn Storage and Warehouse Company.

"How much of your time each day," I asked, "have you given, upon an average, to your professional duties?"

"Only a moderate number of hours. I do not believe in overwork. The affairs of life are not important enough to require it, and the body cannot endure it. Just an ordinary day's labor of eight or ten hours has been my standard."

"Your official duties never drew you wholly from the political field, I believe?"

"Entirely, except special needs of the party, when I have been urged to accept one task after another. I believe that every man's energies should be at the disposal of his country."

"On the political side, what do you think is the essential thing for success?"

"The very things that are essential anywhere else—honesty, consistency and hard work."

"It requires no strain of character, no vacillation?"

"For twenty-five years," answered Mr. Depew, "I was on all occasions to the front in political battles, and I never found that political opinions or activity made it necessary to break friendships or make them."

Mr. Depew's political career is already so well known that it need not be reviewed here.

After three years of service as vice-president of the New York Central Railroad, he was elevated, in 1885, to the presidency. While thus given a position of great influence in the business world, his growing reputation made him eligible for greater political honors than any for which he had yet been named. In 1888 he was the presidential candidate of the Republicans of New York state, at the national convention of the party, and received the solid vote of his state delegation, but withdrew his name. President Harrison offered him the position of secretary of state, to succeed Mr. Blaine, but he declined.

OPPORTUNITIES OF TO-DAY.

"What do you think of the opportunities to-day? Has the recent war aided us?"

"It is the best thing for the young men of to-day that could have happened! The new possessions mean everything to young men, who are going to be old men by and by. We, as a nation, are going to find, by the wise utilization of the conditions forced upon us, how to add incalculably to American enterprise and opportunity by becoming masters of the sea, and entering with the surplus of our manufactures the markets of the world. The solid merchants are to undertake the extension of American trade, but the young men will be called in to do the work under their guidance. The young man who is ready is naturally the one chosen."

"You think a tide of prosperity waits for every young American?"

"It may not exactly wait, but he can catch it easily."

"It is said," I went on, "that any field or profession carefully followed, will bring material success. Is that the thing to be aimed at?"

"Material success does not constitute an honorable aim. If that were true, a grasping miser would be the most honorable creature on earth, while a man like Gladstone, great without money, would have been an impossibility. The truth is that material success is usually the result of a great aim, which looks to some great public improvement. Some man plans to be an intelligent servant of some great public need, and the result of great energy in serving the public intelligently is wealth. It never has been possible to become notable in this respect in any other way."

"It is often said that the excellent opportunities for young men are gone."

"If you listen to ordinary comment," said Mr. Depew, "you can come to believe that almost anything is dead—patriotism, honor, possibilities, trade—in fact, anything, and it's all according with whom you talk. There was a belief, not long ago, that the great orators were dead, and had left no successors. Papers and magazines were said to supply this excellent tonic. Yet orators have appeared, great ones, and in the face of the beauty and grace and fire which animates some of them, you read the speeches of the older celebrities, and wonder what was in them that stirred men."

"And this field is also open to young men?"

"Not as a profession, of course, but as a means to real distinction, certainly. The field was never before so open. I have listened to Stephen A. Douglas, with his vigorous argument, slow enunciation, and lack of magnetism; to Abraham Lincoln, with his resistless logic and quaint humor; to Tom Corwin, Salmon P. Chase, William H. Seward, Charles Sumner, and Wendell Phillips; and, as I look back and recall what they said, and the effect which they produced, and then estimate what they might do with the highly cultivated and critical audiences of to-day, I see the opportunity that awaits the young man here. Only Wendell Phillips strikes me as having possessed qualities which are not yet duplicated or surpassed."

THERE IS MORE THAN ONE KIND OF SUCCESS.

"You recognize more than one kind of success in this world, then?"

"Yes; we can't all be presidents of the United States. Any man is successful who does well what comes to his hand, and who works to improve himself so that he may do better. The man with the ideal, struggling to carry it out, is the successful man. Of course, there are all grades of ideals, and the man with the highest, given the proportionate energy, is the most successful. The world makes way for that kind of young man."

"Do you consider that happiness in the successful man consists in reflecting over what he has done or what he may do?"

"I should say that it consists in both. No man who has accomplished a great deal could sit down and fold his hands. The enjoyment of life would be instantly gone if you removed the possibility of doing something. When through with his individual affairs, a man wants a wider field, and of course that can only be in public affairs. Whether the beginner believes it or not, he will find that he cannot drop interest in life at the end, whatever he may think about it in the beginning."

"The aim of the young man of to-day should be, then—?"

"To do something worth doing, honestly. Get wealth, if it is gotten in the course of an honorable public service. I think, however, the best thing to get is the means of doing good, and then doing it."

XIX

A CHANCE-FOUND BOOK THE TURNING POINT IN A UNITED STATES SENATOR'S CAREER.

HE wasn't much of a boy to look at, this Dolliver boy of ten, trudging off to school every morning in the West Virginia hamlet of Kingwood, where the mountains are so brown in winter and so green in summer. To the master of the little subscription school he was Jonathan Prentiss Dolliver; to the comrades of sport and study he was just plain "Prent," a sturdy little chap, whose hair refused to stay combed, whose clothes showed the rough-and-tumble of play, whose love for the mountains far exceeded his love of arithmetic.

Somebody lost a copy of the "Congressional Record" about that time,—a bound volume, containing many speeches of senators and representatives. "Prent" found it. His boyish imagination was fired. Hour after hour he pored over its pages, committing to memory several of the passages in the speeches.

One day the school committee called,—an auspicious event in the little schoolhouse. Young Dolliver was asked to give a declamation. To the astonishment of all, the boy performed his task with force, vigor, clearness and almost eloquence. Where did he get it?

"O, I can talk," he declared; "dad's a preacher, you know."

Thus climbed into his first forum the witty, eloquent, magnetic Dolliver, a United States senator from the state of Iowa at forty years of age.

The match of ambition having been thus applied, the young lad studied to greater advantage. A superb mother made sacrifices to aid him. How these American mothers have ever helped! He took a course at the State University at Morgantown, West Virginia. This was in 1875, and Prentiss was only seventeen when he stepped forth with his diploma in his hand.

A SCHOOL TEACHER AT EIGHTEEN.

At eighteen, he was a country school teacher himself. The scene is laid in Victor Center, Illinois, in a yellow schoolhouse; and, while it is only a stepping-stone in a career full of more exciting episodes, it is worth while to note that the youth of eighteen was able to do what his predecessors had failed to accomplish,— make an orderly, successful school out of a very turbulent lot of youngsters. On one occasion he quelled a fight by simply looking at the combatants.

The law, and the wide, free west captured the young man a few years later, the former for a profession, the latter for a home. Fort Dodge, Iowa, welcomed the little family in 1880, and there the future senator wrestled with life's serious problems in earnest. Inevitably he was drawn into politics, that field which always has use for men of active brain and silvery tongue. Dolliver had both. James G. Blaine, for whom he delivered scores of speeches, predicted, in 1884, that this dark-haired young orator of the west would enjoy a conspicuous future. The prophecy was not long in reaching fulfilment. From 1890, when he was first elected to congress, until 1900, when he took his seat in the senate, he rose steadily in importance as a great leader and debater, until he had no superior in the great forum of the nation.

His wit is one of the most attractive of his gifts. He can tell a story with wonderful effect. His keen sense of humor would have made him a comedian, if nature had not cast his other faculties in a more serious mould. Therefore, his fun only crops out at times.

When I asked him when and where he first began to consider himself famous, he said:—

"My first term in congress gave me my first sense of exaltation. The people up in the Iowa hills had a little lake, and they named it after me. Then a new postoffice was named in my honor, and a colored woman named her baby after me. I began to think of engaging a niche in some temple of fame.

"But, in my second term, I was disillusioned. A climatic disturbance dried up the lake, free delivery wiped out the postoffice, and the child died,—and I found myself back at the very place whence I had started!"

THE STRANGE RESULT OF A LECTURE.

A few years ago Mr. Dolliver was invited to deliver a lecture in St. Paul and Minneapolis, Minnesota, before the Young Men's Christian Association Lyceum. In each city, the hall was crowded wherein he spoke, some fifteen hundred young men attending. His topic was, "Chances for Young Men."

"That," said he to me, "was a favorite topic with me. I believed in young men, and liked to talk with them, knowing full well that if one can stir them up to energy and ambition, he is doing a grand work in the world.

"Well, I have not changed my opinion since the delivery of that lecture; but, when I got back to Washington to resume my congressional duties, a week later, I began to hear from those particular young men. Letters began to pour in on me. They came in bunches of twos and threes; then in dozens, and finally in basketfuls. Every St. Paul and Minneapolis young man who had heard me declare that this is the young men's age, wrote that he fully agreed with me,—and asked me to get him a government job!"

Mr. Dolliver's services to his party were particularly great in the controversy over the Porto Rican change of front by the administration. The president had, in his message to congress, in December 1899, favored the extending of unrestricted trade opportunities to the Porto Ricans; but, later, seeing that such a course was opposed by many influential persons, and by several strong arguments, he advised the imposition of light duties and the application of the proceeds to the island's own use. In the conflict which at once arose in congress, Dolliver's strong and eloquent plea alone saved the measure from defeat.

HIS IDEA OF GENUINE SUCCESS.

When I asked him what the true idea of success is, he replied, without a moment's hesitation:

"Money-making is the cheapest kind of success. It doesn't indicate the highest development, by any means. I will give you a simple illustration, embodied in an incident which occurred this very day. A friend of mine, a professional gentleman of high mental attainments, had been offered a salary of ten thousand dollars a year by a corporation engaged in transportation. He was strongly tempted to take it, for he is working for the government at a salary of only five thousand dollars. He admitted to me, however, that he is capable of far greater usefulness, in his present work, than he would be in the employment of the railroad. Thereupon I strongly advised him to reject the larger offer, and he has done so. My reason was simply that money does not measure one's place in the world, one's mental triumphs, or one's usefulness to humanity."

"But money is a helpful factor in life," I urged, "and is considered indispensable, nowadays, in climbing up the ladder."

"Well," he replied, "if I had a son and a hundred thousand dollars, I would keep them apart."

In the senate a new member is not supposed to take part in debates, or even discussions. The atmosphere is not only dignified, but frozen. I strongly anticipate, however, that there will be a thawing out before long. The presence of Mr. Dolliver ought to act like an old-fashioned depot stove in a cold-storage room.

XX

VARIED BUSINESS TRAINING THE FOUNDATION OF A LONG POLITICAL CAREER.

THOMAS COLLIER PLATT has succeeded in business and in politics in a phenomenal manner. The reason is, he has had the native sagacity, energy and working ability of two ordinary men, and has fairly earned his place as a senator of the United States, as one of the political leaders of the nation, and as president of the United States Express Company.

Last summer, as I sat on the porch of the Oriental Hotel at Manhattan Beach, for Mr. Platt's return from his office, he came up the steps two at a time, with the elasticity of a man of forty. As I waited for him in the Fifth Avenue Hotel the other day, he came into the lobby looking very much jaded. He said: "I am very tired, after a week's session of the senate at Washington. I have had a very busy day in New York. Come up to my room."

Members of the legislature, local politicians, statesmen of national renown, sent their cards to the senator's room before we were fairly seated. Wearied amid this great press, Mr. Platt took time to say some things about himself, and to indicate some of the elements of his success as an encouragement and inspiration to young men in the struggle of life.

"Where were you born?"

"In Owego, Tioga County, New York.

"My ancestors were Americans. They were Yankees that came from Connecticut and Massachusetts to New York state."

"Do you believe in hereditary tendencies?"

"I do, most certainly. Blood tells. There is nothing so absolutely true as that blood tells in cattle, horses and men. My father was a devoted, consistent Presbyterian. The preachers almost counted my father's house a home when I was a boy. My father was my ideal of a man every way. He was one of the few men I ever saw whose everyday life completely harmonized with the Christian profession."

"In your Puritan home, you had to toe the mark, did you not?"

"Yes, my parents were strict; but very tender. They never used the rod, because we were such exceptionally good children. We did not need it. I never saw father or mother raise their hand against a child. My father was a lawyer. He afterward became interested in real estate, taking charge of extensive timber and farm lands in the northwest, owned by a gentleman in Philadelphia."

HIS START AS A BOY.

"To what do you attribute the start you got as a boy on the road to success?"

"To the principles of truth, honor, love, and labor, which were instilled into my mind in our quiet village home."

"Where were you educated?"

"I attended the Owego Academy. There was nothing out of the ordinary line in teacher or scholar. In the academy I prepared for Yale College, which I entered in 1849. Ill health compelled me to give up my college course at the close of my sophomore year. Our class contained some of the most distinguished men ever graduated from the college. Wayne McVeigh, Edmund Clarence Steadman, Isaac Brumley, Judge Shiras, of the Supreme Court of the United States; Andrew D. White, ambassador to the court of Berlin, were among the number. Yale has grown marvelously since my day, and the student now has increased opportunity for knowledge, but I do not think that the grade of talent to-day is any better than in our time. In 1876, Yale conferred on me the degree of master of arts."

"Would you advise a young man, having a business life in view, to attend college?"

"I would! The intellectual discipline, the social advantages, the mental stimulus will be of profit to a young man entering business in times of great enterprises and heated competitions."

ALWAYS FOND OF READING.

"Were you a reader of books?"

"I have always been fond of reading, and have read books to advantage, but for forty years I have been so engaged with business and politics that I have not had the time to gratify my taste for literature, which is strong. Reading is of great advantage to a young man,—that is, the reading of good books.

"I was fortunate in my early friendships. A man's character and success are greatly effected by his friends. A man is known by the company he keeps. It used to be that a man was known by the newspaper he read. That is not so now."

"Why?"

"Because there are so many and so cheap that a man can and does take and read more than one. I read them all,—those which agree and those which disagree with me politically."

"You are reputed to have been a fine singer when a young man."

"I had a voice which gave me much delight and seemed to please others. I was for many years the leader of the Owego Glee Club, which was very popular. We used to be called for as far as Elmira, Ithaca, Auburn, and Binghamton. With Washington Gladden to write the verses, our glee club to sing them, and Benjamin Tracy, a young lawyer of the town, to make the speeches, we gave considerable inspiration to the social and political gatherings of our community."

A TASTE OF MINING LIFE

"What was your first venture in business?"

"On my return from Yale, I started a retail drug store in my native town, and continued it for fifteen years. I then branched out in the lumber business in Michigan. I became connected with several local enterprises, among them the bank, and a wagon factory."

"You invested in a western mine, did you not?"

"Yes! I owned a third interest in a mine at Deadwood, and in the winter of 1877 I decided to go out and see it. It was my first trip west, and I was not prepared for the hardships. I had to ride sixty hours from the end of the railroad to the camp. The Indians were on the war path and had killed a passenger on the stage that preceded ours. As I started to enter the coach, the driver said: 'Are you armed?' 'No,' said I. Taking a gun from the top of the stage, he gave it to me, and said, 'You will need it.' I told him I was a tenderfoot and did not know how to shoot. He showed me, and I took the gun with me. Luckily I did not need it. About the first thing I saw when I reached the camp was an example of frontier justice. Men, with a rope, were hunting for those who had been guilty of holding up the stage. I found the claim in which I was interested to be one of the richest in the vicinity, according to indications. We spent $60,000 in working the claim. I was offered half a million dollars for my interest in the property, which I declined. Just as we got to paying expenses, the mine played out."

"Did you make any of your money in speculation?"

"I never made much money any way, and I never made any in speculation, or in politics. My political experience has cost me—not brought me money."

"How happened you to come to New York?"

"I came to New York as the general manager of the United

States Express Company, and soon after, in 1879, I was elected president, which position I have held ever since."

The United States Express Company began business in 1854, and had in New York City eight wagons and twenty men, including officers. Its mileage was less than 600 miles. It now operates 30,000 miles of railroads, which is a larger mileage than that of any other single express company in the country. It has ten thousand employees and five thousand offices. In New York City alone it has six hundred horses and two hundred and fifty wagons; and other great cities of the country are correspondingly well equipped. For a dozen years the company has had the entire responsibility of carrying all government money and securities, except in a few states and territories, and it has transported hundreds of millions of gold and silver and paper money without the loss of a penny to the government. The executive ability, tireless industry, ceaseless vigilance and courteous and honest dealing of President T. C. Platt has had much to do with the success of the company.

THE ELEMENTS OF SUCCESS.

"What do you consider essential elements for success in business?"

"Adaptability to the calling, hard work, strict attention to business and honest dealing.

"Young men should remember that it is not the amount made, but that which is saved that indicates financial success. The habit of economy is important in getting along in the world."

"When did you turn your attention to politics?"

"Very early in my history, and I have been in its seething, boiling steam about ever since. I was first elected clerk of my county, and soon after was sent to congress, where I served two terms. I was elected to the United States senate in 1881, and again two years ago this last January."

"It is said that the speech you made on the Treaty of Paris was your maiden speech in the senate."

"It was."

"Why should a man who can make such a speech as that have been silent so long?"

"I am dragged almost to death with my hard work, and I have had no time to prepare fine speeches. I have tried to do my duty in my appropriate sphere as a representative of my state in the senate."

"To what do you attribute your political success?"

"To fidelity to the political principles professed, and especially to my loyalty to my friends."

ADVICE TO YOUNG MEN.

"Would you advise a young man to enter the political field?"

"By no means! I should advise him to keep out of it. It is vexatious, unsatisfactory and unremunerative. I have requested my sons to keep out of politics, and they have wisely heeded the request."

"Do you not think that it is the duty of a young man to hold office or in some way bear his share of the burdens of state?"

"Certainly I do. That is a different thing. I referred to the undesirable calling of a professional politician."

"What would you call the essential elements of success in life?"

"Not one thing, or two things, but a number of them harmoniously blended, and crowned by a true sterling character. True success is not in making money, nor in securing power, nor in winning praise. It is in the building up of true manhood that merits and enjoys these things and employs them for the benefits and happiness of mankind."

"I forgot to ask you about your health?"

"It has never been robust, but it has been good. I have been very careful in my habits, and have preserved what bodily energy

I needed for my life plans. Bodily vigor is necessary to the highest success in any business or profession."

MR. PLATT'S CHARACTERISTICS.

The senator spoke like the courteous gentleman that he is. His bearing is simplicity and sincerity personified. He made answer to my questions in a voice as delicate as a woman's, giving no hint of the dynamite behind it. I understand that it is his habit to economize his strength and use no more on each occasion than is really required. Mr. Platt is a serious man and yet he has a deep vein of humor. He likes a good joke and tells one well. He has a hearty laugh. He has great patience, but makes a hard fight when provoked. He is not tyrannical in victory or vengeful in defeat. He has a knowledge of human nature, a keen insight into men's motives, and has skill in playing upon them. He is a master in adjusting himself to events. He has a masterful will, but a remarkable faculty also for disarming instead of exciting antagonism. Altogether he seems well qualified to be a leader of men.

XXI

A MAGNATE, THE COURAGE OF HIS CONVICTIONS MAKE HIM A REFORMER.

AT the time of the Civil war Tom L. Johnson was just old enough to begin to realize the significance of events; he could remember his family's former affluence, and this memory served as a spur to urge him to the rehabilitation of broken fortunes. At the outbreak of the conflict his father, A. W. Johnson, had joined the Confederate army as a colonel, removing his wife and children, from the Kentucky homestead near Georgetown, to the south, and finally to Staunton, Virginia, for greater safety. There the boy Tom, who was born in 1854, spent four of the most impressionable years of his life, and there he earned his first dollar.

HIS FIRST SPECULATION.

"I am glad I was old enough to remember my home before the war," he said, in speaking of his early life. "Rightly or wrongly, I attach great importance to this fact as a constant incentive in my career. The thought of regaining the position which we had previously held was always with me."

The five weeks immediately following Lee's surrender were a golden time to Tom financially; in that period, he earned eighty-eight dollars, enough to carry the family (which consisted of his parents and two younger brothers), back to Kentucky. This was the way he did it: There was, of course, great thirst for news in Staunton, as all over the country, but only once a day was Staunton in railway communication with the outside world.

The boy saw his chance for a monopoly in newspapers and periodicals, and he straightway cornered the market. This he was enabled to do through the friendship of the conductor of Staunton's unique train, who refused to furnish papers to anyone else. For five weeks he held his monopoly, selling dailies at fifteen cents and illustrated periodicals at twenty-five cents each.

When Johnson ceased to enjoy these exclusive privileges, he was already a small capitalist, besides having learned a lesson that was not without profit in after life. He had eighty-eight dollars in silver.

"I tell you, that seemed like a lot of sure 'nough money," he said, with a smile, "to us who had been paying one hundred dollars in Confederate notes for a hat."

AT WORK IN A ROLLING MILL.

Three years after he went to work in Louisville as clerk in an iron rolling mill, on a very small salary. In the same office with him was another lad, Arthur Moxham, who later became his business partner. For economical reasons, the managers of the mill decided that the services of one of the boys could be dispensed with, and it then came to a choice between them. Moxham was the one retained, and Johnson was turned out to commence over again. At the time, this looked like a misfortune, but it was really the best thing that could have happened. Before long, an opening with Louisville's ramshackle, broken-down-old-mule street railway presented itself, and the discharged mill clerk started on the career which was to lead to fortune.

A FORTUNATE MISFORTUNE.

"The decision which retained Moxham in the mill and turned me adrift," he said, "was both a wise and a fortunate one. Moxham was better suited to the position than I was, and, moreover, I was thus thrown into the work for which I was adapted."

Quickly, the boy, who was then nearing manhood, passed from one place to another in the company's service until, after a few years, he became superintendent. Then he set about building up the railway and putting it on a paying basis. By a wise system of improving the accommodations and reducing the expenses, he was successful in this effort, and he forthwith began to look around for fresh fields for his ambition. But, in the meantime, like most men who are conscious of their strength and ability to cope with the world, and like many who are not, he had entered upon matrimony. His bride was his cousin, Miss Margaret J. Johnson, of Louisville, Kentucky.

At the time of his marriage, Tom L. Johnson was but twenty, and was just beginning to get a secure footing in business. But he was not content with his limited scope of action. Moreover, his employers wanted to help him forward, recognizing his ability. Of his own initiative, Biderman Du Pont, one of the owners of the railway, offered to his *protégé a loan of* $30,000, with which to try his fortune. The possibility of security was, of course, out of the question.

"Take it, Tom," he said, "and if you live, I know you'll pay it back; if you die, why, I'll be out just so much. But I'm gambling on your living."

"And later," remarked Mr. Johnson, "I had the pleasure of associating two of Mr. Du Pont's sons with me in business matters, and thus enjoyed the satisfaction of partially repaying his kindness." With the generous loan, the young financier organized a triumvirate for the purchase of the street railways of Indianapolis, thus taking the first step in the course which led him in turn to absorb the lines of Cleveland, Detroit, St. Louis, Brooklyn and other cities. In Indianapolis, he pursued, with benefit to himself, the system which had been successful in Louisville,—cheap fares and good accommodations, with increased transfer privileges.

From that time on his career is an illustration of the benefits of expansion. The days of the cable and electric cars came, and the new inventions were immediately extended to the lines under his control. By that time he had become strong enough to conduct his operations independently in his own behalf, or in conjunction with Moxham,—whose retention in the mill, by the way, had been but of temporary benefit to him, owing to the failure of the concern.

Like other practical men who have risen from the bottom of the ladder, Mr. Johnson familiarized himself with every detail of his business, even to the mechanical difficulties involved. This he proved by inventing a brake for cable-cars, which came into extensive use.

"PROGRESS AND POVERTY" CHANGED HIS WHOLE LIFE.

One day, while traveling, Mr. Johnson came across a book which was destined to influence his career vitally. This book was Henry George's "Progress and Poverty." There, he thought, was the solution of the great social questions of the age, and from that moment he was an ardent "single-taxer." Indeed, the desire to benefit his fellowmen by opening their eyes to what he considered the truth, had become his first consideration in life, more important even than his business. Forthwith he set about to convert his father and partner, and when, soon thereafter, the chance for action on a larger stage presented itself, he was himself irresistibly impelled to seize it, despite distrust in his own ability. Owing to his uniform plan of considering the comfort of the public in the operation of his railway lines, he had earned for himself unsought popularity in the city of Cleveland, where rival companies had practiced a reactionary system of niggardliness and indifference. The reward came not only in financial prosperity, but also in the form of an unexpected nomination to congress.

HIS VOLUNTEER GERMAN FRIEND.

News of this honor reached Mr. Johnson while fishing, and his first impulse was to decline to run. But further thought led to a change of decision. Having decided, he acted. From that time until the election, he delivered a succession of public speeches, and the man who had distrusted his ability to address an audience suddenly found that he was an orator.

At every one of his tent meetings was to be seen a stout old German, who always occupied a front seat, and who evidently felt a proprietary interest in the speaker, which he manifested by liberal and loud interjections of "Bully Boy!" On one occasion, after a meeting, the German happened to be sitting next to Miss Johnson in the trolley car on the return trip. "Do you see that stout man down there?" he said; addressing her; "well, that's my friend, Tom Johnson. He's a great man; I know him well. And that lady next to him, that's his wife."

"Indeed," replied Miss Johnson, "and I happen to be his daughter."

The old German was not one whit abashed. Springing to his feet, he held out his hand. "And I'm delighted to make your acquaintance, Miss Johnson!" he cried, at the top of his voice; "I'm delighted to meet any one belonging to Tom Johnson. Bully boy!"

Like his German admirer, the people stood by Mr. Johnson, and he was elected a member of the Fifty-second and Fifty-third

Congresses, in which he distinguished himself by his frank criticism of the administration.

HIS FIRST SPEECH IN CONGRESS.

Mrs. Johnson's account of her husband's first speech in Congress is as dramatic and vivid as Baudet's description of the trial in the "Nabob." Like the Nabob's mother, she was in attendance unknown to the principal actor; but, in her case, this was due to intention, not accident.

"I was alone in the stall of the gallery," she said, "save for one other woman, who was there evidently merely from curiosity. I was choking, trembling from excitement. There was a great, inarticulate noise in the chamber, the banging of desk-lids, the calling of members to pages, the murmur of voices in conversation. Groups were scattered about the room; members were reading; no one was paying the slightest attention to the proceedings. Then Mr. Johnson arose, and I felt my heart stand still. Surely they would stop the noise, if only from common courtesy. But there was not an instant's cessation in the hubbub; everything continued exactly as before. He began to speak, but I could hardly catch the sound of his voice. I leaned forward and gripped the rail; the confusion would distract him; he would break down. Oh, how I hated those men who had no consideration for anyone but themselves. I felt the eyes of the other woman on me, sympathetically, pitying. Suddenly, someone cried 'S-sh!' and there was an instant's cessation in the noise. But only for an instant. I was bending forward over the rail, my eyes fixed on the speaker, hoping, praying for his success. Suddenly, W. C. Breckenridge, who was sitting directly in front of him, lifted his eyes and caught sight of me, and started to rise to come up into the gallery. I raised my hand and motioned him back, for I feared Mr. Johnson might look up and see me. Mr. Breckenridge sank back in his seat again, and I breathed a sigh of relief."

TOM REED LISTENED.

"Then a wonderful thing happened. A great, massive figure arose on the Republican side of the house and came over and took a seat directly in front of the speaker. He had come over to hear what Mr. Johnson was saying, and when Tom Reed came across to listen to a Democrat, everyone else listened, you may be sure. A hush fell on the house that remained unbroken until the speaker sat down in a burst of applause. That was the happiest day of my life."

A PEN PICTURE OF TOM JOHNSON.

Mr. Johnson is short and stout, with clear-cut, strong features. His face is that of an orator, the eye clear and direct, the forehead high and commanding. The broad nose-bridge indicates physical strength, and the firm mouth and chin, strength of character. In face, he resembles William Jennings Bryan, but a strong sense of humor belies deeper resemblance. Unlike most rich men, he knows when he has enough, and to this conclusion, it seems, he has now arrived.

"At the age of forty-five," he said to me, in his apartments at the Waldorf-Astoria, "I am fortunate enough to be able to retire from business and to devote myself to other pursuits. Except for two small matters, I may be said to be already out of business, and I have no intention of going into anything new. From now on I shall give all my energies to spreading the single-tax theory, either here or in England, where it seems to be making rapid progress. Exactly how this will be done, I don't know. I have always been a Democrat, and am one still, and I believe in organization; but whether or not I shall work within party lines, I am not yet prepared to say. Still, I have my own ideas, although it is rather my custom to act than to talk in advance."

Those who know Mr. Johnson will agree with him, I think.

EDUCATION AND LITERATURE

XXII

A BACKWOODS BOY WORKS HIS WAY THROUGH COLLEGE AND BECOMES UNIVERSITY PRESIDENT.

AT ten years of age he was a country lad on a backwoods farm on Prince Edward's Island.

At thirteen, he had become a clerk in a country store, at a salary of thirty dollars a year.

At eighteen, he was a college student, supporting himself by working in the evenings as a bookkeeper.

At twenty, he had won a scholarship in the University of London, in competition with all other Canadian students.

At twenty-five, he was professor of philosophy, Acadia College, Nova Scotia.

At thirty-eight he was appointed President of Cornell University.

At forty-four, he was chairman of President McKinley's special commission to the Philippines.

In this summary is epitomized the career of Jacob Gould Schurman. It is a romance of real life such as is not unfamiliar in America. Mr. Schurman's career differs from that of some other self-made men, however. Instead of heaping up millions upon millions, he has applied his talents to winning the intellectual prizes of life, and has made his way, unaided, to the front rank of the leaders in thought and learning in this country. His career is a source of inspiration to all poor boys who have their own way to make in the world, for he has won his present honors by his own unaided efforts.

President Schurman says of his early life:—

"It is impossible for the boy of to-day, no matter in what part of the country he is brought up, to appreciate the life of Prince Edward's Island as it was forty years ago. At that time, it had neither railroads nor daily newspapers, nor any of the dozen other things that are the merest commonplaces nowadays, even to the boys of the country districts. I did not see a railway until late in my 'teens. I was never inside a theater until after I was twenty. The only newspaper that came to my father's house was a little provincial weekly. The only books the house contained were a few standard works,—such as the Bible, Bunyan's 'Pilgrim's Progress,' Fox's 'Book of Martyrs,' and a few others of that class. Remember, too, that this was not back at the beginning of the century, but little more than a generation ago, for I was born in the year 1854.

"My father had cleared away the land on which our house stood. He was a poor man, but no poorer than his neighbors. No amount of land, and no amount of work could yield much more than the necessaries of life in that time and place. There were eight children in our family, and there was work for all of us.

"Our parents were anxious to have their children acquire at least an elementary education; and so, summer and winter, we tramped the mile and a half that lay between our house and the district school, and the snow often fell to the depth of five or six feet on the island, and sometimes, when it was at its worst, our father would drive us all to school in a big sleigh. But no weather was bad enough to keep us away.

"That would be looked upon as a poor kind of school, nowadays, I suppose. The scholars were of all ages, and everything from A,-B,-C, to the Rule of Three, was taught by the one teacher. But whatever may have been its deficiencies, the work of the school was thorough. The teacher was an old-fashioned drillmaster, and whatever he drove into our heads he put there to stay. I went to this school summer and winter until I was thirteen, and by that time I had learned to read and write and spell and figure with considerable accuracy.

"At the age of thirteen, I left home. I hadn't formed any definite plans as to my future. I merely wanted to get into a village and to earn some money.

"My father got me a place in the nearest town,—Summerside,—a village of about one thousand inhabitants. For my first year's work I was to receive thirty dollars and my board. Think of that, young men of to-day! Thirty dollars a year for working from seven in the morning until ten at night! But I was glad to get the place. It was a start in the world, and the little village was like a city to my country eyes."

HE ALWAYS SUPPORTED HIMSELF.

"From the time I began working in the store until to-day, I have always supported myself, and during all the years of my boyhood I never received a penny that I did not earn myself. At the end of my first year, I went to a larger store in the same town, where I was to receive sixty dollars a year and my board. My salary was doubled; I was getting on swimmingly.

"I kept this place for two years, and then I gave it up, against the wishes of my employer, because I had made up my mind that I wanted to get a better education. I determined to go to college.

"I did not know how I was going to do this, except that it must be of my own efforts. I had saved about eighty dollars from my storekeeping, and that was all the money I had in the world.

"When I told my employer of my plan, he tried to dissuade me from it. He pointed out the difficulties in the way of my going to college, and offered to double my pay if I would stay in the store."

THE TURNING POINT OF HIS LIFE.

"That was the turning-point in my life. On one side was the certainty of one hundred and twenty dollars a year, and the prospect of promotion as fast as I deserved it. Remember what one hundred and twenty dollars meant in Prince Edward's Island, and to me, a poor boy who had never possessed such a sum in his life. On the other side was my hope of obtaining an education. I knew that it involved hard work and self-denial, and there was the possibility of failure in the end. But my mind was made up. I would not turn back. I need not say that I do not regret that early decision, although I think that I would have made a successful storekeeper.

"With my eighty dollars capital, I began to attend the village high school, to get my preparation for college. I had only one year to do it in. My money would not last longer than that. I recited in Latin, Greek and algebra, all on the same day, and for the next forty weeks studied harder than I ever had before or have since. At the end of the year I entered the competitive examination for a scholarship in Prince of Wales College, at Charlotte Town, on the Island. I had small hope of winning it, my preparation had been so hasty and incomplete. But when the result was announced, I found that I had not only won the scholarship from my county, but stood first of all the competitors on the Island.

"The scholarship I had won amounted to only sixty dollars a year. It seems little enough, but I can say now, after nearly thirty years, that the winning of it was the greatest success I have ever had. I have had other rewards, which, to most persons, would seem immeasurably greater, but with this difference: that first success was essential; without it I could not have gone on. The others I could have done without, if it had been necessary."

For two years young Schurman attended Prince of Wales College. He lived on his scholarship and what he could earn by keeping books for one of the town storekeepers, spending less than one hundred dollars during the entire college year. Afterward, he taught a country school for a year, and then went to Acadia College in Nova Scotia to complete his college course.

A SPLENDID COLLEGE RECORD.

One of Mr. Schurman's fellow-students in Acadia says that he was remarkable chiefly for taking every prize to which he was eligible. In his senior year, he learned of a scholarship in the University of London offered for competition by the students of Canadian colleges. The scholarship paid five hundred dollars a year for three years. The young student in Acadia was ambitious to continue his studies in England, and saw in this offer his opportunity. He tried the examination and won the prize in competition with the brightest students in the larger Canadian colleges.

During the three years in the University of London, Mr. Schurman became deeply interested in the study of philosophy, and decided that he had found in it his life work. He was eager to go to Germany and study under the great leaders of philosophic thought. A way was opened for him, through the offer of the Hibbard Society in London, of a traveling fellowship with two thousand dollars a year. The honor men of the great English universities like Oxford and Cambridge were among the competitors, but the poor country boy from Prince Edward's Island was again successful, greatly to the surprise of the others.

At the end of his course in Germany, Mr. Schurman, then a doctor of philosophy, returned to Acadia College to become a teacher there. Soon afterward, he was called to Dalhousie University, at Halifax, Nova Scotia. In 1886, when a chair of philosophy was established at Cornell, President White, who had once met the brilliant young Canadian, called him to that position. Two years later, Dr. Schurman became Dean of the

Sage School of Philosophy at Cornell; and, in 1892, when the president's chair became vacant, he was placed at the head of the great university. At that time, he was only thirty-eight years of age.

President Schurman is a man of great intellectual power, and an inspiring presence. Though one of the youngest college presidents in the country, he is one of the most successful, and under his leadership Cornell has been very prosperous. He is deeply interested in all the affairs of young men, and especially those who, as he did, must make their own way in the world. He said, the other day:—

"Though I am no longer engaged directly in teaching, I should think my work a failure if I did not feel that my influence on the young men with whom I come in contact is as direct and helpful as that of a teacher could be."

COLLEGE-BRED MEN ARE IN DEMAND

"It is true that there is an increasing, and just now, an unusual demand for college-bred men in all walks of life. The prescribed preliminaries to legal and medical education are, step by step, approaching graduation from college, and have reached it, in some instances, while these professional courses themselves have been extended and deepened, till they are now nearly or quite on a par with the old liberal training with which they are co-ordinated in the modern university. As to engineers,—fifteen years ago, the manufacturers of machinery had to be coaxed to take those pioneers, the Cornell men, into their shops and give them a chance. But where one went, many followed. Last spring, when the class of 1900 came to graduation, every student in this branch was eagerly bid for two or three times over. One great electrical firm alone asked to be given the entire class. There is observable, too, a gradual increase in the call for college-bred teachers in the public schools, and this demand will grow by what it feeds upon.

"All this is but the sign and symbol of an increasing complexity and organization in our civilization. Rough-and-ready methods are going out, and the untrained handy-man with them. In all directions, as expanding American manufactures and commerce come into competition with those of Europe, it is daily more obvious that the higher skill and intelligence, making the closest use of its resources, will win. Nowadays, to do the work of the world as the world will have it done, and will pay for having it done, requires that a man be trained to the exactitude of scientific methods, and that he be given the wide mental outlook and the special training which he can acquire in the university, and nowhere else."

XXIII

A "JACK OF ALL TRADES" MASTERS ONE AND BECOMES THE POET OF THE PEOPLE.

JAMES WHITCOMB RILEY and I were at breakfast together, and the appearance of his cup of steaming coffee, into which he hastened to drop four full-sized blocks of sugar, threw the "Hoosier" poet into a train of reflections, for which he presently found expression. "They don't make coffee any more," he observed, in an almost aggrieved tone. "It is a lost art. You don't see any more the clear, transparent beverage that mother used to make. It's thick and murky, and, worse than all, it does no good to protest."

It was a fortunate circumstance, however, this recalling a youthful remembrance, for it led him at once into a lively discussion of that part of his career,—his early struggles,—which possess for the average person, and often for the subject himself, far more interest and fascination than any later triumphs, no matter how complete. It is doubtful if there is in the literary world, to-day, a personage whose boyhood and young manhood can approach in romance and unusual circumstances that of the author of "The Old Swimmin' Hole." It was almost as if it were all a chapter from a fairy tale, to see the poet sitting there, calm and dignified, and to listen to his slow speech, in well-modulated voice, and still attempt to realize of what circumstances he had been a factor, what experience he had passed through. All tradition was against his accomplishing anything in the world. How, indeed, said the good folks of the little town of Greenfield, Indiana, could anything be expected of a boy who cared nothing for school, and deserted it at the first opportunity, to take up a wandering life.

It is a wonder of wonders that from such a beginning should spring a poet whose ideals are among the noblest in American literature. "Ike Walton's Prayer," it would seem, must have been spoken from the poet's heart.

IKE WALTON'S PRAYER.

I crave, dear Lord,
  No boundless hoard
  Of gold and gear,
    Nor jewels fine,
    Nor lands, nor kine,
    Nor treasure-heaps of anything.
Let but a little hut be mine
Where at the hearthstone I may hear
    The cricket sing,
    And have the shine
Of one glad woman's eyes to make,
For my poor sake,
  Our simple home a place divine:—
  Just the wee cot—the cricket's chirr—
  Love, and the smiling face of her.

I pray not for
  Great riches, nor
  For vast estates, and castle halls,—
Give me to hear the bare footfalls
    Of children o'er
    An oaken floor,
New rinsed with sunshine, or bespread
With but the tiny coverlet
    And pillow for the baby's head;

And pray thou, may
The door stand open and the day
Send ever in a gentle breeze,
With fragrance from the locust trees,
And drowsy moan of doves, and blur
Of robins' chirps, and drone of bees,
With after hushes of the stir
Of intermingling sounds, and then
   The good-wife and the smile of her
   Filling the silences again—
      The cricket's call,
         And the wee cot,
      Dear Lord of all,
         Deny me not!

I pray not that
   Men tremble at
      My power of place
         And lordly sway,—
   I only pray for simple grace
   To look my neighbor in the face
      Full honestly from day to day—
   Yield me his horny palm to hold,
      And I'll not pray
For gold:—
The tanned face, garlanded with mirth,
It hath the kingliest smile on earth—
The swart brow, diamonded with sweat,
Hath never need of coronet.
   And so I reach
      Dear Lord to Thee,
   And do beseech
      Thou givest me
The wee cot, and the cricket's chirr,
Love, and the glad sweet face of her!

THROWN ON HIS OWN RESOURCES.

The boy's father, like almost all fathers, had aspirations. He wanted the boy to follow in his footsteps, in the legal profession, and he held out alluring hopes of the possibility of scaling even greater heights than any to which he had yet attained. Better still,—from the standpoint of the restless James,—he took the youngster with him as he made his circuit from court to court. These excursions, for they were indeed such to the boy, sowed deep in his heart the seed of a determination to become a nomad, and it was not long until he started out as a strolling sign-painter, determined upon the realization of his ideals. Oftentimes business was worse than dull, and, on one occasion, hunger drove him for recourse to his wits, and lo, he blossomed forth as a "blind sign-painter," led from place to place by a little boy, and showered with sympathy and trade in such abundance that he could hardly bear the thought of the relinquishment of a pretense so ingenious and successful, entered on at first as a joke.

Then came another epoch. The young man fell in with a patent-medicine man, with whom he joined fortunes, and here the young Indianian, who had been scribbling more or less poetry ever since he first essayed to compose a four-line valentine upon a writing table whose writing surface was almost as high as his head, found a new use for his talent, for his duties in the partnership were to beguile the people with joke and song, while his co-worker plied the sales of his cure-all; and, forsooth, there were many times when, but for his poetic fancy, Riley might have seen his audience dwindle rapidly away. It was while thus engaged that he had the opportunities which enabled him to master thoroughly the "Hoosier" dialect. When the glamour of the patent-medicine career had faded somewhat, Riley joined a band of strolling Thespians, and, in this brief portion of his life, after the wont of players of his class, played many parts.

At length he began to give a little more attention to his literary work, and, later, obtained a place on an Indianapolis paper, where he published his first poems, and be it said that they won their author almost instant success.

COURTSHIP

WHY HE LONGED TO BE A BAKER.

When I drew Riley out to talk still further of those interesting days, and the strange experiences which came to him therein, the conversation finally turned on the subject of his youthful ambitions. "I think my earliest remembered one," he said, "was an insatiate longing to become a baker. I don't know what prompted it, unless it was the vision of the mountains of alluring 'goodies,' which, as they are ranged in the windows of the pastry shops, appear doubly tempting to the youth whose mother not only counsels moderation, but enforces it.

"Next, I imagined that I would like to become a showman of some sort, and then my shifting fancy conjured up visions of how grand it would be to work as a painter, and decorate houses and fences in glowing colors, but finally, as I grew a little older, there returned my old longing to become an actor. When, however, my dreams were realized, and I became a member of a traveling theatrical company, I found that the life was full of hardships, with very little chances of rising in the world. I never had any literary ambition whatever, so far as I can remember. I wrote, primarily, simply because I desired to have something to read, and could not find selections that exactly suited me. Gradually I found a demand for my little efforts springing up, and so my brother, who could write legibly, transcribed them."

THE SUPERSTRUCTURE DEPENDS ON THE FOUNDATION.

"Mr. Riley," I said, "I came here to see you to-day in behalf of the thousands of people who are seeking to make progress, or gain a start in business or professional life, and I suppose that the tastes of some of them incline to the literary field. Can't you give me your idea of the prime requisites for success in the field of letters?"

"The most essential factor is persistence,—the determination never to allow your energy or enthusiasm to be dampened by the discouragements that must inevitably come. I believe that he is richer for the battle with the world, in any vocation, who has great determination and little talent, rather than his seemingly more fortunate brother with great talent, perhaps, but little determination. As for the field of literature, I cannot but express my conviction that meteoric flights, such as have been taken, of recent years, by some young writers with whose names almost everybody is familiar, cannot fail to be detrimental, unless the man to whom success comes thus early and suddenly is an exceptionally evenly-balanced and sensible person. Many persons have spoken to me about Kipling's work, and remarked how wonderful a thing is the fact that such achievements could have been possible for a man comparatively so young. I say, not at all. What do we find when we investigate? Simply that Kipling began working on a newspaper when he was only thirteen years of age, and he has been toiling ever since. So you see, even that case, when we get at the inner facts, confirms my theory that every man must be 'tried in the fire,' as it were. He may begin early or late, and in some cases the fight is longer than in others, but of one thing I feel sure, that there is no short-cut to permanent, self-satisfying success in literature, or anything else."

A LITERARY LIFE MEANS WORK.

When he was asked for his opinion on the subject of the expansion of Indiana literature, Mr. Riley said:—

"I do not know what I should say about Indiana literature and the causes of its growth. I think, possibly, the reason it has attracted such wide attention, and expanded in so many directions, is that it drew inspiration and received impetus from having been lampooned and made fun of by every cultured 'Tom, Dick, and Harry' of the outside world.

"Personally, the world has always been kind to me, but I do not know that I expected kindness.

"It is glorious to be barred,—to suffer the whips and scorn of self-accredited superiors! It roused us, this superciliousness, to our real worth, and it inspired us to put forth our best efforts. That excellence in literature is found in Indiana I am thankful for, and I am glad that I have outlived the ridicule, and that others have recognized, of late, this special excellence of the work of our authors, and given credit most generously.

"I am sure that the same excellence will be found in our neighboring western states, and that we, in turn, will not withhold from them encouragement and recognition. Illinois has already developed some rare poets. Ohio, too, ranks high in western literature.

"The beginner, with his youthful imagination just 'ramping it,' is too sensitive to the pricks of criticism. He stands in awe of the self-constituted critic, until he cannot see anything else, and, necessarily, loses sight of the value of ideas, which count more than all else. He can never make up the loss in years. Indeed, he can never regain it. It is expecting to be a writer in six months or a year that makes him think himself a failure.

"A literary life means work. He who would write must learn that, and learn to work hard. Look at Bernhardt's art; look at the amount of hard work she goes through every day to make it perfect. How many writers do as she does? No good thing was ever done quickly,—nothing of any value. The capacity for hard work has had much to do with the development of Indiana literature."

A COLLEGE EDUCATION IS AN ADVANTAGE.

Answering other questions, the poet said: "A college education for the aspirant for literary success is, of course, an advantage, provided he does not let education foster a false culture that will lead him away from his true ideals and the ideals he ought to cling to. There is another thing that the young man in any artistic pursuit must have a care for, and that is, to be practical. This is a practical world, and it is always ready to take advantage of this sort of people, so that if he wishes what we might call domestic happiness, he might as well make up his mind to a dual existence, as it were, and must try to cultivate a practical business sense, as well as an artistic sense. We have only a few men like Rudyard Kipling and F. Hopkinson Smith, who seem to combine these diverse elements of character in just the right proportions, but I believe that it is unfortunate for the happiness and peace of mind of our authors and artists and musicians that we have not more of them."

Riley's poetry is popular because it goes right to the feelings of the people. He could not have written as he does, but for the schooling of that wandering life, which gave him an insight into the struggle for existence among the great unnumbered multitude of his fellow men. He learned in his travels and journeys, in his hard experience as a strolling sign-painter and patent-medicine peddler, the freemasonry of poverty. His poems are natural; they are those of a man who feels as he writes. As Thoreau painted nature in the woods, and streams, and lakes, so Riley depicts the incidents of everyday life, and brightens each familiar lineament with that touch that makes all the world kin. One of his noblest poems is "Old Glory." It speaks the homely, sterling patriotism of the common people.

"The Little Coat" illustrates his wonderful power to touch the heart.

THE LITTLE COAT.

Here's his ragged "roundabout,"
Turn the pockets inside out;
See: his pen-knife, lost to use,
Rusted shut with apple-juice;
Here, with marbles, top and string,
Is his deadly "devil-sling,"
With its rubber, limp at last,
As the sparrows of the past!
Beeswax—buckles—leather straps—
Bullets, and a box of caps,—
Not a thing of all, I guess,
But betrays some waywardness—
E'en these tickets, blue and red,
For the Bible verses said—
Such as this his memory kept—
            "Jesus wept."
  * * * * * *

Here's the little coat—but O!
Where is he we've censured so!
Don't you hear us calling, dear?
Back! come back, and never fear.
You may wander where you will,
Over orchard, field and hill;
You may kill the birds, or do
Anything that pleases you!
Ah, this empty coat of his!
Every tatter worth a kiss;
Every stain as pure instead
As the white stars overhead;
And the pockets—homes were they
Of the little hands that play
Now no more—but, absent, thus
            Beckon us.

XXIV

A FARM BOY WHO DEVOURED BOOKS WRITES ONE OF THE GREATEST POEMS OF THE CENTURY.

THE international discussion of "The Man with the Hoe" had hardly subsided, when popular interest was revived by the remarkable declaration of the author, Mr. Edwin Markham, that he had spent ten years in its production.

Who is this magician of the pen, this man of mystery, who carries his readers, in a single sentence, through "a storm of stars," and, in another, kneels with them in dreamy sympathy beside "the brother to the ox,"—who mixes up the critics in a hopeless tangle of doubt, and puzzles the public by the erratic chronology of his mental processes?

The widespread interest in the personality of the poet may justify the attempt of the writer to get at the "true inwardness" of his life-story. This has not yet been told.

This handsome dreamer, whose eyes are softer than a fawn's, and whose gray-tinged locks give an unwonted majesty to his mien, is only about fifty years old. Yet, in his span of life, he has been engaged in half a score of vocations, ranging from the exciting and strenuous to the peaceful and poetic. The discovery that he was once a village blacksmith promises to lend interest to a new phase of his distinguished career.

THE MAN WITH THE HOE.

Written after seeing
Millet's World-Famous Painting.

*"God made man in His own image, in the
image of God made He him."—Genesis.*

Bowed by the weight of centuries he leans
Upon his hoe and gazes on the ground,
The emptiness of ages in his face,
And on his back the burden of the world.
Who made him dead to rapture and despair,
A thing that grieves not and that never hopes,
Stolid and stunned, a brother to the ox?
Who loosened and let down this brutal jaw?
Whose was the hand that slanted back this brow?
Whose breath blew out the light within this brain?

Is this the Thing the Lord God made and gave
To have dominion over sea and land;
To trace the stars and search the heavens for power;
To feel the passion of Eternity?
Is this the dream He dreamed who shaped the suns
And pillared the blue firmament with light?
Down all the stretch of Hell to its last gulf
There is no shape more terrible than this—
More tongued with censure of the world's blind greed—
More filled with signs and portents for the soul—

More fraught with menace to the universe.
What gulfs between him and the seraphim!
Slave of the wheel of labor, what to him
Are Plato and the swing of Pleiades?
What are the long reaches of the peaks of song,
The rift of dawn, the reddening of the rose?

Through this dread shape the suffering ages look;
Time's tragedy is in that aching stoop;
Through this dread shape humanity betrayed,
Plundered, profaned and disinherited,
Cries protest to the Judges of the World,
A protest that is also prophesy.

O masters, lords and rulers in all lands,
Is this the handiwork you give to God,
This monstrous thing, distorted and soul-quenched?
How will you ever straighten up this shape;
Touch it again with immortality;
Give back the upward looking and the light;
Rebuild in it the music and the dream;
Make right the immemorial infamies,
Perfidious wrongs, immedicable woes?

O masters, lords and rulers in all lands,
How will the Future reckon with this Man?
How answer his brute question in that hour
When whirlwinds and rebellion shake the world?
How will it be with kingdoms and with kings—
With those who shaped him to the thing he is—
When this dumb Terror shall reply to God
After the silence of the centuries?

ONE OF THE GREAT POEMS OF THE CENTURY.

No other poem published in America in many years has so stirred the emotions of the people, commanded so much attention and created so much comment as "The Man with the Hoe." It and Kipling's "Recessional" are regarded as the great poems of the closing years of the century. The critics have hailed "The Man with the Hoe" as a prominent piece of political literature, because of the breadth and depth and vital importance of the theme, and the fervor and noble dignity of its treatment. Yet the poem has been misinterpreted and assailed. It has been said to be an affront to manual labor. The only answer Mr. Markham has thus far made to his critics he dictated to the writer. He also spoke, for the first time for publication, of his mother, and her all-pervading influence on his early life, of his youthful days, and of his own experience with the hoe.

Mr. Markham's poetry proves that his paramount quality is his deep sympathy with suffering. The most marked thing in his personality is his humanity, which effuses, so to speak, in a spontaneous geniality and unaffected interest in others. He laughs easily and tells a story extremely well.

HIS MOTHER WAS BOTH PRACTICAL AND POETIC.

"I am a very serious man at heart," he remarked to me, "but, fortunately, I have a sense of humor. I will confess that the attention attracted by 'The Man with the Hoe' has surprised me, and the comments of some of the gentlemen who have condescended to criticise the poem are amusing. They seem to miss entirely its true spirit and meaning, and yet speak with most complacent confidence. I,— O, you want me to start at the beginning of my life and proceed in an orderly manner, do you? Well, I have said little for print about my early days, but get out your pencil and I will dictate you something.

"That most important event, my birth, occurred in Oregon City, Oregon, on April 23, 1852. My schooling began when I was about four years old, in a primitive little school in my native town.

"While he instilled in my youthful mind the principles of the alphabet and other important knowledge, it was the influence of my mother,—my father having died,—that dominated me. She was, in some respects, the most extraordinary woman I have ever known,—a woman of strong likes and dislikes, and capable of holding on to a purpose to the end. She kept a large store of general merchandise in Oregon City, and conducted the business with remarkable energy. But, despite her hard common sense and practical ability, she was known as the 'Woman Poet of Oregon.' It was from her, of course, that I got my own poetical bent. Her poetry was full of feeling and earnestness, and was impressed with a strong religious spirit. It was published chiefly in newspapers at the time, and I presume I am the only person in the world who now has any of it."

HE GAINED VALUABLE DISCIPLINE ON A FARM.

"When I was still a small boy, mother moved to California. She settled in a little wild valley amid the hills in the central part of the state, on a sheep range that she had bought. I was chief herder. All day long I followed the herd over ridge and hollow, and along the hillsides into the blue distance. I absorbed woodcraft and weather-wit, and a love of nature which has been one of the predominating influences of my life.

"After a few years, we turned our place into a cattle range and farm, with myself as chief farmer. I was just entering my 'teens' then. I fenced and plowed the land straggling up the little valley, and learned every detail of a farmer's work and life. The hoe, the shovel, the scythe, the cradle, the reaper, the threshing machine, the grafting knife,—these are all old friends of mine. When I began to near young manhood, I became a thresher, going from farm to farm, helping to thresh out the grain after the harvest home, and often sleeping at night in hay-mows.

BYRON'S POEMS INSPIRED HIM.

"Meanwhile, I devoured all the poetry I could find. I read Byron's poems more than any other's, because a complete set of his works was at hand, and as a result of his influence I wrote, when about sixteen, a very ambitious poem called, 'A Dream of Chaos.' This was only one of my youthful indiscretions in the poetical line. No, I don't believe the general public will ever be asked to read them. It has been kind to me, and deserves fair treatment."

"But, Mr. Markham, did you not find that your hard farm labor tended to crush out the poetry, and finer feelings generally?"

ANSWERING HIS CRITICS.

"Oh, you are now getting on ticklish ground, for it is here that the critics of 'The Man with the Hoe' congregate and jubilate. Let me say briefly, though, in answer to you and to them, that I believe in labor, that I believe in its humanizing and redeeming power. Indeed, from a religious point of view, I believe that a man's craft furnishes the chief basis of his redemption. While one is making a house, he is making himself. While he chisels the block of marble he is invisibly shaping his own soul. And it does not matter much what a man does,—whether he builds a poem or hoes in a garden. The chief thing is the way we do our work. It must be done thoroughly, and in the spirit of loving service. Work of this order is a perpetual prayer. The doer is elevated by such work.

"But, while all this is true, it is also true that excesses are evils,—that overwork and underpaid work tend to break down instead of build up. Work is good for the child, but I can put such heavy burdens upon him as to deform his body and stunt his mind.

"'The Man with the Hoe' is, of course, the type of industrial oppression in all lands and in all parts of labor. He is the man who has been chained to the wheel by the fierce necessity for bread,—the man with no time for rest, no time for study, no time for thought, no time for the mighty hopes that make us men. The poem is not a protest against labor; it is a protest against the degradation of labor."

SEED SOWN LONG AGO.

Speaking of the writing of this poem, Mr. Markham said that he sketched the outline of it fourteen years ago, upon seeing a photograph of Millet's famous painting, "The Man with the Hoe." When he saw the picture itself four years afterward, he further elaborated the idea, but did not write it out in complete form until Christmas week, 1900. He then spent three or four days on it, and sent it to the San Francisco Examiner, where it was published for the first time on the eighth of January 1901.

Within a few months, the volume, "The Man with the Hoe and other Poems," was issued by Doubleday and McClure, of New York, and met with so large a sale that it was soon in its fifth edition. It has been very favorably received.

Mr. Markham paid his way through the state normal school at San Jose, and afterward through Christian college at Santa Rosa, California. He has done important educational work in that state as a superintendent and principal of schools in various places, and is now head master of the Tompkins observation school in Oakland. Inducements have been offered him to deliver a series of lectures throughout the country, and he has received many requests for literary work, with some of which he will comply.

> The world is well lost when the world is wrong,
>   No matter how men deride you;
> For if you are patient and firm and strong,
>   You will find in time, though the time be long,
>   That the world wheels round beside you.
>
> —Ella Wheeler Wilcox.

XXV

A FAMOUS AUTHORESS TELLS LITERARY ASPIRANTS THE STORY OF HER STRUGGLE FOR RECOGNITION.

BORN and reared in Wisconsin, Ella Wheeler Wilcox, although a resident of New York, is still faithful to the ideals and aspirations of the young and vigorous western state in which she first saw the light. She began writing at an early age, and still has in her possession childish verses, composed when she was only eight years old.

She was, however, far from any literary center; she had no one upon whom she might rely for advice as to her methods, and she had no influential friends, for her family was not a wealthy one. The usual difficulties, so familiar to all beginners, met her at every step; discouragements were endured day after day, and year after year. After a while, she began writing for various periodicals. Her first poems appeared in the New York Mercury, the Waverly Magazine, and Leslie's publications. It was from the publishing house of Frank Leslie she received her first check. Her income from literary work was very small and recognition came quite slowly. But courage, and patience, and fortitude, finally won the day.

HOW HER BEST POEMS WERE WRITTEN.

One of her most famous poems, beginning, "Laugh and the World Laughs with You," was written about February, 1883, at Madison, Wisconsin. She had talked with a friend who had been bereaved by death in her household; later, while dressing for an inaugural ball, given in honor of the governor of Wisconsin, she was startled to think how soon the mind turns from stories of sorrow to scenes of gayety. Thus she formed the idea of this famous poem. It originally appeared in the New York Sun, and the author received five dollars for it. Subsequently, an attempt was made to pirate the verses as the composition of another; but the effort was, happily, a complete failure. The poem embodying the idea,—

"A question is never settled
Until it is settled right,"

with which W. J. Bryan concludes his book, was written by her after hearing a gentleman make a remark in those words at the conclusion of a heated argument, on the single-tax question. The gentleman was afterward told that Lincoln had made use of this exact expression, years ago. But neither the gentleman in question, nor Mrs. Wilcox herself, had ever heard the expression before.

"The Two Glasses," one of her brightest poems, was written at the age of eighteen. Although this was a "temperance poem," she had never, up to that time, seen a glass of beer or wine. This poem, too, was pirated by one who pretended to be the author.

"The Birth of the Opal" was suggested by Herman Marcus, the Broadway jeweler, who advanced the idea of the opal being the child of the sunlight and moonlight.

"Wherever You Are," originally appeared in Leslie's Popular Monthly. A young man who had served a term in Auburn Prison read this poem, and it became the means of his reformation. Mrs. Wilcox lent him a helping hand, and he is to-day a hard-working, honest, worthy man.

She regards the poems, "High Noon," "To An Astrologer," and "The Creed," as probably her best efforts.

It will thus be noted that she does not prefer the more fervid poems of passion, written in her early youth.

THE CREED.

>Whoever was begotten by pure love,
>   And came desired and welcomed into life,
>Is of immaculate conception. He
>Whose heart is full of tenderness and truth,
>Who loves mankind more than he loves himself,
>And cannot find room in his heart for hate,
>May be another Christ. We all may be
>The Saviors of the world, if we believe
>In the Divinity which dwells in us,
>And worship it, and nail our grosser selves,
>Our tempers, greeds, and our unworthy aims
>Upon the cross. Who giveth love to all,
>Pays kindness for unkindness, smiles for frowns,
>And lends new courage to each fainting heart,
>And strengthens hope and scatters joy abroad,
>He, too, is a Redeemer, Son of God.

Mrs. Wilcox lives in New York City from November to May, and in her cottage at Short Beach, Connecticut, during the rest of the year. Her husband, R. M. Wilcox, is a clear-headed business man, of polished manners, kind and considerate to all whom he meets,—one who, in short, is deservedly popular with all the friends of the happy couple. The summer house at Short Beach is especially charming. It is in full view of the Long Island Sound, with a fine beach in front, and a splendid sweep of country at the rear.

SHE IS A PRONOUNCED OPTIMIST.

As to "literary methods," Mrs. Wilcox has few suggestions to make, except to recommend hard work, conscientiously performed. She is untiring in her own efforts at rewriting, revising and polishing her productions, and cannot rest until every appearance of crudeness and carelessness is effaced. Her manuscripts are always neat, always carefully considered, and never prepared in undue haste. She believes that no writer can succeed who is a pessimist. She is, therefore, an optimist of the most pronounced type, and believes that all poems should be helpful not hurtful; full of hope, and not of despair; bright with faith, and not clouded by doubt.

"What is your view of the first duties of a young author?" she was asked, and replied:

"The first thing necessary for you to do is to find out your own motive in choosing a literary career. If you write as the young bird sings, you need no advice from me, for your thoughts will find their way out, as natural springs force their way through rocks, and nothing can hinder you. But if you have merely a well-defined literary ability and taste, you should consider carefully before undertaking the difficult task of authorship.

"An author should be able to instruct, entertain, guide or amuse his readers. Otherwise, he has no right to expect their attention, time or money. If it is merely a question of money, you would be wise to wait until you have a comfortable income, sufficient to maintain life during the first ten years of literary pursuits. Save in rare cases of remarkable genius, literature requires ten years of apprenticeship, at least, before yielding support to its followers. But be sure that you help,—not harm, humanity. To the author, of all men, belongs the motto, '*Noblesse oblige.*'"

DO NOT FEAR CRITICISM.

"Unless you are so absorbed in your work that you utterly forget the existence of critics or reviewers, you have no right to call yourself a genius. Talent thinks with fear and fawning of critics; genius does not remember that they exist. One bows at the shrine of existing public opinion, which is narrow with prejudice. The other bows at the shrine of art, which is as broad as the universe."

"How do you think a young author should proceed to obtain recognition?"

"In regard to the practical method of getting one's work before the public, I would beg that you would not send it to any well-known author, asking him or her to 'read, criticize, correct, and find a publisher for you.' If such a thought has entered your head, remember that it has entered the heads of five hundred other amateurs, and the poor author is crushed under an avalanche of badly-written manuscripts, not one of which he has time to read. No editor will accept what he does not want, through the advice of any author, however famous.

"Do not attempt to adopt the style of anyone else. Unless you feel that you can be yourself, do not try to be anybody. A poor original is better than a good imitation, in literature, if not in other things.

"Expect no aid from influential friends in any way. The more wholly you depend upon yourself, the sooner will you succeed.

"It is absolute nonsense to talk about 'influence' with editors or publishers. No one ever achieved even passing fame or success in literature through influence or 'friends at court.' An editor might be influenced to accept one article, but he would never give permanent patronage through any influence, however strong.

"As I receive so many hundreds of letters asking how I found my way into print, and through what influences, it may be pardonable for me to say a few words regarding my own experiences. In the first place, I never sent a manuscript to any human being in my life, to ask for an opinion or influence. I always send directly to the editors, and I am not aware that any influence was ever used in my behalf. I have often had an article refused by six editors and accepted by the seventh. An especially unfortunate manuscript of mine was once rejected by eight periodicals, and I was about to consign it to oblivion, when, at a last venture, I sent it to the ninth. A check of seventy-five dollars came to me by return mail, with an extremely complimentary letter from the editor, requesting more articles of a similar kind."

MERIT IS NOT ALWAYS DISCOVERED QUICKLY.

"Very few authors have lived to attain any degree of fame without receiving back their cherished yet unwelcome manuscripts from the hands of one or more unappreciative editors before they met the public eye.

"It is reported of 'David Harum' that six publishers rejected it previous to its final publication.

"Archibald Gunter's book, 'Mr. Barnes of New York,' went the rounds of the various publishing houses, only to be rejected by all. Then Mr. Gunter rose to the occasion, published it himself, and reaped a small fortune from its sales.

"Many a successful short story and poem passes through the 'reading' department of a half-dozen magazines and weeklies without having its merit discovered until a seventh editor accepts it.

"Poems of my own, which have later met much favor from the public, I have seen return with a dejected and dog-eared air, from eight or nine offices, whither they had gone forth, like Noah's dove, seeking for a resting place. A charming bit of verse, written by a friend of mine, took twenty-one journeys from the maternal hand to the editor's table before it found an appreciative purchaser.

"If the young writer will stop and consider that each editor has his own individual ideas of what he wants, both in verse and prose, and that, just as no two faces are alike, no two minds run in the same groove,—he may be hopeful for the ultimate acceptance of the darling of his brain, if he will persevere. Of course, this refers to a writer who possesses actual talent."

EDITORS ARE ANXIOUS FOR GOOD ARTICLES.

"No more absurd idea ever existed than that of the efficacy of 'influence' in literature. An editor will buy what he thinks his readers will appreciate. He will not buy anything which he feels will fall dead on his audience. He may purchase one—possibly two, manuscripts,—to oblige a friend, but it will end there; and one or two manuscripts, so purchased, can never make name or fame for their author.

"It would be just as reasonable to talk about 'influence with a dry-goods merchant,' and to expect to make him purchase undesired goods from a manufacturer for friendship's sake, as to think an editor can be influenced by a friend at court.

"Editors are employed by the owners of periodicals to select and publish material which will render the periodical a paying concern. The editor who does not do this may lose his position and his salary.

"He is on the watch for attractive matter—and desires to find new material. He is delighted when he discovers a new poet or author. Being mortal, and having but one mind, he can judge of the poems and stories sent to him only from an individual standpoint.

"He not infrequently lets genius slip through his hands, and accepts paste imitations. But he does it ignorantly, or carelessly, not wilfully; or he may have in his collection of accepted manuscripts something similar, which would prevent his use of a poem or sketch at that particular juncture.

"The reasons why an editor declines a good manuscript are innumerable. It is impossible for him to explain them to each applicant for his favor. Nothing indicates the crudity of an author more than a request to criticize a manuscript and point out its defects; for frequently the very first verse or the very first page of a poem or romance decides its fate, and the editor returns it without reading further. Sometimes its length prevents any possibility of its being used in that particular periodical, while it might be just what another magazine would desire."

PERSEVERANCE COUNTS IN AUTHORSHIP.

"The young writer who decides absolutely upon a literary career, and is confident of his mental equipment for his profession, should read all the current periodicals, magazines, and weeklies, American and English, and observe what style of literature they publish. Then he should make a list of them, and send his poem or his narrative first to the magazine which he feels it is best suited for; if it returns, let him proceed to speed it forth again, after giving it another reading; and so on, until it has finished the circuit of, perhaps, fifty periodicals. This habit of perseverance will be worth something, even if he never sells that manuscript.

"If he is still confident of his powers, let him write in another vein, and proceed in the same manner. This persistency, backed by talent, must win in the long run.

"If he feels he wants criticism, let him apply to some of the literary bureaus which make a business of criticism and revision.

"Very few authors have time to give to this work, nor are they, as a rule, the best judges of the merit of another writer's productions. After all, the secret of a writer's success lies within him. If he is well equipped, he will win, but not otherwise."

WILL-POWER

There is no chance, no destiny, no fate,
Can circumvent, or hinder, or control
The firm resolve of a determined soul.
Gift counts for little; will alone is great;
All things give way before it, soon or late.
What obstacle can stay the mighty force
Of the sea-seeking river in its course,
Or cause the ascending orb of day to wait?
Each well-born soul must win what it deserves,
Let the fool prate of Luck! The fortunate
Is he whose earnest purpose never swerves,
Whose slightest action or inaction serves
The one great aim.
Why, even death stands still
And waits, an hour, sometimes, for such a will!

XXVI

A PRINTER'S BOY, SELF TAUGHT, BECOMES THE DEAN OF AMERICAN LETTERS.

"I SHOULD like, Mr. Howells," said I, by way of opening my interview with the famous novelist, "to learn your opinion concerning what constitutes success in life. You should have the American view?"

"Not necessarily," said the novelist, seating himself.

"Do you share the belief that everything is open to the beginner who has sufficient energy and perseverance?"

"Add brains, and I will agree," said Mr. Howells with a smile. "A young man stands at the 'parting of two ways,' and can take his path this way or that. It is comparatively easy then, with good judgment. Youth is certainly the greatest advantage which life supplies."

"You began to carve out your place in life under conditions very different from those of to-day?"

"Yes. I was born in a little southeastern Ohio village,—Martin's Ferry,—and, of course, I had but little of what people deem advantages in the way of schools, railroads, population, and so on. I am not sure, however, that compensation was not had in other things."

"Do you consider that you were specially talented in the direction of literary composition?"

"I should not say that. I think that I came of a reading race, which had always loved literature in a way. My inclination was to read."

"Would you say that, with a special leaning toward a special study, and good health, a fair start, and perseverance, anyone can attain to distinction?"

EARLY IDEALS.

"That is a probability, only. You may be sure that distinction will not come without those qualities. The only way to succeed, therefore, is to have them; though having them will not necessarily guarantee distinction. I can only say that I began with a lofty ideal, without saying how closely I have held to it. My own youth was not specially marked by advantages. There were none, unless you can call a small bookcase full of books, which my home contained, an advantage. The printing office was my school from a very early date. My father thoroughly believed in it, and he had his belief as to work, which he illustrated as soon as we were old enough to learn the trade he followed. We could go to school and study, or we could go into the printing office and work, with perhaps an equal chance of learning; but we could not be idle."

"And you chose the printing office?"

"Not wholly. As I recall it, I went to and fro between the schoolhouse and the printing office. When I tired of one, I was promptly given my choice of the other."

"Then you began life in poverty?"

"I suppose that, as the world goes now, we were poor. My father's income was never above twelve hundred a year, and his family was large; but nobody was rich then. We lived in the simple fashion of that time and place."

"You found time to read?"

"My reading, somehow, went on pretty constantly. No doubt my love for it won me a chance to devote time to it."

"Might I ask how much time you devoted each day to your literary object?"

"The length varied with varying times. Sometimes I read but

little. There were years of the work, of the over-work, indeed,—which falls to the lot of many, that I should be ashamed to speak of except in accounting for the fact. My father had sold his paper in Hamilton, and had bought an interest in another at Dayton, and at that time we were all straining our utmost to help pay for it."

"And that left you little time?"

"In that period very few hours were given to literature. My daily tasks began so early, and ended so late, that I had little time, even if I had the spirit for reading. Sometimes I had to sit up until midnight, waiting for telegraphic news, and be up again at dawn to deliver the papers, working afterward at the case; but that was only for a few years."

"When did you find time to seriously apply yourself to literature?"

ACQUIRING A LITERARY STYLE.

"I think I did so before I really had the time. Literary aspirations were stirred in me by the great authors whom I successively discovered, and I was perpetually imitating the writings of these,—modeling some composition of my own after theirs, but never willing to own it."

"Do you attribute your style to the composite influence of these various models?"

"No doubt they had their effect, as a whole, but individually I was freed from the last by each succeeding author, until at length I came to understand that I must be like myself, and no other."

"Had you any conveniences for literary research, beyond the bookcase in your home?"

"If you mean a place to work, I had a narrow, little space, under the stairs at home. There was a desk pushed back against the wall, which the irregular ceiling sloped down to meet, behind it, and at my left was a window, which gave a good light on the writing leaf of my desk. This was my workshop for six or seven years,—and it was not at all a bad one. It seemed, for a while, so very simple and easy to come home in the middle of the afternoon, when my task at the printing office was done, and sit down to my books in my little study, which I did not finally leave until the family were all in bed. My father had a decided bent in the direction of literature; and, when I began to show a liking for literature, he was eager to direct my choice. This finally changed to merely recommending books, and eventually I was left to my own judgment,—a perplexed and sorrowful mistaken judgment, at times."

"In what manner did you manage to read the works of all your favorite authors?"

"Well, my hours in the printing office began at seven and ended at six, with an hour at noon for dinner, which I used for putting down such verses as had come to me in the morning. As soon as supper was over, I got out my manuscripts, and sawed, and filed, and hammered away at my blessed poems, which were little less than imitations, until nine, when I went regularly to bed, to rise again at five. Sometimes the foreman gave me an afternoon off on Saturday, which I devoted to literature."

"Might I ask concerning your next advance in your chosen work?"

"Certainly. As I recall it, my father had got one of those legislative clerkships, in 1858, which used to fall sometimes to deserving country editors, and together we managed and carried out a scheme for corresponding with some city papers. Going to Columbus, the state capital, we furnished a daily letter giving an account of the legislative proceedings, which I mainly wrote from the material he helped me to gather. The letters found favor, and my father withdrew from the work wholly."

"How long were you a correspondent?"

HIS POEMS ALWAYS WERE REJECTED.

"Two years. At the end of the first winter, a Cincinnati paper offered me the city editorship, but one night's round with the reporters at the police station satisfied me that I was not meant for that kind of work. I then returned home for the summer, and spent my time in reading, and in sending off poems, which regularly came back. I worked in my father's printing office, of course; but, as soon as my task was done, went home to my books, and worked away at them until supper. Then a German bookbinder, with whom I was endeavoring to read Heine in the original, met me in my father's editorial room, and with a couple of candles on the table between us, and our Heine and the dictionary before us, we read until we were both tired out."

"Did you find it labor?"

"I fancy that reading is not merely a pastime, when it is apparently the merest pastime. It fatigues one after the manner of other work, and uses up a certain amount of mind-stuff; and I have found that, if you are using up all the mind-stuff you have, much or little, in some other way, you do not read, because you have not the mind-stuff for it. You cannot say more of any other form of work."

"Then it might be said that you worked at separate and equally difficult tasks, constantly?"

"Perhaps not equally difficult, but, certainly, constantly."

"Rather a severe schooling to give one's self, don't you think it?"

Mr. Howells smiled. "It was not without its immediate use. I learned how to choose between words, after a study of their fitness; and, though I often employed them decoratively, and with no vital sense of their qualities, still, in mere decoration, they had to be chosen intelligently, and after some thought about their structure and meaning. I would not imitate great writers without imitating their method, which was to the last degree intelligent. They knew what they were doing, and, although I did not always know what I was doing, they made me wish to know, and ashamed of not knowing. The result was beneficial."

"It is very evident that you recovered your health, in spite of your toil?"

HIS FIRST EDITORIAL POSITION.

"Oh, yes. I got back health enough to be of use in the printing office at home, and was quietly at work there, when, to my astonishment, I was asked to come and take a place upon a Republican newspaper at the capital. I was given charge of the news department. This included the literary notices and the book reviews, and I am afraid that I at once gave my prime attention to these."

"When did you begin to contribute to the literature of the day?"

"If you mean, when did I begin to attempt to contribute, I should need to fix an early date, for I early had experience with rejected manuscripts. One of my pieces, which fell so far short of my visions of the immense subjects I should handle as to treat of the lowly and familiar theme of spring, was the first thing I ever had in print. My father offered it to the editor of the paper I worked on in Columbus, where we were then living, and I first knew what he had done when, with mingled shame and pride, I saw it in the journal. In the tumult of my emotions, I promised myself that if ever I got through that experience safely, I would never suffer anything else of mine to be published; but it was not long before I offered the editor a poem, myself."

"When did you publish your first story?"

"My next venture was a story in the Ik Marvel manner, which it was my misfortune to carry into print. I did not really write it, but composed it, rather, in type, at the case. It was not altogether imitated from Ik Marvel, for I drew upon the easier art of Dickens, at times, and helped myself out in places with bald parodies of 'Bleak House.' It was all very well at the beginning, but I had not reckoned with the future sufficiently to start with any clear ending in my mind; and, as I went on, I began to find myself more and more in doubt about it. My material gave out; my incidents failed me; the characters wavered, and threatened to perish in my hands. To crown my misery, there grew up an impatience with the story among its readers; and this found its way to me one day, when I overheard an old farmer, who came in for his paper, say that he 'did not think that story amounted to much.' I did not think so, either, but it was deadly to have it put into words; and how I escaped the mortal effect of the stroke I do not know. Somehow, I managed to bring the wretched thing to a close, and to live it slowly down."

AN EXPERIENCE IN COLLABORATION.

"My next contribution to literature was jointly with John J. Piatt, the poet, who had worked with me as a boy in the printing office at Columbus. We met in Columbus, where I was then an editor, and we made our first literary venture together in a volume entitled, 'Poems of Two Friends.' The volume became instantly and lastingly unknown to fame; the west waited, as it always does, to hear what the east should say. The east said nothing, and two-thirds of the small edition of five hundred copies came back upon the publisher's hands. This did not deter me, however, from contributing to the periodicals, which, from time to time, accepted my efforts."

"Did you remain long, as an editor, in Columbus?"

"No; only until 1861, when I was appointed consul at Venice. I really wanted to go to Germany, that I might carry forward my studies in German literature; and I first applied for the consulate at Munich. The powers at Washington thought it quite the same thing to offer me Rome, but I found that the income of the Roman consulate would not give me a living, and I was forced to decline it. Then the president's private secretaries, Mr. John Nicolay and Mr. John Hay, who did not know me, except as a young westerner who had written poems in the 'Atlantic Monthly,' asked me how I would like Venice, promising that the salary would be put up to $1,000 a year. It was really put up to $1,500, and I accepted. I had four years of nearly uninterrupted leisure at Venice."

"Was it easier when you returned from Venice?"

"Not at all. On my return to America my literary life took such form that most of my reading was done for review. I wrote at first a good many of the lighter criticisms in 'The Nation,' and then I went to Boston, to become assistant editor of 'The Atlantic Monthly,' where I wrote the literary notices for that periodical for four or five years."

"You were eventually editor of the 'Atlantic,' were you not?"

"Yes, until 1881; and I have had some sort of close relation with magazines ever since."

"Would you say that all literary success is very difficult to achieve?" I ventured.

"All that is enduring."

"It seems to me ours is an age when fame comes quickly."

"Speaking of quickly made reputations," said Mr. Howells, meditatively, "did you ever hear of Alexander Smith? He was a poet who, in the fifties, was proclaimed immortal by the critics, and ranked with Shakespeare. I myself read him with an ecstacy which, when I look over his work to-day, seems ridiculous. His poem, 'Life-Drama,' was heralded as an epic, and set alongside of 'Paradise Lost.' I cannot tell how we all came out of this craze, but the reading world is very susceptible of such lunacies. He is not the only third-rate poet who has been thus apotheosized, before and since. You might have envied his great success, as I certainly did; but it was not success, after all; and I am sure that real success is always difficult to achieve."

"Do you believe that success comes to those who have a special bent or taste, which they cultivate by hard work?"

"I can only answer that out of my literary experience. For my own part, I believe I have never got any good from a book that I did not read merely because I wanted to read it. I think this may be applied to anything a person does. The book, I know, which you read from a sense of duty, or because for any reason you must, is apt to yield you little. This, I think, is also true of everything, and the endeavor that does one good,—and lasting good,—is the endeavor one makes with pleasure. Labor done in another spirit will serve in a way, but pleasurable labor brings, on the whole, I think, the greatest reward."

THE REWARDS OF LITERATURE.

"You were probably strongly fascinated by the supposed rewards of a literary career?"

"Yes. A definite literary ambition grew up in me, and in the long reveries of the afternoon, when I was distributing my case in the printing office, I fashioned a future of overpowering magnificence and undying celebrity. I should be ashamed to say what literary triumphs I achieved in those preposterous deliriums. But I realize now that such dreams are nerving, and sustain one in an otherwise barren struggle."

"Were you ever tempted and willing to abandon your object of a literary life for something else?"

"I was once. My first and only essay, aside from literature, was in the realm of law. It was arranged with a United States senator that I should study law in his office. I tried it a month, but almost from the first day, I yearned to return to my books. I had not only to go back to literature, but to the printing office, and I gladly chose to do it,—a step I never regretted."

"You started out to attain personal distinction and happiness, did you not?"

"I did."

WHAT TRUE HAPPINESS IS.

"You have attained the first,—but I should like to know if your view of what constitutes happiness is the same as when you began?"

"It is quite different. I have come to see life, not as the chase of a forever-impossible personal happiness, but as a field for endeavor toward the happiness of the whole human family. There is no other success.

"I know, indeed, of nothing more subtly satisfying and cheering than a knowledge of the real good will and appreciation of others. Such happiness does not come with money, nor does it flow from a fine physical state. It cannot be bought. But it is the keenest joy, after all, and the toiler's truest and best reward."

XXVII

A FAMOUS NOVELIST ATONES FOR WASTED SCHOOL DAYS BY SELF-CULTURE.

IN his study, a curiously-shaped building without the accompaniment of a window, and combining in equal proportions the Byzantine, Romanesque and Doric styles of architecture, the gray-haired author of "Ben Hur," surrounded by his pictures, books and military trophies, is spending, in serene and comfortable retirement, the evening of his life. As I sat beside him and listened to the recital of his earliest struggles and later achievements, I could not help contrasting his dignified bearing, careful expression, and gentle demeanor, with another occasion in his life, when, a vigorous, black-haired young military officer, in the spring of 1861, he appeared, with flashing eye and uplifted sword, at the head of his regiment, the gallant and historic Eleventh Indiana Volunteers.

General Wallace never repels a visitor, and his greeting is cordial and ingenuous.

"If I could say anything to stimulate or encourage the young men of to-day," he said, when I had explained the object of my visit, "I would gladly do so, but I fear that the story of my early days would be of very little interest or value to others. So far as school education is concerned, it may be truthfully said that I had but little, if any; and if, in spite of that deficiency, I ever arrived at proficiency, I reached it, I presume, as Topsy attained her stature,—'just growed into it.'"

HE WAS A CARELESS STUDENT.

"Were you denied early school advantages?" I asked.

"Not in the least. On the contrary, I had most abundant opportunity in that respect. My father was a lawyer, enjoying a lucrative practice in Brookville, Indiana,—a small town which bears the distinction of having given to the world more prominent men than any other place in the Hoosier state. Not long after my birth, he was elected lieutenant-governor, and, finally, governor of the state. He, himself, was an educated man, having been graduated from the United States Military Academy at West Point, and having served as instructor in mathematics there. He was not only an educated man, but a man of advanced ideas generally, as shown by the fact that he failed of a re-election to congress in 1840, because, as a member of the committee on commerce, he gave the casting vote in favor of an appropriation to develop Morse's magnetic telegraph. Of course, he believed in the value, and tried to impress upon me the necessity of a thorough school training; but, in the face of all the solicitude and encouragement which an indulgent father could waste on an unappreciative son, I remained vexatiously indifferent. I presume I was like some man in history,—it was Lincoln, I believe,—who said that his father taught him to work, but he never quite succeeded in teaching him to love it.

"My father sent me to school, and regularly paid tuition,—for in those days there were no free schools; but, much to my discredit, he failed to secure anything like regular attendance at recitations, or even a decent attempt to master my lessons at any time. In fact, much of the time that should have been given to school was spent in fishing, hunting and roaming through the woods."

HE LOVED TO READ.

"But were you thus indifferent to all forms of education?"

"No, my case was not quite so hopeless as that. I did not desert the schools entirely, but my attendance was so provokingly irregular and my indifference so supreme, I wonder now that I was tolerated at all. But I had one mainstay; I loved to read. I was a most inordinate reader. In some lines of literature, especially history and some kinds of fiction, my appetite was insatiate, and many a day, while my companions were clustered together in the old red brick schoolhouse, struggling with their problems in fractions or percentage, I was carefully hidden in the woods near by, lying upon my elbows, munching an apple, and reveling in the beauties of Plutarch, Byron or Goldsmith.

"Did you not attend college, or the higher grade of schools?"

"Yes, for a brief period. My brother was a student in Wabash College,—here in Crawfordsville,—and hither I also was sent; but within six weeks I had tired of the routine, was satiated with discipline, and made my exit from the institution. I shall never forget what my father did when I returned home. He called me into his office, and, reaching into one of the pigeon-holes above his desk, withdrew therefrom a package of papers neatly folded and tied with the conventional red tape. He was a very systematic man, due, perhaps, to his West Point training, and these papers proved to be the receipts for my tuition, which he had carefully preserved. He called off the items, and asked me to add them together. The total, I confess, staggered me."

A FATHER'S FRUITFUL WARNING.

"'That sum, my son,' he said, with a tone of regret in his voice, 'represents what I have expended in these many years past to provide you with a good education. How successful I have been, you know better than anyone else. After mature reflection, I have come to the conclusion that I have done for you in that direction all that can reasonably be expected of any parent, and I have, therefore, called you in to tell you that you have now reached an age when you must take up the lines yourself. If you have failed to profit by the advantages with which I have tried so hard to surround you, the responsibility must be yours. I shall not upbraid you for your neglect, but rather pity you for the indifference which you have shown to the golden opportunities you have, through my indulgence, been enabled to enjoy.'"

"What effect did this admonition have on you? Did it awaken or arouse you?"

"It aroused me, most assuredly. It set me to thinking as nothing before had done. The next day, I set out with a determination to accomplish something for myself. My father's injunction rang in my ears. New responsibilities rested on my shoulders, as I was, for the first time in my life, my own master. I felt that I must get work on my own account. After much effort, I finally obtained employment from the man with whom I had passed so many afternoons strolling up and down the little streams in the neighborhood, trying to fish. He was the county clerk, and he hired me to copy what was known as the complete record of one of the courts. I worked for months in a dingy, half-lighted room, receiving for my pay something like ten cents per hundred words. The tediousness and regularity of the work was a splendid drill for me, and taught me the virtue of persistence as one of the avenues of success. It was at this time I began to realize the deficiency in my education, especially as I had an ambition to become a lawyer. Being deficient in both mathematics and grammar, I was forced to study those branches evenings. Of course, the latter was a very exacting study, after a full day's hard work, but I was made to realize that the time I had spent with such lavish prodigality could not be recovered, and that I must extract every possible good out of the golden moments then flying by all too fast."

HIS FIRST LITERARY EFFORT.

"Had you a distinct literary ambition at that time?"

"Well, I had always had a sort of literary bent or inclination. I read all the literature of the day, besides the standard authors, and finally began to devote my odd moments to a book of my own,—a tale based on the days of the crusades. When completed it covered about three hundred and fifty pages, and bore the rather high-sounding title, 'The Man-at-Arms.' I read a good portion of it before a literary society to which I belonged; the members applauded it, and I was frequently urged to have it published. The Mexican War soon followed, however, and I took the manuscript with me when I enlisted; but before the close of my service it was lost, and my production, therefore, never reached the public eye."

"But did not the approval which the book received from the few persons who read it encourage you to continue writing?"

"Fully fifty years have elapsed since then, and it is, therefore, rather difficult, at this late day, to recall just how such things affected me. I suppose I was encouraged thereby, for, in due course of time, another book which turned out to be 'The Fair God,'—my first book to reach the public,—began to shape itself in my mind. The composition of this work was not, as the theatrical people would say, a continuous performance, for there were many and singular interruptions, and it would be safe to say that months, and, in one case, years, intervened between certain chapters. A few years after the war, I finished the composition, strung the chapters into a continuous narrative, leveled up the uneven places, and started East with the manuscript. A letter from Whitelaw Reid, then editor of the New York 'Tribune,' introduced me to the head of one of the leading publishing houses in Boston. There I was kindly received, and, delivered my manuscript, which was referred to a professional reader, to determine its literary, and also, I presume, its commercial value.

"It would be neither a new nor an interesting story to acquaint the public with the degree of anxious suspense that pervaded my mind when I withdrew to await the reader's judgment. Every other writer has, I assume, at one time or another, undergone much the same experience. It was not long until I learned from the publisher that the reader reported in favor of my production. Publication soon followed, and for the first time, in a literary sense, I found myself before the public, and my book before the critics."

"How long after this did 'Ben Hur' appear, and what led you to write it?"

THE ORIGIN OF "BEN HUR."

"I began 'Ben Hur' about 1876, and it was published in 1880. The purpose, at first, was a short serial for one of the magazines, descriptive of the visit of the wise men to Jerusalem as mentioned in the first two verses of the second chapter of Matthew. It will be recognized in 'Book First' of the work as now published. For certain reasons, however, the serial idea was abandoned, and the narrative, instead of ending with the birth of the Savior, expanded into a more pretentious novel and only ended with the death scene on Calvary. The last ten chapters were written in the old adobe palace at Sante Fe, New Mexico, where I was serving as governor. It is difficult to answer the question, 'what led me to write the book?' or why I chose a piece of fiction which used Christ as its leading character. In explanation, it is proper to state that I had reached an age in life when men usually begin to study themselves with reference to their fellowmen, and reflect on the good they may have done in the world. Up to that time, never having read the Bible, I knew nothing about sacred history; and in matters of a religious nature, although I was not in every respect an infidel, I was persistently and notoriously indifferent. I did not know, and, therefore, did not care. I resolved to begin the study of the good book in earnest.

CONVERTED WHILE WRITING HIS OWN BOOK.

"I was in quest of knowledge, but I had no faith to sustain, no creed to bolster up. The result was that the whole field of religious and biblical history opened up before me, and, my vision not being clouded by previously formed opinions, I was enabled to survey it without the aid of lenses. I believe I was thorough and persistent. I know I was conscientious in my search for the truth. I weighed, I analyzed, I counted and compared. The evolution from conjecture into knowledge, through opinion and belief, was gradual but irresistible; and at length I stood firmly and defiantly on the solid rock. Upward of seven hundred thousand copies of 'Ben Hur' have been published, and it has been translated into all languages from French to Arabic; but, whether it has ever influenced the mind of a single reader or not, I am sure its conception and preparation, if it has done nothing more, has convinced its author of the divinity of the lowly Nazarene who walked and talked with God."

XXVIII

A SOCIAL LEADER, HAVING "EYES THAT SEE," EARNS LITERARY LAURELS.

MRS. BURTON HARRISON, the gifted American authoress, is a charming woman socially. She is unaffected in manner, and easy and graceful in conversation. When I called, I was ushered into her library and study, and was entertained in the same delightful way in which her books are written. Indeed, she told me that she writes without effort, and endeavors to do so naturally.

It was a pretty story she told me of her childhood days in Old Virginia, where she spent the greater part of her time in reading standard works, and in dreaming of an almost unformed ambition. "Even in my youngest years," she said, "I used to make up fairy tales. Later, I put my thoughts on paper."

"And what was your first experience in a literary way?" I asked.

"When I was about seventeen years old, I sent a love story to the 'Atlantic Monthly.' It was lurid and melancholy," she said, with a smile. "It was returned in due course of time, and across its face was written, in very bright ink, 'This is far better than the average, and ought to be read through,' from which I inferred that only the first page had been read. But I was encouraged even by that."

HER FIRST NOVEL.

"My next attempt was a novel, which I called 'Skirmishing.' It was destroyed in a fire, for which I have ever since felt grateful."

Miss Constance Cary (her maiden name), next went abroad with her widowed mother, and spent some years in traveling and in completing her education.

"It was not until after I returned to America," she said, "and was married to Mr. Harrison, that I was again bold enough to take up my pen. I wrote a little article, which I called 'A Little Centennial Lady.' It was published in 'Scribner's Magazine,' and had so favorable a reception that I was encouraged to write 'Golden Rod,' a story of Mount Desert, which appeared later in 'Harper's Magazine.'"

BOOKS SHE ENJOYED.

"My books that I have enjoyed most, if a writer may enjoy her own work, have not been those dealing with New York social life, but my tales of the south. Charles A. Dana, of the New York 'Sun,' was unconsciously responsible for my 'Old Dominion.' He gave me the agreeable task of editing the 'Monticello Letters,' and from them I gleaned a story which outlined my 'Old Dominion.' But the editors cry for stories of New York social life, to gratify the popular demand."

Mrs. Harrison's books are so well known that it is unnecessary to dwell on their acknowledged merit, vividness, and truthfulness to life. To the general public, there is something fascinating about a New York social story, dealing with the millionaire's club life, woman's teas, and love's broken lances. Besides the general desire for a good social novel, there is a morbid, unsatiated desire to pry into the doings, customs and manners of the rich.

It is with agreeable expectations that one picks up one of Mrs. Harrison's books; it is almost with the knowledge that you will be entertained.

HER CHARACTERS ARE FROM LIFE.

On a former call, she told me that her New York stories are built on her observations, and that the characters are so changed as not to antagonize her friends, for she enters the best society through her family ties and her well-earned prestige.

"It is very peculiar," she continued, "how, in writing a story, the characters govern me, not I the characters. I may have the outline and ending of a book in my mind, but the characters take everything into their hands, and walk independently through the pages. I have always found it best to obey. The ending of 'Anglomaniacs,' which caused so much adverse criticism, was not as I had planned. I was helpless under the caprices of the characters. At first, I was displeased at the ending; but now, looking back upon it, I am well satisfied."

"Then the characters to you become real, and you are entirely under their spell, merely chronicling what to you appears real?"

IN LOVE WITH HER WORK.

"Yes, if I did not believe in them, I would be unable to write; for the time being, I am living and observing a dozen lives. There is much satisfaction in doing so correctly. I am in love with my work, and am a hard worker."

For the past few months, Mrs. Harrison has been idle, by the advice of her physicians, and has spent the season abroad, traveling over the continent.

"But all the time, I am turning little romances over in my mind, and when I can no longer keep my pen from paper,

I suppose I shall sit down and write," she said. "Last winter, I was under a pretty heavy strain, and my overworked condition compelled me to rest for a while."

Many amusing little instances touching upon her work have come to her attention.

"One morning," said Mrs. Harrison, "after my husband had successfully defended a client, the man grasped his hand very warmly, and, to my husband's amazement, said, 'Well, Mr. Harrison, I want to tell you what we think of your wife. She's the finest writer in the English language, that's what my daughter says. She says there are no books like hers.'

"'Which one does she like most?' asked my husband, immensely pleased.

"'Well,' he replied, 'I can't just answer that, but I think it's "Your Eyre."'

"Once I received a rather startling letter from a western ranchman. It said, 'Your book has been going the rounds, but it always comes back, and I have threatened to put a bullet in the hide of the man who does not return it.' I was greatly pleased with that letter.

"The most gratifying letter I ever received was from a man in a prison. He begged to be supplied with all I had written.

"Perhaps he was a man who had been in society, and there is a little story connected with his imprisonment."

SHE IS A GENTLE, FORCEFUL WOMAN.

Mrs. Harrison has made many close friends through her books. Once she was with a party of friends in a Madrid gallery. Her name was mentioned, and a Spanish lady came forward, and introduced herself, at the same time expressing her admiration for her.

"She is now one of my dearest friends," concluded Mrs. Harrison.

Just then, a colored man appeared in her library, bearing a tray,—for afternoon tea,—so I arose, although she asked me to have a cup of tea, fearing that I might be intruding, and expressed my wish that she would soon be at her desk again.

"I suppose I shall," she said, "for it is irksome being idle."

Such is Mrs. Harrison's disposition. Indeed, it is hard to imagine her idle. Orders are pouring in upon her, which through her present weak health, she is forced to decline.

But what is my impression about her? She is a gentle, forceful woman, whose energy and painstaking have placed her in the front rank of American writers. Without the latter attributes, her talent would have fallen to the ground.

ART

XXIX

PAINSTAKING, THE SECRET OF A CELEBRATED PAINTER'S SUCCESS.

UNDOUBTEDLY the best-known American artist is Edwin Austin Abbey. He has done more than any other man to spread the fame of American art in Europe. He has proceeded, step by step, from his early youth, when he earned fifteen dollars a week as a "hack-artist," until he ranks as the greatest living decorative painter. The history of his life is an inspiration to students, as it furnishes striking evidence of what hard work and self-confidence can accomplish in the field of art. Mr. Abbey advanced gradually from water-colors and pen-sketching to oil-painting, pastel and fine decorative work. Although he is a very prolific artist, he has maintained a surprising degree of excellence. His work breathes forth his personality, and shows the character of the man; there is confidence in every line. His taste is as fine, as his art and execution are perfect, and he has an extraordinary degree of comprehension and receptivity, due to his American blood.

Mr. Abbey has scholarly ability and intense application, but they would have availed him little if they had not seconded a talent of the most unusual order, and an individuality which is so personal that it may be said of him that he resembles no other living painter. It is only natural that he should have gained success in his chosen line of work, for his heart has been in it from his boyhood days. His earnest efforts have always been appreciated both in Europe and America. Only two seasons after he went to live in England, he was elected a member of the Royal Institute of Painters in Water Colors. In 1889, he received a first-class medal at the Paris Exposition, and, in 1896, he was honored by an associate membership in the Royal Academy. Two years later he was received into full membership, though John R. Sargent, his fellow-countryman, had to wait three years. Mr. Abbey was honored by King Edward VII with a commission to paint the coronation scene in Westminster Abbey, and by the Pennsylvania legislature with a commission to decorate the new state capitol at Harrisburg.

A MOST INTERESTING STUDIO.

During a recent trip to England, I determined to visit Mr. Abbey, and obtain from him some message for his young countrymen who are beginning where he began thirty years ago. He has a beautiful country house known as Morgan Hall, in Gloucestershire, an attractive English county. In this house is the largest private studio in the whole country, built especially for the preparation of the Boston Library decorations, which Mr. Abbey recently completed. It measures twenty-five by fourteen yards, and has a high ceiling. In this room I observed a number of great easels, for Mr. Abbey usually has several pictures in progress at one time, but they occupied only a fraction of the space. It would be hard to imagine a studio more perfectly equipped for work. Great tapestries hung from heavy frames, not for ornamentation, but for study; carved oak doors and panels were resting against the walls, and scattered everywhere were casts of curious architecture. Priceless armor was displayed on every side, and along the walls were a number of canvases which had been used for studies, or paintings which had not been completed. There were chests filled with velvets, brocades and silks of various ancient periods. All these things are accessories of Mr. Abbey's craft and nothing more. He uses them in working out the details of his historical paintings. There were trestles full of elaborate studies and half-finished drawings standing about, and, tacked upon the walls were photographs of pictures of many interesting periods.

Mr. Abbey has also a vast collection of costumes. They are of all periods, and one might suppose himself in the stock room of some great theater. All these costumes help in depicting the dress worn at some great event which the artist desires to put upon canvas. Mr. Abbey is very accurate and careful in his work, and has never been challenged in any details of fact, of costume, of architecture, or of accessory. It must not be supposed that any of these costumes and decorations are copied in the paintings; they are merely suggestions for invention.

Mr. Abbey's industry and energy are prodigious, so that I was quite prepared to find him at work when I visited his studio. Although the artist has lived abroad for many years, he is thoroughly American in his personality, and I might have been talking with him at a Philadelphia studio, instead of in the heart of England.

HE WAS NOT A PRECOCIOUS BOY.

"There was nothing at all extraordinary about my boyhood," he said, in answer to a question. "I was very much like other boys, perhaps less promising than most. I remember that my parents complained because I was unable to fix my ambition upon any single profession, and they urged that I must have some definite aim in life. When I appeared unable to decide for myself, they undertook to decide for me and to formulate plans for my future. They suggested that I enter the ministry, but I had an instinct which told me that I was fitted for no such career. I told them then that art offered a greater attraction, and they were willing that I should begin studying. I entered the Academy of Fine Arts in Philadelphia, and was delighted with my undertaking from the very beginning.

"Of course I was interested in all that pertained to art, and especially in drawing in black and white. I read all publications which printed work of this sort, and especially 'Punch' and 'The Graphic,' so that they had no inconsiderable share in my instruction in the use of a pencil. I used to observe the styles of the different artists and study the best in each.

"In 1871, my father suggested that it was time to decide whether or not I was to earn my livelihood as an artist, and I decided that it should be my life-work. I was fortunate in obtaining employment in the art department of Harper and Brothers, in New York City. I was only nineteen years old at the time, and was filled with enthusiasm over my work. I was anxious to learn as much as possible, and Harper's was an excellent place for me. I was given a great variety of work, and received every encouragement for earnest effort. Every improvement in my drawings was appreciated. Several boys who worked with me at that time have since become famous in the art world, notably Reinhart and Alexander. Even the boys who swept out the office were gaining an excellent start, for one of them has since become one of the most famous Franco-American painters, practicing in Paris."

HIS WORK WAS ENCOURAGED.

"My first published drawing represented the demolition of the Vendome Column in Paris by the French Commune, and I shall never forget my pleasure at seeing it in 'Harper's Weekly.' It doesn't matter how old we get, we're sure to remember our first appearance. I received many congratulations for my effort and continued my work with enthusiasm.

"The young artists in Harper's offices were given all sorts of subjects to do, pictorial, illustrative and reportorial, and this variety has been of the utmost value to me. There was one sort of work, however, that I preferred above all others. When only a lad I fell in love with the classic literature of England; Goldsmith was always one of my favorite authors, and whenever I had spare time I devoted it to illustrating some of the stories that I had read. I was especially fond of English history, so you can imagine my delight when it was decided that I was to illustrate the works of Herrick for 'Harper's Monthly,' with a view to ultimate publication in book form.

"It was then that I first came to England. I thought it advisable to live for a time in the English country, and I settled for two years in one of the most picturesque districts of Worcestershire. I need not tell you that I enjoyed that visit, and, when I returned to America, in 1880, it was only to remain eight months and to arrange my affairs so that I could return here. Although I had lost none of my regard for the land of my birth, I felt that, if I was to draw pictures from English history, England was the place for me to live in, so here I have been ever since, save for occasional journeys to America and the Continent."

Mr. Abbey breathed a sigh of relief as he finished the narrative of his early days. "But this doesn't bring you up to date," I said, "and the most interesting story is about what you've done since." But the artist shook his head. "It's simply a record of steady work," he said; "you already know about the chief paintings I have done in late years."

"Of course," I said, "you are doing nothing now but painting in oils?"

"That's all," replied Mr. Abbey, "and my contracts will prevent me from doing any other kind of work in the near future. I didn't begin painting in oils until I had been working many years; the

'Mayday Morn,' my first exhibit, was not shown until 1890. It seems quite the usual thing for artists to take up oils after they are known chiefly by black and white or water colors."

HE ALWAYS TAKES PAINS.

"It is well known that you spend much time in preparing the subjects of your paintings," I said, "but there aren't many artists who worry about the technical details as you do."

"I won't say that I worry about them," replied Mr. Abbey. "An artist should study for his profession just as a man should prepare for the law or medicine, and should never consider that natural ability is all that he requires for success. He should have a knowledge of architecture and sculpture as well as of the principles of drawing; in short, he should carefully learn what may be called 'the grammar of his profession.'

"When I am to paint a subject which is mythological, I am at pains to absorb the atmosphere of the period, and to learn something of the geography in which the legendary figures moved. I visit the scene of the story, obtain every picture which will give me a knowledge of the dress of the period, and I am not satisfied until I have exhausted every possible source of information. It is well known that Sir Frederick Leighton constantly refreshed his mind and memory by visiting the classic scenes of his paintings.

"Some artists have been known to go so far as to paint a scene as an artist living in the period of the story would have painted it. I regard this as rather extreme. It is well to have the details perfect, but modern art has some advantage of technique and color which are not to be despised. I would not have you believe that technical efficiency is the greatest essential in an artist's qualifications, only it is a valuable asset when added to natural ability and earnestness of purpose."

PERSISTENCE AND HARD WORK COUNT.

Mr. Abbey has invariably practiced what he advises other artists to do. Before beginning the decorative paintings for the delivery room of the Boston Library, he spent many months traveling in Italy, collecting information which might aid him in the paintings of the Holy Grail. But in the end he decided that the scene should not be in Italy at all, and his effort went for nothing, as far as that particular series was concerned. He spent four years of unsurpassable toil, study and application in completing the first five of the pictures, and when they were done the public was not slow to appreciate the effort he had evidently put forth. Mr. Abbey could not have chosen a subject more worthy of his talent. He has confidence in his ideas of what is best in art, is full of mediæval feeling, and is endowed,—in spite of his sunny, hopeful temperament,—with an appreciation of the tragedy underlying so much of human life. In historical pictures, he considers no toil too great to make sure of accuracy, and his university training has been of the greatest assistance to him in his work.

"No artist can be too well educated," he said, during my conversation with him; "every bit of information is sure to be of use to him sooner or later, in one painting or another."

"I am glad," he said, "if I can encourage anyone to hard work, for surely that is the chief aid to success in any career. The young person who believes that an artist's life is a bed of roses, and that he needs only to ply the brush a few hours each day, is mistaken. He must be scholarly by nature, must have a wide and minute acquaintance with art, and must never consider that he has learned it all if he hopes for lasting fame. I might add that he must also have earnest convictions regarding his work, and the courage to carry them out. Given these qualifications, combined with talent, of course, any person should succeed as well in the field of art as in any other profession, providing he is willing to give a reasonable time to study and preparation. Although the world may call him master, the true artist will never regard himself as other than a student."

XXX

A SCHOOL GIRL, NOT AFRAID OF DRUDGERY, BECOMES AMERICA'S FOREMOST WOMAN ILLUSTRATOR.

IN the heart of Philadelphia's great business quarter, on lower Chestnut street, there stands a five-story, red brick building which is about as reserved looking as Philadelphia business structures can be, and before which, in the street below, the tide of traffic rumbles and clatters and clangs from early morning until night. It doesn't look much like a place where a person could be free enough from noise and other distractions to exercise a fine artistic taste.

Yet it was here, I was informed, that Alice Barber Stephens had her studio, and to this I was bound. Mrs. Stephens takes rank with A. B. Frost, Howard Pyle, A. B. Wenzell, C. D. Gibson and others, and there are those who put her before several of these. I remember looking over a book of her drawings, published by some New York house, entitled "The American Woman in the Home," and admiring exceedingly the gentle, refined appearance of the mothers, the excellent sedateness and sympathetic beauty of the young married daughters, and the quiet modesty of the girls in these pictures.

You would say, looking at these drawings, "Here is a plain, commonplace, genuine person, who illustrates." She has swept, sewed, performed the duty that lay nearest. You can see it in the sketches. She paints because she likes to, and as well as she can. She has no thought of immortality, nor imagines that she will be hailed as a marvel, but simply believes it is well and interesting to do good work.

Considering these things, I made my way one afternoon up several flights of stairs,—artists must have the sky-light, you know,—to a door labeled A. B. Stephens, which was opened by a tall, slender, reserved-looking woman, who smiled as she admitted that she was Alice Barber Stephens. After a sentence or two of explanation, an invitation was extended to enter.

ART IGNORES NOISE.

It was as if one had dropped a stage curtain upon the rattling, excited scene without. Comfortable chairs were scattered about. Screens and tall bric-a-brac cases of oriental workmanship divided spaces and filled corners. A great square of sunshine fell from a sky-light, and in one corner a Dutch clock slowly ticked. The color of the walls was a dull brick red, and against them stood light brown shelves, holding white and blue china vases, jugs and old plates. Sketches in ink, wash and color were here and there on the wall, and in one place a large canvas showing Market street, Philadelphia, near City Hall, on a rainy day, gave a sombre yet rather pleasing touch.

Mrs. Stephens had returned to her easel, on which was a large sketch in black and white, showing a young rake, with his body bent forward, his elbows resting on his knees, his face buried in his hands,—the picture of despair. Some picture for a novel it was, the title of which might easily have been "The Fool and His Money."

"You won't mind my working," said Mrs. Stephens, and I hastened to explain that I wouldn't, and didn't.

She put touches here and there on the picture, as we talked of women in art, and the conversation did not seem to distract her attention from the work in hand, which advanced rapidly.

GIRLS' CHANCES AS ILLUSTRATORS.

"Don't you believe it is easier, to-day, for a young girl to succeed in illustrating than it is for a young man?"

"Well, possibly," she answered. "Neither girl nor boy can succeed without aptitude and the hardest kind of work, but girls are rather novel in the field, and their work may receive slightly more gentle consideration to begin with. It would not be accepted, however, without merit."

"Hasn't the smaller remuneration which women accept something to do with the popularity of the woman illustrator?"

"Very little, if any," she answered. "I find that women are about as quick, perhaps more so, than men, to demand good prices for clever work, although they have less of the egotism of men artists."

"You judge from your own case," I suggested.

"Not at all. I never possessed cleverness. It was need and determination with me, and I can honestly say that all I have gained has been by the most earnest application. I never could do anything with a dash. It was always slow, painstaking effort; and it is yet."

"Do you ever exhibit?" I asked.

"No," said Mrs. Stephens, "not any more. There was a time when I had an ambition to shine as a painter, and as long as I had that ambition I neither shone as a painter nor made more than a living as an illustrator. I made up my mind, however, that I was not to be a great woman painter, and I decided to apply myself closely to the stronger, illustrative tendency which fascinated me. From that time on my success dates, and I am rather proud now that I was able to recognize my limitations."

"Did you find that in marrying you made your work more difficult to pursue?" I ventured, for her interesting home life is a notable feature of her career.

"I cannot say that I did. There is more to do, but there is also a greater desire to do it. I love my boy, and I take time to make his home life interesting and satisfying. When he was ill, I removed my easel from the studio to a room adjoining the sick-chamber at the house, and worked there."

HOW SHE BEGAN.

Her instinct for art seems to have been a gift direct. As a very little girl her facility with the pencil delighted her teachers, and after the regular exercises of the day she was allowed to occupy her time drawing whatever fancy or surroundings might suggest. At seven years of age her parents removed to Philadelphia, and there the young artist encountered school regulations which rather debarred her from following her beloved pastime. But her talent was so pronounced that one day in every week was allowed her in which to attend the School of Design—an arrangement that continued until she entered the grammar school.

A few years later she became a regular student at this School of Design, where she took a course of wood engraving, but did not relax her study of drawing. As an engraver she became so successful that her work soon became remunerative, and gave her means to enter the Pennsylvania Academy of Fine Arts. At the same time her progress as an engraver was so marked that her efforts were brought to the attention of the art editor of "Scribner's Magazine," for whom, to illustrate an article on the academy, she engraved the "Woman's Life Class," from her own drawing. Soon her drawings gave her a reputation, and she abandoned engraving. Her first published drawings were for school-book illustrations, from which her field widened and her work came into great demand.

In 1887 she was married and spent ten months abroad, studying for a part of the time in Paris in the school of Julien and of Carlo Rossi, devoting the remainder of her stay in travel.

Upon her return she was prevailed upon to become an instructor in the Philadelphia School of Design, where she introduced life-class study, which has met with marked success.

XXXI

A SCHOOLBOY'S SKETCHES REVEAL THE BENT OF A TALENTED ILLUSTRATOR.

FREDERIC REMINGTON'S drawings and paintings of ranch life are so full of action and so vigorously drawn that they have attracted attention all over the United States and abroad, wherever true art is honored. No living artist can equal Remington in bringing into life, as it were, on the very canvas, a bucking broncho, or the sweeping charge of a force of Uncle Sam's cavalry. One fairly sees the dust on the scorching alkali plains, and hears the quick clatter of the horse's hoofs as he strikes the ground, and gathers his legs again.

And yet, with all his success, Mr. Remington is most unassuming. I went to New Rochelle, where he has a cosy place on the crest of a hill. He was in his studio, which is an addition to the house; and, as I descended a few steps, he rose from before his easel to greet me. His working coat was covered with paint, and he held a brush in his left hand. He had not been warned of my mission, and seemed almost startled.

"I cannot shake hands," he said, looking at me, "mine are soiled; I am a painter, you know."

He sat down, hanging one arm over the back of his chair.

"Don't write about me, but speak of my art!" said Mr. Remington.

"But you and your art are one," I replied, looking around the studio, and to its walls hung with Indian relics. "Most of your pictures are from experiences of your own in the great far west, are they not?"

"Yes, but not all," was the reminiscent reply.

"And those trophies?" I added, glancing at them.

"O, I bought most of them. That jacket I bought from a mounted policeman. Pretty, isn't it? I am able to depict the western country and life, because I have been there."

REMINGTON'S SCHOOLBOY EFFECTS.

"When did you first take up art?"

"I studied some art at the Yale Art School, and a little at the Art League. When I was a schoolboy, I was forever making sketches on the margin of my school-books, but I never really studied it much, although my dream was to be an artist. At nineteen, I caught the fever to go west, and incidentally to become rich. That was my idea; art came second. I ranched it, and got into Indian campaigns. I have always been fond of horses and out-of-door life, and I got plenty of it there, with every opportunity to study the rough life, the lay of the country, and the peculiar atmosphere."

"Mr. Remington," I asked, "how do you get that 'devil-may-care' look in the faces of your cowboys and soldiers?"

His face lighted up, and a deep twinkle came into his eyes. He glanced across the room at just such a picture as I had described. He took his pipe out of his mouth and laid it on the window sill.

REMINGTON'S ATTENTION TO DETAIL.

"Kipling says that, 'a single man in a barrack is not a plaster saint,' and that is about it. That cavalryman posed for me on his horse. But not all of my work is from life. I go west for three months every year, and gather a lot of sketches and then work them up. Those color sketches there,—a chief and his daughter,—are from life. You see I was able to get all the color. Yet I like to depict white men best; they are more interesting."

My eyes rested on an unfinished picture, toward which, every now and then, Mr. Remington turned a thoughtful gaze as if trying to think of something. It was a birch-bark canoe, with a figure at either end; the water was smooth, and the shore was wooded. One person in the motionless canoe was fishing.

"Is that from memory?" I asked of the artist.

"Partly," he said, with a smile. "I used to see a good many photographs of trout fishing in the Adirondacks; lines taut, and then hurling a trout through the air, to land it in the canoe. So once I thought I would try it myself. I went up there and fished for two weeks in the rain. I am trying to think how to make the rain appear to strike and bounce from the water. You know how water looks when it is raining,"—and there came into his face a thoughtful and studious look, showing how carefully he weighed every detail of his work.

Mr. Remington rises early, has breakfast at seven, and works until three, when he takes his customary horseback ride across the country.

"Do you work from inspiration?" I asked.

"I do not know what you mean, exactly. I must have a study in my mind, and then I work it out. Some mornings I can do but little; but I am kept exceedingly busy with constant orders to fill, besides illustrating my own articles."

HOW HIS WAR PICTURES ARE MADE.

"That painting of the charge of the Rough Riders up San Juan hill, and your other Cuban pictures, must have been interesting work."

"I saw Roosevelt just before but not during the charge. But when you see one, you see all. The fighting to-day is done in long, thin lines; the solid formations are no longer used. It makes too great a target. You are never out of range, for the bullets carry a mile and a half. Most of the fighting is done lying down, the front line advancing, and the others harassing the enemy. To me there was nothing enjoyable about it. A correspondent is worse off than the soldier. He has no means of transportation. Fortunately, in Cuba, I secured a horse the day before the battle. I made a great number of sketches, but lost one of my sketch books while crawling on my hands and knees through the long grass. It contained many bits of action, which I wanted. I suppose it was spoiled, or maybe someone found it. But in my younger days, I actually enjoyed being in the midst of an Indian fight. The climate is so different, and entirely to my liking, out west."

We rose and viewed the studio.

"How do you get that peculiar alkali, yellowish air of the plains?" I asked, as we stood before an example of Mr. Remington's art.

"Only by having lived there, and after a dint of study. That is a dust study."

"And those blue shadows are correct?"

COLOR OF THE PLAINS.

"Yes; you cannot have a black shade out in the open, and the atmosphere there causes that particular shade. That one above, though, which is also a study, shows an almost steel gray shadow, while that other one is still darker. These are 'color notes,' of Indian ponies, and bronchos. There is no crest or arch to their necks. They are really degenerated horses, but they can go."

On a pedestal was a casting of the "Broncho Buster."

"You must have modeled in clay before you did that."

"No, that was my first attempt. I had never put my hands to clay before. Painting and modeling are about the same. You must know anatomy in both. I never intended to have it cast, but some of my friends, on seeing it, said I should, so I had it done. 'Bunkie,' which means, in the army, 'comrade,' is my second work."

It was only in 1885 that Mr. Remington turned his whole attention to art. On leaving Yale, where he was more devoted to football than to study, he served for a brief period as confidential clerk to Governor Cornell, at Albany. But that life was too prosaic; and, in 1880, he caught the fever, "to go west." He went to Montana, and became a "cow-puncher." Later, he made money on a Kansas mule ranch, and was cowboy, guide and scout in the southwest. When he had run through what he had earned, he returned to Kansas City, where the shops displayed his first work. They possessed the now well-known Remington style, but the colors were daubed on so that they looked like chromos, although the drawings had that muscular dash and action for which his work is noted.

HIS FIRST SKETCH.

"My first drawing," said Mr. Remington, "appeared in Harper's. It was redrawn by them, but it had in it that which they liked."

In the meantime he had married, and he started east with his wife. They arrived in New York with just three dollars. After engaging a small room, he made a bee-line for Harper's with a number of sketches. They were accepted on the spot, and since then there has been no more successful illustrator than Frederic Remington among the celebrated artists of America.

XXXII

REBUFFS AND DISAPPOINTMENTS FAIL TO REPRESS A GREAT CARTOONIST'S GENIUS.

TO-DAY Homer C. Davenport is the "first cartoonist" of America, and yet he is but thirty-five years old. Mr. Davenport has a small place in Roseville, on the outskirts of Newark, New Jersey. He is a tall, handsome man, with large, humorous eyes, beneath heavy eyelids, that give him an expression of perpetual thought.

"I suppose you want to see my studio?" Mr. Davenport said. We went upstairs.

"This is it," he said, with a chuckle.

It was merely a small, square room, with a few framed pictures on the papered walls, and a desk in the corner. There was no easel in the room, but I saw a drawing-board under the desk.

DAVENPORT'S UNIQUE STUDIO.

"You work on that board, when on the desk?"

"Yes."

"You are disappointed," said his sister, with a smile. "It is not what you expected."

It wasn't. I had expected to see a typical studio, with unfinished cartoons, and the usual artistic surroundings.

Mr. Davenport laid an unfinished cartoon on the desk, representing a chariot race, and laughed when he explained what it would be and mean; and this told me that he enters heartily in whatever he draws, which is requisite to success in art as well as in other things. Then we adjourned to another room and sat about a wood fire.

"Tell me of your beginning," I said.

"Well, I was born in Oregon, thirty-five years ago, on my father's farm. As a child, I was perpetually drawing, and to my father I owe much, for it was he who encouraged me, my mother dying when I was very young. I would lie flat on my stomach, and draw on the floor, if I had no paper. As I spent hours this way, the habit became injurious to my digestive organs, so a flat cushion was made for me. I was a hopelessly poor student, doing more drawing on my slate and on the margins of my books than studying. To sit in school for any length of time made me sick and nervous, so my father called on the schoolmaster and gave instructions that, whenever I got tired, I should be allowed to draw, or to go home."

HE DREW CARTOONS IN SCHOOL.

"This was rather demoralizing to the school, for even then I drew cartoons. Finally, I was taken away, and my father painted a blackboard, four feet high by fifteen feet long, on the side of a room in the farm-house, where, with plenty of chalk, I drew to my heart's content. I would draw all day."

"And you received no instructions in drawing?"

"I never had a lesson in my life. It was my father's ambition for me to become a cartoonist. When, in later years, I did anything that he considered particularly good, he would carry me off to Portland, and I would submit it to the Portland 'Oregonian,' where my attempts were always laughed at. Then, much crestfallen, I would return to the farm.

"'Now, my boy,' my father would say, 'that is good enough to be printed,' and off I would go again.

"At length, the news spread that I had a job on the Portland

'Oregonian.' The whole town became interested, and when the day arrived for my departure, the band of which I was a member, and many of the townspeople, escorted me with due honor to the railroad station."

HIS FIRST DISAPPOINTMENT.

"'Well,' I heard some say, 'I guess we will never see him again. He's too big for this place.'

"I was on the Portland 'Oregonian' just one day.

"'What's the sense of this?' I was asked. 'You can't draw,' and back I went.

"I had before me the mortification of meeting the righteous disgust of my friends. On my way back to Silverton, I heard that they were short of a brakeman at the Portland end, so I beat my way back to Portland, and, walking into the office, offered myself.

"'What!' said the man. 'What do you know about braking? I would like to know who sent you on such a fool's errand?' and he raved and stamped, and swore he would discharge everyone on the train. But on the next train, I went out as head brakeman. All the elements got together,—it rained and snowed and froze, and when I got to Silverton, almost frozen, I slipped from the train and tramped home, a much disheartened young man.

"But just to show my father I had something in me, and wanted to make my way in life, I asked to be sent to an institution of learning, where I stayed just one week. Then I got a place attending to the ink roller in the local printing office, where the town paper was published, which, to this day, I do not think can be beaten,"—and Mr. Davenport laughed in his hearty way.

AT TEN DOLLARS A WEEK.

"Finally, my star rose on the horizon. I went to San Francisco, and was taken on trial on the 'Examiner.' I remember the day well,—February 2, 1892. For one mortal week, I simply hung around the office. Then I was put to work at ten dollars a week. But I proved unsatisfactory. I drew the man over me aside.

"'Look here,' I said, 'I can't draw. I want you to write to my father and tell him what a failure I am, and that his belief that I am an artist is the delusive mistake of a fond parent.' He sat down to write, and, as he was doing so, my fingers, always itching to draw, were at work with a pencil in sketching horses, on a piece of paper on the table.

"'When did you do that?' he asked, picking up the paper.

"'I did it just now,' I replied, sheepishly.

"'What? Do it again.'

"I did so. He looked at me curiously.

"'Wait a bit,' he said. He took the paper into the office. 'Come in here,' he said, 'the boys won't believe it. Do some more.'

"'Davenport,' said the manager, 'you are too old to strike a path for yourself. You must put yourself in my hands. Do nothing original, not one line.' If the manager caught me doing so, he tore it up.

"I remember one time, Ned Hamilton, a star writer on the 'Examiner,' some others, and myself, were sent to a Sacramento convention. I drew what I considered very good likenesses, and that night, when I retired, with a fire burning brightly in the room where we all bunked, I fairly kicked my heels in delight, in anticipation of the compliments of the 'Examiner.' I was awakened by the tearing of a paper, that sent the cold shivers up and down my back. Ned Hamilton was grumbling, and throwing my labor into the fire.

"'If you can't do better than that,' he said, 'you ought to give up.'

"I almost wept, but it took any conceit I might have had out of me, and the next day I did some work that was up to the mark."

HE WAS DISCHARGED IN CHICAGO.

"But my walking papers came in due time, and I went to the 'Chronicle.' It almost took my breath away when they offered me twenty dollars a week. Before I was discharged from there, I had risen to a higher salary. I went to Chicago, and got on the Chicago 'Herald,' at thirty-five dollars a week. I was there during the World's Fair. It seemed to me the principal thing I did was to draw horses. But the greatest blow of all was when the Chicago 'Herald' discharged me. It seemed as if everything were slipping from beneath my feet. I went back to San Francisco and got on the 'Chronicle' again. It was then, and not till then,—1894,—that I was allowed any freedom. All that I had been asking an outlet for found vent, and my cartoons began to attract attention.

"William R. Hearst, of the 'Examiner,' asked, in one of his editorial rooms: 'Who is that Davenport, on the "Chronicle," who is doing us up all the time?'

"'Oh, we bounced him; he's no good,' was the reply.

"'Send for him!' said Mr. Hearst.

"No attention was paid to the order. Mr. Hearst finally sent for me himself. I was engaged at forty-five dollars a week. Then a thing happened that I will never forget, for no raise before or since ever affected me to such a degree.

"I drew a cartoon of Senator 'Steve' White and his whiskers. The whiskers so pleased Mr. Hearst, that he called me in and said that my pay would be raised five dollars a week. I went home that night, and woke up my wife to tell her the glad news. She fairly wept for joy, and tears trickled down my own cheeks, for that increase meant appreciation that I had been starving for, and I felt almost secure,—and all on account of Senator 'Steve' White's whiskers."

Here Mrs. Davenport, who had brought us two large books, in which she had fondly pasted all of her husband's work, said:—

"Yes, no subsequent increase, no matter how large, has ever equaled that five-dollar advance."

IN CLOVER AT LAST.

Mr. Hearst, as soon as he bought the New York "Journal," telegraphed to the "Examiner:" "Send Davenport." He is now receiving a very large salary, and his work is known throughout the world.

Two years ago, Mr. Davenport went abroad and drew sketches of the members of the houses of parliament, and Mr. Phil. May, the English artist, became his fast friend.

In Washington, Senator Hanna insisted upon meeting Mr. Davenport, and shaking him by the hand. He was the first to immortalize Mr. Hanna, with that checkered suit of dollar marks.

Such is the man and artist, Homer C. Davenport, who, in 1894, had not drawn a public cartoon, and who, to-day, has a world-wide reputation, and the esteem of even those whom he has caricatured, and who cannot help enjoying their own exaggerated portraits. Davenport's success has come rapidly, but not until he had sustained reverses that would have discouraged any man of a less resolute character.

XXXIII

BEING HIMSELF IN STYLE AND SUBJECTS, THE SECRET OF AN ARTIST'S WONDERFUL POPULARITY.

NOTHING in the studio of Charles Dana Gibson suggests that it is a studio, excepting the alien circumstance that it is artistic. Such proof tends to puzzle the casual-minded, whose mind is trained to look upon any sky-lighted room furnished like a pound party, and occupied by artists, or brokers, or bachelor wholesale dealers,—as a studio.

Mr. Gibson's studio is a real room, devoted to stern facts, and is, therefore, beautiful. It has no furniture that is not essential. Even the large rugs, woven of moss and mist and fire, hang on the walls like coverings, and not by way of decoration. The wood is heavy and dark. There are no pictures.

Mr. Gibson talks while he works. His easel stands squarely beneath the skylight, and, as he sat before it the other day, a picture grew under his hand while he talked about the making of an illustrator. Everything he said was emphasized by the slow growth of the glorious creature, who was there to show, from her pretty tilted pompadour to the hem of the undoubted creation she was wearing, that what the famous illustrator insisted may be done by skill and hard work can assuredly be accomplished.

"When anyone asks me," said Mr. Gibson, "what to do to become a successful illustrator, I always assure him that he has thought about the matter and doubtless knows far more about it than I do, for I know of no rule to follow to become what one was born to be, and I certainly know of none to prevent one from failing at something for which he has no talent.

"If a man knows how to draw, he will draw; and all the discouragements and all the bad teachers in the world cannot turn him aside. If he has no ability, he will drift naturally into school-teaching and buying stocks, without anybody's rules to direct him either way.

"The main thing is to have been born an artist."

Mr. Gibson said this quite simply, as if he were advising a course in something, or five grains of medicine.

"If you were that," he went on, "you yourself know it far better than anyone can tell you, and you know also, in your heart, that neither wrong teaching nor anything but idleness can prevent your success. If you are not a born artist, you may not know it. I think I can soon say something about the way to find your limitations, but no one can say much to help a born genius. His genius is largely, indeed, that he knows how to help himself."

Lightly leaving the student of illustrating adequately provided with having been born a genius, Mr. Gibson went on to tell what should be his education before he begins to study art, and upon this he put on record an opinion which is a departure from current belief.

A NATURAL ARTIST WILL NEVER REQUIRE AN INSTRUCTOR.

"I do not think," he said, "that the previous training of a student who begins studying illustrating has much to do with his career. It seems to me that his actual previous education matters very little. If he wants to learn, he will learn. If he does not, he will not. If he does not want to learn, his attempt at an education will profit him very little. His gift for illustrating, if he has it, is a thing not more dependent upon his education than upon his surroundings. While there are instances in which an education forced upon a pupil has been acknowledged by him afterward to mean much to him, there are also cases in all arts of which we say that contact with the schoolmen would not have been an advantage."

Mr. Gibson said this quite tranquilly, as if it were not an idea at odds with all other accepted statements that the thorough education of an artist is the best foundation for anything he may undertake.

"That leaves a good deal of work for the pupil's master," I suggested.

"Master!" exclaimed Mr. Gibson, with almost a frown; "what is a master? Have we any masters now? It seems to me that the word has lost its old meaning, and that there is no longer such a thing as a 'master.' Suppose we say 'teacher' instead! And then let me add this: I do not believe the teacher matters in the least."

"Don't you think," I demanded, "that a pupil would make better progress with you for a teacher than he would with somebody whose work had no value?"

IF YOU DO NOT SEE YOUR MISTAKES, NO ONE ELSE CAN.

"Not a bit," he said, promptly. "To tell the truth, I think the teaching of drawing is an over-estimated profession. It doesn't seem to me as if I could teach,—as if I would feel it would be exactly honest to teach. Why, see for yourself,—what can a teacher do?"

Mr. Gibson laid down his pencil, but he continued thus:—

"I was for a year at the Art League, and two years in Paris. In Paris we used to sit in rows at canvases, like this. We saw our teacher for half an hour, twice a day. He would come and spend less than two minutes beside the chair of each of us, and what would he do? Point out a mistake, or a defect, or, rarely, an excellence, which, if we had any talent at all, we could see perfectly well for ourselves. This last is the important point.

"If you are a born illustrator, you will know your own mistakes better than anyone can tell you about them. If you do not see your mistakes, nobody can ever help you to be anything. All the teachers in all the art schools cannot help you if you cannot see your mistakes. I said I could help a pupil to know his own limitations. Well, that is the way. If your own work looks quite finished and perfect to you, or if it looks wrong but you cannot tell exactly what is the inaccuracy or lack, you may depend upon it that you were not born to be an illustrator.

"That is true in anything. The writer, the sculptor and the musician have to stand this test. What sort of musician would a man be who could not detect a discord? You can see it easily enough with that illustration. Well, your illustrator must see a bad bit of drawing, or bad composition, just as quickly as a born piano player can tell if he has played without expression. It is just as true in art as it is in ordinary matters. The snow-shoveler must know when his sidewalk is clean, the typewriter when the words are correctly spelled, the cook when her pastry tastes right,—or they are all discharged forthwith. Well, one expects no less of an illustrator than of a cook."

THE VALUE OF ARTISTIC INDIVIDUALITY.

Mr. Gibson returned to his board, and what he said next was wonderfully extra-illustrated by the girl—"Gibson" to her finger-tips,—who looked up at him.

"The whole value of your work is its individuality," he said, "and for that you are obliged to depend absolutely upon yourself. Obviously nobody can show you how to be original.

"Now take the simple example of a copy book. Do you remember how the letters used to look, and the elaborate directions which accompanied every writing lesson? The 'a's,' and so on, must be just of a height. The 't's' must be twice as high. The 'l's' and the 'h's' must be a quarter-length or so above those. Well, as a matter of fact, who writes like that? Nobody. If anyone did he would simply be laughed at, and justly so. His handwriting would mean nothing. It would have no individuality. Everybody simply keeps the letters in mind and forms them to suit himself, and after a time he has a writing which he can never change by any chance. That has become the way he writes.

"Well, it is just the same in illustrating. I might tell you all that I know about drawing; any teacher might tell you all he knows; but, gradually, by observation and the assertion of your own personality, you will modify all these forms, and will find yourself drawing one special way. That is the way you draw, and you can never change it in essence, though you may go on improving it forever.

"Now, to my mind, just so much instruction in drawing is necessary as is needed to tell the child who is learning to write which letter is which, and how to pronounce and recognize it. That once learned, the child will go its own sweet way and develop a handwriting such as no one in the world can exactly duplicate. So it is with drawing. When the first fundamental instructions are over,—which anyone who can draw can give you,—you are your own master, and will draw or not, as you were born to do.

"Remember that I am not saying that I regret the time I spent studying, either here or in Paris. I am only telling you what I regard as necessary for one who wants to learn.

"Now, just as the way to learn to write is to write, so the way to learn to draw is to draw. I think it is best to begin with objects in the room, and with figures,—any objects, any figures,—it does not matter. But draw one over and over again; draw it from all sides; draw it big, and draw it little, and draw it again. Then go to something else, and then come back to it later the same day. Put them all away till the next day, and then find the mistakes in them. Here is something to remember, and something which ought to hearten many a discouraged student quite blue because of what really should have encouraged him: Do not be discouraged at the mistakes you can find in your own work, unless you find only a small number. The more mistakes you can detect, the better able you are to draw. Do not leave a thing until you are satisfied, after going back to it every day for weeks, that you can draw it no better. Then, if you come upon it the next year, and still see no room for improvement,—well, then there is still room for discouragement about yourself."

WHILE STUDYING ART, ONE SHOULD WORK INCESSANTLY.

"In all this work, observe one rule: Never mind about drawing a thing as you may possibly have been told to do in the course of instruction. Draw it the way it looks to you. You will see it differently as you go back to it again and again. If you do not see it differently, you cannot see your own mistakes, and that is positive proof that for you fame is waiting at some other door,— or, at any rate, that it will not come to you from art.

"How much ought one to work? All the time. Draw all the time. Look all the time for something to draw. In the beginning, never pass anything without wresting from it its blessing, so to speak. Before you pass, be sure you can draw it; and the only way to be sure of that is to draw it several times. The objects in a room are a little simpler than figures, at first, but figures are the most interesting, and you must draw whatever interests you. If you would rather draw crawfish and bootjacks than men and women, draw crawfish and bootjacks. It really doesn't so much matter what you draw; the point is that you draw. But it is important to you that you develop a taste for drawing something special,—and of that you need have no fear if you are a born artist. If you are not, as I said, it doesn't matter.

"I always feel that any general talk about the way to succeed, in any art one selects, is rather unnecessary. I cannot repeat too often that I believe, if the student has it in him to draw, he will not need to be told to persevere, or to work hard, or to be careful of bad influences in his work, or to avoid imitation,—he will do all these as naturally as he will hold a pencil. Holding a pencil, by the way, is another example of what I just spoke of. Do you remember that they used to tell us just how our fingers must hold the pen, and how the whole arm ought to move? 'What will they think of you,' they said, 'when you get out in the world, if you hold your pencil like that?' As a matter of fact, nobody gives the matter a thought, and hardly one of us holds a pencil that way. It is so with many of the *formulae* of an art. But isn't it curious that I never did get out of holding my pencil that prescribed way? I do happen to hold my pencil correctly."

"Maybe you held some of the other *formulae* the same way," I suggested, "and they are influencing you."

"Oh, well," said Mr. Gibson, "so far as the pencil goes, I fancy, perhaps, that I draw in spite of the way I hold it rather than because of it."

Then he made a small retraction of his remark.

"There is one class of teachers," he said, "that I count,—pictures. Pictures are always at hand,—and good work is the best teacher in the world. A pupil in New York ought to go to the art gallery often and often, and sit there and steep himself in what he sees. Let him go to study definite pictures, too,—but just to sit and absorb,—as one sits in a garden, or before an old tower, or by the sea,—without sketching, only just looking,—that is the best instruction you can pay for on either continent."

The picture of the girl on the board was practically complete, with its high little chin and haughty mouth and fearless eyes, and it seemed so alive that getting to be a great illustrator appeared hopeless by the side of it.

"How long," I asked, "does it take, normally, to find out if you're a born artist or not?"

Mr. Gibson laughed and took it the other way.

"A very long time," he said, regretfully, "and some of us even go down blind to our graves."

"May it not be inferred from your idea that the born illustrator has little need of a teacher, that he also has little need of a sojourn in the art atmosphere of Paris?" I asked.

"It certainly may be," replied Mr. Gibson quickly. "A young man or woman can now learn just as much art in some of our great cities, like New York or Philadelphia, as abroad. Our art schools are as good as those of Paris. In fact, they are superior in some respects, and I am very sure that the average American art student is, in general, better off in the United States.

"There are, of course, the magnificent galleries of Europe, with which every artist should be familiar, but there need be no special hurry to study these. It is much more advisable, I think, for the young artist to become imbued with the spirit of our own art, and to acquire a distinctively American style, before subjecting himself to the influence of the painters of the Old World.

"I have little patience with the American who, in his art, becomes a foreigner. If he does, he is not accepted as representative either abroad or in this country. The time has come when a man or woman may take much pride in being a true American artist. We are no longer mere imitators. We are forging ahead into leadership, and I venture to predict that this century will see New York the art center of the world."

XXXIV

A "PRINTER'S DEVIL" WHOSE PERSEVERANCE WINS HIM WELL-EARNED REPUTATION AS A FUN-MAKER.

THE felicity of F. Opper's caricatures is marvelous. His drawings for the Dinkelspiel stories, by George V. Hobart, in the New York "Morning Journal" have drawn to him the pleased attention of those whom he has caused to laugh at the happy expressions of his characters,—at the ridiculous expressions of the characters,—during Mr. Dinkelspiel's "gonversationings," particularly at Mr. Dinkelspiel's earnest look.

He is a caricaturist of the "first water," and in this connection I may say that a caricature too carefully drawn often loses its humor. Still Mr. Opper has proved his ability to finish a drawing smoothly. Those familiar with the back numbers of "Puck" will concede this and much more.

His life is an example of determination. I called, by appointment, at his house in Bensonhurst (near Bath Beach), a pretty suburb within the precincts of Greater New York. We stepped into his library.

He drew my attention to the pictures on the four walls of the room. "Those are all 'originals,' by contemporaries," he said, "and there is one by poor Mike Woolf. We were intimate friends, and I attended his funeral."

STUDIES OUT HIS IDEAS.

The conversation turned toward Mr. Opper himself, and I asked:—

"How is it you can conceive so many ridiculous ideas and predicaments?"

"It is a matter of study," he replied. "I work methodically certain hours of the day, but very seldom at night. We will say it is a political cartoon on a certain occurrence that I am to draw. I deliberately sit down and study out my idea. When it is formed, I begin to draw. I never commence to draw without a conception of what I am going to do."

"And when did you first put pencil to paper?" I asked.

"Almost as soon as I could creep. I was born in Madison, Ohio, in 1857, and as far back as I can remember, I had a determination to become an artist. My path often swerved from my ambition, on account of necessity, but my determination was back of me, and whenever an obstacle was removed I advanced thus much farther toward my goal.

"I went to the village school till I was fourteen years of age, and then I went to work in the village store. Both at school and in the store, every spare moment found me with pencil and paper, sketching something comical; so much so, indeed, that I became known for it."

A PRINTER'S DEVIL.

"I remained in the store for a few months, and then went to work on the weekly paper, and acted the part of a 'printer's devil.' Afterward, I set type. In about a year, the idea firmly possessed me that I could draw, and I decided that it was best to go to New York. But my self-esteem was not so great as to rate myself a full-fledged artist. My idea was to obtain a position as a compositor in New York, to draw between times, and gradually to land myself where my hopes all centered. So my disappointment was great when, on arriving in the city, I discovered that, to become a compositor, I must serve an apprenticeship of three years. I was in New York, in an artistic environment, and had burned my bridges; accordingly I looked for a place, and obtained one in a store. One of my duties there was to make window cards, to advertise the whole line, or a particular lot of goods. I decorated them in my best fashion."

GOOD USE OF LEISURE TIME.

"All the leisure I had to myself, evenings and holidays, I spent in making comic sketches, and I took them to the comic papers,—to the 'Phunny Phellow,' and 'Wild Oats.' I just submitted rough sketches. Soon the editors permitted me to draw the sketches also, which was great encouragement. I met Frank Beard, and called on him, by request, and he proposed that I come into his office. So I left the store, after having been there eight or nine months, and ceased drawing show-cards for the windows. I drew for 'Wild Oats,' 'Harper's Weekly,' 'Frank Leslie's,' and the 'Century,' which at that time was Scribner's publication; and later for 'St. Nicholas.'"

It was then that Mr. Opper had an offer from "Leslie's" to work on the staff at a salary, which he accepted.

"I was only a little over twenty years of age," he continued. "I was a humorous draughtsman, and a special artist, also; going where I was directed to make sketches of incidents, people and scenes."

Six years before, Mr. Opper had left the village school with a burning determination to become an artist. It can be seen how well he sailed his bark,—tacking and drifting, and finally beating home with the wind full on the sails.

This shows what determination will do.

HIS CONNECTION WITH "PUCK."

"Three years later," said Mr. Opper, "I had an offer from the publishers of 'Puck' to work for them,—a connection which I severed not long ago, although I still hold stock in the company. I not only made my own drawings, but furnished ideas for others. I have always furnished my own captions, inscriptions and headings. Indeed, they are a part of a cartoon, or other humorous work. I think that I may say that 'Puck' owes some of its success to me, for I labored conscientiously."

Mr. Opper walked over to a mantelpiece for two books of sketches, which he handed me to look at. They contained sketches of the country places he had visited on his summer wanderings.

"And you use these?" I asked.

"Yes; if I want a farmer leaning over a fence with a cow in the distance. I can use that barnyard scene And that bit of a country road can be made useful. So can that corncrib with the tin pans turned upside down on the posts supporting it, to keep the rats off. That old hay-wagon, and that farmer with a rake and a large straw hat can all be worked in. I always carry a sketch-book with me, no matter where I go."

THE "SUBURBAN RESIDENT."

On "Puck," Mr. Opper was the originator of the "suburban resident," who has since been the subject of much innocent merriment,—the gentleman with the high silk hat, side whiskers, glasses, an anxious expression, and bundles, and always on the rush for a train.

"I enjoyed those," said Mr. Opper, with a laugh, "before I became a suburban myself."

XXXV

"A SQUARE MAN IN A ROUND HOLE" REJECTS $5,000 A YEAR AND BECOMES A SCULPTOR.

"MY LIFE?" repeated F. Wellington Ruckstuhl, one of the foremost sculptors of America, as we sat in his studio looking up at his huge figure of "Force." "When did I begin to sculpture? As a child I was forever whittling, but I did not have dreams then of becoming a sculptor. It was not till I was thirty-two years of age. And love,—disappointment in my first love played a prominent part."

"But as a boy, Mr. Ruckstuhl?"

"I was a poet. Every sculptor or artist is necessarily a poet. I was always reaching out and seeking the beautiful. My father was a foreman in a St. Louis machine shop. He came to this country in a sailing ship from Alsace, by way of the Gulf, to St. Louis, when I was but six years old. He was a very pious man and a deacon in a church. One time, Moody and Sankey came to town, and my father made me attend the meetings. I think he hoped that I would become a minister. But I decided that 'many are called, but few are chosen.' Between the ages of fourteen and nineteen, I worked in a photographic supply store; wrote one hundred poems, and read incessantly. I enlarged a view of the statue of Nelson in Trafalgar Square, London, into a 'plaster sketch,' ten times as large as the picture, but still I did not know my path. I began the study of philosophy, and kept up my reading for ten years. My friends thought I would become a literary man. I wrote for the papers, and belonged to a prominent literary club. I tried to analyze myself. 'I am a man,' I said, 'but what am I good for? What am I to make of this life?' I drifted from one position to another. Every one was sorry to part with my services, for I always did my duties as well as they can be done. When I was twenty-five years of age, the girl to whom I was attached was forced by her mother to marry a wealthy man. She died a year afterward, and I 'pulled up stakes,' and started on a haphazard, reckless career. I went to Colorado, drifted into Arizona, prospected, mined and worked on a ranch. I went to California, and at one time thought of shipping for China. My experiences would fill a book. Again I reached St. Louis. For a year I could not find a thing to do, and became desperate."

MADE HIS FIRST SKETCH AT TWENTY-FIVE.

"And you had done nothing at art so far?" I asked.

"At that time I saw a clay sketch. I said to myself, 'I can do as well as that,' and I copied it. My second sketch admitted me to the St. Louis Sketch Club. I told my friends that I would be a sculptor. They laughed and ridiculed me. I had secured a position in a store, and at odd times worked at what I had always loved, but had only half realized it. Notices appeared in the papers about me, for I was popular in the community. I entered the competition for a statue of General Frank R. Blair. I received the first prize, but when the committee discovered that I was only a bill clerk in a store, they argued that I was not competent to carry out the work, although I was given the first prize medal and the one hundred and fifty dollars accompanying it."

"But that inspired you?"

"Yes, but my father and mother put every obstacle in the way possible. I was driven from room to room. I was not even allowed to work in the attic." Here Mr. Ruckstuhl laughed. "You see what genius has to contend with. I was advanced in position in the store, till I became assistant manager at two thousand dollars a year. When I told the proprietor that I had decided to be a sculptor, he gazed at me in blank astonishment. 'A sculptor?' he queried, incredulously, and made a few very discouraging remarks, emphasized with dashes. 'Why, young man, are you going to throw up the chance of a lifetime? I will give you five thousand dollars a year, and promote you to be manager if you will remain with me.'"

HE GAVE UP A LARGE SALARY TO PURSUE ART.

"But I had found my life's work," said Mr. Ruckstuhl, turning to me. "I knew it would be a struggle through poverty, till I attained fame. But I was confident in myself, which is half of the battle."

"And you went abroad?"

"Yes, with but two hundred and fifty dollars," he replied. "I traveled through Europe for five months, and visited the French Salon. I said to myself, 'I can do that, and that,' and my confidence grew. But there was some work that completely 'beat' me. I returned to America penniless, but with a greater insight into art. I determined that I would retrace my steps to Paris, and study there for three years, and thought that would be sufficient to fully develop me. My family and friends laughed me to scorn, and I was discouraged by everyone. In four months, in St. Louis, I secured seven orders for busts, at two hundred dollars each, to be done after my return from France. That shows that some persons had confidence in me and in my talent.

"O, the student life in Paris! How I look back with pleasure upon those struggling, yet happy days! In two months, I started on my female figure of 'Evening,' in the nude, that now is in the Metropolitan Museum of Art. I finished it in nine months, and positively sweat blood in my work. I sent it to the Salon, and went to Italy. When I returned to Paris, I saw my name in the paper, with honorable mention. I suppose you can realize my feelings; I experienced the first flush of victory. I brought it to America, and exposed it in St. Louis. Strange to say, I rose in the estimation of even my family. My father actually congratulated me. A wealthy man in St. Louis gave me three thousand dollars to have my 'Evening' put into marble. I returned with it to Paris, and in a month and a quarter it was exhibited in the Salon. At the world's Fair at Chicago, it had the place of honor, and received one of the eleven grand medals given to American sculptors. In 1892, I came to New York. This statue of 'Force' will be erected, with my statue of 'Wisdom,' on the new Hall of Records in New York."

We gazed at it, seated and clothed in partial armor, of the old Roman type, and holding a sword across its knees. The great muscles spoke of strength and force, and yet with it all there was an almost benign look upon the military visage.

"There is force and real action there, withal, although there is repose," I said in admiration.

THE INSPIRATION THAT COUNTS.

"Oh," said Mr. Ruckstuhl, "that's it, and that is what it is so hard to get! That is what every sculptor strives for; and, unless he attains it, his work, from my point of view is worthless. There must be life in a statue; it must almost breathe. In repose there must be dormant action that speaks for itself."

"Is most of your work done under inspiration?" I asked.

"There is nothing, and a great deal, in so-called inspiration. I firmly believe that we mortals are merely tools, mediums, at work here on earth. I peg away and bend all my energies to my task. I simply accomplish nothing. Suddenly, after considerable preparatory toil, the mist clears away; I see things clearly; everything is outlined for me. I believe there is a conscious and a subconscious mind. The subconscious mind is the one that does original work; it cannot be affected by the mind that is conscious to all our petty environments. When the conscious mind is lulled and silenced, the subconscious one begins to work. That I call inspiration."

"Are you ever discouraged?" I asked out of curiosity.

"Continually," replied Mr. Ruckstuhl, looking down at his hands, soiled with the working clay. "Some days I will be satisfied with what I have done. It will strike me as simply fine. I will be as happy as a bird, and leave simply joyous. The following morning, when the cloths are removed, I look at my precious toil, and consider it vile. I ask myself: 'Are you a sculptor or not? Do you think that you ever will be one? Do you consider that art?' So it is, till your task is accomplished. You are your own critic, and are continually distressed at your inability to create your ideals."

Mr. F. Wellington Ruckstuhl is fifty years of age; neither short nor tall; a brilliant man, with wonderful powers of endurance, for his work is more exacting and tedious than is generally supposed.

"I have simply worked a month and a quarter on that statue," he said. "Certain work dissatisfied me, and I obliterated it. I have raised that head three times. My eyes get weary, and I become physically tired. On such occasions I sit down and smoke a little to distract my thoughts, and to clear my mind. Then my subconscious mind comes into play again," he concluded with a smile.

Mr. Ruckstuhl's best known works are: "Mercury Teasing the Eagle of Jupiter," which is of bronze, nine feet high, which he made in Paris; a seven-foot statue of Solon, erected in the Congressional Library at Washington; busts of Franklin, Goethe and Macaulay, on the front of the same library; and the eleven-foot statue of bronze of "Victory," for the Jamaica soldiers' and sailors' monument. In competition, he won the contract for an equestrian statue of General John F. Hartranft, ex-Governor of Pennsylvania, which he also made in Paris. It is considered the finest piece of work of its kind in America. Besides this labor, he has made a number of medallions and busts.

"Art was in me as a child," he said; "I was discouraged whenever it beckoned me, but finally it claimed me. I surrendered a good position to follow it, whether it led through a thorny road or not. A sculptor is an artist, a musician, a poet, a writer, a dramatist, to throw action, breath and life, music and a soul into his creation. I can pick up an instrument and learn it instantly; I can sing, and act, so I am in touch with the sympathies of the beings that I endeavor to create. You will find most sculptors and artists of my composite nature.

"There," said Mr. Ruckstuhl, and he stretched out his arm, with his palm downward, and moved it through the air, as he gazed into distance, "you strive to create the imagination of your mind, and it comes to you as if sent from another world.

"You strive. That is the way to success."

XXXVI

DURING LEISURE HOURS HE "FOUND HIMSELF" AND ABANDONED THE LAW FOR ART.

THERE is a charming lesson in the way Henry Merwin Shrady, the sculptor, "found himself." A few years ago, this talented artist, whose splendid buffalo and moose ornamented the entrance of the Pan-American Exposition at Buffalo, was employed as an assistant manager in the match business of his brother-in-law, Edwin Gould. It was by attempts at self-improvement through painting in oil, during leisure hours, that he discovered his capacity for art, and, finally, for sculpture of a high order of merit.

"I always secretly wished," he said modestly, "to become a great painter, and, with that in view, dabbled in oils from childhood. My family wished me to study medicine, but my nature revolted at the cutting of flesh; so, after a course at Columbia University, I studied law. An attack of typhoid fever, caught at a Yale-Harvard boat race, after my graduation, incapacitated me for work for a year. Then I went into the match business, instead of practicing law.

"After business hours and on holidays, I taught myself painting. I have never taken a lesson in drawing, in painting, or in sculpture, in my life. I joined the Bronx Zoölogical Society, that I might the better study animals, and it was at these gardens that I made the sketches for my buffalo and moose."

Mr. Shrady taught himself the art of mixing oils, and then, in spare hours, called on William H. Beard, at his studio, for the delineator of "The Bulls and Bears of Wall Street" to criticise his sketches. Once Mr. Beard said, prophetically, "Some day you will forsake all for art."

A PET DOG HIS FIRST PAINTING.

The young artist had, at his home, a fox-terrier, of which he was very fond. He painted a picture of the dog, and his wife, thinking it an excellent piece of work, offered it clandestinely for exhibition at the National Academy of Design. It was accepted. Great was his astonishment when he recognized it there. It was sold for fifty dollars. His next serious attempt was caused by a little rivalry. His sister brought from abroad an expensive painting of some French kittens. He instantly took a dislike to the kittens, and said he would paint her some Angora ones. To make satisfactory sketches, he carried a sketch-book in his pocket, on his walks to and from his office, pausing on the pavements before the different fanciers' windows to sketch the kittens within. This picture was also accepted by the National Academy of Design. But he refused an offer to sell it, as he had promised it to his sister, Mrs. Gould, for a Christmas present.

"It was on account of the almost impossible feat of getting colorings at night," he said, "that I turned to modeling in clay. I wanted to do something to improve as well as amuse me. I modeled a battery going into action, but did not finish it till persuaded to do so by Alvin S. Southworth, a special correspondent of a New York paper in the Crimean War, and friend of my father, Dr. Shrady. It was to gratify him that I finished it. A photograph of it, reproduced in 'The Journalist,' attracted a gentleman in the employ of the firm of Theodore B. Starr. He called upon me, and encouraged me to have it made in Russian bronze. That house purchased it, and advised me to enter the field, as they saw prospects for American military pieces."

Mr. Shrady sketched the gun-carriage and harness for his

battery in the Seventh Regiment armory, to which regiment he has belonged for seven years; and his own saddle horse was his model for the horses of the battery.

One day Carl Bitter, the sculptor, dropped in at Starr's, while Mr. Shrady was there. He noticed the small bronzes,—the buffalo and the moose. "I think we can use them at the Buffalo Exposition," he said. Mr. Bitter offered the sculptor the use of his studio, in Hoboken, and, in six weeks, by rising at half past five in the morning, and working ten hours a day, he enlarged his buffalo to eight feet in height, and his moose, a larger animal, to nine feet. Then glue molds were taken of both of them, with the greatest care.

"I had never enlarged, or worked in plaster of Paris before," said Mr. Shrady. "They gave me the tools and plaster, and told me to go to work. I didn't know how to proceed, at first, but eventually learned all right. I think I could do such work with more ease now," he added, "for that was practical experience I could not get in an art school."

Since then, Mr. Shrady has made a realistic cavalry piece, "Saving the Colors,"—of two horsemen, one shot and falling, and the other snatching the colors; also, "The Empty Saddle,"— of a cavalry horse, saddled and bridled, and quietly grazing at a distance from the scene of the death of his rider. This was exhibited at the Academy of American Artists. The Academy of Fine Arts, of Philadelphia, requested Mr. Shrady to exhibit at its exhibition in January, 1902.

The youthful sculptor has the gift of giving life, expression and feeling to his animals, which, some say, is unsurpassed.

A UNIQUE EXPERIMENT WITH A HORSE.

"I do not believe," said he, "in working from an anatomical figure, or in covering a horse with skin and hair after you have laid in his muscles. You are apt to make prominent muscles which are not really prominent. Once I soaked a horse with water, and took photographs of him, to make a record of the muscles and tendons that really show. They are practically few, except when in active use. In an art school you learn little about a horse. The way which I approve is to place a horse before you, study him and know him, and work till you have reproduced him. No master, standing over your shoulder, can teach you more than you can observe, if you have the soul. Corot took his easel into the woods, and studied close to nature, till he painted truthfully a landscape. Angelo's best work was that done to suit his personal view.

"Talent may be born, but it depends upon your own efforts whether it comes to much. I believe that if your hobby, desire, or talent, whichever you wish to call it, is to paint or model, you can teach yourself better than you can be taught, providing you really love your work, as I do."

Thus did Mr. Shrady desert a mechanical life he disliked, and start on a promising career. He is still young, slight, and with delicate features. His heart is tender toward animals, and he refuses to hunt. His chief delight is in riding the horse which has figured so prominently in his work. His success proves two things: the value of leisure moments, and the wisdom of turning a hobby into a career.

AMUSEMENT

XXXVII

DEFORMED IN BODY, HIS CHEERFUL SPIRIT MAKES HIM THE ENTERTAINER OF PRINCES.

A SCORE of years ago, seated on a bench in Bryant Park, a hungry lad wept copious tears over his failure to gain a supper or a night's lodging. A peddler's outfit lay beside him. Not a sale had he made that day. His curiously diminutive body was neatly clad, but his heart was heavy. He was dreadfully hungry, as only a boy can be.

"Oh, see the funny little man!" exclaimed a quartet of little girls, as they trooped past the shrinking figure. "Mamma! Come and buy something from him!"

Down the steps of a brown stone mansion came a young matron, curiosity shining out of her handsome eyes. The boy looked up and smiled. The lady did not buy anything, but her mother's heart was touched, and before she hurried home with her little girls, she gave him five cents.

Last winter, two members of the Lamb's Club were about to part on the club steps. One was "The Prince of Entertainers and the Entertainer of Princes," Marshall P. Wilder. The other was a distinguished lawyer.

"Come and dine with me to-night, Mr. Wilder," said the latter. "You have never accepted my hospitality, but you have no engagements for to-night, so come along."

Ten minutes later, the great entertainer was presented to the wife of his host and to four beautiful young women.

A curious thrill passed over the guest as he looked into those charming faces. They seemed familiar. A flash of memory carried him back to that scene in the park. He turned to the hostess:—

"Do you remember,"—his voice trembled,—"a little chap in the park years ago, to whom you were kind,—'a funny little man,' the children called him, and you gave him five cents?"

"Yes, yes, I do remember that,—and you—?"

"I am the funny little man."

It was indeed true. The hungry boy had not forgotten it, though wealth and fame had come to him in the meanwhile. In a little private diary that no one sees but himself, he has five new birth dates marked, those of the mother and her four daughters. "Just to remember those who have been kind to me," is the only explanation on the cover of the book.

What a brightly interesting story is Wilder's, anyway! Who else in all this great, broad land has made such a record,—from a peddler's pack to a fortune of one hundred thousand dollars,—and all because he is merry and bright and gay in spite of his physical drawbacks. His nurse dropped him when he was an infant, but for years the injury did not manifest itself. At three he was a bright baby, the pride of the dear old father, Doctor Wilder, who still survives to enjoy his son's popularity in the world of amusement-makers. It was no fault of the doctor that Marshall was obliged to go hungry in New York. Doctor Wilder lived and practiced in Hartford, where his son ought to have stayed, but he didn't. At five he was handsome and well formed, but at twelve he stopped growing. The boys began to tease him about his diminutive stature.

"I don't think I've grown very much since,—except in experience," he said the other day in the course of a morning chat in his handsome bachelor apartments. "I thought, by leaving home, I might at least grow up with the country."

"But you didn't grow, after all?"

"No, I haven't found the country yet that can make me grow up with it. I guess I'll have to be satisfied with being a plain expansionist." [Mr. Wilder is nearly as broad as he is long.]

"How did you happen to choose the amusement profession?" I asked.

NATURE'S LAW OF COMPENSATION.

"I was always a good mimic," he replied, "and I found my talents lay in that direction. I created a new business, that of story-teller, imitator of celebrated people, and of sleight-of-hand performer, all without the aid of costumes, depending solely on my facial expression to give point to the humor. Nature had certainly tried to make amends for her frowns by giving me facial power,—the power to smile away dull care. There is a niche in life for everyone, a place where one belongs. Society is like a pack of cards. Some members of it are kings and others are knaves, while I,—I discovered that I was the little joker."

Mr. Wilder is a bubbling fountain of wit, whose whimsicalities are no less entertaining to himself than to his hearers. As he quaintly expresses it, they are "ripples from the ocean of my moods which have touched the shore of my life." His disposition is so cheery that children and dogs come to him instantly. Eugene Field has the same trait.

HOW HE TOOK JOSEPH JEFFERSON'S LIFE.

His first appearance on any stage was made in "Rip Van Winkle," when he was a boy. Joseph Jefferson carried him on his back as a dwarf. The great "Rip" has remained his steadfast friend ever since. Only a few years ago, Wilder left New York to fulfil a church entertainment engagement in Utica. He got there at three in the afternoon. Mr. Jefferson's private car was on the track, containing himself, William J. Florence, Mrs. John Drew, Viola Allen, and Otis Skinner. They hailed him instantly and induced him to pass the afternoon in the car and to take dinner with them. His church engagement was over at half past eight, and at Mr. Jefferson's invitation he occupied a box at the opera house. The house happened to be a small one, while the church had been crowded to the doors. After the theater, the Jefferson party again entertained the humorist in the car, keeping him until his train left, half an hour after midnight. As Mr. Wilder was leaving, Mr. Jefferson pretended to get very angry and said: "What do you think, my friends? Here we have entertained this ungrateful young scamp all the afternoon, and invited him to dinner. Then he goes up to town and plays to a big audience, leaving me only a very poor house. Then he comes down here, partakes of our hospitality again, and before leaving takes my life!" Suiting the action to the word, Mr. Jefferson handed the young man a copy of his "Life and Recollections."

His first attempt at wit was at a little church in New York, where he was one of the audience. A tableau was being given of "Mary, Queen of Scots," and in order to make it realistic they had obtained a genuine butcher's block and a cleaver. As the executioner stood by, the lights all turned low, and his dreadful work in progress, a shrill voice arose from the darkened house:—

"Save me a spare-rib."

His readiness in an emergency was shown at Flint, Michigan, when he was before an unresponsive audience. As luck would have it, the gas suddenly went out.

"Never mind the gas," he called to the stage manager. "They can see the points just as well in the dark." After that he was *en rapport*.

The greatest gift God ever made to man, he admitted to me in strict confidence, is the ability to laugh and to make his fellowmen laugh. This more than compensates, he adds, for the reception he gets from some of the cold audiences in New Jersey.

I asked him what was the funniest experience he had ever had.

"In a lodge room one night with Nat Goodwin," he replied. "It was, or ought to have been, a solemn occasion, but there was a German present who couldn't repeat the obligation backward. Nat stuffed his handkerchief into his mouth. I bit my lip trying to keep from laughing. I knew what an awful breach of decorum it would be if we ever gave way to our feelings. We had almost gained perfect control of ourselves, and the beautiful and impressive ceremony was half over, when that confounded Dutchman was asked once more to repeat the oath backward. He made such work of it that I yelled right out, while Nat had a spasm and rolled on the floor. Did they put us out? Well, I guess they did. It took seven or eight apologies to get us back into that lodge."

Equally funny was his experience in London. It was on the occasion of the visit of the Ancient and Honorable Artillery, of Boston. A big dinner was to be given, and the American ambassador and the Prince of Wales were to be there. I asked Wilder to tell me the story of his visit.

"I received an invitation," he began, "through my friend, B. F. Keith, who was a member of the Ancient and Honorable Artillery, and who happened to be in London. The uniforms were something gorgeous. The members stood in two long lines, awaiting the coming of the prince, who is always punctual. I was dressed in my usual boy-size clothes, a small American flag stuck in my Tuxedo coat. I walked around restlessly. The major-domo was a very grand personage, with a bearskin hat on one end and long boots on the other. He must have been eight or ten feet high. He chased me to the rear of the room several times,—evidently not knowing who I was,—but every time he turned his back I would bob out again, sometimes between his legs. The prince came, and almost the first thing he did was to walk across the floor to me and say: 'Hullo, little chap. I am very glad to see you.'

I had met him before. Then Henry Irving bore down on me and shook my hand, and so did Mr. Depew and others. By this time the major-domo had shrunk in size.

"Who the Dickens is that little chap, anyway?" he asked.

"'Sh! He belongs to the American army,' was the answer. 'He's a great marshal or something over there!'"

Wilder is big-hearted. "The biggest fee I ever received," he stated in reply to my inquiry, "was the satisfaction I saw depicted on a poor man's face. It was on a railway train. A life-prisoner was being taken, after a long man-hunt in Europe and America, out to Kansas City. I never saw so dejected a face. I devoted four or five hours to brightening him up, and when I left he was smiling all over. I had succeeded in making him forget his misery for at least four hours!"

A wealthy gentleman of New York pays Mr. Wilder a stated sum every year to "cheer up" the inmates of hospitals and similar institutions.

XXXVIII

ENERGY AND EARNESTNESS WIN AN ACTOR FAME.

"WHO will play the part?" asked A. M. Palmer, anxiously, looking over the members of his "Parisian Romance" company one night when the actor who had been playing 'Baron Cheval' failed to appear.

"I will," spoke up an obscure young player, a serious, earnest man who had been "utility" for the company only a short time.

It was Richard Mansfield, and the part was given him. It had not been a conspicuous part up to that hour, but that night Mr. Mansfield made it a leading one. He saw in it opportunities for a deeper dramatic portrayal, for an expression of intense earnestness, and for that finished acting which ennobles any part in a play, however humble. Before the performance was over, he had opened the eyes of the company and the public to the fact that a new actor of great talent had come to the front at a bound.

In his beautiful home in New York, the other day, I found him surrounded by the evidences of wealth and artistic taste.

"So you represent Success," he exclaimed. "Well, I am pleased to have you call. Success pays few calls, you know. Ordinarily, we have to pursue it and make great efforts to keep it from eluding us."

Mr. Mansfield made this remark with a quizzical, yet half-tired smile, as if he had himself found the chase exhausting.

HOW TO FIND SUCCESS.

"Yes," he went on, "success is a most fleet-footed—almost a phantom—goddess. You pursue her eagerly and seem to grasp her, and then you see her speeding on in front again. This is, of course, because one is rarely satisfied with present success. There is always something yet to be attained. To speak personally, I never worked harder in my life than I am working now. If I should relax, I fear that the structure which I have built up would come tumbling about my ears. It is my desire to advance my standard every year,—to plant it higher up on the hill, and to never yield a foot of ground. This requires constant effort. I find my reward, not in financial returns, for these are hardly commensurate with the outlay of labor; nor in the applause of others, for this is not always discriminative or judicious; but in the practice of my art. This suggests what, it seems to me, is the true secret of success.

"Love your work; then you will do it well. It is its own reward, though it brings others. If a young man would rather be an actor than anything else, and he knows what he is about, let him, by all means, be an actor. He will probably become a good one. It is the same, of course, in many occupations. If you like your work, hold on to it, and eventually you are likely to win. If you don't like it, you can't be too quick in getting into something that suits you better."

HE BEGAN AS A DRY GOODS CLERK.

"I began as a dry goods clerk in Boston, and was a very mediocre clerk. Afterward I became a painter in London, and was starving at that. Finally, like water, I found my level in dramatic art."

The thing about Mr. Mansfield which most inspires those

who come in contact with him is his wonderful store of nervous energy. It communicates itself to others and makes them keen for work.

"I cannot talk with him five minutes," said his business representative, "before I want to grab my hat and 'hustle' out and do about three days' work without stopping. For persons who have not, or cannot absorb, some of his own electric spirit, he has little use. He is a living embodiment of contagious energy."

His performances before audiences constitute a comparatively small portion of his work. It is in his elaborate and painstaking preparation that the labor is involved, and it is to this—to the minute preliminary care that he gives to every detail of a production,—that his fine effects and achievements before the footlights are, in considerable measure, due.

HE GIVES INFINITE ATTENTION TO DETAIL.

The rehearsals are a vital part of the preparatory work, and to them Mr. Mansfield has devoted a great deal of time. For weeks, between the hours of eleven in the morning and four in the afternoon, he remains on the stage with his company, seated in a line four or five deep on either side of him, like boys and girls at school, deeply engrossed in impressing upon the minds of individual members of the company his own ideas of the interpretation and presentation of the various parts. Again and again, until one would think he himself would become utterly weary of the repetition, he would have an actor repeat a sentence. Not until it is exactly right is Mr. Mansfield satisfied. Nothing escapes his scrutiny. At dress rehearsals he may see, to mention a typical case, a tall man and a small one of no special importance in the play standing together, and the tall one may be made up to have a sallow complexion and beard. Mr. Mansfield glances at them quickly. Something is wrong. He hastens up to the smaller one and suggests that, for the sake of contrast, he make himself up to look stout and to have a smooth face. The improvement is quite noticeable. Mr. Mansfield carefully notes the effect of light and shadow on the scenery; and sometimes, at the last moment, will seize the brush and add, here and there, a heightening or a softening touch.

An incident of his early youth will tend to illustrate his spirit of self-reliance. His mother was an eminent singer who frequently appeared before royal families in Europe, and usually had little Richard with her. On one occasion, after her own performance before royalty in Germany, the little Crown Prince, who was about the same age as Richard, and an accomplished boy, played a selection on the piano, and played it well. When he had left the piano, the company was very much surprised to see Master Richard Mansfield take his place, without an invitation, and play the same music, but in a considerably better manner than had the Crown Prince. When the boy had become a youth, he was compelled to support himself; and, having come to this country, he obtained a position as a clerk in the Jordan & Marsh establishment in Boston. Meanwhile, he was devoting all his spare time to studying painting. He afterward tried to make a living at it in London, and failed. He was finally given an opportunity as a comedian in "Pinafore." He had the small part of Joseph. It was but a short time afterward when he entered the employ of Mr. Palmer and got the chance of his lifetime.

XXXIX

A FATHER'S COMMON SENSE GIVES AMERICA A GREAT BANDMASTER.

KIPLING essayed to write verses at thirteen, and John Philip Sousa entered his apprenticeship in a military band at the age of twelve. The circumstances, which he related to me during a recent conversation, make it clear, however, that it was not exactly the realization of any youthful ambition. "When I was a youngster of twelve," said the bandmaster, "I could play the violin fairly well. It was in this memorable year that a circus came to Washington, D. C., where I then lived, and remained for two days. During the morning of the first day, one of the showmen passed the house and heard me playing. He rang the bell, and when I answered it, asked if I would not like to join the show. I was at the age when it is the height of every boy's ambition to join a circus, and was so delighted that I readily agreed to his instructions that I was to take my violin, and, without telling anyone, go quietly to the show grounds late the next evening.

"I couldn't, however, keep this stroke of good fortune entirely to myself, so I confided it to my chum, who lived next door. The effect was entirely unanticipated. He straightway became so jealous at the thought that I would have an opportunity to witness the circus performance free that he told his mother, and that good woman promptly laid the whole matter before my father."

IN THE MARINE BAND.

"At the time I was, of course, ignorant of this turn of affairs; but early the next morning my father, without a word of explanation, told me to put on my best clothes, and, without ceremony, bundled me down to the office of the Marine Band, where he entered me as an apprentice. The age limit at which admission could be gained to the band corps was fourteen years, and I have always retained the two years which my father unceremoniously added to my age at that time."

Sousa is of Spanish descent, his father having emigrated from Spain to Portugal by reason of political entanglements. Thence came the strange fact that, during the recent war, American troops marched forward to attack Spaniards to the music of marches written by this descendant of their race. The director's remark that his family was one of the oldest in Spain was supplementary to an amused denial of that pretty story which has been so widely circulated to the effect that the bandmaster's name was originally John Philipso, and that when, after entering the Marine Band, he signed it with the "U. S. A." appended, some intelligent clerk divided it into John Philip Sousa.

HIS FIRST SUCCESSFUL WORK.

In discussing his opera, "El Capitan," which, when produced by De Wolf Hopper several seasons ago, achieved such instantaneous success, the composer remarked that it was the sixth opera he had written, the others never reaching the dignity of a production.

As Sousa is preëminently a man of action, so his career and characteristics are best outlined by incidents. One in connection with his operatic composition strikingly illustrates his pluck and determination. Before he attained any great degree of prominence in the musical world, Sousa submitted an opera to Francis Wilson, offering to sell it outright for one thousand five hundred dollars. Wilson liked the opera, but the composer was not fortified by a great name, so he declined to pay more than one thousand dollars for the piece. The composer replied that he had spent the best part of a year on the work, and felt that he could not take less than his original demand. Wilson was obdurate, and Sousa ruefully put the manuscript back into his portfolio.

Some time afterward a march which the bandmaster sent to a well-known publishing house caught the public favor. The publishers demanded another at once. The composer had none at hand, but suddenly thought of the march in his discarded opera, and forwarded it without waiting to select a name.

While he was pondering thoughtfully on the subject of a title, Sousa and a friend one evening went to the Auditorium in Chicago, where "America" was then being presented. When the mammoth drop curtain, with the painted representation of the Liberty Bell was lowered, the bandmaster's companion said, with the suddenness of an inspiration: "There is a name for your new march." That night it was sent on to the publishers.

Up to date, this one selection from the opera for which Francis Wilson refused to pay fifteen hundred dollars has netted its composer thirty-five thousand dollars.

A MAN WHO NEVER RESTS.

Sousa has practically no vacations. Throughout the greater part of the autumn, winter and spring, his band is *en tour* through this country and Canada, giving, as a rule, two concerts each day, usually in different towns. During the summer, his time is occupied with daily concerts at Manhattan Beach, near New York. Despite all this, he finds time to write several marches or other musical selections each year, and for several years past has averaged each year an operatic production. Any person who is at all conversant with the subject knows that the composition of the opera itself is only the beginning of the composer's labor, and Sousa has invariably directed the rehearsals with all the thoroughness and attention to detail that might be expected from a less busy man.

The bandmaster is a late riser, and in that, as in other details, the routine of his daily life is the embodiment of regularity and punctuality. In reply to my question as to what produces his never-failing good health, he said: "Absolute regularity of life, plenty of sleep, and good, plain, substantial food."

His idea of the most valuable aids, if not essentials to success, may be imagined. They are "persistence and hard work." The "March King" believes that it is only worry, and not hard work, that kills people, and he also has confidence that if there be no literal truth in the assertion that genius is simply another name for hard work, there is at least much of wisdom in the saying.

Many persons who have seen Sousa direct his organization make the assertion that the orders conveyed by his baton are non-essential,—that the band would be equally well-off without Sousa. This never received a fuller refutation than during a recent concert in an eastern city. Two small boys in seats near the front of the hall were tittering, but so quietly that it would hardly seem possible that it could be noticed on the stage, especially by the bandmaster, whose back was, of course, toward the audience. Suddenly, in the middle of a bar, his baton fell. Instantly, every sound ceased, not a note having been sounded after the signal, which could not have been anticipated, was given. Wheeling quickly, the leader ordered the troublesome youngsters to leave the hall, and almost before the audience had realized what had happened, the great organization had resumed the rendition of the selection, without the loss of a chord.

HOW SOUSA WORKS.

In answer to my inquiry as to his methods of work, the director of America's foremost band said:—

"I think that any musical composer must essentially find his periods of work governed largely by inspiration. A march or a waltz depends perhaps upon some strain that has sufficient melody to carry the entire composition, and it is the waiting to catch this embryo note that is sometimes long.

"Take my experience with 'The Stars and Stripes Forever.' I worked for weeks on the strain that I think will impress most persons as the prettiest in the march. I carried it in my mind all that time, but I could not get the idea transferred to paper just as I wanted. When I did accomplish it, there was comparatively little delay with the remainder."

When I asked him about his future work, Mr. Sousa said:—

"I of course have commissions to write several operas, and I am at work on a musical composition which I hope to make the best thing that I have ever attempted."

His temperament is well illustrated by an incident on a western railroad. The Sousa organization, which had been playing in one of the larger cities, desired to reach a small town in time for a matinée performance, but, owing to the narrow policy of the railway officials, the bandmaster was obliged to engage a special train, at a cost of $175.

In the railway yard stood the private coach of the president of the system, and just before the Sousa train pulled out, the discovery was made that the regular train, to which it had been intended to attach the president's car, was three hours late. A request was made of the bandmaster that he allow the car to be attached to his train; but Sousa, with that twinkle in his eye which every person who has seen him must have noticed, simply smiled, and, with the most extravagant politeness, replied: "I am sorry, gentlemen, but, having chartered this train for my especial use, I am afraid I shall have to limit its use to that purpose."

PHILANTHROPY

XL

BLIND, DEAF, AND DUMB, PATIENT EFFORT
WINS FOR HER CULTURE AND RARE WOMANHOOD.

"I AM trying to prove that the sum of the areas of two similar polygons, constructed on the two legs of a right triangle, is equal to the area of a similar polygon constructed on the hypotenuse. It is a very difficult demonstration," she added, and her expressive face, on which every passing emotion is plainly written, looked serious for a moment, as she laid her hand upon the work about which I had asked.

Helen Keller, the deaf and blind girl, whose intellectual attainments have excited the wonder and admiration of our most prominent educators, is well known to all readers, but Helen Keller, the blithesome, rosy-cheeked, light-hearted maiden of nineteen, whose smile is a benediction, and whose ringing laugh is fresh and joyous as that of a child, is not, perhaps, so familiar.

HELEN KELLER AT HOME.

By kind permission of her teacher, Miss Sullivan, I was granted the privilege of an interview with Miss Keller at her residence on Newbury street, Boston, where she was busily at work preparing for the entrance examinations to Radcliffe College.

After a cordial greeting, Miss Sullivan, whose gracious, kindly manner makes the visitor feel perfectly at home, introduced me to her pupil. Seated on a low rocking-chair, in a large, sunny bay-window, the young girl, fresh as the morning, in her dainty pink shirt-waist over a dress of plain, dark material, with the sunshine glinting through her waving brown hair, and kissing her broad white forehead and pink cheeks, made a picture which one will not willingly forget. On her lap was a small red cushion, to which wires, representing the geometrical figures included in the problem on which she was engaged, were fastened. Laying this aside at a touch from Miss Sullivan, she arose, and, stretching out her hand, pronounced my name softly, with a peculiar intonation, which at first makes it a little difficult to understand her words, but to which the listener soon becomes accustomed. Of course, her teacher acted as an interpreter during our conversation, though much of what Helen says is perfectly intelligible even to the untrained ear.

"Yes," she said, "it is a very difficult problem, but I have a little light on it now."

HER AMBITION.

"What will your ambition be when your college course is completed?" I asked.

"I think I should like to write,—for children. I tell stories to my little friends a great deal of the time now, but they are not original,—not yet. Most of them are translations from the Greek, and I think no one can write anything prettier for the young. Charles Kingsley has written some equally good things, like 'Water Babies,' for instance. 'Alice in Wonderland' is a fine story, too, but none of them can surpass the Greek tales."

Many of our advanced thinkers are fond of advancing the theory that the medium of communication in the future will not be spoken words, but the more subtle and genuine, if mute, language of the face, the eyes, the whole body. Sarah Bernhardt forcibly illustrates the effectiveness of this method, for even those who do not understand a word of French derive nearly as much pleasure from the great actress's performances as those who are thoroughly familiar with the language. Helen Keller's dramatic power of expression is equally telling.

She is enthusiastic in her admiration of everything Greek. The language, the literature, the arts, the history of the classic land fascinate and enthrall her imagination.

"Oh, yes," she exclaimed, eagerly, in answer to my query if she expected to go to Greece sometime, "it is one of my air castles. Ever since I was as tall as that," (she held her hand a short distance from the floor) "I have dreamed about it."

"Do you believe the dream will some day become a reality?"

"I hope so, but I dare not be too sure,"—and the sober words of wisdom that followed sounded oddly enough on the girlish lips,—"the world is full of disappointments and vicissitudes, and I have to be a little conservative."

"Which of your studies interest you most?"

"Latin and Greek. I am reading now Virgil's 'Eclogues,' Cicero's 'Orations,' Homer's 'Iliad' and 'Odyssey,'" she said, and ran rapidly over a list of classic books which she likes.

Her readiness to perceive a joke and her quickness to detect the least carelessness in language are distinguishing traits, which she illustrated even during our brief conversation. Commenting on her love of everything pertaining to Greece, I remarked that a believer in the doctrine of metempsychosis might imagine that she possessed the soul of an old Greek. Instantly she noticed the little slip, and, laughing gayly, cried: "Oh, no, not the soul of an *old* Greek, the soul of a *young* Greek."

Helen's merriment was infectious, and we all joined heartily in the laugh, Miss Sullivan saying, "She caught you there," as I was endeavoring to explain that, of course, I meant the soul of an ancient Greek.

While taking so deep an interest in matters intellectual, and living in a world of her own, penetrated by no outward sight or sound, Miss Keller's tastes are as normal as those of any girl of nineteen. She is full of animal spirit, dearly loves a practical joke, is fond of dancing, enjoys outside exercise and sport, and has the natural desire of every healthy young maiden to wear pretty things and look her best.

In answer to a question on this latter subject, she said:—

"I used to be very fond of dress, but now I am not particularly so; it is such a bother. We ought to like dress, though, and wear pretty things, just as the flowers put on beautiful colors. It would be fine," she continued, laughing gleefully, "if we were made with feathers and wings, like the birds. Then we would have no trouble about dress, and we could fly where we pleased."

"You would fly to Greece, first, I suppose?"

"No," she replied, and her laughing face took on a tender, wistful look, "I should go home first, to see my loved ones."

HEREDITY AND CHILDHOOD.

Miss Keller's home is at Tuscumbia, Alabama, where she was born on June 27, 1880. Some of the best blood of both the north and the south flows in her veins, and it is probable that her uncommon mental powers are in no small degree due to heredity. Her father, Arthur H. Keller, a polished southern gentleman, with a large, chivalrous nature, fine intelligence and attractive manners, was the descendant of a family of Swiss origin, which had settled in Virginia and mixed with some of the oldest families in that state. He served as a captain in the Confederate army during the Civil War, and, at the time of Helen's birth, was the owner and editor of a paper published at Tuscumbia. On the maternal side she is descended from one of the Adams families of Massachusetts, and the same stock of Everetts from which Edward Everett and Reverend Edward Everett Hale sprang.

Helen Keller was not born deaf and blind, although, at the age of eighteen months, when a violent fit of convulsions deprived her of the faculties of seeing and hearing, she had not attempted to speak. When a child, she was as notable for her stubbornness and resistance to authority as she is to-day for her gentleness and amiability. Indeed, it was owing to an exhibition of what seemed a very mischievous spirit that her parents sought a special instructor for her. Having discovered the use of a key, she locked her mother into a pantry in a distant part of the house, where, her hammering on the door not being heard by the servants, she remained imprisoned for several hours. Helen, seated on the floor outside, felt the knocking on the door, and seemed to be enjoying the situation intensely when at length jailer and prisoner were found. She was then about six years old, and, after this escapade, Mr. and Mrs. Keller felt that the child's moral nature must be reached and her mental powers cultivated, if possible.

HELEN'S FIRST TEACHER.

On the recommendation of Dr. Alexander Graham Bell, inventor of the telephone, Michael Anagnos, director of the Perkins Institute for the Blind at South Boston, sent Miss Annie Mansfield Sullivan to Tuscumbia to undertake the difficult task of piercing the veil behind which the intelligence of the little girl lay sleeping. How well this noble and devoted teacher has succeeded in her work is amply evidenced by the brilliancy and thoroughness of her pupil's attainments.

Miss Sullivan's method of instruction was similar to that adopted by Dr. Samuel G. Howe in teaching Laura Bridgman. She used the manual alphabet, and cards bearing, in raised letters, the names of objects. At first, the pupil violently resisted the teacher's efforts to instruct her, and so determined was her opposition, Miss Sullivan declares, that, if she had not exercised physical force and a determination even more strenuous than that of her refractory pupil, she would never have succeeded in teaching her anything. Night and day she was at her side, watching for the first gleam of conscious mind; and at length, after seven weeks of what she says was the hardest work she had ever done, the faithful teacher received her reward in the sudden dawning of the child's intelligence. All at once, the light seemed to burst in upon her wondering soul; she understood then that the raised letters which she felt on the cards and the groups of manual signs on her hands, represented words, or the names of familiar objects. The delight of the pupil and teacher was unbounded, and from that moment Helen's education, though still demanding the greatest patience and loving care on the part of her teacher, was a comparatively easy matter.

With the awakening of her intellectual faculties, she seemed literally to have been "born again." The stubborn, headstrong, self-willed, almost unmanageable child became patient, gentle and obedient; and, instead of resisting instruction, her eagerness to learn was so great that it had to be restrained. So rapid was her progress that, in a few weeks, anyone who knew the manual alphabet could easily communicate with her, and in July, 1887, less than a year from the time Miss Sullivan first saw her, she could write an intelligent letter.

PREPARING FOR COLLEGE.

In September, 1896, accompanied by her teacher, Miss Keller entered the Cambridge School for Girls, to prepare for Radcliffe College, and in June, 1897, passed the examinations of the first preparatory year successfully in every subject, taking "honors" in English and German. The director of the school, Arthur Gilman, in an article in "American Annals of the Deaf," says: "I think that I may say that no candidate in Harvard or Radcliffe College was graduated higher than Helen in English. The result is remarkable, especially when we consider that she had been studying on strictly college preparatory lines for one year only. She had, it is true, long and careful instruction, and she has had always the loving ministration of Miss Sullivan, in addition to the inestimable advantage of a concentration that the rest of us never know. No other, man or woman," he adds, "has ever, in my experience, got ready for those examinations in so brief a time."

Mr. Gilman, in the same article, pays the following well-deserved tribute to Miss Sullivan, whose work is as worthy of admiration as that of her pupil:—

"Miss Sullivan sat at Helen's side in the classes (in the Cambridge School), interpreting to her, with infinite patience, the instruction of every teacher. In study hours, Miss Sullivan's labors were even more arduous, for she was obliged to read everything that Helen had to learn, excepting what was prepared in Braille; she searched the lexicons and encyclopedias, and gave Helen the benefit of it all. When Helen went home, Miss Sullivan went with her, and it was hers to satisfy the busy, unintermitting demands of the intensely active brain; for, although others gladly helped, there were many matters which could be treated only by the one teacher who had awakened the activity and had followed its development from the first. Now, it was a German grammar which had to be read, now a French story, and then some passage from 'Cæsar's Commentaries.' It looked like drudgery, and drudgery it would certainly have been had not love shed its benign influence over all, lightening each step and turning hardship into pleasure."

Miss Keller is very patriotic, but large and liberal in her ideas, which soar far beyond all narrow, partisan or political prejudices. Her sympathies are with the masses, the burden-bearers, and, like all friends of the people and of universal progress, she was intensely interested in the Peace Congress.

Speaking on the subject, she said: "I hope the nations will carry out the project of disarmament. I wonder which nation will be brave enough to lay down its arms first!"

"Don't you hope it will be America?"

"Yes, I hope so, but I do not think it will. We are only just beginning to fight now," she went on, sagely, "and I am afraid we like it. I think it will be one of the old, experienced nations, that has had enough of war."

HER IDEAL OF A SUCCESSFUL CAREER.

I asked Miss Keller what she considers most essential to a successful career.

She thought a moment, and then replied, slowly, "Patience, perseverance and fidelity."

"And what do you look upon as the most desirable thing in life?"

"Friends," was the prompt reply to this broad general question; and, as she uttered the word, she nestled closely to the friend who has so long been all in all to her.

"What about material possessions?" I asked; "for instance, which would you place first,—wealth or education?"

"Education. A good education is a stepping-stone to wealth. But that does not imply that I want wealth. It is such a care. It would be worse than dressing. 'Give me neither poverty nor riches, but give me contentment,'" she quoted, with a smile.

The future of this most interesting girl will be followed with closest attention by educators, psychologists, and the public generally. There is little doubt that the time and care spent on her education will be amply justified; and that she will personally illustrate her own ideal of a successful career,—"To live nobly; to be true to one's best aspirations,"—is the belief of all who know her.

XLI

JAY GOULD'S CHUM CHOOSES "HIGH THINKING, NOT MONEY MAKING," AND WINS SUCCESS WITHOUT RICHES.

WHEN I visited the hill-top retreat of John Burroughs, the distinguished lover of nature, at West Park, New York, it was with the feeling that all success is not material; that mere dollars are nothing, and that the influential man is the successful man, whether he be rich or poor. John Burroughs is unquestionably both influential and poor. On the wooden porch of his little bark-covered cabin I waited, one June afternoon, until he should come back from the woods and fields, where he had gone for a ramble. It was so still that the sound of my rocker moving to and fro on the rough boards of the little porch seemed to shock the perfect quiet. From afar off came the plaintive cry of a wood-dove, and then all was still again. Presently the interpreter of out-door life appeared in the distance, and, seeing a stranger at his door, hurried homeward. He was without coat or vest, and looked cool in his white outing shirt and large straw hat. After some formalities of introduction, we reached the subject which I had called to discuss, and he said:—

"It is not customary to interview men of my vocation concerning success."

"Any one who has made a lasting impression on the minds of his contemporaries," I began, "and influenced men and women——"

"Do you refer to me?" he interrupted, naively.

DIFFERENT WAYS OF BEING SUCCESSFUL.

I nodded and he laughed. "I have not endowed a university nor made a fortune, nor conquered an enemy in battle," he said.

"And those who have done such things have not written 'Locusts and Wild Honey' and 'Wake, Robin.'"

"I recognize," he said, quietly, "that success is not always where people think it is. There are many ways of being successful, and I do not approve of the mistake which causes many to consider that a great fortune acquired means a great success achieved. On the contrary, our greatest men need very little money to accomplish the greatest work."

"I thought that anyone leading a life so wholly at variance with the ordinary ideas and customs would see success in life from a different point of view," I observed. "Money is really no object with you?"

"The subject of wealth never disturbs me."

"You lead a very simple life here?"

"Such as you see."

The sight would impress anyone. So far is this disciple of nature away from the ordinary mode of the world that his little cabin, set in the cup-shaped top of a hill, is practically bare of luxuries and the so-called comforts of life. His surroundings are of the rudest, the very rocks and bushes encroaching upon his back door. All about, the crest of the hill encircles him, and shuts out the world. Only the birds of the air venture to invade his retreat from the various sides of the mountain, and there is only a straggling, narrow path, which branches off a dozen times before it takes the true direction. In his house are no decorations but such as can be hung upon the exposed wood. The fireplace is of brick, and quite wide; the floor, rough boards scrubbed white; the ceiling, a rough array of exposed rafters, and his bed a rudely constructed work of the hand. Very few and very simple chairs, a plain table and some shelves for books made the wealth of the retreat and serve for his ordinary use.

"Many people think," I said, "that your method of living is an ideal example of the way people ought to live."

"There is nothing remarkable in that. A great many people are very weary of the way they think themselves compelled to live. They are mistaken in believing that the disagreeable things they find themselves doing, are the things they ought to do. A great many take their idea of a proper aim in life from what other people say and do. Consequently, they are unhappy, and an independent existence such as mine strikes them as ideal. As a matter of fact, it is very natural."

A WORTHY AIM IN LIFE.

"Would you say that to work so as to be able to live like this should be the aim of a young man?"

"By no means. On the contrary, his aim should be to live in such a way as will give his mind the greatest freedom and peace. This can be very often obtained by wanting less of material things and more of intellectual ones. A man who achieved such an aim would be as well off as the most distinguished man in any field. Money-getting is half a mania, and some other 'getting' propensities are manias also. The man who gets content comes nearest to being reasonable."

"I should like," I said, "to illustrate your point of view from the details of your own life."

"Students of nature do not, as a rule, have eventful lives. I was born in Roxbury, New York, in 1837. That was a time when conditions were rather primitive. My father was a farmer, and I was raised among the woods and fields. I came from an uncultivated, unreading class of society, and grew up amid surroundings the least calculated to awaken the literary faculty. Yet I have no doubt that daily contact with the woods and fields awakened my interest in the wonders of nature, and gave me a bent toward investigation in that direction."

"Did you begin early to make notes and write upon nature?" I questioned.

"Not before I was sixteen or seventeen. Earlier than that, the art of composition had anything but charms for me. I remember that while at school, at the age of fourteen, I was required, like other students, to write 'compositions' at stated times, but I usually evaded the duty one way or another. On one occasion, I copied something from a comic almanac, and unblushingly handed it in as my own. But the teacher detected the fraud, and ordered me to produce a twelve-line composition before I left school. I remember I racked my brain in vain, and the short winter day was almost closing when Jay Gould, who sat in the seat behind me, wrote twelve lines of doggerel on his slate and passed it slyly over to me. I had so little taste for writing that I coolly copied that, and handed it in as my own."

JAY GOULD WAS HIS CHUM.

"You were friendly with Gould then?"

"Oh, yes; 'chummy,' they call it now. His father's farm was only a little way from ours, and we were fast friends, going home together every night."

"His view of life must have been considerably different from yours."

"It was. I always looked upon success as being a matter of mind, not money; but Jay wanted the material appearances. I remember that once we had a wrestling match, and as we were about even in strength, we agreed to abide by certain rules,— taking what we called 'holts' in the beginning and not breaking them until one or the other was thrown. I kept to this in the struggle, but when Jay realized that he was in danger of losing the contest, he broke the 'holt' and threw me. When I remarked that he had broken his agreement, he only laughed and said, 'I threw you, didn't I?' And to every objection I made, he made the same answer. The fact of having won (it did not matter how), was pleasing to him. It satisfied him, although it wouldn't have contented me."

"Did you ever talk over success in life with him?"

"Yes; quite often. He was bent on making money and did considerable trading among us schoolboys,—sold me some of his books. I felt then that my view of life was more satisfactory to me than his would have been. I wanted to obtain a competence, and then devote myself to high thinking instead of to money-making."

"How did you plan to attain this end?"

HE BEGAN WRITING AT SIXTEEN.

"By study. I began in my sixteenth or seventeenth year to try to express myself on paper, and when, after I had left the country school, I attended the seminary at Ashland and at Cooperstown, I often received the highest marks in composition, though only standing about the average in general scholarship. My taste ran to essays, and I picked up the great works in that field at a bookstore, from time to time, and filled my mind with the essay idea. I bought the whole of Dr. Johnson's works at a second-hand bookstore in New York, because, on looking into them, I found his essays appeared to be of solid literature, which I thought was just the thing. Almost my first literary attempts were moral reflections, somewhat in the Johnsonian style."

"You were supporting yourself during these years?"

"I taught six months and 'boarded round' before I went to the seminary. That put fifty dollars into my pocket, and the fifty paid my way at the seminary. Working on the farm, studying and teaching filled up the years until 1863, when I went to Washington and found employment in the Treasury Department."

"You were connected with the Treasury, then?"

"Oh, yes; for nearly nine years. I left the department in 1872, to become receiver of a bank, and subsequently for several years performed the work of a bank examiner. I considered it only as an opportunity to earn and save up a little money on which I could retire. I managed to do that, and came back to this region, where I bought a fruit farm. I worked that into a paying condition, and then gave all my time to the pursuit of the studies I like."

"Had you abandoned your interest in nature during your Washington life?"

"No; I gave as much time to the study of nature and literature as I had to spare. When I was twenty-three, I wrote an essay on 'Expression,' and sent it to the 'Atlantic.' It was so Emersonian in style, owing to my enthusiasm for Emerson at that time, that the editor thought some one was trying to palm off on him an early essay of Emerson's which he had not seen. He found that Emerson had not published any such paper, however, and printed it, though it had not much merit. I wrote off and on for the magazines."

The editor in question was James Russell Lowell, who, instead of considering it without merit, often expressed afterward the delight with which he read this contribution from an unknown hand, and the swift impression of the author's future distinction which came to him with that reading.

WHAT NATURE STUDY REALLY MEANS.

"Your successful work, then, has been in what direction?" I said.

"In studying nature. It has all come by living close to the plants and animals of the woods and fields, and coming to understand them. There I have been successful. Men who, like myself, are deficient in self-assertion, or whose personalities are flexible and yielding, make a poor show in business, but in certain other fields these defects become advantages. Certainly it is so in my case. I can succeed with bird or beast, for I have cultivated my ability in that direction. I can look in the eye of an ugly dog or cow and win, but with an ugly man I have less success.

"I consider the desire which most individuals have for the luxuries which money can buy, an error of mind," he added. "Those things do not mean anything except a lack of higher tastes. Such wants are not necessary wants, nor honorable wants. If you cannot get wealth with a noble purpose, it is better to abandon it and get something else. Peace of mind is one of the best things to seek, and finer tastes and feelings. The man who gets these, and maintains himself comfortably, is much more admirable and successful than the man who gets money and neglects these. The realm of power has no fascination for me. I would rather have my seclusion and peace of mind. This log hut, with its bare floors, is sufficient. I am set down among the beauties of nature, and in no danger of losing the riches that are scattered all about. No one will take my walks or my brook away from me. The flowers, birds and animals are plentifully provided. I have enough to eat and wear, and time to see how beautiful the world is, and to enjoy it. The entire world is after your money, or the things you have bought with your money. It is trying to keep them that makes them seem so precious. I live to broaden and enjoy my own life, believing that in so doing I do what is best for everyone. If I ran after birds only to write about them, I should never have written anything that anyone else would have cared to read. I must write from sympathy and love,—that is, from enjoyment,—or not at all. I come gradually to have a feeling that I want to write upon a given theme. Whenever the subject recurs to me, it awakens a warm, personal response. My confidence that I ought to write comes from the feeling or attraction which some subjects exercise over me. The work is pleasure, and the result gives pleasure."

"And your work as a naturalist is what?"

"Climbing trees to study birds, lying by the waterside to watch the fishes, sitting still in the grass for hours to study the insects, and tramping here and there, always to observe and study whatever is common to the woods and fields."

"Men think you have done a great work," I said.

"I have done a pleasant work," he said, modestly.

"And the achievements of your schoolmate Gould do not appeal to you as having anything in them worth aiming for?" I questioned.

"Not for me. I think my life is better for having escaped such vast and difficult interests."

The gentle, light-hearted naturalist and recluse came down the long hillside with me, "to put me right" on the main road. I watched him as he retraced his steps up the steep, dark path, lantern in hand. His sixty years sat lightly upon him, and as he ascended I heard him singing. Long after the light melody had died away, I saw the serene little light bobbing up and down in his hand, disappearing and reappearing, as the lone philosopher repaired to his hut and his couch of content.

WHY HE IS RICH WITHOUT MONEY.

It must not be inferred that Mr. Burroughs has no money. As an author, he has given us such delightful books, dear to every lover of nature, as "Wake, Robin," "Winter Sunshine," "Locusts and Wild Honey," "Fresh Fields," "Indoor Studies," "Birds and Poets," "Pepacton," "Signs and Seasons," "Riverby," "Whitman," and "The Light of Day," published by Houghton, Mifflin & Company.

His writings produce goodly sums, while his vineyards and gardens produce as much as he needs; but the charm of it all is, he knows not the unrest of eagerly seeking it. His is one of the very infrequent instances in which a man knows when he has enough, and really and truthfully does not care for more. Nor is he a "hayseed" in the popular application of that expressive term. When he goes to the city, as he occasionally does (just to reassure himself that he prefers life in the country), he is not met at the station by gentlemen in loud checked suits; he carries no air of the rustic with him. As an Irish wit recently put it, "When in Paris, he does as the parasites do," and he conducts himself and clothes himself as a well regulated citizen should.

So John Burroughs is rich, not in money, but in thought, in simplicity, in the knowledge that he is making the best of life. He has found out that money is not everything, that all the money in the world will not buy a light heart, or a good name,—that there is a place for every one, and in that place alone can a man be of service to himself or others,—that there alone can he be successful; there only can he be "rich without money!"

XLII

A MILLIONAIRE'S DAUGHTER MAKES INHERITED WEALTH A BLESSING TO THOUSANDS.

MISS HELEN MILLER GOULD has won a place for herself in the hearts of Americans such as few people of great wealth ever gain. She is, indeed, one of the best known and most popular young women of New York, if not in the world. Her strong character, common sense, and high ideals, have made her respected by all, while her munificence and kindness have won her the love of many.

Her personality is charming. Upon my arrival at her Tarrytown home, I was made to feel that I was welcome, and everyone who enters her presence feels the same. The grand mansion, standing high on the hills overlooking the Hudson, has a home-like appearance that takes away any awe that may come over the visitor who looks upon so much beauty for the first time.

Chickens play around the little stone cottage at the grand entrance, and the grounds are not unlike those of any other country house, with trees in abundance, and beautiful lawns. There are large beds of flowers, and in the gardens all the summer vegetables were growing.

Miss Gould takes a very great interest in her famous greenhouses, the gardens, the flowers, and the chickens, for she is a home-loving woman. It is a common thing to see her in the grounds, digging and raking and planting, for all the world like some farmer's girl. That is one reason why her neighbors all like her; she seems so unconscious of her wealth and station.

A FACE FULL OF CHARACTER.

When I entered Lyndhurst, she came forward to meet me in the pleasantest way imaginable. Her face is not exactly beautiful, but has a great deal of character written upon it, and is very attractive, indeed. She held out her hand for me to shake in the good old-fashioned way, and then we sat down in the wide hall to talk. Miss Gould was dressed very simply. Her gown was of dark cloth, close-fitting, and her skirt hung several inches above the ground, for she is a believer in short skirts for walking. Her entire costume was very becoming. She never over-dresses, and her garments are neat, and, naturally, of excellent quality.

HER AMBITIONS AND AIMS.

In the conversation that followed, I was permitted to learn much of her ambitions and aims. She is ambitious to leave a great impression on the world,—an impression made by good deeds well done, and this ambition is gratifying to the utmost. She is modest about her work. "I cannot find that I am doing much at all," she said, "when there is so very much to be done. I suppose I shouldn't expect to be able to do everything, but I sometimes feel that I want to, nevertheless." Her good works are numerous and many-sided. For a number of years, she has supported two beds in the Babies' Shelter, connected with the Church of the Holy Communion, New York, and the Wayside Day Nursery, near Bellevue Hospital, has always found in her a good friend. Once a year she makes a tour through the day nurseries of New York, noting the special needs of each, and often sending checks and materials for meeting those needs.

A MOST CHARMING CHARITY.

One of her most charming charities is "Woody Crest," two miles from Lyndhurst, a haven of delight where some twoscore waifs are received at a time for a two-weeks' visit. She has a personal oversight of the place, and, by her frequent visits, makes friends with the wee visitors, who look upon her as a combination of angel and fairy godmother. Every day, a wagonette, drawn by two horses, takes the children, in relays, for long drives into the country. Amusements are provided, and some of those who remain for an entire season at Woody Crest are instructed in different branches. Twice a month some of the older boys set the type for a little magazine which is devoted to Woody Crest matters. There are several portable cottages erected there, one for the sick, one for servants' sleeping rooms, and a third for a laundry.

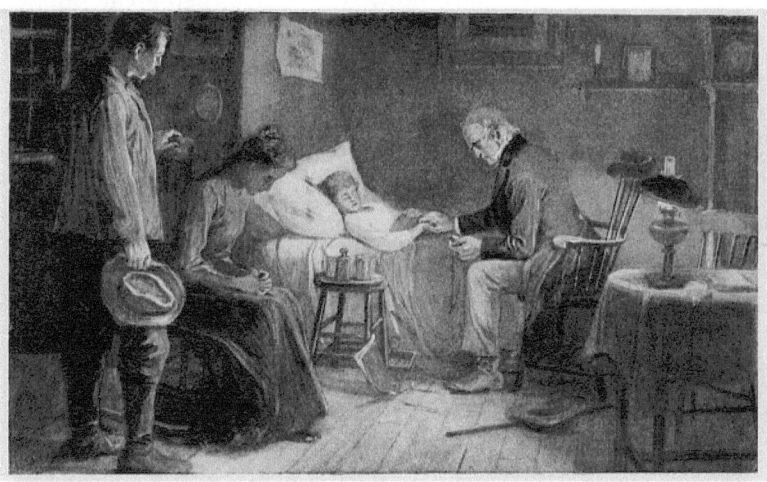

DOMESTIC TRIALS

Miss Gould's patriotism is very real and intense, and is not confined to times of war. Two years ago, she caused fifty thousand copies of the national hymn, "America," to be printed and distributed among the pupils of the public schools of New York.

"I believe every one should know that hymn and sing it," she declared, "if he sings no other. I would like the children to sing it into their very souls, till it becomes a part of them."

She strongly favors patriotic services in the churches on the Sunday preceding the Fourth of July, when she would like to hear such airs as "America," "Hail Columbia," and "The Star-Spangled Banner," and see the sacred edifices draped in red, white and blue.

UNHERALDED BENEFACTIONS.

Miss Gould has a strong prejudice against letting her many gifts and charities be known, and even her dearest friends never know "what Helen's doing now." Of course, her great public charities, as when she gives a hundred thousand dollars at a time, are heralded. Her recent gift of that sum to the government, for national defense, has made her name beloved throughout the land; but, had she been able, she would have kept that secret also.

I tried to ascertain her views regarding the education of young women of to-day, and what careers they should follow. This is one of her particular hobbies, and many are the young girls she has helped to attain to a better and more satisfactory life.

HER MEANS OF EDUCATION.

"In the first place," she said, "I believe most earnestly in education for women; not necessarily the higher education about which we hear so much, but a good, common school education. As the years pass, girls are obliged to make their own way in the world more and more, and to do so they must have good schooling."

"And what particular career do you think most desirable for young women?"

"Oh, as to careers, there are many that young women follow, nowadays. I think, if I had my own way to make, I should fit myself to be a private secretary. That is a position which, I think, attracts nearly every young woman; but, to fill it, she must study hard and learn, and then work hard to keep the place. Then I think there are openings for young women in the field of legitimate business. I've always held that women know as much about money affairs as men, only most of them haven't had much experience. In that field there are hundreds of things that a woman can do."

THE EVIL OF IDLENESS.

"But I don't think it matters much what a girl does so long as she is active, and doesn't allow herself to stagnate. There's nothing, to my mind, so pathetic as a girl who thinks she can't do anything, and is of no use to the world. Why, it's no wonder there are so many suicides every day!"

She is consulted by her agents in regard to all her affairs. "I have no time for society," she said, "and indeed I do not care for it at all. It is very well for those who like it," she added, for she is a tolerant critic.

Her life at Tarrytown is an ideal one. She runs down to the city at frequent intervals, to attend to business affairs, for she manages all her own property; but she lives at Lyndhurst. She entertains but few visitors, and in turn visits but seldom.

I will not attempt to specify the numerous projects of charity that have been given life and vigor by Miss Gould. I know her gifts in recent years have passed the million-dollar mark.

Would you have an idea of her personality?

If so, think of a good young woman in your own town, who

loves her parents and her home; who is devoted to the church; who thinks of the poor on Thanksgiving Day and Christmas; whose face is bright and manner unaffected; whose dress is elegant in its simplicity; who takes an interest in all things, from politics to religion; whom children love and day-laborers greet by fervently lifting the hat; and who, if she were graduated from a home seminary or college, would receive a bouquet from every boy in town. If you can think of such a young woman, and nearly every community has one, (and ninety-nine times out of a hundred she is poor,) you have a fair idea of the impression made on a plain man from a country town in Indiana by Miss Gould.

Helen Miller Gould is just at the threshold of her beautiful career. What a promise is there in her life and work for the coming century!

She has given much of her fortune for the Hall of Fame on the campus of the New York University, overlooking the Harlem River. It contains tablets for the names of fifty distinguished Americans, and proud will be the descendants of those whose names are inscribed thereon.

The human heart is the tablet upon which Miss Gould has inscribed her name and her "Hall of Fame" is as broad and high as the Republic itself.

XLIII

A SELF-MADE MERCHANT SOLVES THE PROBLEM OF PRACTICAL PHILANTHROPY

LATE one afternoon, I stopped to converse with a policeman in Central Park. Another policeman came up. Nathan Strauss was mentioned. "Well, I tell you," said the first policeman, stamping his foot, "there is a man!

"Charities! He's the only man in New York City who gives real charities. Why, when others want to give, they go to him, and have him do it for them. He knows what's what. I tell you, he's the most respected man in New York City;" and the other said, "That's right."

Go on the east side, and ask about Nathan Strauss, and you will hear what is as pleasant as it is rare,—the poor giving a rich man unstinted praise. But do not speak to Mr. Strauss about his work as charity; he dislikes to have it called by that name.

PRACTICAL BENEFICENCE NOT MERE CHARITY.

The greatest blessing that he has conferred on New York, is helping the poor to get pure, sterilized milk. No work of beneficence ever before showed such surprising results. It has reduced the death rate of infants over fifty per cent. Formerly, almost seventy-five per cent. of the children of the very poor died.

It was in the summer of 1893 that Mr. Strauss opened his first milk depot, at which milk was sold for four cents a quart; one and one-half cents a bottle for sterilized pure milk; one cent a bottle (six ounces,) for modified milk, and one cent a glass for pure milk.

It was a loss to the benefactor, but he established other depots throughout the unhealthy portions of the city and in the parks. Doctors received blanks to fill out for milk for those unable to purchase, and to such it was given free. A doctor's prescription was honored. What followed? The death rate was reduced.

At the instigation of his son,—who died from a cold contracted in distributing coal,—coal yards had been established on the docks and elsewhere. The dealers at that time were retailing coal at ten cents and fourteen cents a basket, which made the price from twelve dollars to sixteen dollars per ton. At Mr. Strauss' depots, five-cent tickets procured twenty and twenty-five pounds; ten-cent tickets, forty and fifty pounds, and so on. Most of the coal was carried in baskets on the shoulders and backs of those who, in some cases, had walked miles to obtain it. During the last financial panic, grocery stores were started, where five cents procured a large amount of food. Lodging houses were opened, while a clean bed and a breakfast of coffee and bread could be procured for five cents, and lunch rooms where two cents purchased bread and coffee and corned beef.

The great financier, J. Pierpont Morgan, asked Mr. Strauss to be permitted to assist him in the grocery stores, and a large central depot was rented at 345 Grand street, for which Mr. Morgan furnished the money and Mr. Strauss acted as manager.

Although all these charities in which Mr. Strauss has been interested have entailed a steady loss, a great number of those he benefited and benefits are under the impression that he does not sustain a loss, and that they merely buy for less than they would pay elsewhere.

HE DOES NOT WOUND THEIR SELF-RESPECT.

This is exactly the impression he desires them to possess, in his own words:—

"I do not wish to make a single one feel that he is receiving charity, or is in any way a pauper. Such an impression is harmful, and lowers the standard of those who have a right to consider that they are the sinews of the country. I wish them to feel only that they are buying at low prices. Suppose that those who buy five cents' worth of groceries and trudge a distance for them, are able to pay a little more. The mere fact that they walk far to save a few cents, proves that their hard-earned pennies are precious, and that there is the necessity of getting all that can be obtained for their money."

HE IS A KEEN, ENERGETIC MANAGER.

Such is the keynote of Mr. Strauss' love for humanity: He is not a "lord bountiful," but a generous man, unsolicitous of thanks. There are many records of him having helped individuals. Two young men in his employ were threatened with an early death from consumption. He sent them to a sanitarium in the Adirondacks for a year, when they returned sound in health. During their absence, their salaries were paid to their families.

In business, Mr. Strauss is a strict disciplinarian. He believes that every man should attend strictly to duty, and this is the fundamental secret of his success. In his own words, "Any man, with the ordinary amount of business instinct, can succeed. To succeed, you must be honest, believe in your own ability, and, after having selected your path in life, stick to it through thick and thin. With ordinary mental endowments, there is no reason why any young man should fail.

"Do I think the chances of to-day are as great as some years ago? They are greater. The thing is to take advantage of opportunities and utilize them to the best of your ability. Chances, or opportunities, come to everyone, often, in a lifetime. They should be recognized. Never let one slip; but weigh the possibilities. The great trouble is, a great many young men do not bestir themselves. They fall into a rut, and lack 'ginger.' This is a bustling world, and every youngman should be wide-awake and on the lookout, constantly giving conscientious attention to duty. Duty, integrity and energy are the watchwords, and will direct you on the road to success. Remember, the opportunities of to-day are as great as ever!"

ONWARD, EVER; UPWARD, ALWAYS.

But though Mr. Strauss is a tireless worker, he finds time for a little recreation. He is one of the best gentleman drivers in New York, and he delights to race on the speedway. Still, the background of his life is charity. For many years, he desired to establish a sterilizing plant on Randall's Island, for the benefit of waifs and foundlings taken there. The death rate was very high. At length he gained his point, and a recent unsolicited letter from the matron contained the gratifying statement "that the death rate, since the installation of the plant, has been reduced fully fifty per cent."

In such deeds, Nathan Strauss delights. His life is one of perpetual attention to duty and to business, and he encourages others who would succeed, by saying: "Go at it with a will, and stick to your ambitious aspirations through thick and thin!"

Mr. Strauss himself is an excellent example of the success of the principle which he urges upon others as a rule of life. His whole career has been distinguished by tireless energy and industry, and the interests which are under his control have never suffered for any lack of careful and thorough attention. He has always been deliberate and consistent in adopting and adhering to any policy, public or private, and never deserts those whom he has seen fit to honor with his confidence, save on absolute proof of their unworthiness.

DIVINITY

XLIV

A VARIED CAREER DEVELOPS THE RESOURCEFUL HEAD OF A GREAT INSTITUTIONAL CHURCH AND COLLEGE.

IT was misfortune that proved the fortunate turning-point for Dr. Russell H. Conwell, the pastor of the largest church in America, and president of Temple College, which has upward of 8,000 students. He had not been unsuccessful prior to his ordination to the ministry; on the contrary, he had been a successful newspaper man and lawyer, and had served with distinction in the Civil War. But, in the panic of 1873, he lost most of his investments. I quote his own words:—

"I then wondered,—being always of a religious temperament,—why I should make money my goal."

We sat in his study, and he spoke thus of his interesting life:—

"I was born at South Worthington, Hampshire County, Massachusetts, February 15, 1843, on my father's farm, called the 'Eagle's Nest,' on account of its high and rocky surroundings. At an early age, I went to school, and, when I grew older, worked on the farm. I was sometimes laughed at because I always carried a book around with me, studying and memorizing as I worked.

Yet I was dull and stupid, never stood high in my classes, and could not grasp a subject as quickly as others. But I would stick to it. I am just as dull now, but I preserve my old habit of stick-to-it-iveness. If I am driving a tack and it goes in crooked, I lift it out, straighten it, and send it home. That is one of my golden rules that I force myself to obey."

HE ENLISTED AT EIGHTEEN.

"I went to Wilbraham, and, in 1861, entered Yale College, taking up law, but the breaking out of the war interrupted my studies. I enlisted, but, being only eighteen years of age, my father made me 'right about face', and come home. If I could not fight, I could speak, and I delivered orations all over my native state, and was in some demand in Boston. Finally, in 1862, I could stand the strain no longer, and my father, already greatly interested in the war, permitted me to go to the field.

"I returned a colonel, suffering from a wound, campaigns and imprisonment, and entered the law school of the Albany University, from which I was graduated in 1865.

"I married and moved to the great far west, to the then small town of Minneapolis. There I suffered the usual uphill experiences and privations of a young lawyer trying to make his way single-handed. I opened a law office in a two-story stone building on Bridge square. My clients did not come, and poverty stared my wife and me in the face. I became an agent for Thompson Brothers, of St. Paul, in the sale of land warrants.

"Fortune favored me in business, and I also became the Minneapolis correspondent of the St. Paul 'Press.' I acquired some real estate, and took part in politics. Having once dipped into journalism, I started a paper of my own called 'Conwell's Star of the North.' Then the sheriff made his appearance, and turned the concern over to a man with more capital. Next, I brought the Minneapolis daily 'Chronicle' to life. It united with the 'Atlas,' and the combined papers formed the foundation for the great journal of Minneapolis, the 'Tribune.'"

HOUSEKEEPING IN TWO SMALL ROOMS.

"I continued to practice law. My wife and myself lived in two small rooms. The front one was my office, and the back one, kitchen, parlor, sitting room and bedroom. I had never fully recovered from my wound received in the war. I knew Governor Marshall, and it was he who appointed me emigration commissioner for the state of Minnesota. My duties, of course, took me to Europe."

When Dr. Conwell arrived in Europe, his health, that had been breaking down, gradually gave way, and he gave up his place as commissioner. For awhile, he rested; then, for several months, he attended lectures at the University of Leipsic. That pilgrimage was followed by a number of other journeys across the Atlantic to the principal countries of Europe, and to northern Africa.

"In 1870," continued Dr. Conwell, "I made a tour of the world as special correspondent for the New York 'Tribune' and the Boston 'Traveler.' I then exposed the iniquities of Chinese contract immigration. I next returned to Boston and law, and became editor of the Boston 'Traveler.'"

"But, doctor, had you never entertained a desire to enter the ministry?" I asked.

"All my life I studied theology. The question was before me always: Shall it be law or the ministry? The change came after I had lost considerable money in the panic of 1873. Then came death into my home, and the loss of my first wife. I turned to missionary work in Boston. As time rolled on, I became more interested. But the turning-point was really brought about by a law case. There was a meeting house in Lexington, Massachusetts, in 1877, dilapidated and old. The congregation had left it, so the few old persons who remained decided that it should be sold.

They wished to consult a lawyer, and called me to Lexington. Standing on the platform, I asked the few present to vote upon the question. The edifice had been dear to some of them, and they hemmed and hawed, and couldn't decide.

"At length, I suggested that they put new life into the place. But interest in the building as a place of worship seemed to have departed, although they did not care to see it torn down."

HOW HE ENTERED THE MINISTRY.

"On the spur of the moment, I said that, if they would gather there the following Sunday morning, I would address them. A few came at first, then more. We had to rent a hall in another place. I suggested that they should get a pastor.

"To my surprise, they replied that if I would be their pastor, they would erect a new church.

"I studied for the ministry. One day, I startled the quaint village of Lexington by demolishing the little old church with an axe. The people were aroused by my spirit, and gave donations for a new church. I worked with the men we hired to construct it, and afterward attended the Newton Theological Seminary. Seventeen years ago, I came to Philadelphia as pastor of this church, which then worshipped in a basement some squares away."

"But Temple College, Doctor; how was that started?"

"About fourteen years ago a poor young man came to me to ask my advice how to obtain a college education. I offered to be his teacher. Then others joined until there were six. The number was gradually enlarged to forty, when the idea came to me to found a people's college. Certain gentlemen became interested, and we erected Temple College, which was then connected with this church, but now is a separate and distinct institution. We hope shortly to have it like the New York University. We have rented a number of outside buildings, and have a law school and a seminary. About four thousand attend the evening classes, while four thousand attend the special day classes."

HE IS ALWAYS STUDYING SOMETHING.

"How do you manage to keep up in all the studies?" I asked. "Do you carry text-books around with you in your pockets?"

"Yes, and I always have. I study all the time. I have acquired several languages in that way."

"When do you prepare your sermons?"

"I have never prepared a lecture or a sermon in my life, and I have lectured for thirty-seven years. I seldom use even notes. When in the pulpit, I rivet my attention on preaching, and think of nothing else.

"Application in the most severe form, and honesty, are the means by which true success is attained. No matter what you do, do it to your utmost. You and I may not do something as well as someone else, but no stone should be unturned to do it to the best of our individual ability. I have had a varied life, and many experiences, and I attribute my success, if you are so pleased to call it, to always requiring myself to do my level best, if only in driving a tack in straight."

XLV

AN INSPIRING PERSONALITY WINS A NOTED PREACHER FAME.

ONE of the brightest examples of early success in life is Frank W. Gunsaulus, D.D., one of the sincerest friends of young men striving to climb upward, that America has produced. Chicago has helped him, and he has helped Chicago, to do great things. During his six years of ministry in that city, before he left the pulpit and became president of Armour Institute, he founded two notable institutions and raised over $7,000,000 in money for charitable purposes. On the stormiest of Sunday evenings, after a newspaper announcement that he will speak, an audience two thousand five hundred strong will gather to hear him. It was not an uncommon sight, during one of his series of winter sermons, for men anxious to hear the splendid orator, to be lifted through windows of Central Music Hall, when no more could get in at the doors. His most conspicuous labor has been the founding of the famous Armour Institute of Technology, which now has twelve hundred students, and of which he is the president.

CAN A PREACHER BE A POWER?

I found him in the president's office of Armour Institute.

"Do you think," I said, "that it is more difficult for a preacher to become a power in a nation than it is for a merchant, a lawyer, or a politician?"

"Rather hard to say," he answered. "There are prejudices

against and sympathies in favor of every class and profession. I think, however, that a preacher is more like a doctor in his career. He is likely to make a strong local impression, but not apt to become a national figure. Given powerful convictions, an undertaking of things as they are to-day, and steady work in the direction of setting things right, and you may be sure a man is at least heading in the direction of public favor, whether he ever attains it or not."

"How did you manage to do the work you have done, in so short a time?"

"In the first place, I don't think I have done so very much; and, in the second place, the time seems rather long for what I have done. I have worked hard, however.

"I thought to be a lawyer in my youth, and did study law and oratory. My father was a country lawyer at Chesterfield, Ohio, where I was born, and was a member of the Ohio Legislature during the war. He was a very effective public speaker himself and thought that I ought to be an orator. So he did everything to give me a bent in that direction, and often took me as many as twenty miles to hear a good oration."

MEN WHO INFLUENCED HIM.

"I admired Fisher Ames, to begin with, and, of course, Webster. I think Wendell Phillips and Bishop Matthew Simpson, whom I heard a few times, had the greatest influence on me. I considered them wonderful, moving speakers, and I do yet. Later on, Henry Ward Beecher and Phillips Brooks attracted my admiration."

"Did you have leisure for study and time to hear orations when you were beginning life?"

"In early years I attended the district school. From the twelfth to my eighteenth year, I worked on the farm and studied nights. For all my father's urgings toward the bar, I always felt an inward drawing toward the ministry, because I felt that I could do more there. My father was not a member of any church, though my mother was an earnest Presbyterian. Without any prompting from my parents, I leaned toward the ministry, and finally entered it of my own accord. I was fortunate enough to find a young companion who was also studying for the ministry. We were the best of friends and helped each other a great deal. It was our custom to prepare sermons and preach them in each other's presence. Our audience in that case, unlike that of the church, never hesitated to point out errors. The result was that some sermons ended in arguments between the audience and the preacher, as to facts involved."

HE DID NOT PRETEND TO PIETY.

"I was graduated from the Ohio Wesleyan Seminary in debt. I had no reputation for piety, and I don't remember that I pretended to any. I had convictions, however, and a burning desire to do something, to achieve something for the benefit of my fellowmen, and I was ready for the first opportunity."

"Was it long in coming?"

"No, but you would not have considered it much of an opportunity. I took charge of a small church at Harrisburg, Ohio, at a salary of three hundred and twenty dollars a year. In preaching regularly I soon found it necessary to formulate some kind of a theory of life,—to strive for some definite object. I began to feel the weight of the social problem."

ARE THE DICE OF LIFE LOADED?

"One important fact began to make itself plain, and that was that the modern young man is more or less discouraged by the growing belief that all things are falling into the hands of great corporations and trusts, and that the individual no longer has much chance. My father had been more or less of a fatalist in his view of life, and often quoted Emerson to me, to the effect that the dice of life are loaded, and fall according to a plan. My mother leaned to the doctrine of Calvin,—to predestination. I inherited a streak of the same feeling, and the conditions I observed made me feel that there was probably something in the theory. I had to battle this down and convince myself that we are what we choose to make ourselves. Then I had to set to work to counteract the discouraging view taken by the young people about me."

"You were a Methodist, then?"

"Yes, I was admitted to preach in that body, but it was not long before I had an attack of transcendentalism, and fell out with the Methodist elder of my district. The elder was wholly justified. He was a dry old gentleman, with a fund of common sense. After one of my flights, in which I advocated perfection far above the range of humankind, he came to me and said: 'My dear young man, don't you know that people have to live on this planet?' The rebuke struck me as earthly then, but it has grown in humor and common sense since.

"I left voluntarily. I knew I was not satisfactory, and so I went away. I married when I was twenty. I preached in several places, and obtained a charge at Columbus, Ohio."

A MINISTER'S TRUE IDEAL.

"When did you begin to have a visible influence on affairs, such as you have since exercised?"

"Just as soon as I began to formulate and follow what I considered to be the true ideal of the minister."

"And that ideal was?"

"That the question to be handled by a preacher must not be theological, but sociological."

"How did this conviction work out at Columbus?"

"The church became too small for the congregation, and so we had to move to the opera house.

"My work there showed me that any place may be a pulpit,—editorial chair, managerial chair, almost anything. I began to realize that a whole and proper work would be to get hold of the Christian forces outside the ecclesiastical machine and get them organized into activity. I was not sure about my plan yet, however, so I left Columbus for Newtonville, Massachusetts, and took time to review my studies. There I came under the influence of Phillips Brooks. When I began once more to get a clear idea of what I wanted to do, I went to Baltimore, on a call, and preached two years at Brown Memorial Presbyterian Church.

"I came to Chicago in 1872. Plymouth Church offered an absolutely free pulpit, and an opportunity to work out some plans that I thought desirable."

HIS WORK IN CHICAGO.

"How did you go about your work in this city?"

"The first thing that seemed necessary for me to do was to find a place where homeless boys of the city who had drifted into error and troubles of various kinds could be taken into the country and educated. I preached a sermon on this subject, and one member gave a fine farm of two hundred and forty acres for the purpose. Plymouth Church built Plymouth Cottage there, and the Illinois Training School was moved there, and other additions were made, gradually adding to its usefulness."

"The church grew under your ministration there, did it not?"

"You can leave off that about me. It grew, yes, and we established a mission."

"Was there not a sum raised for this?"

"Yes; Mr. Joseph Armour gave a hundred thousand dollars to house this mission, and the church has since aided it in various ways."

"This Armour Institute is an idea of yours, is it not?"

"Well, it is in line with my ideas in what it accomplishes. It is the outcome of Mr. Armour's great philanthropy."

"Do you find, now that you have experimented so much, that your ideals concerning what ought to be done for the world were too high?" I asked.

"On the contrary," answered Dr. Gunsaulus, "I have sometimes felt that they were not high enough. If they had been less than they are, I should not have accomplished what I have."

"What has been your experience as to working hours?"

"I have worked twelve and fourteen, at times even eighteen hours a day, particularly when I was working to establish this institution, but I paid for it dearly. I suffered a paralytic stroke which put me on my back for nine months, and in that time you see I not only suffered, but lost all I had gained by the extra hours."

HOW TO MEET GREAT EMERGENCIES.

"You believe in meeting great emergencies with great individual energy?"

"There doesn't seem to be any way out of it. A man must work hard, extra hard, at times, or lose many a battle."

"You have mingled in public affairs here in Chicago, also, have you not?"

"Yes, I have always tried to do my share."

"You believe the chances for young men to-day are as good as in times gone by?"

"I certainly do. That is my whole doctrine. The duties devolving on young men are growing greater, more important, more valuable all the time. The wants of the world seem to grow larger, more urgent every day. What all young men need to do is to train themselves. They must train their hands to deftness, train their eyes to see clearly, and their ears to hear and understand. Look at the call there is going to be upon young men when this country will be organizing its new possessions and opening up new fields of activity. What the world needs is young men equipped to do the work. There is always work to be done."

"You think, in your own field, there is a call for energetic young men?"

"It never was greater. A young preacher who looks around him, studies the conditions, finds out just a few of the ten thousand important things that are going begging for someone to do them, and then proceeds to work for their accomplishment, will succeed beyond his wildest dreams.

"The world looks for leaders, it looks for men who are original, able and practical; and all I have got to say to a young man is simply to find out clearly all about a need in a certain direction, and then lead on to the alleviation of it. Money, influence, honor, will all follow along after, to help."

XLVI

FROM THE FORGE TO THE PULPIT,
A LIFE OF DEVOTION AND APPLICATION.

"SO you want me to tell you of myself,—to 'blaw my ain harn,' as we used to say in old Yorkshire. Well, I'm not in love with the undertaking, for what we call a self-made man usually shows that he has made a pretty poor fist of it when he begins to describe the job himself. However, if an outline of my life be of service, I give it gladly. The beginning was in the hamlet of Ilkley, Yorkshire, England, seventy-five years ago. I was born well; that is, I was born of simple, hard-working folk who inspired in me very early a hearty respect for work. My mother was a noble woman. I can see the old home now,—the bit of grass in front, the plum tree, the whitewashed walls, and within, the two rooms with floor of flags, the old prints on the walls, the highly polished chairs and bureau, the tall clock that was always too fast at bedtime and in the morning, and always too slow at mealtime, the little shelf of books,—Bunyan, 'Robinson Crusoe,' Goldsmith, and the Bible, full of pictures. Until I was eight years old, I went to school to old Willie Hardie, who tried to find in me the spring of what we called the humanities in the same way that they used to try to locate a spring of water, namely: with a hazel rod."

THE RIVALS: BOOKS AND THE MAIDEN.

"All the schooling I ever had under the master was finished in my eighth year, when I went to earn my own living in a linen factory. There was an article of faith in our good home creed about which both my father and mother were of one mind,— the boys must learn a trade. So, after six years in the factory, I was apprenticed to the village blacksmith. I was a hard-working, conscientious boy, but full of mischief and fond of fun. I had, however, a ravenous appetite for books. I remember once, when quite small, I stood for a long time before a shop window with a big English penny in my hand, debating whether I should spend it for a particular kind of candy, of which I was very fond, or for a little paper-covered book of travels. At length I went in and bought the book. At meals I used to read, and even when I was courting the lass whom I made my wife, I read all the books in her father's house. I am surprised she did not give me the mitten, and it would have served me right, too.

"Books were not only pleasing to me, but were my passion. Give a young man or maiden a passion for anything,—for books, business, painting, teaching, farming, mechanics or music, I care not what, and you give him or her a lever with which to lift their world, and a patent of nobility, if the thing they do is noble. So I call my reading my college course. It was not an adequate college nor an adequate course, and there have been times when I felt a trifle sad that there should have been no chance for me at a good, all-round education. But there is a chance in the everlasting hunger to read books, and it is with reading as it is with eating,— you grow choice when there is a plenty. You instinctively learn to distinguish what is sweet and wholesome and what is neither, and then you read as you eat,—only the best.

"A great sorrow came to me in 1849. As a result of it, I found my way into a Methodist meeting house, and began to express what I felt. From a few words, uttered standing by my seat in the meeting, I began to preach at irregular intervals; and when I did, it became the custom, after a while, for some one to go through the village, ringing a bell and calling out: 'The blacksmith is going to preach this morning.' The working people came to hear me because I was one of themselves. Then they would have me preach regularly,—at nothing a Sunday and find myself.

"Sometimes I would forget the flight of time and preach for two hours or more. As I look back upon the poor mortals who sat under my ministrations for such a length of time, I am reminded of the judge who, when asked how long a sermon ought to last, replied: 'About twenty minutes, with leanings to the side of mercy.'"

THE LIGHT THAT LED OVER THE SEA.

"My only worldly ambition was to make my way as a blacksmith, but one day there came to me in a flash the thought that I must go to America, where I would have to bow to no class, but would be as good a man as any. Many times in my life these sudden burstings of light, half thought, half feeling, have come to me; and, when they do come, I cease to reason about the matter. I simply obey the impulse with all the power of my will. It would have taken tremendous difficulties to have kept me from embarking for this country after the flash came, and so, one fine spring morning in 1850, I and my little family, with our small store of worldly goods, went aboard the old ship 'Roscius,' made ourselves as comfortable as we could in the steerage, and a month later were in New York.

"I had made up my mind to settle in the vicinity of Philadelphia, and there I soon found work at the anvil. It was lucky I did, for, when we reached our destination, my whole capital amounted to only about twenty dollars. We made ourselves a little home, and I worked at my trade for the next nine years, except during the panic of 1857, when I carried the hod and broke stone on the turnpike for a dollar a day. Meanwhile, I was preaching o' Sundays, again at nothing a Sunday. In 1859, I was asked to devote myself altogether to preaching,—to go to Chicago as a minister to the poor. Well, I went. I said good-by forever to the anvil, in whose ringing voice I had heard so many years the old sermon on the nobility of work."

GENIUS IS DEVOTION AND APPLICATION.

"Before I had been in Chicago a great while, some people got together and built a church, and appointed me pastor of it, hardly so much as saying to me 'by your leave.' It was named the Unity Church, and I remained in charge of it till 1879, when I came to New York to preach in the Church of the Messiah.

"Here I have since remained. My life, you see, is divided into two sections,—forty years in the pulpit, twenty-one years at the anvil. I have worked on long lines, and I will say to young men that, when your homes and your schools have done all they can for you, and you begin the work of life, you must take hold with a will and be content to work hard on long lines. People say that such and such a person has genius for what he or she takes in hand, and that is the secret of the success attained. But I say that genius means strong devotion and steadfast application. You may imagine that you can go from the bottom to the top of the ladder at one jump, but it is not true. Going up the ladder at one jump is like the toy monkey that goes up at a jump and comes down head first. The men and women who achieve true success are all hard climbers. They work in one direction. Our course must not be like a cow-path, all over the pasture and into the woods, for that may mean through the woods into the wilderness.

"I want to say, too, that, if we expect to do well in this life, we must keep well, by all the means in our power;—eat well, and sleep well eight hours out of the twenty-four. Young men should choose, as early as they can, a good and true woman for a wife, and look forward to a noble family of children. My ambition was to have seven, and the all-wise Father gave me nine. If a young man has good mental and physical health and works hard, his life will be sweet and clean. He will do his day's work well and his life's work well, and at the end he will be able to say, with Adam in the play:—

"'Though I look old, yet am I strong and lusty,
For in my youth I never did apply hot and rebellious liquors to my blood,
And did not with unbashful forehead woo
The means of weakness and debility.
Therefore my age is lusty winter, frosty, but kindly.'"

CANADIANS

XLVII

CANADA'S LEADING CONSERVATIVE EXTOLS "THE COUNTRY OF THE TWENTIETH CENTURY."

THOUGH he lost his fight against Sir Wilfrid Laurier for the Premiership of Canada in the general election of 1904, Robert Laird Borden is still one of the Dominion's important figures.

He is in the prime of life. He has conspicuous ability, remarkable energy and an indomitable will. What a man with this combination of qualities sets his mind upon he usually obtains. Mr. Borden freely acknowledges his ambition to reach the top notch of political success, and there are a great many Canadians who believe that he will yet be Premier.

His party, in spite of his defeat, has strong faith in him, and his opponents, now triumphant, admit that he is formidable—a menace to their continuing success. They feel that under the scrutiny of Borden, who is notably quick to detect weak spots in the armor of the enemy, and to drive home strong thrusts, they must put their best foot front. Thus, even in defeat, Mr. Borden is a power.

My first impression of him was obtained in Montreal. He was walking through a hotel rotunda with the long, swift strides that bespeak much physical energy. His head was bowed and his eyes were knit. He struck me at the moment as being a personification of determination and concentration. It was a little later, in his room, that I had my talk with him. Mr. Borden's head is large. His brow rises straight up from heavy brows and eyes which are deep-set and rather small, and twinkle with shrewdness and good nature. The lower part of his face is heavy, indicating the strength of will and purpose which have carried him to the front in Canadian politics.

"I am much interested in success," he said with a smile. "Indeed, the air in Canada nowadays is charged with it. We have a feeling that a far larger part of the success of Canada lies in the future rather than in the past. While the United States developed more in the nineteenth century than any other country in the world, we believe that Canada will show similar industrial advances within the next quarter of a century. We entertain the idea that ours will prove to be the country of the twentieth century. It is not yet as widely known as it should be that we have a somewhat larger area in land than the United States and that this land is not rendered sterile by the winter reign of the mythical personage called 'our lady of the snows,' but is capable of remarkable productivity.

"We are looking forward and not backward, and therefore I am not particularly interested in the unimportant events of long ago; but if you must know, I will say that I was born in the village of Grand Pre, in Nova Scotia, in 1854. Some of my ancestors had lived in the United States. One of them, my great-grandfather, was the law partner of Pierpont Edwards, in New Haven, Conn. They had one of the largest practices in that section of the country, but when the Revolutionary War broke out my forefather remained loyal to King George. He migrated with his family to Nova Scotia, and there the family has since remained.

"Yes, my village is the one which Longfellow has described in his poem 'Evangeline'; and yet, taking full advantage of his poetical license, Longfellow put much in his picture that is purely imaginary. It is, however, a little community whose inhabitants lead the simple life, acquire robust physiques, and strong opinions of right and wrong.

"I know of no better environment than one like this for the passing of the days of early youth. The impressions stamped on the mind of a boy by such people and surroundings never forsake him. However different from the simple beliefs of these villagers his standpoint may eventually become, these first teachings remain what might be called the oak rafters of his philosophy.

"I feel that not a little of whatever I have achieved is due to the fact that the years of my boyhood and youth were spent in an environment of simplicity. I was an industrious student, and when I was about fourteen I was made a teacher in the Acadia Villa Academy in my native country. It was in this school that I had obtained my preliminary education, and I presume I did right in returning to the institution as teacher the modicum of knowledge I had acquired. When I was still in my teens I went to the United States and became an instructor in Glenwood Institute in New Jersey. This proved to be excellent training for me. I think that an experience of this kind is one of the best things in the world for a young man, for the reason that the necessity in it to command others teaches him the more easily to command himself. It increases his dignity, self-reliance and self-respect.

"I decided, however, that I did not care to make teaching my life work, and so I returned to Nova Scotia in 1874 and began the study of law in the offices in Halifax of the firm of Weatherby & Graham. In 1878 I was called to the bar and a few months afterwards was offered a partnership by J. P. Chapman, of Kentville, now a county court judge.

"Together we worked up quite a large practice, but owing to certain circumstances I entered the firm of Thompson, Graham & Tupper. It was not long afterward that the senior member of the firm, Sir John Thompson, became judge of the Supreme Court, and in the course of time Sir Charles Tupper, one of the other members, was called to the cabinet of Sir John A. McDonald.

Subsequently Mr. Graham, the third member of the firm, became Judge in Equity for the Province of Quebec.

"I believe that a large part of anything I have achieved has been due to the fact that I was associated with able men during the impressible period of young manhood. While I did not realize it at that time, I have often thought since that one of the most fortunate circumstances in my life was my close contact with these men. By this means I not only absorbed a greater knowledge of the law than otherwise would have been the case, but also became imbued with certain principles that I have always retained.

"The calling of these gentlemen to high places under the Government left me to the position of senior partner, and the firm name eventually became Borden, Ritchie, Parker & Chisholm. We did a large business, and on the strength of this I was elected and held for several years the position of president of the Nova Scotia Barristers Society. It was in 1896 that I first entered politics, representing Halifax as the Conservative party's candidate for the Dominion Parliament."

"To what in particular, Mr. Borden," I inquired, "do you attribute the fact that you speedily arose to leadership of your party in Parliament?"

Mr. Borden pondered a moment, and then said:

"I can hardly answer that question, but I will say that perhaps the influence I have been able to gain in Parliament has been due to the fact that I have had very strong convictions on all public questions, and have let slip few opportunities to express them. I am usually able to maintain the positions I take in argument, for the reason that I am always careful to fortify myself with facts and with as extensive a general knowledge of the subject as possible before going into a debate or going before the House on any particular issue.

"I believe I have the reputation of being a hard worker. However this may be, I will say that I have always made it a rule to give painstaking attention to seemingly unimportant details in my legal cases, and have frequently won them on this account. This habit, acquired in my youth, of looking after small matters, has made it much easier for me to take care of the large affairs of my clients and of my party since I have entered politics. I know of no surer road to both general and political success than the obvious highway of hard work, coupled, of course, with common sense.

"While the law is the profession which most naturally leads the young man into the political arena, I always like to see the farmer in politics, for the reason that the latter usually has a certain strong simplicity and a degree of sense that often discounts and renders weak in comparison the learning and polish of the professional man. The farmers will be the dominating class in the development of the Northwest, and I hope to see more and more of them in politics."

In his contact with his fellow-men Mr. Borden's manner is marked by a quiet dignity and cordiality that has won him many friends. While he has numerous political enemies, there are few men in the Dominion who are as popular personally. Mr. Borden likes to meet and exchange views with the average citizen. A little story is told of him in his recent campaign which is characteristic. It seems that he was on a night journey on a train and could not sleep. A like wakefulness afflicted a young man in the same car, and at midnight they found themselves together in the smoking compartment. Talk began at once, and throughout the dragging hours these two discussed the great questions of the day. The young man, who had just returned from the States, did not recognize his companion, and the next morning in Montreal he remarked to his friends upon his very interesting fellow-traveler of the night before. He said that they had chiefly talked politics and that his acquaintance had been so convincing that he had been won over to the Conservative party. He described his fellow-passenger, and very much to his astonishment was informed that the latter was Mr. Borden himself.

XLVIII

AN EMINENT SCHOLAR ADVOCATES THE UNION OF CANADA AND THE UNITED STATES.

CANADA'S "grand old man" is Professor Goldwin Smith. With all his opinions Canadians do not agree, but they are united in their admiration for his qualities as a man and a scholar. A mention of his name brings an expression of liking and pride to the face of every intelligent resident of the Dominion. A mention of his well-known belief that Canada and the United States will eventually be one brings a smile which well expresses the average Canadian's feeling that their leading philosopher's idea of the union of the great commonwealths is too abstract and remote to arouse alarm in the patriotic breast.

In spite of this difference of opinion the people of the Dominion highly appreciate Professor Smith's notable attainments as a student and a writer. They realize that from his vantage point of long residence in both England and the United States, as well as in Canada, and from his careful and enlightened study of the problems of these countries, his outlook is perhaps broader than that of any other man in Canada. Professor Smith, now in his eighty-first year, lives in an ideal way in his Toronto residence, The Grange. It was here that I called on him.

The Scotch lodgekeeper and his wife, in their quaint little home at the gate, were quite in keeping with the air of dignified calm which enfolds The Grange. The house, standing well back in the grounds, is representative of the best architecture of a century ago. It suggests reminiscence and contemplation. It has the mellow atmosphere of the past. When approaching it along the gravel walk you feel that you have left behind the hurly burly of everyday life; that this is a most fitting abode for one who stands apart from the crowd to watch the currents of life flow by.

As the house is, so is the man. Tall, slender and a trifle bent in figure, with a thin ascetic face, Professor Smith impressed me as a man who contemplates calmly and critically, but with a very kindly eye, as from high ground, the agitations and excitements of the times. I made a remark to him as to the quietude of his surroundings.

"Yes, I am very fond of the old place," he replied, his eyes kindling with interest. "I am proud of it. You have noticed that all of the woodwork is black walnut, which was the prevailing mode in interior decorations in the early part of the nineteenth century. I have permitted nothing to be changed. I am fond of old things, perhaps, because I am old myself."

"Your activities make it rather difficult to believe that statement," I said.

"Well, I have always tried to retain a youthful spirit," answered Professor Smith, with the engaging smile which is characteristic of him, "and I have been able to keep a fair amount of physical vigor by means of plenty of exercise and regularity in my mode of living. I have always been very fond of walking, and have done a great deal of it. While I am not as industrious in this respect as I used to be, I make a point of driving out in my carriage every afternoon. I rarely let anything interfere with this, because it has a tendency to give me new vitality both in spirit and body."

"While your house is old, Professor Smith," I remarked, "this country in which you live, Canada, is young."

"Yes, we have not progressed as rapidly as the United States; we are yet, in many respects, a people of beginnings. Canadians look forward to the future with very optimistic spirit. We see possibilities of great industrial and agricultural development."

"The average Canadian does not look as far into the future as you do yourself."

"No, perhaps not," smilingly replied Professor Smith. "I

believe that the great majority of our people are not at all in sympathy with my opinion that Canada will eventually become a part of the United States. I have, however, long held this belief. It has been my idea for many years that the whole continent of North America should be, and will be eventually, given up to republican institutions. It has been said of me that I left Great Britain in order to be able to live in the republican atmosphere of the New World. While this is not altogether true, I am wonderfully interested in the great experiment of a government by the people which is now being tried by the United States.

"I think the experiment will prove a success, and that in the end all of the commonwealths on this side of the Atlantic will come sufficiently under the influence of this form of government to embrace it. The Old World powers are by degrees losing their dependencies in the New World. I long ago said, for example, that Spain's hold upon Cuba was becoming weaker and weaker, and would sooner or later become altogether relaxed. I believe that this is likewise true of Great Britain in her relationship with Canada. A wide ocean divides the mother country from her great colony in North America, while merely an artificial boundary line divides us from the powerful republic to the South.

"The bond between Canada and the United States is gradually becoming closer in spite of the little intervening frictions which from time to time arise. I am aware that many Canadians express an antipathy for the United States, but this amounts to little more than talk. Young Canadians have been for many years seeking opportunities in the United States, and at the present time many thousands of agriculturists from the Western States are annually migrating into our Northwest to take advantage there of the productivity of the virgin soil. Numerous American capitalists are investing their money on our side of the line, and thus the commercial connection is constantly becoming closer.

"As a matter of fact, there is in some particulars more intimate union between Canada and the United States than between some of our own provinces. I have often said to my friends that the beginning of wisdom in regard to Canada is the realization of the fact that the natural avenues of traffic and communication lie north and south rather than east and west. We must remember that between various parts of the Dominion nature has set up very formidable barriers, great lakes, high mountains, and wide expanses of uncultivated territory. We must not forget, furthermore, that there are two distinct races in Canada, different in religion, sympathies and general characteristics. Thus it will be seen that without compactness in territory and without a homogeneous spirit among the people, Canada is not a united country. She needs the United States and, by the same token, the United States needs Canada. While I don't expect to see it in my own time, I feel justified in prophesying that the passing years of the twentieth century will bring an equal union between our country and the States. Together they will rise to greater heights of power, influence and civilization than any nation has yet attained.

"I like to see Canadians go to the United States and I like to see young Americans come to Canada. A young man should always have courage to seek the fields which seem to be most promising for him. I am inclined to think that a changed environment is a stimulus to his energy and ambition. A knowledge of the different sections certainly gives him a broader outlook and adds materially to his equipment for the battle of life."

XLIX

AFTER FAILURE AS A GROCER, HE BECOMES THE ABLEST ADMINISTRATOR QUEBEC HAS EVER HAD.

"THE busiest man in Canada," exclaimed a friend in close touch with the government, when I told him that I desired to meet the Hon. S. N. Parent, Premier of the Province of Quebec.

"Parent, you know," continued my informant, "is not only Premier of the Province, but is also mayor of the City of Quebec, minister of lands, mines and fisheries, president of the company that is building a seven-million-dollar bridge across the St. Lawrence, director in the Quebec Railway Light and Power Company, director in the Grand Trunk Railway, and a lawyer with the largest practice in the Province."

This information as to his surprising range of activities, bespeaking a man of remarkable achievement, made me more than ever anxious to talk with Mr. Parent, and I said so to my friend.

"Well," he exclaimed, "the premier is personally one of the most approachable men alive, but all day long in the ante-rooms of his various offices there are crowds waiting to see him. He never appears in the streets of Quebec on foot, but always in his cab, for the simple reason that if he were walking so many persons would stop him that he would be hours getting to his destination. His lieutenants hedge him in, but once past them you are all right."

"What would be a good time and place to call on him?"

"In answer to that I will give you an outline of his movement for his business day, and you may judge for yourself. Promptly every morning at half-past seven he arrives at his law office in Lower Town and sees clients there until ten o'clock, when he goes to the City Hall to take up his work as Mayor. Here he keeps in close touch with every detail of city administration.

"It has been said that not a nail is driven on public property without his knowledge. This, of course, is an exaggeration, but it is the truth that he is the first mayor Quebec has had in sixty years who has been able to run the municipal government without an annual deficit in the treasury. And yet with all his economy he has instituted numerous public improvements. On the strength of this work for Quebec he has several times been reëlected Mayor and has held the office for eleven years.

"After an hour at the City Hall he is driven to Parliament House, where he transacts the business of the Province until half-past one. Here, in addition to his general work, he gives special attention to the land and fisheries department, which he has made the most important in the provincial government. He has so developed it that it yields a larger income than any other.

"Mr. Parent takes a light luncheon at half-past one, and remains in Parliament House until four o'clock, when he returns to his law office, where he gives himself up to cases and to his financial interests until seven. Now comes a dinner which is hardly more hearty than his luncheon, and after this he attends the meetings of committees, which assemble in the evening chiefly to suit his convenience. This schedule is as regular as clockwork. The Premier makes a point of letting nothing interfere with it. Exactly at the times and places I mention you can find him."

Armed with this knowledge, and with a letter of introduction, I sought the Premier at the House of Parliament—a stately building of massive stone, standing out against the sky on the heights of the "Gibraltar of America," and commanding a huge panoramic view of the Lower Town, of the St. Lawrence and St. Charles rivers, of the Isle of Orleans, the wide valley of St. Anne and the sweeping lines of the Laurentian Mountains.

The ante-room was crowded, as I had been told it would

be, but an attendant at once took in my letter and almost immediately returned.

"The Premier cannot see you to-day," he said, "but will be very glad to meet you at this office at twelve sharp to-morrow. If you would accept a little word of advice," he added, official manner giving way to French-Canadian courtesy, "I would say that it would be well to be exactly on time. By five minutes past twelve, if you are not here, the Premier will be engaged with some one else, and then your opportunity will be gone. He never spends time in waiting. This is what you might call one of his peculiarities."

I was on time. At precisely twelve an official passed out of the inner room and I was invited in. As the Premier swung about in his chair with the quick glance and motion that are characteristic with him, I saw a man with a high forehead, a prominent nose, keen gray eyes and a small mustache. His age is fifty-three, but he appears much younger.

"I am interviewing the most successful men in Canada," I said, "and so, naturally, have called on you."

Mr. Parent smiled, with a slight shrug of his shoulders, but made no comment.

"Would you mind telling me how you made your start toward success?"

The light of reminiscence came into the Premier's eyes and his smile was more pronounced. After a very brief pause he said:

"You flatter me by the use of that word success; but if you want to know how I began my career I will assure you that I began it with a failure. My father was a merchant across the river in Beauport, where I was born, and before I was old enough to appreciate how much I did not know I branched out into business for myself. I started a grocery store. It failed, and I decided that I was unfit to be a successful grocer.

"A fair education gained at the normal school enabled me to obtain a place in a law office of S. B. Langois here in Quebec. After I had been with him a short time he strongly advised me to take up law as a profession. I was beginning to feel a pronounced inclination in this direction, and, stimulated by his encouragement, I began to study hard. I took the course at Laval University, and after graduation commenced to practice chiefly at first in the police courts.

"Gradually my clients increased in numbers and my cases in importance. Politics had always interested me. I became somewhat active in this field, and, although I have never tried to practice the art of oratory, for which I have no gift, I was elected to the County Council of Quebec in 1890. Three years later I was made Mayor of the city and not long afterwards Premier of the Province. My career since then has been largely official and a matter of record."

"It is said that you have given the province and the city the best business administration they have ever had. You know more about business now than when you ran the grocery store, for instance."

"Oh, yes," laughed Mr. Parent, "a great deal more. For one thing, I have learned that the price of a business success is eternal vigilance. I have found that the only way to conduct affairs of a municipality along strictly business lines is to watch the committees—to watch their every move. It is in these bodies that the financial leaks are most likely to occur. Not having to carry the main responsibility for public expenditures, committees are inclined to be too generous, too confident of the resources of the treasury. I have no doubt that this is as true in your country, the United States, as in Canada.

"We have ten committees which are meeting constantly. During the eleven years I have been in office I have not missed a single meeting, which is one of the main causes, I think, of whatever success I may have had as a public administrator."

"Your position as the representative of a large population of both French and English must have its difficulties," I remarked.

"These are not nearly as great as you might imagine," quickly replied the Premier. "I don't pretend to try to please everybody, but I do try to treat all alike. I myself, as you know, am of French descent. French was the language of my childhood, but whether a man is English, or Scotch, or French-Canadian, whether he is a Protestant or Catholic, has absolutely no weight with me in my attitude toward him in the discharge of my official duties.

"We French hold to our language and customs because we are proud of them, but there is complete sympathy between the two races in the Province of Quebec. The Anglo-Saxon Canadian admires the French-Canadian because of his honesty, industry and thrift, and the latter admires the former for virtues too numerous to mention. A union between the two, already close, is constantly becoming closer, and it gives me pleasure to think that perhaps I have done something to advance this movement for the common good.

"We are all working for the prosperity and progress of the province and city of Quebec. In this connection the possibilities are so great that even if we were inclined to racial prejudices, which is not true, we would realize that we could not afford to entertain them.

"Quebec is on the threshold of a new era. The great bridge across the St. Lawrence will bring important improvements in the railroad facilities of the city. The harbor, already one of the finest in existence for vessels of large tonnage, will be made even better by the extension of the dock system and by other projects now in hand. The Grand Trunk Pacific Railway, which is about to be built across the continent, will have its eastern terminus at Quebec, and will bring to us for export to the markets of the world a vast quantity of the products of the great Northwest. All this will mean a remarkable stimulus to our city.

"As for the province as a whole, the fertility of the soil, particularly in the neighborhood of Lake St. John, warrants the prediction that it will become the granary of Eastern Canada. The enormous water powers within our boundaries, harnessed for the generation of electricity, will mean the rise of many industries. There is, moreover, an immense wealth of money to be gathered from the many thousands of miles of territory which offer pulp wood for paper making. Year by year the pulp industry is extending, but it is as yet at the very beginning of its development. It will bring many millions of dollars to the province and its people. Young men now at the outset of their careers will grow rich from the new industrial activities.

"But in Quebec we have not yet been educated up, or down, to the idea that the most desirable thing in the world is wealth. We have other standards of success. None of us have what would be considered from the American point of view great riches, and we are well content that this is so. Money, of course, is an excellent thing, and we have no prejudices against its possession, but we are in no feverish haste to acquire it. For example, none of our professional men or politicians are very rich. Political life here offers practically no financial opportunities. The politician who attempted corrupt practices would find himself in an isolated position. There would be no coterie to support him. He would be subjected to adverse opinion that would quickly terminate his career. In my administration of public affairs in the province and city of Quebec there has not been, I am happy to say, five cents' worth of scandal.

"No, as yet, at least, we are not worshippers of the golden calf. All we want in our careers and community is a healthy progress. We desire to keep the city of Quebec, for instance, abreast of the times, to infuse her veins with new blood, but certainly not at a sacrifice of the flavor of the past which makes her the most interesting and picturesque city on the continent. We respect the old, and intend to keep it and the new in harmonious balance."

"How were you impressed with Mr. Parent?" inquired my friend when I informed him that I had had my interview.

"Excellently well," I answered.

"I knew you would be. He is a high grade man, and is very representative of the French-Canadians of this generation. He believes in progress, but not in haste. He has good intentions, and the ability to carry them out. He is much more of a listener than a talker, but when he says a thing, or makes a promise, you may depend upon it."

"You have found, haven't you, that his political opponents admit that they respect him? I thought so. It has been said here in Quebec that in his character there is the combination of the canniness of the Scot, the progressive energy of the Englishman, the conservatism and sentiment of the French-Canadian, and the geniality of the Irish gentleman."

L

CANADA'S LEADING ECONOMIST TELLS HER SONS TO SEEK FORTUNE IN HER OWN DOMAIN.

SIR WILFRID LAURIER, Premier of Canada, said that in matters pertaining to railways the Hon. Andrew George Blair was the Dominion's greatest authority. Whenever in Canada you mention the name of Mr. Blair, whether among his friends or political opponents, the comment is,—an able man.

Since his entrance into political life in 1878, after twelve years of notably successful practice as a lawyer in his native city of Fredericton, New Brunswick, he has continually risen. Though defeated in his first candidacy for the New Brunswick House of Commons, he was elected the second time he ran, in 1879, and since then has always been victorious at the polls.

As a matter of course, through the force of his personality and without apparent effort, he became leader of the minority in the New Brunswick House, and this minority he changed from weakness to strength. His personal following grew so steadily that in 1883 the majority was defeated and Mr. Blair became Premier of the Province. In three general elections, those of 1886, 1890 and 1894, his leadership was sustained. "By this time," remarked a friend of his to me, "Blair was the whole thing in the Province of New Brunswick."

However this may have been, it is true that Mr. Blair had become a figure of national prominence. Long before this he had attracted the attention of Sir Wilfrid Laurier, and when the latter became Premier of the Dominion in 1896 he made Mr. Blair a member of his Cabinet, appointing him to the important place of Minister of Railways and Canals.

It was in this position that he acquired the mastery of railroad problems that has made him Canada's leading authority on transportation. In 1903, because he disagreed with the governmental powers on the subject of the projected Grand Trunk Pacific line across the continent, he resigned his portfolio.

But it very soon became evident that Mr. Blair was a man with whose services it was difficult to dispense. For the purpose of regulating the railroads in their relations with the public more specifically than had been possible by the Ministry of Railways and Canals a Board of Railway Commissioners was provided for by Parliament early in 1904. Mr. Blair had been very active in advocating the organization of the committee, and it was obvious that there was no man in Canada who could approach him in fitness for the place of chairman. Yet his opposition to the government in its great scheme for the new transcontinental road was a very formidable objection to his selection. This difficulty caused much hesitation on the part of the ruling spirits, but in the end it was decided that the Government could not get along without Mr. Blair, and so he was appointed chairman of the committee. After a few months of very successful work he resigned his place, an act which threw the party in power into a state of astonishment and consternation.

In his office in Ottawa I called upon Mr. Blair, and was at once impressed with what might be called his bigness. His face, the lower part of which is covered with the luxuriant growth of beard which is characteristic of the Scotchman, is broad. His forehead is high and wide. His eyes are unusually large. He speaks slowly, and every word has weight.

If one were to make a military comparison it might be said that he has much more of the blunt strength of the cannon than of the glittering sharpness of the sword. And yet this military simile, except at times of heated debate in the House of Parliament, or when his indignation is aroused, is not a fair one, for no man's ordinary manner is more quiet and benign. His energy is not obtrusive, nor of the kind called nervous. It seems to have a far deeper source than this. The truth is, Mr. Blair impressed me as possessing more of the equipment of the scholar and philosopher than of the lawyer giving and parrying quick thrusts in court litigation, or of the politician devising ways and means to hold and increase his power. It is difficult to imagine him indulging in airy flights of eloquence calculated to arouse the admiration of the crowd. Indeed, he never indulges in what is ordinarily called oratory. He depends for effectiveness in his speeches upon the force of fact and logic, with which in Parliament he has shattered numerous soaring bubbles of forensic sentiment.

"I don't care to talk about myself," he remarked to me. "Those good friends of mine who differ with me on matters of public policy are doing that. But I have no objection to saying something on the topic of success, although the subject is so vital and has such an intimate relationship to a young man's ambitions and career that I should have liked to have a little time to consider it.

"I will say, however, that I have been strongly impressed within very recent times with the fact that it is no longer necessary for young Canadians to go to the United States to seek their success. At one time there were much greater opportunities for them there than here, and Canada lost many of her best minds and most promising youths. Not a few of these have achieved distinction in the States, and many young Canadians, inspired by their example, are still seeking fame and fortune across the border. But a larger number are now coming in this direction. The tide has turned. Men with capital, in money or in brains, are beginning to realize that in this twentieth century Canada is the land of opportunities.

"Even in the profession of law, which feels the effect of new conditions rather less quickly than do commercial pursuits, there has been a marked advance toward more business and larger fees. For electrical, mechanical and civil engineers there is more and more work in Canada because of the constant installation of new manufacturing plants and the extension of the railway systems.

"In the field of railroad construction in particular, on account of the necessity of thousands of miles more of track in the new territory which is being opened up, there will be a great deal of work for young men within the next few years. I do not myself believe that it is necessary to build new lines with the haste thought advisable in some quarters, but it is inevitable that sooner or later the country will be covered by a network of railroads. All this railway building and the resulting development of new communities will mean, of course, business and professional openings for a great number of energetic men.

"This will be especially true of our immense Northwest, which is virtually a new country of a wonderful productivity in grain and minerals, and of a vastness in territory difficult to imagine. In the flourishing little city of Edmonton, in the province of Alberta, I happened to meet a man not long ago who was installing mills for the grinding of wheat in the territory to the north, and asked him as to the location of the most northerly mill that he was building. In reply he mentioned a place which, to my astonishment, was over twelve hundred miles north of Edmonton. From this you will see that there are wheat fields nearly sixteen hundred miles north of the boundary line between Canada and the United States.

"The climate here is tempered by the winds which come through the passes of the Rocky Mountains from the warm Japanese current of the Pacific. This makes it possible to grow wheat in the region just east of the Rockies at a latitude much higher than in the section farther east, where the balmy winds do not reach, but the fact that there are wheat fields sixteen hundred miles north of the border will give you an idea of the marvelous extent of the wheat growing country of northwestern Canada.

"I have not the slightest doubt that in the course of the next twenty-five years a great commonwealth will have been developed here, and this means that many thousands of young men who are honest and energetic and wide awake enough to see and seize their chances will acquire comfortable competencies for themselves and families. Some will unquestionably make large fortunes.

"I do not, however, regard the accumulation of a great deal of money as a criterion of success. I think that a man who has been able to build for himself a comfortable home, presided over by a good wife and enlivened with the presence of a moderate number of children, is apt to be far more content with his lot than the man who must carry the burden of a great fortune.

"In the Northwest the conditions will not be such as to enable a man to amass the fabulous wealth which has marked the industrial development of the United States. For one thing, we are so regulating our railroads in their relations to the public that it will be quite impossible for favored shippers to obtain the preferences in freight rates which, in the United States, have been the chief source of the menacing wealth of certain conspicuous capitalists.

"To make impossible all discrimination in rates on the part of railroads has been one of my principal cares in the discharge of my official duties as Minister of Railways and as Chairman of the Railway Commission. If it can be truthfully said that I have accomplished something in this direction I shall feel that my labors have not been in vain."

"What," I inquired, "do you consider the chief requisite of success in political life?"

Mr. Blair paused, and turned his eyes reflectively toward the window. "This is a difficult question," he answered slowly. "There are, of course, numerous qualities that combine to give a man success in politics as in any other pursuit. But I am sure that the prime essential of the man who is ambitious to hold any lasting influence in political life is character.

"If he possesses character he is bound to gain and maintain the respect, not only of his friends, but even of his enemies, and will be able to keep himself afloat on the tempestuous sea of politics long after those who have not been able to resist the temptations of a political career have been engulfed.

"In Canada the political life carries with it no great financial rewards. The young man who enters politics and devotes himself zealously to affairs of state must not expect affluence. If his aim in life is to acquire riches he should by all means keep clear of the political arena until, at least, he has made his success in business."

In his administration in the office of Minister of Railways and of Chairman of the Railway Commission, Mr. Blair showed a pronounced simplicity and unconventionality in his methods. His aim being to accomplish as much as possible, he went straight to the mark, with little regard for formality or red tape. Many times, in his work of railway supervision, he has traversed the length and breadth of Canada, preferring to see conditions for himself rather than to judge of them on hearsay evidence. A single episode may be given as characteristic of his manner of obtaining results. There had been numerous complaints about the dangers of a certain crossing on one of the railways. Some of these complaints had been sent to the office of the Commission, but in the ordinary routine of business some time would have elapsed before action upon them could be taken. Meanwhile the railroad was doing nothing in the matter, and the lives of many children were daily in danger. Mr. Blair, however, had heard unofficially of the crossing. One day he happened to meet on a train the superintendent of the road in question. The train was approaching the dangerous place, when Mr. Blair suddenly remarked to the superintendent: "By the way, Mr. ——, I have heard that you have a bad crossing on the line not far from here. Let us get out and take a look at it."

The superintendent acquiesced, and when the crossing was reached the train was stopped and the two gentlemen alighted. For a few moments they surveyed the woods that concealed the approach of trains and the other conditions which made the crossing hazardous.

"I think we have seen enough, Mr. ——," remarked the Chairman. When they had resumed their seats in the car he said, "Now, see here, it is just as obvious to you as it is to me that this place should at once be made safer. It can be done easily. I wish you would interest yourself personally in the matter." Within a day or two a gang of workmen had made the crossing safe.

LI

A DISTINGUISHED EDUCATOR HAS FOUND CONTENTMENT IN THE SIMPLE LIFE.

"MY life has been very quiet," said Dr. James Loudon, president of the University of Toronto, which is the largest educational institution in Canada. "When I was graduated from this University in the early sixties I became associated with it as an instructor, and have never had any other professional connection.

"My birthplace was the city of Toronto, and my parents, like those of so many people in this province of Ontario, were Scotch. I might remark, parenthetically, that I think the infant that opens its eyes upon the world with Scotch blood in its veins has already made a pretty fair start in life. The typical Scotchman is shrewd and patient, and is the fortunate possessor of that sense of humor which does so much to smooth the way, both for himself and for those about him, and is so conducive to a sane philosophy. Patience, I have always thought, is a particularly valuable asset for the man who desires steady progress in his life."

"The truth of this is exemplified in your own career," I suggested.

"Perhaps so," replied Dr. Loudon. "I well remember Toronto when it was a comparative village, and I have seen it develop into the present brisk and impressive city. I remember, too, our University when its attendance was very small, and I have seen it steadily expand until now it has over twenty-five hundred students, and its influence has become widespread. I myself have been carried up with the general growth. For many years I was professor of mathematics in the University, and have made a special study of the science of physics. Finally, in 1892, chiefly on the ground of long service, I was made the president.

OUT OF DEBT AT LAST

"Our progress here has been preëminently healthy—a substantial process of construction from the foundations up. If, from my observation of this development, any wisdom for young men can be gleaned, I would say to them, eliminate impatience and haste from your plans in building the structure of your career. Build slowly, keeping a careful eye upon the quality and placing of every beam and stone. It is by this method only that you will be able to construct an edifice that will be permanently satisfactory to yourself and impressive to the world.

"A conspicuous evil in the present day life of North America is hurry. Young men, in haste to achieve success, force themselves. The able ones rise with a rapidity which, I think is the reverse of beneficial in the long run. A reaction, an aftermath, is apt to come. Their mental and physical elasticity is apt to prematurely disappear, with the result that they will too soon find themselves past the summit of their careers and traveling the declivity on the other side. The great cities on this continent, and particularly those of the United States, have a voracious appetite for the vitality of youth. They develop a man, yes, but they also exhaust him.

"The mistake of this lies principally in the industrial and social pace of the present. Young men, influenced by the city life about them, spend a good deal more money on their living and enjoyment than they did in the days of my own youth, and in their keen desire to keep in the hunt, so to speak, they seek the goal of wealth cross-lots instead of by the more roundabout but much safer highway. The young women who become their wives have great power in the matter of keeping them away from the dangerous short-cuts. A wife should have an intimate knowledge of the varying conditions in her husband's business, in order that she may properly adjust her expenditures to these conditions. This seems obvious, but the wife's failure in this respect has been the cause of the undoing of many a man.

"The spirit of materialism and commercialism which is so marked has been, perhaps, a necessary factor in the development of the resources of this continent, but I believe that it is gradually losing its position as the commanding influence in our New World civilization, and that it will become a subordinate element in a broader and higher attitude toward life."

"This development will come sooner, I think, in the United States than in Canada, for the reason that the former country has had the start of us in the evolution. The rough work of subduing rebellious nature, of clearing land, of breaking virgin soil for agriculture, of building railroads, has been nearly completed across the border, while on our side it is just beginning. We have a great Northwest, still in large degree a wilderness, to cover with farms and homes and the other appurtenances of civilization. We have yet large sections of our East to dot with the towns and the industries which this territory will bountifully support.

"It is only within a very few years that we have begun to take hold of this work with the zeal and determination that brings success. With this twentieth century there has been born in Canada a new spirit of enterprise. Even here in the University its effects have been strongly felt. It was not long ago that a large proportion of our graduates became teachers, or entered some other professional sphere, and in these fields most of them sought their opportunities in the United States. At the present time the majority of our students have turned toward commercial, mechanical or scientific pursuits, and they are finding their openings within our own domain. The standard of pecuniary compensation is advancing, not only in commerce but also in the professions. For example, even as comparatively a short time as a decade ago the largest fees or salaries for legal services never rose above a very few thousand dollars. Now we often hear of Canadian lawyers receiving many thousands in single fees or in yearly salaries from railroad, banking and other corporations. The general tendency is in this direction, and it is a direct result of our industrial expansion. The interests of Canadian employers of brains and labor are becoming larger. They want more men, and better trained men, and are willing to pay them more than in former years.

"Since a university does not completely fulfil its functions unless it keeps in touch with the life of the people and the currents of broad activity, we of the University of Toronto are aiming to keep pace with the new development in Canada. We are equipping young men for many practical pursuits, and are even establishing close relationships with numerous specific industries. Often of late we have had applications from employers for young men capable of assuming responsibilities. We keep track of the demand for youthful brains and university training, and make a point of being always ready to supply it. A notable factor in the practical work of the university is the Agricultural College, which is located at Guelph, Ontario, and controls 550 acres of land, upon which all phases of farming are carried on and taught to nearly six hundred students. We feel that this college is doing work which is very important. Much of the future wealth of Canada will be derived from agriculture, and especially from wheat growing in the Northwest, where hard wheat, the finest in the world, can be produced in sufficient quantities to supply all the markets of the earth. To adequately develop the possibilities of this territory we must have scientific farmers, and this is the kind we are doing our best to train.

"But with all this effort along material lines, we are by no means forgetting at the University of Toronto what we used to call the broad humanities. The play of the spirit, the exercise of the imagination, the stimulus of literature and art, a tolerant and cheerful philosophy are, after all, the things which make life worth living."

LII

BEGINNING AS TELEGRAPH OPERATOR HE BUILT THE CANADIAN PACIFIC.

"WHAT is success?" questioned Sir William Van Horne, half-reclining within the hospitable arms of a big chair in his luxurious residence in Shelbrooke Street, Montreal.

"You, Sir William, should surely know," I remarked. "You are accredited by the world with being very familiar with it."

"There are numerous subjects upon which the world and I do not agree," replied, with a smile, the famous railroad builder.

"What is success?" he repeated slowly. "You might say, of course that it is the achievement of a purpose, but in the selection and formation of your purpose you may have made a failure, and then the whole is failure.

"Is contentment success? I am sure it is not. Is wealth? Not by any means. Is power? Not at all."

Sir William was silent for a moment.

"The truth is," he said suddenly, "the word success is one of the hardest in the language to define, and I won't attempt it. I should say however, that a man's real success in life can be pretty accurately measured by his usefulness as a member of society.

"He may be rich or poor, courted or ignored, but if he does things which at once or eventually make for progress in the world he is most assuredly a success. If, for example, he discovers something new in science, invents a valuable article, paints a great picture, writes a great book, develops a great industry, or——"

"Or builds a great railroad?" I interrupted.

Sir William smiled, and after a pause remarked, "I suppose

you intend that to be a personal allusion, but we are not discussing personalities. I will say, however, that some of the men whom down in the States you call captains of industry have my admiration. I care very little whether they give money to charity, whether their work is colored by an active consciousness of its value to anybody outside of their families, their friends and themselves. Most of the men of this stamp are just in their dealings, and it is to their initiative force that the United States owes her material greatness. They have started wheels of industry that have given honest work and many of the comforts of life to millions of self-respecting men. They are rich, yes, and we say that riches do not constitute success. Nevertheless, these men have achieved it in one of its highest forms."

It was very plain from his manner that in making these remarks Sir William's thoughts were quite remote from his own career. Yet he himself is one of the most conspicuous and striking representatives on the continent of the class of men he was discussing. His humble start as a small boy in a railway station, contrasted with his present place as a giant in the field of railroading, indicates the height of his own achievement. His career has been a long series of upward steps.

At an age when most boys are playing marbles in short trousers, young Van Horne, forced by the death of his father to earn his own living, obtained a place as general utility boy at a railroad station in the county in Illinois in which in 1843 he was born. Here he saw and seized his first opportunity; that is, he taught himself telegraphy. With this knowledge and a robust personality as his only assets, he journeyed to Chicago and found a position as telegraph operator in the offices of the Illinois Central Railroad. But he did not long hold this place. The telegraphic keys were too small for him. Before he was twenty-two he had gone over to the Chicago & Alton road and was dispatching trains—work of so responsible a character that no railroad company would think for an instant of entrusting it to the ordinary inexperienced youth. But the chief requisite of the train despatcher is care, and care was only one of young Van Horne's conspicuous qualities. He had a combination of others that overshadowed it and brought him promotion to the place of superintendent of telegraphy.

His work was still too easy for him, so they made him a division superintendent. He was now where the officials of other lines could see him, and the Wabash road took him away from the Chicago & Alton to make him their general manager. He was about thirty years old at this time, but he was already looming so large among the railroad men of the Middle West that when the directors of the Southern Minnesota Railway, which was in the hands of a receiver, bethought themselves to look about for a man who could rehabilitate their road, their eyes fell upon young Van Horne, and they asked him if he thought the line could be made to pay.

He replied that he thought so, and gave his reasons. They then asked him to assume the management of the moribund property. He liked then, as he does now, this kind of a job. There were chances in it far above the mere satisfactory performance of routine duty. There were opportunities here to create, to develop, to quicken into new life; and the young man's instincts were all in this direction. So he took hold with enthusiasm, and put the company on a paying basis with a rapidity that amazed the stockholders who made him president. He went back to the Chicago & Alton in 1878 as general manager.

In a lifetime of work very few railroad men achieve as much as this, but Van Horne was still in his thirties and was just beginning. The Canadian Government had been trying for several years to push from the Ottawa Valley a road of steel across its vast domain to the Pacific Ocean, and it had found the task too much for it. Surveys had been made, but there had been comparatively little work of actual construction. Finally, in 1880, it was decided to allow the project to become a private enterprise, and in 1881, under the auspices of Sir Donald Smith, now Lord Strathcona, the Canadian Pacific Railroad Company was organized.

After Sir Donald had found the immense amount of money that was required, his greatest care was to find a man to take charge of the construction, much of it through unknown wildernesses, of the longest railway that had ever been projected. The length of the proposed line and the nature of the country through which it was to pass, made this the most stupendous railway undertaking the world had seen. It was necessary to procure a man fitted for a Herculean task. Sir Donald took stock with the railroad men of the New World and decided that the most promising of them all was William C. Van Horne.

The latter went into the work like a football player bucking the line on a university team. An army of men was hired. At an average speed of three miles a day for many months the steel rails were pushed into the vast forests and the trackless prairies of the Northwest. At last the workmen, urged incessantly by the directing mind of General Manager Van Horne, attacked the Rocky Mountains, and under the charges of picks and powder the mountains made way. At the end of the third year the summit of the Rockies had been reached, and before another twelve months had gone by the forbidding passes in the Selkirks were thundering and trembling from the assaults of dynamite.

The last rail of the main line was laid in November, 1885. In the meantime the company had been acquiring branch connections, and before the end of the year was in possession of nearly forty-five hundred miles of track. Before another six months had passed a great system was fully equipped and Canada had her railway from the Atlantic to the Pacific.

The contract had called for the completion of the road in ten years. Van Horne and his men had finished it in five. Since then the system has been extended until now it embraces nearly ten thousand miles of track, and steamship lines cross the Atlantic and Pacific oceans. One may travel eighteen thousand miles on the route and property of the Canadian Pacific. Cities and towns, many thousands of farms and factories, have sprung up along the way. A new commonwealth in the Northwest has been developed. And it has been done under the general direction of Sir William C. Van Horne.

This is why Canadians, when asked to name living men who have done most to develop the Dominion, couple his name with that of Lord Strathcona. The latter, then Sir Donald Smith, had the courage to assume a burden of railway construction that had proved too heavy for the Government. He thus made possible Canada's only transcontinental railway. Lord Strathcona financed the road, but Sir William Van Horne built it. The latter was its president from 1888 until 1899, when, the creative work being done, the chief difficulties surmounted, he resigned the presidency in favor of Sir Thomas Shaughnessy, and assumed work of less detail as chairman of the board of directors.

Plain William C. Van Horne became Sir William in 1894, when he was knighted by the queen for his high value as a worker in her domains in North America. Being nothing if not democratic, he was inclined, until he became used to it, to wax jocular about his title.

"I'll wager," he is reported to have said one day soon after he had received it, "that my old friends among the railroad boys down in Chicago, who used to call me Bill, will make some pointed remarks when they learn that I am Sir William now."

His bluff geniality is one of the things that Canada likes best about Sir William. She claims him as a citizen, since his greatest work has been done and he has lived for years within her boundaries. She is proud of him and he is proud of her.

"Very few people," he said to me, "have more than a faint idea of the marvelous resources and possibilities of this country. In the provinces of Quebec and Ontario the innumerable streams rushing down from the mountains offer sufficient water power to run the factories of a nation. A beginning has been made here that will eventually lift this locality into one of the leading industrial and electrical centers of the continent. In the making of paper in particular it will be preëminent. Much of the pulp wood used in paper manufacturing has thus far been obtained from Maine, but the supply there will be exhausted in less than five years, and then the paper makers must come to Canada for their supply of pulp. There are already extensive pulp wood industries in the Province of Quebec, but these are bound to be greatly multiplied."

"It is in the Northwest, however, where millions of acres of land await only the plow and seed to produce the finest wheat in the world, that the most inviting opportunities for young men are to be found. The Canadian Northwest is much as was the great region of the United States west of the Mississippi River fifty years ago. It is a country at the outset of its development—a country which needs and will adequately reward the vigorous efforts of young manhood."

"In your field of railroad building I presume there will be great opportunities?" I remarked.

"Undoubtedly," replied Sir William.

"Is the railroad business a good one for a young man?"

"It is as good as any," answered Sir William thoughtfully, "if a young man is content to work for a salary all his life. But he should not be content with this. The salary habit is a bad one, very easy to acquire, and very hard to shake off. The man with his stipend every week is apt to settle into a groove. He adjusts his mode of life to his Saturday envelope. It gets to be about the most important thing in his existence. He becomes tied up to it, and is afraid to make a move that will disturb this pleasant union. Always acting under the direction of somebody higher up, he loses his power of initial effort, and never develops to the full extent of his possibilities. He is likely to be a dependent all his life. If after long years of service he loses his place, as often happens, he is nearly helpless.

"I should say to the young man, strike out for yourself as soon as you can. Don't be afraid to take a chance. Most of the interest of life lies in its uncertainties. You will have your tumbles, of course, but the exercise of standing on your own legs will give you strength to get up again and push on. One of the drawbacks about a salaried place is that a man is apt to lose keen interest in his work, and interest is at the foundation of energy, of concentration of inspiration, even, of all the elements, in brief, that go to make up an adequate performance.

"If you are interested, you will be working with vigor long after most other men have knocked off, tired out, as they imagine. I don't care to talk about myself, but I will say that whatever my efforts have amounted to they have been impelled by strong interest. The man who feels no enthusiasm for his work will never accomplish anything worth while. Work that is interesting does more than all the doctors to keep men alive and young. I endorse what Russell Sage says about vacations. I don't believe in them. When a man who has worked hard for many years decides that he has earned a long vacation, and retires from business, it almost invariably means the beginning of the end for him.

"There is nothing strange in this. He has suddenly cut off the interests of a lifetime, and no longer has momentum to carry him along the road of life. On the other hand, look at the old men who have not retired. Russell Sage himself is an excellent illustration; but in his city, New York, where the business pace is supposed to be very swift and wearing, there are many others—patriarchs to whom the allotted span of threescore years and ten is beginning to look like comparative youth, and yet who still are handling great interests. If they had stopped work when they had made fortunes, most of them would have been long since dead.

"Several years ago a London physician of Lord Strathcona informed him that he was in a bad way; that his friends would be mourning his loss in a week unless he permitted himself to relax. In less than a month the death of the doctor made it impossible to withdraw his injunction, so Lord Strathcona has been on the go ever since. He is over eighty now, and is so vigorous that he thinks nothing of taking little business trips from London across the Atlantic and the continent of North America to Vancouver.

"I believe in recreation of course, but I think it should be of a kind that involves activity of the brain. My own mental rest I find in painting pictures. I am very fond of doing landscapes. This takes my mind into a sphere rather remote from railway earnings and expenditures, and is refreshing."

Sir William showed me a number of his paintings. Some were hung on his walls among those of well-known landscape artists, and in the comparison they suffered not a particle. I commented upon this fact.

"You can't be much of a judge of art," he answered with a smile. In this matter, however, many good judges are agreed. It is remarkable that a rough and ready man of affairs, a captain of industry in the true sense, should be able to paint pictures of a quality that many a professional artist might well envy. But Sir William has even wider interests than railroad building and painting. He is largely identified with financial enterprises of great magnitude in the UnitedStates, and at present is much absorbed in developing the resources of Cuba, upon which island he believes there are opportunities among the finest in the world for men of either large or small capital.

In addition to these pursuits he is a botanist and geologist of wide and accurate knowledge, and has for years been a close student of the civilization and art of the Orient. Nothing delights him more than a conversation on the art products of China, and he takes great pleasure in showing his friends beautiful specimens in his large collection of Oriental pottery and pictures. Supplement to these interests those of the practical farmer and you will have a partial idea of the range of accomplishments of a man who was making his living at the age of thirteen, and is self-taught.

Sir William has an extensive farm not far from Winnipeg. On a recent occasion, when the agriculturists of the region were holding a meeting to discuss their relations with the Canadian Pacific Railway, and to air some little grievances which they thought they had, Sir William was present, and was called upon to make a speech. He slowly arose, and the tillers of the soil settled back in their chairs to listen to words of great weight and finality from the master spirit of the road.

"I am inclined to think, gentlemen," said Sir William in one of his opening sentences, "that we farmers are pretty well treated by this road." From this point the agriculturists were with him to a man, and they left the hall with the feeling that their interests could not be otherwise than well looked after by the railroad company, since at the head of it they had a fellow-farmer.

LIII

AN IMMIGRANT BOY BECOMES A NATIONAL FIGURE IN REFORM.

THERE died recently in Ohio a man who made a high place for himself in the community. He won a strong hold on the hearts of the working people. He commanded also the respect and support of the majority of law-abiding citizens. I refer to Samuel Jones, late head executive and reform mayor of Toledo. His fame spread fast without the bounds of the municipality, and throughout the nation. He became as widely known as Governor Pingree, of Michigan, as a friend of the people, and for his peculiar yet practical ideas of municipal, social and industrial reform. He also won distinction as an able writer and fluent speaker on the social and economic conditions which affect our national life so strongly to-day.

Besides having been a conspicuous philanthropist, reformer, public officer, orator and writer, it is to be noted that Mayor Jones was, first and last, a successful man of business. He was president of the Acme Oil Company; an inventor and manufacturer of a successful patent—the Acme sucker-rod—an implement for pumping oil wells. He made a fortune as a successful operator in oil, and did it without influence or backing—by dint of industry, honesty and push, starting as a penniless boy, with only such education as he could acquire by himself.

A man of large heart and broad mind, his life presents a stimulating, wholesome example of the self-made, conscientious man of wealth impelled by Christian sympathy, and stung into action by what appeared to him to be the stress of political, industrial and social injustice. He embraced the opportunity which his social position afforded, of carrying out and putting into practice some ideas, of which, quoting Heine, he said: "They have taken possession of me, and are forcing me into the conflict whether I will or not."

As showing the man, a few incidents are apropos. On going to his factory, one morning, during the hard winter of 1896, Mr. Jones found that some of his office help had affixed a sign to the outside door, "No help wanted." This he ordered taken away as being contrary to the spirit of the institution. "Men who apply for work should have at least a decent reception," he said; "maybe we can help them by kind words, even if we have no work for them."

During the years of financial depression the prosperity of the oil business was affected by the conditions prevalent throughout the country. Mr. Jones issued an order that his work-people should not suffer. "Keep a little flour in the barrel and see that they have coal enough to keep them warm," was the order.

LOVED BY HIS EMPLOYEES.

He loved to tell how, returning from a trip to Europe, the warmest welcome (and that which shows the popularity of the man) was that given by a crowd of his employees gathered at the Toledo depot to greet him as the train rolled in.

The election of Mr. Jones to the mayoralty of Toledo is an interesting story. He was the candidate nominated in the spring of 1897 to bridge the chasm between the two opposing factions in the Republican party. The saloons, corporations and rings of the city were marshaled against him, but his stout supporters, the wage-earners and the law-abiding people, carried the day after a lively campaign.

The frankness and plainness of Mr. Jones pleased the people as well as his eight-hour day and his ideas of social equality. His messages as mayor to the common council of Toledo were models of businesslike integrity and acumen, showing a vital interest in the welfare of the city, and the value of having a practical and upright business man at the head of civic affairs. Among measures pertinent and practical for the city's self-government advocated by the mayor were a single-chambered board, city bids, the wage system, a municipal lighting plant, the abolishment of the contract system, the establishing of a purchasing agency to stop the waste of department buying, park and street improvements, etc.

His address before the annual convention of the League of American Municipalities, at Detroit, on "Municipal Ownership" was characterized as the best of the convention, and attracted wide attention. It was repeated at Chicago by request.

Mayor Jones was accorded a warm reception in Boston. He addressed the Twentieth Century Club at a dinner; he was banqueted by the Mayors' Organization of Massachusetts; he dined with Mayor Quincy, who is something of a reformer himself; and he gave utterance to his views at a public mass-meeting of Boston's best people. But with characteristic modesty, he looked upon such invitations merely as new opportunities to spread the new gospel, and not in any sense as the means of bringing fame or glory to himself.

The story of Mr. Jones's successful career carries with it encouragement and example for the young man who starts in life with no capital but manliness, courage, persistency, and a willingness to work.

BORN IN A HUMBLE HOME.

Mr. Jones was born in 1846, in Wales. Of his humble home he says: "It could scarcely be dignified by the name of cottage, for, as I saw it a few years ago, it seemed a little barren hut, though still occupied." It was in memory of this modest birthplace over the sea, which is known as *Tan y Craig* (under the rock), that

Mr. Jones named his handsome Toledo mansion Tan y Oderwen (under the oak).

Perhaps the following autobiographical statement will serve better than anything I could write to present his life story:

"I came with my parents to America when I was three years old, and I have often heard them tell of the tedious voyage of thirty days in an emigrant sailing ship, and the subsequent voyage over the Erie Canal to central New York, where they settled in Lewis County. My parents were very poor and very pious. The poverty in our family was so stringent that it was necessary for me to go out and work, and I bear upon my body to-day the marks of the injustice and wrong of child labor.

"At the age of eighteen I heard of the opportunities in the oil regions in Pennsylvania, and at once made my way to Titusville. I landed there with fifteen cents in my pocket, and without an acquaintance in the State. For three days I went through one of the most trying experiences of any young man's life—living without money and seeking work among strangers. I had promised to write to my mother, and I used hotel stationery to fulfil my promise, but was without the necessary three cents then needed to purchase a postage stamp. This was one of the hardest financial problems of my life. I overcame it through stratagem. Seeing a man on the way to the post-office with a bundle of letters I inquired of him: 'Are you going to the post-office?' 'Yes, sir,' he said. 'Will you have the kindness to mail this for me?' At the same time I put my hand into my empty pocket in search of the necessary coin, fumbling my pocket-knife and keys a moment. The gentleman kindly said: 'Never mind, I'll stamp it,' and the revenue was provided which took my first letter to my mother.

THE LAND OF OPPORTUNITIES.

"But I was on the right track; I was in a land of opportunities. I soon found work and a business that was to my taste; a business, too, that the good Providence has removed in part, at least, from the domain of the competitive destroyer—the business of producing crude petroleum from the earth.

"Since 1870 I have been more or less of an oil producer. In 1866, I came to the Ohio oil fields and began the business of producing oil at Lima. Since that time I have followed it both in Ohio and Indiana, and to some extent in Pennsylvania and West Virginia. In 1893 I invented some improvements in appliances for producing oil, and, finding manufacturers unwilling to make the articles, fearing there would be no profit, I concluded to undertake their manufacture. This brought me in contact with labor conditions in a city for the first time in my life. As a rule, labor in the oil fields had enjoyed large wages compared with similar classes outside. I found men working in Toledo for a fraction of a dollar a day. I began to wonder how it was possible for men to live on such a small sum of money in a way becoming to citizens of a free republic. I studied social conditions, and these led me to feel very keenly the degradation of my fellow-men, and I at once declared that the 'going wages' rule should not govern in the Acme Sucker-Rod Company, which is the firm name of our business. I said that the rule that every man is entitled to such a share of the product of his toil as will enable him to live decently, and in such a way that he and his children may be fitted to be citizens of the free republic, should be the rule governing the wages of our establishment.

"To break down the feeling of social inequality, we began to 'get together,'—that is, we had little excursions down the bay. We invited our workmen and their families, and also some other people who live in big houses and do not work with their hands. We sought to mix them, to let them understand that we were all people—just people, you know.

GOOD WILL AND FELLOWSHIP IN BUSINESS.

"As our business increased, we took in new men. We made no special effort to select. We asked no questions as to their habits, their morals, their religion or their irreligion. We were ignoring the sacred rule of business, getting along in a sort of free and easy way, occasionally giving the boys a word of caution, printed on the envelopes; then, perhaps, a little letter expressing good will and fellowship. Then we came to feel the need of a rule to govern the place. We thought, to that extent, we ought to be like other people. So we had the following printed on a piece of tin and nailed to the wall. It's there to-day:

"'The Rule Governing This Factory: Therefore, whatsoever ye would that men should do unto you, do ye even so unto them.'

"In 1895, at Christmas time, we made a little cash dividend, accompanying it with such a letter as we believed would be helpful. In 1896, we repeated the dividend and the letter. In 1897 and 1898 we did the same."

In response to the query as to how he would regulate property interests, Mayor Jones said:

"If you will read the Fourth of Acts and see how property was regarded and treated by the early Christians, you will read what I believe to be the one scientific way in which property can be handled for the good of all. The manifest destiny of the world is to realize brotherhood. We are brothers, not competitors."

"What would you advise the rising generation to do to bring about such a realization?"

"That is an important question," replied the mayor. "Well, I am free to answer that I think by far the best thing that the Acme Sucker-Rod Company has done has been to open the adjoining corner lot as a Golden Rule park and playground. Here is a spot of God's green earth in the heart of the industrial part of our city that is as free to the people as when the red Indian trod there.

And I am sure that the healthful play of the children and the delightful studies of the older ones as we discuss the questions of brotherhood, golden rule, and right relations generally, in our Sunday afternoon meetings, will do more to bring about the era of peace and good will than all else that has been done there. And now we have added Golden Rule Hall, where we may continue these studies, for we must first understand our disease before we can apply the remedy.

TRYING TO LEARN HOW TO HELP EACH OTHER.

"How delightful are the hours which we pass together in the study of the question of right social relations! How much like men it makes us feel to think that we are spending a part of our time in trying to learn how we can help each other; that is, help all the people, instead of devoting it all to the piggish business of helping ourselves!

"As an outgrowth of that spirit, during the past year, we have: our coöperative insurance; the Co-operative Oil Company; the Tuesday Night Social Study Club; and the Equality Club.

"Our experience has been progressive, and, I believe, profitable, in a moral as well as a material way. I have learned much of my relation to my fellow-men. I have learned that we are all dependent on each other.

"In introducing the shorter workday and trying to establish living wages we have tried to acknowledge, in some measure, the relation of brotherhood that exists between us and all other men; for we must remember that this bond is only limited by the confines of the globe itself."

"When I first took office I ignored the professional politicians. Some of my friends expostulated with me. They assured me that I was ruining my future. I answered that I did not want a future based upon a disregard of the principle that an office-holder should faithfully serve the people. I told them that I would be glad to sacrifice my chances for a second term as mayor, if I could be equal to the responsibilities that were pressing upon me. They laughed, and called me impracticable—a dreamer. And yet, my way, so far, has proved successful, even from their standard of success, which, in some particulars, is quite remote from my own. My political experience has been of great encouragement to me. It has made me feel that, despite the seeming success of mere self-seekers, honesty of purpose in the discharge of public duties will, in the end, prevail.

YOUNG MEN IN POLITICS.

"And because I believe this is true, I hope to see earnest, honest young men go into politics. If they have strong convictions of what is right, and force of character enough to hold to these convictions against the many wrongful pressures and influences of political life, they will achieve success of the best kind.

"To-day, more than ever before in its history, the country needs men of this kind. Conditions have come into existence which must be changed. From an experience of years in practical business, I say that the young man now starts in commercial life heavily handicapped. In almost every line of business, he must fight great accumulations of capital, that usually either crush him or make a hireling of him. It has been said that the very name of America is a synonym of opportunity. It was so once, but my experience has taught me that this is entirely true no longer.

EVILS OF CONCENTRATION.

"In my opinion, the reason for the present hard conditions for the rank and file of men is the concentration of business within a few hands. This is a vast subject, and I do not intend to discuss it now. I only want to say that the remedy for the evil, which is felt most keenly by young men trying to succeed in life, lies largely in their own hands. Let them interest themselves in politics and insist, in the first place, that public utilities in cities, such as gas works and street-car lines, which all the people must use, and which bring in great revenues, be conducted for the benefit of the people at large, instead of for a few individuals. This would be only the first step to bring about improvement, but it would be a very important one. The present conditions may be worse before they are better, but, sooner or later, the problem will be solved. I have too much faith in the American people not to be sanguine of the future. And even now, although fortunes cannot be acquired as easily as they used to be, there are ample opportunities to acquire true success in life.

A WRONG CONCEPTION OF SUCCESS.

"The trouble with a great many young men is that they have a wrong conception of success. Large numbers imagine it lies in mere money-making. Yet the average millionaire is not a happy or even a contented man. He has been so engrossed from his youth in piling up dollars that he has had no time for the cultivation of the higher qualities of his mind and heart, in the exercise of which the only true happiness is to be found. You may remember that Emerson said: 'Happiness lies only in the triumph of principle.'

"Of course, a certain amount of money is a necessity, and more of it enables one to enjoy many things which would be an impossibility without it. I am not advising any young man not to do all he can in a legitimate way to make money; but, if he is successful, he must be careful to keep money his servant, and not let it become his master.

SLAVES OF WEALTH.

"Many rich men are the slaves of their own wealth, and their sons, growing up without a purpose in life, never know what real living is. I knew what poverty was when I was a young man, and few have suffered from it more than I. Yet now I am thankful for it, because it made me work. To live, we must work, and one must work to live. It is not birth, nor money, nor a college education, that makes a man; it is work. It has brought me commercial success. I am a practical man, yet I can never express too earnestly my thankfulness that I learned from my good mother to set up usefulness as my standard of success—usefulness to others as well as to myself."

LIV

A "FORTY-NINER" WHO SEIZED OPPORTUNITIES OTHERS FAILED TO SEE.

I FOUND Mr. Armour in his crowded office at 205 La Salle street, Chicago, an office in which a snowstorm of white letters falls thickly upon a mass of dark desks, and where brass and lamps and electrical instruments abound, yet not much more than do the hurrying men. Such a mobilization of energy to promote the private affairs of one man I had never seen.

"Is Mr. Armour within?" I asked, supposing, since it was but 9:30 A.M., that he had not arrived.

"He is," said the attendant, "and has been since half-past seven."

"Does he usually arrive so early?" I inquired.

"Always," was the significant reply.

I presented my letters, and was soon informed that they were of no avail there. Mr. Armour could see me only after the crush of the day's affairs—that is, at 6 P.M., and then in the quiet of the Armour Institute, his great philanthropic school for young men and women. He was very courteous, and there was no delay. He took my hand with a firm grasp, evidently reading with his steady gaze such of my characteristics as interested him and saying at the same time, "Well, sir."

"Mr. Armour," I said, "will you answer enough questions concerning your life to illustrate for our readers what success means?"

The great Hercules of American industry visibly recoiled at the thought of implied notoriety, having, until the present time, steadily veiled his personality and general affairs as much as possible from public gaze.

"I am only a plain merchant," he answered.

A BOY'S CHANCE TO-DAY.

"Do you consider," I said, "that the average American boy of to-day has equally as good a chance to succeed in the world as you had when you began life?"

"Every bit, and better. The affairs of life are larger. There are greater things to do. There was never before such a demand for able men."

"Were the conditions surrounding your youth especially difficult?"

"No. They were those common to a very small New York town in 1832. I was born at Stockbridge, in Madison County. Our family had its roots in Scotland. My father's ancestors were the Robertsons, Watsons and McGregors of Scotland; my mother came of the Puritans who settled in Connecticut."

"Dr. Gunsaulus says," I ventured, "that all these streams of heredity set toward business affairs."

INHERITED QUALITIES.

"Perhaps so. I liked trading as well. My father was reasonably prosperous and independent for those times. My mother had been a school-teacher. There were six boys, and, of course, such a household had to be managed with the strictest economy in those days. My mother thought it her duty to bring to our home some of the rigid discipline of the schoolroom. We were all trained to work together, and everything was done as systematically as possible."

"Had you access to any books?"

"Yes, the Bible, 'Pilgrim's Progress,' and a history of the

United States."

It is said of the latter, by those closest to Mr. Armour, that it was as full of shouting Americanism as anything ever written, and that Mr. Armour's whole nature was colored by its stout American prejudices; also, that it was read and re-read by the Armour children, though of this the great merchant would not speak.

"Were you always of a robust constitution?" I asked.

"Yes, sir. All our boys were. We were stout enough to be bathed in an ice-cold spring, out of doors, when at home. There weren't any bath-tubs and warm water arrangements in those days. We had to be strong. My father was a stern Scotchman, and when he laid his plans they were carried out. When he set us boys to work, we worked. It was our mother who insisted on keeping us all at school, and who looked after our educational needs, while our father saw to it that we had plenty of good hard work on the farm."

"How did you enjoy that sort of life?" I asked.

"Well enough, but not much more than any boy does. Boys are always more or less afraid of hard work."

The truth is, though Mr. Armour laughed it out of court as not worth discussing, that when he attended the district school he was as full of pranks and capers as the best, and traded jack-knives in summer and bob-sleds in winter.

LEAVING THE FARM.

Young Armour was often to be found, in the winter, coasting down the long hill near the schoolhouse; and, later, his experience at the Cazenovia Seminary was such as to indicate that some of the brightest people finish their education rather more suddenly than their family and friends might desire.

"When did you leave the farm for a mercantile life?" I asked.

"I was clerk in a store in Stockbridge for two years, after I was seventeen, but was mixed up with the farm more or less, and wanted to get out of that life. I was a little over seventeen years old when the gold excitement of 1849 reached our town. Wonderful tales were told of gold already found and the prospects for more on the Pacific coast. I was taken with the fever, and brooded over the difference between tossing hay in the hot sun and digging up gold by handfuls, until one day I threw down my pitchfork and went over to the house and told mother that I had quit that kind of work.

"People with plenty of money could sail around Cape Horn in those days, but I had no money to spare, and so decided to walk across the country. That is, we were carried part of the way by rail and walked the rest. I persuaded one of the neighbor's boys, Calvin Gilbert, to go along with me, and we started."

"How did you fare?"

"Rather roughly. I provided myself with an old carpet sack, into which I put my clothes. I bought a new pair of boots, and when we had gone as far as we could on canals and wagons, I bought two oxen. With these we managed for awhile, but eventually reached California afoot."

A MINING VENTURE.

He suffered a severe illness on the journey, and was nursed by his companion, Gilbert, who gathered herbs and steeped them for his friend's use, and once rode thirty miles in the rain to get a doctor. When they reached California he fell in with Edward Croarkin, a miner, who nursed him back to health. The manner in which he remembered these men gives keen satisfaction to the friends of the great merchant.

"Did you have any money when you arrived at the gold-fields?"

"Scarcely any. I struck right out, though, and found a place where I could dig, and I struck pay dirt in a little time."

"Did you work entirely alone?"

"No. It was not long before I met Mr. Croarkin at a little mining camp called Virginia. He had the next claim to mine, and we became partners. After a little while he went away, but came back in a year. We then bought in together. The way we ran things was 'turn about.' Croarkin would cook one week and I the next, and then we would have a clean-up every Sunday morning. We baked our own bread, and kept a few hens, which kept us supplied with eggs. There was a man named Chapin who had a little store in the village, and we would take our gold dust there and trade it for groceries."

"Did you discover much gold?" I asked.

"Oh, I worked with pretty good success—nothing startling. I didn't waste much, and tried to live as carefully as I ever had. I also studied the business opportunities around, and persuaded some of my friends to join me in buying and developing a 'ditch'—a kind of aqueduct—to convey water to diggers and washers. That proved more profitable than digging for gold, and at the end of the year the others sold out to me, took their earnings and went home. I stayed and bought up several other water-powers, until, in 1856, I thought I had enough, and so I sold out and came East."

"How much had you made, altogether?"

"About four thousand dollars."

"Did you return to Stockbridge?"

HE ENTERS THE GRAIN MARKET.

"For a little while. My ambition was setting in another direction. I had been studying the methods then used for moving the vast and growing food products of the West, such as grain and cattle, and I believed that I could improve them and make money. The idea and the field interested me and I decided to enter it.

"Well, my standing was good, and I raised the money and bought what was then the largest elevator in Milwaukee. This put me in contact with the movement of grain. At that time John Plankinton had been established in Milwaukee a number of years, and, in partnership with Frederick Layton, had built up a good pork-packing concern. I bought in with those gentlemen, and so came in contact with the work I liked. One of my brothers, Herman, had established himself in Chicago some time before in the grain-commission business. I got him to turn that over to the care of another brother, Joseph, so that he might go to New York as a member of the new firm, of which I was a partner. It was important that the Milwaukee and Chicago houses should be able to ship to a house of their own in New York—that is, to themselves. Risks were avoided in this way, and we were certain of obtaining all that the ever-changing markets could offer us."

"When did you begin to build up your Chicago interests?"

"They were really begun, before the war, by my brother Herman. When he went to New York for us we began adding a small packing-house to the Chicago commission branch. It gradually grew with the growth of the West."

"Is there any one thing that accounts for the immense growth of the packing industry here?" I asked.

"System and the growth of the West did it. Things were changing at startling rates in those days. The West was growing fast. Its great areas of production offered good profits to men who would handle and ship the products. Railway lines were reaching out in new directions or increasing their capacities and lowering their rates of transportation. These changes and the growth of the country made the creation of a food-gathering and delivering system necessary. Other things helped. At that time (1863) a great many could see that the war was going to terminate favorably for the Union. Farming operations had been enlarged by the war demand and war prices. The State banking system had been done away with, and we had a uniform currency, available everywhere, so that exchanges between the East and the West had become greatly simplified. Nothing more was needed than a steady watchfulness of the markets by competent men in continuous telegraphic communication with each other, and who knew the legitimate demand and supply, in order to sell all products quickly and with profit."

QUALITIES THAT BRING SUCCESS.

"Do you believe that system does so much?" I ventured.

"System and good measure. Give a measure heaped full and running over and success is certain. That is what it means to be intelligent servants of a great public need. We believed in thoughtfully adopting every attainable improvement, mechanical or otherwise, in the methods and appliances for handling every pound of grain or flesh. Right liberality and right economy will do everything where a public need is being served."

"Have your methods improved any with years?"

"All the time. There was a time when many parts of cattle were wasted, and the health of the city injured by the refuse. Now, by adopting the best known methods, nothing is wasted, and buttons, fertilizer, glue and other things are made cheaper and better for the world in general out of material that was before a waste and a menace. I believe in finding out the truth about all things—the very latest truth or discovery—and applying it."

"You attribute nothing to good fortune?"

"Nothing!" Certainly the word came well from a man whose energy, integrity and business ability made more money out of a ditch than other men were making out of rich placers in the gold region.

"May I ask what you consider the turning-point of your career?"

"The time when I began to save the money I earned at the gold-fields."

"What trait do you consider most essential in young men?"

"Truth. Let them get that. Young men talk about getting capital to work with. Let them get truth on board, and capital follows. It's easy enough to get that."

"Did you always desire to follow a commercial rather than a professional life?"

"Not always. I have no talent in any other direction, but I should have liked to be a great orator."

THE GENESIS OF A GREAT BENEVOLENCE.

Mr. Armour would say no more on this subject, but his admiration for oratory has been demonstrated in a remarkable way. It was after a Sunday morning discourse by the splendid orator, Dr. Gunsaulus, at Plymouth Church, Chicago, in which the latter had set forth his views on the subject of educating children, that Mr. Armour came forward and said:

"You believe in those ideas of yours, do you?"

"I certainly do," said Dr. Gunsaulus.

"And would you carry them out if you had the opportunity?"

"I would."

"Well, sir," said Mr. Armour, "if you will give me five years of your time, I will give you the money."

"But to carry out my ideas would take a million dollars!" exclaimed Gunsaulus.

"I have made a little money in my time," returned Mr. Armour, and so the famous Armour Institute of Technology, to which its founder has already given sums aggregating $2,800,000, was associated with Mr. Armour's love of oratory.

One of his lieutenants says that Gerrit Smith, the old abolitionist, was Armour's boyhood hero, and that Mr. Armour would go far to hear a good speaker, often remarking that he would have preferred to be a great orator rather than a great capitalist.

"There is no need to ask you," I continued, "whether you believe in constant, hard labor?"

"I should not call it hard. I believe in close application, of course, while laboring. Overwork is not necessary to success. Every man should have plenty of rest. I have."

"You must rise early to be at your office at half-past seven?"

"Yes, but I go to bed early. I am not burning the candle at both ends."

The enormous energy of this man, who was too modest to discuss it, was displayed in the most normal manner. Though he sat all day at a desk which had direct cable connection with London, Liverpool, Calcutta, and other great centers of trade, with which he was in constant connection; though he had at his hand long-distance telephone connection with New York, New Orleans and San Francisco, and direct wires from his room to almost all part of the world, conveying messages in short sentences upon subjects which involved the moving of vast amounts of stock and cereals, and the exchange of millions in money, he was not, seemingly, an overworked man. The great subjects to which he gave calm, undivided attention from early morning until evening were laid aside with the ease with which one doffs his raiment, and outside of his office the cares weighed upon him no more. His mind took up new and simpler things.

"What do you do," I inquired, "after your hard day's work—think about it?"

"Not at all. I drive, take up home subjects, and never think of the office until I return to it."

"Your sleep is never disturbed?"

"Not at all."

A BUSINESS KING.

And yet the business which this man could forget when he gathered children about him and moved in his simple home circle amounted, in 1897, to over $102,000,000 worth of food products, manufactured and distributed. The hogs killed were 1,750,000; the cattle were 1,080,000; the sheep, 625,000. Eleven thousand men were constantly employed, and the wages paid them were over $5,500,000; the railway cars owned and moving about all parts of the country, four thousand; the wagons of many kinds and of large number, drawn by 750 horses. The glue factory, employing 750 hands, made over twelve million pounds of glue! In his private office, it is he who took care of all the general affairs of this immense world of industry, and yet at half-past four he was done, and the whole subject was comfortably off his mind.

"Do you believe in inherited abilities, or that any boy can be taught and trained, and made a great and able man?"

"I recognize inherited ability. Some people have it, and only in a certain direction; but I think men can be taught and trained so that they become much better and more useful than they would be otherwise. Some boys require more training and teaching than others. There is prosperity for everyone, according to his ability."

"What would you do with those who are naturally less competent than others?"

"Train them, and give them work according to their ability. I believe that life is all right, and that this difference which nature makes is all right. Everything is good, and is coming out satisfactorily, and we ought to make the most of conditions, and try to use and improve everything. The work needed is here, and everyone should set about doing it."

When, in 1893, local forces planned to defeat him in the grain market, and everyone was crying that at last the great Goliath had met his David, he was all energy. He had ordered immense quantities of wheat. The opposition had shrewdly secured every available place of storage, and rejoiced that the great packer, having no place to store his property, would suffer immense loss, and must capitulate. He foresaw the fray and its dangers, and, going over on Goose Island, bought property at any price, and began the construction of immense elevators. The town was placarded with the truth that anyone could get work at Armour's elevators. No one believed they could be done in time, but three shifts of men, working night and day, often under the direct supervision of the millionaire, gradually forced the work ahead; and when, on the appointed day, the great grain-ships began to arrive, the opposition realized failure. The vessels began to pour the contents of their immense holds into these granaries, and the fight was over.

The foresight that sent him to New York in 1864 to sell pork brought him back from Europe in 1893, months before the impending panic was dreamed of by other merchants. It is told of him that he called all his head men to New York, and announced to them:

"Gentlemen, there's going to be financial trouble soon."

FOREARMED AGAINST PANIC.

"Why, Mr. Armour," they said, "you must be mistaken. Things were never better. You have been ill, and are suddenly apprehensive."

"Oh, no," he said, "I'm not. There is going to be trouble;" and he gave as his reasons certain conditions which existed in nearly all countries, which none of those present had thought of. "Now," said he to the first of his many lieutenants, "how much will you need to run your department until next year?"

The head man named his need. The others were asked, each in turn, the same question, and, when all were through, he counted up, and, turning to the company, said:

"Gentlemen, go back and borrow all you need in Chicago on my credit. Use my name for all it will bring in the way of loans."

The lieutenants returned, and the name of Armour was strained to its utmost limit. When all had been borrowed, the financial flurry suddenly loomed up, but it did not worry the great packer. In his vaults were $8,000,000 in gold. All who had loaned him at interest then hurried to his doors, fearing that he also was imperiled. They found him supplied with ready money, and able to compel them to wait until the stipulated time of payment, or to force them to abandon their claims of interest for their money, and so tide him over the unhappy period. It was a master stroke, and made the name of the great packer a power in the world of finance.

SOME SECRETS OF SUCCESS.

"Do you consider your financial decisions which you make quickly to be brilliant intuitions?" I asked.

"I never did anything worth doing by accident, nor did anything I have come that way. No, I never decide anything without knowing the conditions of the market, and never begin unless satisfied concerning the conclusion."

"Not everyone could do that," I said.

"I cannot do everything. Every man can do something, and there is plenty to do."

"You really believe the latter statement?"

"There was never more. The problems to be solved are greater now than ever before. Never was there more need of able men. I am looking for trained men all the time. More money is being offered for them everywhere than formerly."

"Do you consider that happiness consists in labor alone?"

"It consists in doing something for others. If you give the world better material, better measure, better opportunities for living respectably, there is happiness in that. You cannot give the world anything without labor, and there is no satisfaction in anything but labor that looks toward doing this, and does it."

LV

THE BLIND YACHT DESIGNER ATTRIBUTES HIS CONQUESTS TO HIS MOTHER'S EARLY CARES.

> Thus with the year
> Seasons return; but not to me returns
> Day, or the sweet approach of even or morn,
> Or sight of vernal bloom, or summer's rose,
> Or flocks, or herds, or human face divine;
> But cloud instead, and ever-during dark,
> Surround me!   *   *   *   *
> So much the rather thou, celestial Light!
> Shine inward, and the mind, through all her powers,
> Irradiate; there plant eyes; all mist from thence
> Purge and disperse; that I may see and tell
> Of things invisible to mortal sight.
>
> —MILTON.

"SHIPSHAPE and Bristol fashion," a hundred years ago, more or less, was a phrase often heard on every sea plowed by American or English keels. Sailors everywhere applied it only to vessels in perfect condition, with bright paint, clean bottoms, spars well scraped, rigging taut, spare ropes neatly coiled, sails without mildew and of perfect set, pumps free, and all the thousand-and-one details that tell of ideal seamanship properly attended to. Those four words paid the highest tribute of the craft to the skill of the hardy mariners sailing from the tidy little port near the head of Narragansett Bay.

Bristol's long streets, bordered from end to end with widespreading, aged trees, and lined with great dwellings of the colonial era, savor of a delightful antiquity which has not had time to grow musty, but has been well cared for by successive generations and has a sufficiently close relation to modern life to kindle a real affection in us of recent growth, not unlike that felt by the toddling urchin for his white-haired and gold-spectacled grandmother. These big, old houses suggest comfortable bank accounts, stored up by ancestors who built ships or who sailed away in them to the Indies—East or West—and returned with rich freights that profited much.

They built well, those ancestors, and their handsome dwellings seem as sound to-day as the everlasting hill which is known in history as Mount Hope. What eight-foot clocks and brass-handled bureaus, and bulky, shining chests, capable of hiding away mountains of housewifely linen; what high-backed chairs with fantastically carved legs; what large four-posters; what cavernous fireplaces; what wainscotings and curling balustrades; what mantel shelves with under ornaments of sturdy filigree; what yawning closets, as big as bedrooms of this year of grace; what sets of unimpeachable china, brought home by those same nautical ancestors; what attic stores of spinning-wheels and old books, and revolutionary papers, breathing vengeance against his majesty, King George; what thousand and one treasures of the keepsake order do not these old mansions possess within their generously proportioned walls, to say nothing of quaint porches and curious doors and pseudo-classical piazza pillars outside of them! That Bristol of the old, prosperous, gable-ended, ship-building, ship-sailing, cargo-discharging and cargo-embarking days has gone; but this Bristol lives on the memories and the proceeds of those happier, wooden-walled, shiver-my-timbers times, draws on her bank accounts, and takes it easy.

Amid scenes like these, one expects to find men and women of culture and general ability, but does not look for world-renowned specialists. No one is surprised at a display of enterprise in a "booming" western town, where everybody is "hustling"; but in a place which has once ranked as the third seaport in America, but has seen its maritime glory decline, a man who can establish a marine industry on a higher plane than was ever before known, and attract to his work such world-wide attention as to restore the vanished fame of his town, is no ordinary person. Moreover, if such a man has laid his plans and done his work in the disheartening eclipse of total blindness, he must possess some qualities of the highest order, whatever faults he may have, and is thus eminently fitted to instruct the rising generation.

Pursuant to this idea, I called at the office of the Herreshoff Manufacturing Company, at Bristol. The building, formerly belonging to the Burnside Rifle Company, is substantial, but unpretentious, and is entered by a short stairway on one side. The furniture throughout is also plain, but has been selected with excellent taste, and is suggestive of the most effective adaptation of means to ends in every detail. On the mantel and on the walls are numerous pictures, most of them of vessels, but very few relating directly to any of the great races for the "America's" cup. The first picture to arrest one's attention, indeed, is an excellent portrait of the late General Ambrose E. Burnside, who lived in Bristol, and was an intimate friend of John B. Herreshoff.

Previous inquiry had elicited the information that the members of the firm were very busy with various large orders, in addition to the rush of work on the "Columbia" and the "Defender"; so it was a very agreeable surprise when I was invited into the tasteful private office, where the blind president sat, having just concluded a short conversation with an attorney.

"Well, sir," said he, rising and grasping my hand cordially, "what do you wish?"

"I realize how very busy you must be, Mr. Herreshoff," I replied, "and will try to be as brief as possible; but I venture to ask a few minutes of your valuable time, with a view to obtaining suggestions and advice from you to young men and women at the threshold of their careers."

"But why select me, in particular, as an adviser?"

This was "a poser," at first, especially when he added, noting my hesitation:

LET THE WORK SHOW.

"We are very frequently requested to give interviews in regard to our manufacturing business; but, as it is the settled policy of our house to simply do our work just as well as we possibly can, and then leave it to speak for itself, we have felt obliged to decline all these requests. We have a very pleasant feeling toward the papers and their representatives, for they have treated us very kindly; but it would be repugnant to our sense of propriety to talk in public about our special industry. 'Let the work show!' seems to us a good motto."

"True," said I. "But the majority of my readers may not care to hear of cutters or 'skimming dishes,' center-boards or fin keels, or copper coils *versus* steel tubes for boilers. They are willing to leave the choice in such matters to you, realizing that you have always proved equal to the situation. What I want now is advice in regard to the great international human race—the race of life—the voyage in which each must be his own captain, but in which the words of others who have successfully sailed the sea before will help to avoid rocks and shoals, and to profit by favoring currents and trade winds. You have been handicapped in an unusual degree, sailing in total darkness and beset by many other difficulties, but have, nevertheless, made a very prosperous voyage. In overcoming such serious obstacles you must have learned much of the true philosophy of both success and failure, and I think you will be willing, like so many other eminent men and women, to help the young with suggestions drawn from your experience."

"I always want to help young people, or old people, either, for that matter, if anything I can say will do so. But what can I say?"

"What do you call the prime requisite of success?"

"I shall have to answer that by a somewhat humorous but very shrewd suggestion of another—select a good mother. Especially for boys, I consider an intelligent, affectionate but considerate mother an almost indispensable requisite to the highest success. If you would improve the rising generation to the utmost, appeal first to the mothers."

"In what way?"

"Above all things else, show them that reasonable self-denial is a thousandfold better for a boy than to have his every wish gratified. Teach them to encourage industry, economy, concentration of attention and purpose, and indomitable persistence."

"But most mothers try to do this, don't they?"

A MOTHER'S MIGHTY INFLUENCE.

"Yes, in a measure; but many of them, perhaps most of them, do not emphasize the matter half enough. A mother may wish to teach all these lessons to her son, but she thinks too much of him, or believes she does, to have him suffer any deprivation, and so indulges him in things which are luxuries for him, under the circumstances, rather than necessaries. Many a boy, born with ordinary intellect, would follow the example of an industrious father were it not that the mother wishes him to appear as well as any boy in the neighborhood. So, without exactly meaning it, she gets to making a show of her boy, and brings him up with a habit of idling away valuable time, to keep up appearances. The prudent mother, however, sees the folly of this course, and teaches her son to excel in study and work rather than in vain display. The difference in mothers makes all the difference in the world to children. Like brooks, they can be turned very easily in their course of life."

"What ranks next in importance?"

"Boys and girls themselves, especially as they grow older, and have a chance to understand what life means, should not only help their parents as a matter of duty, but should learn to help themselves, for their own good. I would not have them forego recreation, a reasonable amount every day, but let them learn the reality and earnestness of existence, and resolve to do the whole work and the very best work of thorough, reliable young men and women."

"What would you advise as to choosing a career?"

"In that I should be governed largely by the bent of each youth. What he likes to do best of all, that he should do and try to do it better than anyone else. That is legitimate emulation. Let him devote his full energy to his work; with the provision, however, that he needs change or recreation more in proportion as he uses his brain more. The more muscular the work, if not too heavy, the more hours, is a good rule; the more brain work, the fewer hours. Children at school should not be expected to work so long or so hard as if engaged in manual labor. Temperament, too, should be considered. A highly organized, nervous person, like a racehorse, may display intense activity for a short time, but it should be followed by a long period of rest; while the phlegmatic person, like the ox or the draft horse, can go all day without injury."

"Would you advise a college course?"

"I believe in education most thoroughly, and think no one can have too much knowledge, if properly digested. But in many of our colleges, I have often thought, not more than one in five is radically improved by the course. Most collegiates waste too much time in frivolity, and somehow there seems to be little restraining power in the college to prevent this. I agree that students should have self-restraint and application themselves, but, in the absence of these, the college should supply more compulsion than is now the rule."

"Do you favor reviving the old apprentice system for would-be mechanics?"

"Only in rare cases. As a rule, we have special machines now that do as perfect work as the market requires; some of them, indeed, better work than can be done by hand. A boy or man can soon learn to tend one of these, when he becomes, for ordinary purposes, a specialist. Very few shops now have apprentices. No rule, however, will apply to all, and it may still be best for one to serve an apprenticeship in a trade in which he wishes to advance beyond any predecessor or competitor."

"Is success dependent more upon ability or opportunity?"

PREPARE TO THE UTMOST: THEN DO YOUR BEST.

"Of course, opportunity is necessary. You couldn't run a mammoth department store on the desert of Sahara. But, given the possibility, the right man can make his opportunity, and should do so, if it is not at hand, or does not come, after reasonable waiting. Even Napoleon had to wait for his. On the other hand, if there is no ability, none can display itself, and the best opportunity must pass by unimproved. The true way is to first develop your ability to the last ounce, and then you will be ready for your opportunity, when it comes, or to make one, if none offers."

"Is the chance for a youth as good as it was twenty-five or fifty years ago?"

"Yes, and no! In any country, as it becomes more thickly populated, the chance for purely individual enterprises is almost sure to diminish. One notices this more as he travels through other and older countries, where, far more than with us, boys follow in the footsteps of their fathers, generation after generation. But for those who are willing to adapt themselves to circumstances, the chance to-day, at least from a pecuniary standpoint, is better than ever before for those starting in life. There was doubtless more chance for the individual boat-builder in the days of King Philip, when each Indian made his own canoe, but there is certainly more profit now for an employee of our firm of boat-builders."

"Granted, however, that he can find employment, how do his chances of rising compare with those of your youth?"

THE MAN IS THE IMPORTANT FACTOR.

"They still depend largely upon the individual. Some seem to have natural executive ability, and others develop it, while most men never possess it. Those who lack it cannot hope to rise far, and never could. Jefferson's idea that all men are created equal is true enough, perhaps, so far as their political rights are concerned, but from the point of view of efficiency in business it is ridiculous. In any shop of one hundred men you will find one who is acknowledged, at least tacitly, as the leader, and he, sooner or later, becomes so in fact. A rich boy may get and hold a place in an office on account of his wealth or influence; but in the works merit alone will enable a man to hold a place long."

"But what is his chance of becoming a proprietor?"

THE DEVELOPMENT OF ABILITY.

"That is smaller, of course, as establishments grow larger and more valuable. It is all bosh for every man to expect to become a Vanderbilt or a Rockefeller, or to be President. But, in the long run, a man will still rise and prosper in almost exact proportion to his real value to the business world. He will rise or fall according to his ability."

"Can he develop ability?"

"Yes, to a certain extent. As I have said, we are not all alike, and no amount of cultivation will make some minds equal to those of others who have had but little training. But, whether great or small, everyone has some weak point; let him first study to overcome that."

"How can he do it?"

"The only way I know of is to—do it. But this brings me back to what I told you at first. A good mother will show one how to guard against his weak points. She should study each child and develop his individual character, for character is the true foundation, after all. She should check extravagance and encourage industry and self-respect. My mother is one of the best, and I feel that I owe her a debt I can never repay. If I have one thing more than another to be thankful for, it is her care in childhood and her advice and sympathy through life. How often have I thought of her wisdom when I have seen mothers from Europe, where they were satisfied to be peasants, seek to outshine all their neighbors after they have been in America a few years, and so bring financial ruin to their husbands or even goad them into crime, and curse their children with contempt for honest labor in positions for which they are fitted, and a foolish desire to keep up appearances, even by living beyond their means and by seeking positions they cannot fill properly."

"You must have been quite young when you began to build boats?"

HE WOULD NOT BE DISCOURAGED.

"About thirteen or fourteen years old. You see, my father was an amateur boat-builder, in a small way, and did very good work, but usually not for sale. But I began the work as a business thirty-six years ago, when I was about twenty-two."

"You must have been terribly handicapped by your blindness?"

"It was an obstacle, but I simply would not allow it to discourage me, and did my best, just the same as if I could see. My mother had taught me to think, and so I made thought and memory take the place of eyes. I acquired a kind of habit of mental projection which has enabled me to see models in my mind, as it were, and to consider their good and bad points intelligently. Besides, I cultivated my powers of observation to the utmost in other respects. Even now I take an occasional trip of observation, for I like to see what others are doing, and so keep abreast of the progress of the age. But I must stop, or I shall get to 'talking shop,' the thing I declined to do at first. The main thing for a boy is to have a good mother, to heed her advice, to do his best, and not get a 'swelled head' as he rises—in other words, not to expect to put a gallon into a pint cup or a bushel into a peck measure. Concentration, decision, industry and economy should be his watchwords, and invincible determination and persistence his rule of action."

LVI

A GREAT VOCALIST SHOWS THAT ONLY YEARS OF LABOR CAN WIN THE HEIGHTS OF SONG.

OF the five internationally famous singers—Melba, Calvé, Nordica, Eames and Lehmann—none is a greater favorite than Madame Lillian Nordica. She has had honors heaped upon her in every music-loving country, including her own, America. Milan, St. Petersburg, Paris, London, and New York in turn accepted her, and the music-lovers of those cities received her with a *furore* of praise. Jewel cases filled with bracelets, necklaces, tiaras and diadems of gold and precious stones, attest the unaffected sincerity of her admirers in all the great music-centers of the world. She enjoys, in addition, the distinction of being one of the first two American women to attain to international fame as a singer in grand opera. When Madame Nordica was in New York fulfilling her part in the most brilliant operatic season the city had ever known, she lived in sumptuous style at the Waldorf-Astoria Hotel, where I met her by appointment. She accepted the statement that the public is interested in the details of her career as most natural, and was pleased to discuss the philosophy of a singer's success from the view-point of its difficulties.

"You would like to know how distinction in the field of art is earned? Well, it is not thrust upon anyone. The material for a great voice may be born in a person—it is, in fact—but the making of it into a great voice is a work of the most laborious character."

"Is the matter of nationality of any advantage to an aspirant?"

"You wish to know——"

"Whether, in some countries, the atmosphere is not very

favorable to a beginner;—the feeling of the public and the general support given to music not particularly conducive to the musical development of, we will say, a young girl with a promising voice."

"Yes. I should judge almost any of the greater European nations would be better in this respect than the United States; not much better, however, because nearly all depends on strength of character, determination, and the will to work. If a girl has these, she will rise as high, in the end, anywhere; perhaps not so quickly in some places, but no less surely."

"You had no European advantages?"

"None whatever."

"Were you born in the West?"

"No. I come of New England stock. You will understand that more readily when I tell you that my real name is Norton. I was born at Farmington, Maine, and was reared in Boston."

"Were your parents musically talented?"

"Not at all. Their opinion of music was that it is an airy, inviting art of the devil, used to tempt men's feet to stray from the solemn path of right. They believed music, as a vocation, to be nearly as reprehensible as a stage career, and for the latter they had no tolerance whatever. I must be just, though, and own that they did make an exception in the case of church music, else I should never have received the slightest encouragement in my aspirations. They considered music in churches to be permissible—even laudable. So, when I displayed some ability as a singer, I was allowed to use it in behalf of religion, and I did. I joined the church choir and sang hymns about the house almost constantly."

"You had a natural bent for singing."

"Yes, but I needed a world of training. I had no conception of what work lies ahead of anyone who contemplates singing perfectly. All I knew was that I could sing, and that I would win my way with my voice if I could."

"How did you accomplish it?"

THERE MUST BE NO PLAY, ONLY STUDY AND PRACTICE.

"By devoting all my time, all my thought, and all my energy to that one object. I devoured church music—all I could get hold of. I practiced new and difficult compositions all the time I could spare."

"Naturally, your efforts attracted attention?"

"Yes, I became a very good church singer; so much so that, when there were church concerts or important religious ceremonies, I was always in demand. Then there began to be a social demand for my ability, and, later, a public demand in the way of concerts."

"At Farmington?"

"Oh, no. At Boston. I forgot to say that my parents removed, while I was still quite young, to Boston."

"Did you give much of your time to public concerts?"

"None at all. I ignored all but church singing. My ambition ran higher than concert singing, and I knew my parents would not consent. I persuaded them to let me have my voice trained. This was not very difficult, because my church singing, as it had improved, became a source of considerable profit, and they saw even greater results for me in the large churches and in the religious field generally. So I went to a teacher of vocal culture."

"Where, if you please?"

"Professor John O'Neill, one of the instructors in the New England Conservatory of Music, Boston, was a fine old teacher, a man with the highest ideals concerning music, and of the sternest and most exacting method. He made me feel, at first, that the world was mine if I would work. Hard work was his constant cry. There must be no play, no training for lower forms of public entertainment, no anything but study and practice. I must work and perfect myself in private, and then suddenly appear unheralded in the highest class of opera and take the world by storm. It was a fine fancy."

"Did you manage to work it out so?"

"No. It wouldn't have been possible. O'Neill was a fine musician. In his mind and heart, all his aspiration was sincere, but it was not to be."

"Were you ambitious enough?"

"Oh, yes! and most conscientious. Under him I studied the physiology of the voice, and practiced singing oratorios. I also took up Italian, familiarizing myself with the language, with all the songs and endless *arias*. In fact, I made myself as perfect in Italian as possible."

"How much time did the training take?"

"Three years."

"And what was the result?"

"Well, I had greatly improved, but was not perfect. Mr. O'Neill employed methods of making me work which discouraged me. He was a man who would magnify and storm over your slightest error, and make light of or ignore your sincerest achievements. If anything, he put his grade of perfection so high that I began to consider it unattainable, and lost heart. Finally, I gave it up and rested awhile, uncertain of everything."

"And then?"

"After I had thought awhile and regained some confidence, I came to New York to see Mme. Maretzek. She was not only a teacher, but also a singer quite famous in her day and knew the world of music thoroughly. She considered my voice to be of the right quality for the highest grade of operatic success, and gave me hope that, with a little more training, I could begin my career. She not only did that, but also set me to studying the great operas, 'Lucia' and the others, and introduced me to the American musical celebrities. Together we heard whatever was worth hearing in New York. When the renowned Brignola came to New York she took me to the Everett House, where he was stopping, and introduced me. They were good friends, and, after gaining his opinion of my voice, we went to hear him sing 'Faust.'

"That was a wonderful thing for me. To hear the great Brignola! It fired my ambition. As I listened, I felt that I could also be great, and that people, some day, might listen to me as enraptured as I then was by him. It put new fire into me and caused me to fairly toil over my studies. I would have given up all my hours if I had been allowed or requested to."

"And then what?"

"Well, so it went until, after several years of study, Madame Maretzek thought I was getting pretty well along and might venture some important public singing. We talked about different ways of appearing, and what I would sing and so on, until finally Gilmore's band came to Madison Square Garden. He was in the heyday of his success then, both popular and famous, and carried important soloists with him. Madame Maretzek decided that she would take me to see him and get his opinion; and so, one day, toward the very last of his Madison Square engagement, we went to see him. Madame Maretzek was on good terms with him also. I remember that she took me in one morning when he was rehearsing. I saw a stout, kindly, genial looking man who was engaged in tapping for attention, calling certain individuals to notice certain points, and generally fluttering around over a dozen odds and ends. Madame Maretzek talked with him a little while and then called his attention to me. He looked toward me.

"'Thinks she can sing, eh? Yes, yes. Well, all right! Let her come right along.'

"Then he called to me:

"I WAS TRAVELING ON AIR."

"'Come right along, now. Step right up here on the stage. Yes, yes. Now, what can you sing?'

"I told him I could sing almost anything in oratorio or opera, if he so wished. He said: 'Well, well, have a little from both. Now, what shall it be?'

"I shall never forget his kindly way. He was like a good father, gentle and reassuring, and seemed really pleased to have me there and hear me. I went up on the platform and told him that I would begin with 'Let the Bright Seraphim,' and he called the orchestra together and had them accompany me."

"You must have been slightly nervous."

"I was at first, but I recovered my equanimity and sang up to my full limit of power. When I was through, he remarked, 'Very good! very good!' and then, 'Now, what else?' I next sang an *aria* from 'Somnambula.' He did not hesitate to express his approval, which was always, 'Very good! very good! Now, what you want to do,' he said, 'is to get some roses in your cheeks and come along and sing for me.' After that he continued his conference with Madame Maretzek, and then we went away together.

"I was traveling on air when I left, I can assure you. His company was famous. Its engagement had been most successful. Madame Poppenheim was singing with it, and there were other famous names. There were only two more concerts, concluding his New York engagement, but he had told Madame Maretzek that if I chose to come and sing on these occasions, he would be glad to have me. I was more than glad of the opportunity and agreed to go. We arranged with him by letter, and, when the evening came, I sang.

"My work made a distinct impression on the audience and pleased Mr. Gilmore wonderfully. After the second night, when all was over, he came to me, and said: 'Now, my dear, of course there is no more concert this summer, but I am going West in the fall. Now, how would you like to go along?'

"I told him that I would like to go very much, if it could be arranged; and, after some negotiation, he agreed to pay the expenses of my mother and myself, and give me one hundred dollars a week besides. I accepted, and when the Western tour began, we went along."

"How did you succeed on that tour?"

"Very well indeed. I gained thorough control of my nerves in that time and learned something of audiences and of what constitutes distinguished 'stage presence.' I studied all the time, and, with the broadening influence of travel, gained a great deal. At the end of the tour my voice was more under my control than ever before, and I was a better singer all around."

HER FIRST EUROPEAN TOUR.

"You did not begin with grand opera, after all?"

"No, I did not. It was not a perfect conclusion of my dreams, but it was a great deal. My old instructor, Mr. O'Neill, took it worse than I did. He regarded my ambitions as having all come to naught. I remember that he wrote me a letter in which he thus called me to account:

"After all my training, my advice, that you should come to this! A whole lifetime of ambition and years of the hardest study consumed to fit you to go on the road with a brass band! Poh!

"I pocketed the sarcasm in the best of humor, because I was sure of my dear old teacher's unwavering faith in me, and knew that he wrote only for my own good. Still, I felt that I was doing wisely in getting before the public, and so decided to wait quietly and see if time would not justify me.

"When the season was over Mr. Gilmore came to me again. He was the most kindly man I ever knew. His manner was as gentle and his heart as good as could be.

"'I am going to Europe,' he said. 'I am going to London and Paris and Vienna and Rome, and all the other big cities. There will be a fine chance for you to see all those places and let Europeans hear you. They appreciate good singers. Now, little girl, do you want to come? If you do, you can.'

"I talked it over with my mother and Madame Maretzek, and decided to go; and so, the next season, we were in Europe."

"Did it profit you as you anticipated?"

"Very much. We gave seventy-eight concerts in England and France. We opened the Trocadero at Paris, and mine was the first voice of any kind to sing there.

"This European tour of the American band really was a great and successful venture. American musicians still recall the *furore* which it created and the prestige which it gained at home. Mr. Gilmore was proud of his leading soloists. In Paris, where the great audiences went wild over my singing, he came to praise me personally in unmeasured terms. 'My dear,' he said, 'you are going to be a great singer. You are going to be crowned in your own country yet. Mark my words: they are going to put diamonds on your brow!'

"At the end of that tour I decided to spend some of my earnings on further study in Italy. Accordingly, I went to Milan, to the singing teacher San Giovanni. On arriving there, I visited the old teacher and stated my object. I said that I wanted to sing in grand opera.

"WHY DON'T YOU SING IN GRAND OPERA?"

"'All right!' he answered; 'let me hear your voice.'

"I sang an *aria* from 'Lucia'; and when I was through, he said dryly: 'You want to sing in grand opera?'

"'Yes.'

"'Well, why don't you?'

"'I need training.'

"'Nonsense!' he answered. 'We will attend to that. You need a few months to practice Italian methods—that is all.'

"So I spent three months with him. After much preparation, I made my *début* as Violetta in Verdi's opera, 'La Traviata,' at the Teatro Grande, in Brescia."

The details of Madame Nordica's Italian appearance are very interesting. Her success was instantaneous. Her fame went up and down the land, and across the water—to her home. She next sang in Gounod's "Faust," at Geneva, and soon afterwards appeared at Navarro, singing Alice in Meyerbeer's "Roberto," the enthusiastic and delighted subscribers presenting her with a handsome set of rubies and pearls. After that she was engaged to sing at the Russian capital, and accordingly went to St. Petersburg, where, in October, 1881, she made her *début* as La Filma in "Mignon."

There, also, her success was great. She was the favorite of the society of the court, and received pleasant attentions from every quarter. Presents were made her, and inducements for her continued presence until two winters had passed. Then she decided to revisit France and Paris.

THIS WAS HER CROWNING TRIUMPH.

"I wanted to sing in grand opera at Paris," she said to me. "I wanted to know that I could appear successfully in that grand place. I counted my achievements nothing until I could do that."

"And did you?"

"Yes. In July, 1882, I appeared there."

This was her greatest triumph. In the part of Marguerite she took the house by storm, and won from the composer the highest encomiums. Subsequently, she appeared with equal success as Ophélie, having been specially prepared for both these rôles by the respective composers, Charles Gounod and Ambroise Thomas.

"You should have been satisfied after that," I said.

"I was," she answered. "So thoroughly was I satisfied that, soon afterwards, I gave up my career and was married. For two years I remained away from the public, but, after that time, my husband having died, I decided to return. I made my first appearance at the Burton Theater in London, and was doing well enough when Colonel Mapleson came to me. He was going to produce grand opera—in fact, he was going to open Covent Garden, which had been closed for a long time, with a big company. He was another interesting character. I found him to be generous and kind-hearted and happy-spirited as anyone could be. When he came to me it was in the most friendly manner. 'I am going to open Covent Garden,' he said. 'Now, here is your chance to sing there. All the great singers have appeared there—Patti, Gerster, Nilsson, Tietjens—now it's your turn—come and sing.'

"'How about terms?' I asked.

"'Terms!' he exclaimed; 'terms! Don't let such little details stand in your way. What is money compared to this? Ignore money. Think of the honor, of the memories of the place, of what people think of it;' and then he waved his arms dramatically.

"Well, we came to terms, not wholly sacrificial on my part, and the season began. Covent Garden had not been open for a long time. It was in the spring of the year, cold and damp. There was a crowded house, though, because fashion accompanied the Prince of Wales there. He came, night after night, and heard the opera through with an overcoat on.

"It was no blessed task for me, or healthy, either, but the Lord has blessed me with a sound constitution. I sang my parts, as they should be sung, some in bare arms and shoulders, with too little clothing for such a temperature. But it was Covent Garden, and so I bore up under it."

"What was the next venture?"

"Nothing much more interesting. The summer after that season I visited Ems, where the De Reszkes were. One day they said: 'We are going to Bayreuth to hear the music, don't you want to go along?'

"I thought it over, and decided that I did. My mother and I packed up and departed. When I got there and saw those splendid performances I was entranced. It was perfectly beautiful. Everything was arranged after an ideal fashion. I had a great desire to sing there, and boasted to my mother that I would. When I came away I was fully determined to carry out that boast."

"Could you speak German?"

"Not at all. I began, though, at once, to study it; and when I could talk it sufficiently I went to Bayreuth and saw Madame Wagner."

THE KINDNESS OF FRAU WAGNER.

"Did you find her the imperious old lady she is said to be?"

"Not at all. She welcomed me most heartily; and when I told her that I had come to see if I could not sing there she seemed much pleased. She treated me like a daughter, explained all that she was trying to do, and gave me a world of encouragement. Finally I arranged to sing and create 'Elsa' after my own idea of it during the season following the one then approaching."

"What did you do meanwhile?"

"I came to New York to fulfil my contract for the season of 1894-1895. While doing that I made a study of Wagner's, and, indeed, of all German music; and when the season was over went back and sang it."

"To Frau Wagner's satisfaction?"

"Yes."

"Have you found your work very exacting?"

"Decidedly so. It leaves little time for anything else."

"To do what you have done requires a powerful physique, to begin with?"

"Yes, I should judge so."

"Are you ever put under extraordinary mental strain?"

"Occasionally."

"In what manner?"

"Why, in my manner of study. I remember once, during my season under Augustus Harris, of an incident of this order. He gave a garden party one Sunday to which several of his company were invited, myself included. When the afternoon was well along he came to me and said: 'Did you ever sing "Valencia" in "The Huguenots"?' I told him I had not.

"'Do you think you could learn the music and sing it by next Saturday night?'

"I felt a little appalled at the question, but ventured to say that I could. I knew that hard work would do it.

"'Then do,' he replied; 'for I must have you sing it.'

"Let me ask you one thing," I said. "Has America good musical material?"

THE MUSICAL TALENT OF AMERICAN GIRLS.

"As much as any other country, and more, I should think. The higher average of intelligence here should yield a greater percentage of musical intelligence."

"Then there ought to be a number of great American women singers in the future?"

"There ought to be, but it is a question whether there will be. They are not cut out for the work which it requires to develop a good voice."

"You think there is good material for great voices in American women, but not sufficient energy?"

"That is my fear, not my belief. I have noticed that young women here seem to underestimate the cost of distinction. It means more than most of them are prepared to give; and when they face the exactions of art they falter and drop out. Hence we have many middle-class singers, but few really powerful ones."

"What are these exactions you speak of?"

"Time, money, and loss of friends, of pleasure. To be a great singer means, first, to be a great student. To be a great student means that you have no time for balls and parties, very little for friends, and less for carriage rides and pleasant strolls. All that is really left is a shortened allowance of sleep, of time for meals and time for exercise."

"Did you ever imagine that people leaped into permanent fame when still young and without much effort on their part?"

"I did. But I discovered that real fame—permanent recognition which cannot be taken away from you—is acquired only by a lifetime of most earnest labor. People are never internationally recognized until they have reached middle life. Many persons gain notoriety young, but that goes as quickly as it comes. All true success is founded on real accomplishment, acquired with difficulty; and so, when you see some one accounted great, you will usually find him to be in the prime of life or past it."

"You grant that many young people have genius?"

"Certainly I do. Many of them have it. They will have waited long, however, before it has been trained into valuable service. The world gives very little recognition for a great deal of labor paid in; and when I earn a thousand dollars for a half hour's singing sometimes it does not nearly average up for all the years and for the labor much more difficult, which I contributed without recompense."

VOLUME TWO

MEN AND WOMEN WHO
HAVE ACHIEVED EMINENCE

SUCCESS MAXIMS

If I were a cobbler, it would be my pride
The best of all cobblers to be;
If I were a tinker, no tinker beside
Should mend an old kettle like me.
—Old Song.

People do not lack strength; they lack will.—Victor Hugo.

Every man stamps his own value upon himself, and we are great or little according to our own will.—Samuel Smiles.

The saddest failures in life are those that come from not putting forth of the power and will to succeed.—Whipple.

As men in a crowd instinctively make room for one who would force his way through it, so mankind makes way for one who rushes toward an object beyond them.—Dwight.

There can be no doubt that the captains of industry to-day, using that term in its broadest sense, are men who began life as poor boys.—Seth Low.

Do noble things, not dream them, all day long,

And so make life, death and the vast forever one grand, sweet song. —Charles Kingsley.

Dost thou love life? Then do not squander time, for that is the stuff life is made of.—Franklin.

The high prize of life, the crowning fortune of a man, is to be born with a bias to some pursuit, which finds him in employment and happiness.—EMERSON.

A man that is young in years may be old in hours, if he have lost no time.—BACON.

The one prudence in life is concentration; the one evil is dissipation; and it makes no difference whether our dissipations are coarse or fine.... Everything is good which takes away one plaything and delusion more, and sends us home to add one stroke of faithful work.—EMERSON.

MEN AND WOMEN
WHO HAVE ACHIEVED EMINENCE

STATESMEN

- Thomas B. Reed
- William Boyd Allison
- George F. Hoar
- Elihu Root
- Theodore Roosevelt
- Henry Cabot Lodge
- Grover Cleveland (*Copyright, 1903, by Rockwood, N.Y.*)
- John Hay
- Richard Olney

CANADIANS OF NOTE

- Sir T. Shaughnessy
- Sir Wm. Van Horne
- Lord Strathcona
- Simon N. Parent
- Sir Wilfrid Laurier
- Robt. L. Borden
- A. G. Blair
- Jas. Loudon
- Goldwin Smith

CANADIANS OF NOTE

- Wm. Peterson
- George W. Ross
- Dr. Wm. Osler
- Lord Mount Stephen
- Sir Geo. Drummond
- George A. Cox
- Timothy Eaton
- William S. Fielding
- Charles Fitzpatrick

LITTLE VISITS WITH GREAT AMERICANS

CAPTAINS OF INDUSTRY

- Charles H. Cramp
- John B. Herreschoff
- Charles M. Hays
- Lewis Nixon
- Andrew Carnegie
- *(Copyright, 1900, by Rockwood, N. Y.)*
- Charles R. Flint
- E. G. Acheson
- J. H. Patterson
- Robert C. Clowry

LITTLE VISITS WITH GREAT AMERICANS

MANUFACTURERS

- C. W. Post
- John W. Wheeler
- Phill. D. Armour
- A. G. Spalding
- Albert A. Pope
- Charles Eastman
- Hugh T. Chisholm
- Theo. L. De Vinne
- W. L. Douglass

LITTLE VISITS WITH GREAT AMERICANS

TRANSPORTATION LEADERS

- August Belmont
- Clement Acton Griscom
- Herbert H. Vreeland
- George Gould
- J. J. Hill
- M. E. Ingalls
- A. J. Cassatt
- Geo. H. Daniels
- George F. Baer (*Copyright, 1901, by F. Gutekunst*)

LITTLE VISITS WITH GREAT AMERICANS

INVENTORS

- Alex. G. Bell
- Santos Dumont
- Wm. Marconi
- Chas. F. Brush
- Thomas Alva Edison
- Peter C. Hewitt
- John P. Holland (*Copyright, 1900, by Rockwood, N.Y.*)
- Hiram Stevens Maxim
- Geo. Westinghouse (*Copyright, 1902, by Gessford, N.Y.*)

MERCHANTS

- Henry Siegel
- Nathan Strauss
- F. W. Woolworth
- Marshall Field
- John Wanamaker
- Sir Thomas Lipton
- Edward Cooper
- Robt. L. Ogden
- W. F. King

LITTLE VISITS WITH GREAT AMERICANS

FINANCIERS

- Henry Clews
- Charles Tyson Yerkes
- Lyman Gage
- John D. Rockefeller
- J. Pierpont Morgan (*Copyright, 1902, by Pach, New York*)
- Russell Sage
- Cornelius Vanderbilt
- Hetty Green
- William Waldorf Astor

LITTLE VISITS WITH GREAT AMERICANS

POLITICAL LEADERS

- Hazen S. Pingree
- William Jennings Bryan
- Thomas C. Platt
- Sam'l M. Jones
- Marcus A. Hanna
- Arthur Pue Gorman
- Tom L. Johnson
- Carter Harrison
- Jos. W. Folk

LAWYERS AND JURISTS

- Wm. Travers Jerome
- John W. Griggs
- Frank S. Black
- Alton Brooks Parker
- Melville W. Fuller
- Oliver Wendell Holmes
- Joseph McKenna
- James B. Dill
- Fred. R. Coudert

LITTLE VISITS WITH GREAT AMERICANS

SOLDIERS AND SAILORS

- Richmond P. Hobson
- Joseph Wheeler
- Fred Funston
- Adna R. Chaffee
- Nelson A. Miles
- Wm. R. Shafter
- Winfield S. Schley
- George Dewey
- Robley D. Evans

LITTLE VISITS WITH GREAT AMERICANS

EXPLORERS AND TRAVELLERS

LITTLE VISITS WITH GREAT AMERICANS

- H. Nansen
- Henry M. Stanley
- A. H. Savage Landor
- Walter Wellman
- Robert Edwin Peary
- Dr. Frederick A. Cook
- E. Burton Holmes
- Evelyn V. Baldwin (*Copyright, 1902, by Rockwood, New York*)
- Sven Hedin

LITTLE VISITS WITH GREAT AMERICANS

EDUCATORS

- Jacob G. Schurman
- W. H. P. Faunce
- Nicholas M. Butler
- E. Benjamin Andrews
- William T. Harris
- Woodrow Wilson
- Arthur T. Hadley
- H. M. McCracken
- Charles Wm. Eliot (*Copyright, 1899, by Notman Photo. Company, Boston*)

LITTLE VISITS WITH GREAT AMERICANS

EDITORS

- Henry M. Alden
- Albert Shaw
- George H. Lorimer
- James M. Buckley
- Edward Bok
- Richard W. Gilder
- Henry Watterson
- George Harvey
- Whitelaw Reid
- (*Copyright, 1892, by Rockwood, N.Y.*)

PUBLISHERS

- Louis Klopsch
- Isaac K. Funk
- John Brisben Walker
- W. R. Hearst
- S. S. McClure
- Joseph Pulitzer
- Frank A. Munsey
- Edward E. Higgins
- F. N. Doubleday

ORATORS

- Champ Clark
- Frank W. Gunsaulus
- A. J. Beveridge
- J. P. Dolliver (*Copyright, by Francis B. Johnston*)
- Joseph H. Choate
- John Warwick Daniel
- Chauncey M. Depew
- Carl Schurz
- W. Bourke Cockran

MUSICIANS

- Reginald DeKoven
- Maud Powell
- Leonora Jackson
- Victor Herbert (*Copyright, by Aime Dupont, N. Y.*)
- John Phillip Sousa
- Maurice Grau (*Copyright, by Aime Dupont, N.Y.*)
- Franz Kneisel
- Theodore Thomas
- Walter Damrosch
- (*Copyright, by Aime Dupont, N.Y.*)

LITTLE VISITS WITH GREAT AMERICANS

SINGERS

- David Bispham
- Adelina Patti
- Lillian Nordica
- Jean de Reszke
- Emma Eames
- Edouard de Reszke
- Zelie de Lussan
- Emma Calvé (*Copyright, by E. W. Histed, 304 Fifth Avenue. N. Y.*)
- Marcella Sembrich

LITTLE VISITS WITH GREAT AMERICANS

ACTORS

- J. K. Hackett
- John Drew
- William Gillette
- Richard Mansfield
- Henry Irving
- E. H. Sothern
- Joseph Jefferson
- William Crane (*Copyright, 1899, by E. Chickering, Boston*)
- Nat C. Goodwin

ACTRESSES

- Ethel Barrymore (*Copyright, 1901, by Burr McIntosh*)
- Maude Adams
- May Irwin (*Courtesy of Colliers Weekly*)
- Mrs. Leslie Carter
- Eleonora Duse
- Mrs. Lillie Langtry
- Viola Allen
- Julia Marlowe
- Virginia Harned

ORGANIZERS AND LECTURERS

- Mary Lowe Dickinson
- Mrs. C. Westover Alden
- Clara Barton
- Herbert Hungerford
- Samuel Gompers
- Francis E. Clark
- E. Thompson-Seton
- John Mitchell
- Thos. Dixon, Jr. (*Copyright, 1901, by Rockwood, New York*)

LITTLE VISITS WITH GREAT AMERICANS

ILLUSTRATORS, DECORATORS AND SCULPTORS

- Charles Mente
- Alice Barber Stephens
- Henry Merwin Shrady
- T. De Thulstrup
- Edwin Austin Abbey (*Copyright, by Elliott and Fry, London*)
- W. De Leftwich Dodge
- Frederic Remington
- Charles Dana Gibson
- F. Wellington Ruckstuhl

CARTOONISTS

- Louis Dalrymple (*Courtesy of Pirie McDonald*)
- R. F. Outcault (*Courtesy of Pirie McDonald*)
- T. S. Allen
- Sydney B. Griffin (*Courtesy of Pirie McDonald*)
- C. G. Bush (*Courtesy of Pirie McDonald*)
- Frederick B. Opper
- Homer Davenport
- Carl E. Schultze
- Eugene Zimmerman

LITTLE VISITS WITH GREAT AMERICANS

HUMORISTS

- George V. Hobart
- Simeon Ford
- Elizabeth M. Gilmer
  "Dorothy Dix"
- Melville De L. Landon
  "Eli Perkins" (*Copyright by Rockwood, N.Y.*)
- Samuel L. Clemens
  "Mark Twain"
- George Ade
- John Kendrick Bangs
- Marshall P. Wilder
- Finley Peter Dunne
  "Mr. Dooley"

LITTLE VISITS WITH GREAT AMERICANS

JOURNALISTS AND WRITERS

- Stewart E. White
- Owen Wister
- David G. Phillips
- Hamlin Garland
- William T. Stead
- C. G. D. Roberts
- Vance Thompson
- Richard Harding Davis
- Stephen Bonsal

LITTLE VISITS WITH GREAT AMERICANS

POETS

- Richard LeGallienne (*Copyright, 1898, Rockwood, New York*)
- Robert Mackay
- John Burroughs
- James W. Riley (*Copyright, by Rockwood, New York*)
- Joaquin Miller (*Copyright, 1902, by Rockwood, New York*)
- Henry Van Dyke (*Copyright, 1902, by Rockwood, New York*)
- Ella Wheeler Wilcox (*Copyright, 1901, by Theo. C Marceau*)
- Edwin Markham (*Copyright, 1899, by Gessford and Van Brunt, New York*)
- Thos. Bailey Aldrich (*Copyright, 1903, by J. E. Purdy, Boston*)

LITTLE VISITS WITH GREAT AMERICANS

AUTHORS

- Charles Major
- Lew Wallace (*Copyright, 1900, by Nicholson Lacey, Crawfordville, Ind.*)
- Thos. Nelson Page
- Rudyard Kipling
- F. Marion-Crawford
- Wm. Dean Howells
- Geo. W. Cable (*Copyright, 1903, by Rockwood, N.Y.*)
- James Lane Allen
- Winston Churchill

NOVELISTS

- Mrs. Pearl Craigie
- Mrs. Mary Wilkins-Freeman
- Sara Orne Jewett
- Amelia Edith Barr
- Mrs. Gertrude Atherton
- Mrs. Burton Harrison (*Copyright, by Rockwood, New York*)
- Mrs. E. S. P. Ward
- Anna Katherine Greene
- Frances H. Burnett

REFORMERS

- Frederick Booth Tucker
- Anthony Comstock (*Copyright, by Rockwood, New York*)
- Elizabeth Cady Stanton (*Copyright, 1902, by Rockwood, New York*)
- William R. George
- Geo. Thorndike Angell
- Susan B. Anthony
- Elbridge T. Gerry
- Wilbur Fisk Crafts
- Charles Henry Parkhurst

PHILANTHROPISTS

- Mrs. Leland Stanford
- Mrs. Phoebe Hearst
- Mrs. Theo. Roosevelt (*Copyright, 1903, by Underwood and Underwood*)
- Darius Ogden Mills (*Copyright, 1902, by Rockwood, New York*)
- Helen Miller Gould
- D. K. Pearsons
- Mrs. Henry Codman Potter
- Anson Phelps Stokes
- Mrs. Russell Sage

LITTLE VISITS WITH GREAT AMERICANS

DIVINES

- Theo. L. Cuyler
- Edward Everett Hale (*Copyright, 1900, by Rockwood. N. Y.*)
- Bishop J. H. Vincent
- Bishop H. C. Potter
- Bishop Wm. Taylor
- B. Fay Mills (*Copyright, 1889, by B. Fay Mills*)
- Russell Conwell
- Lyman Abbott(*Copyright, 1893, by Rockwood, N.Y.*)
- Robert Collyer

VOLUME THREE

ENCYCLOPEDIC BIOGRAPHIES,
OR THE ROMANCE OF REALITY.

SUCCESS MAXIMS

"Never give up: for the wisest is boldest,
Knowing that Providence mingles the cup;
And of all maxims, the best, as the oldest,
Is the stern watchword of 'Never give up!'"
—HOLMES.

I find nothing so singular in life as this: that everything opposing appears to lose its substance the moment one actually grapples with it.—HAWTHORNE.

Perpetual pushing and assurance put a difficulty out of countenance, and make a seeming impossibility give way.—JEREMY COLLIER.

The truest wisdom is a resolute determination.
—NAPOLEON I.

He wants wit, that wants resolved will.—SHAKESPEARE.

When a firm decisive spirit is recognized, it is curious to see how the space clears around a man and leaves him room and freedom.—JOHN FOSTER.

Self-distrust is the cause of most of our failures. In the assurance of strength there is strength, and they are the weakest, however strong, who have no faith in themselves or their powers.—BOVEE.

Self-reverence, self-knowledge, self-control—these three alone lead life to sovereign power.—TENNYSON.

There is no fate! Between the thought and the success, God is the only agent.—BULWER.

Character must stand behind and back up everything— the sermon, the poem, the picture, the play. None of them is worth a straw without it.—J. G. HOLLAND.

I hate a thing done by halves. If it be right, do it boldly; if it be wrong, leave it undone.—GILPIN.

Doing well depends upon doing completely.—PERSIAN PROVERB.

Things don't turn up in this world until somebody turns them up.—GARFIELD.

We live in a new and exceptional age. America is another name for Opportunity. Our whole history appears like a last effort of the Divine Providence in behalf of the human race.—EMERSON.

STATESMEN.

WILLIAM BOYD ALLISON.

William Boyd Allison was born at Perry, Ohio, March 2, 1829. His father, John Allison, was a farmer, and young William spent his boyhood in work on the farm and in attending the district school. At the age of sixteen he studied at the Academy at Wooster and subsequently spent a year at Allegheny college in Meadville, Pennsylvania. After that he made enough money by teaching school to pay for his admission in the Western Reserve college in Hudson, Ohio. He studied law in Wooster, and in 1851 was admitted to the bar. Soon after he became deputy county clerk. His political tastes were made evident early in life. In 1856 he was a delegate to the Republican state convention and supported Fremont for president. In the following year he moved to Ohio, and settled in Dubuque, where he has since resided. He was a delegate at the Chicago Republican Convention which nominated Abraham Lincoln for President. At the beginning of the Civil war he was appointed on the staff of the Governor of Ohio. In 1862 he was elected to the Thirty-eighth congress and was re-elected three times in succession. He was the leading member of the ways and means committee during the Civil war and was of great use to the President and the Secretary of the Treasury in devising plans for raising money. He was elected to the United States senate in 1872. His previous record in the house caused his selection as chairman of the senate committee on appropriations. Mr. Allison has always taken a prominent part in tariff questions and was chiefly instrumental in framing the senate tariff bill of the Fiftieth congress. In 1881 he was offered the position of secretary of the Treasury by President Garfield, but declined, and, in 1888, he was a leading candidate for nomination for the presidency. After the election of Mr. Harrison he was again offered the treasury portfolio, which he again declined. Senator Allison has always held the respect of public men, and has never used his position to enrich himself. His tastes are refined, he is an agreeable host, and popular in both public and private life.

GROVER CLEVELAND.

Grover Cleveland was born at Caldwell, New Jersey, March 18, 1837. His ancestors came from England. His father was a Presbyterian minister and he was named after the Rev. Steven Grover. In 1841 the family moved to Fayetteville, New York, where the future president was educated in the public schools. Between lessons he acted as clerk in a country store. He received further education at a local academy, and was later appointed assistant teacher in the New York Institution for the Blind. In 1855, while helping his uncle, Lewis F. Allen, at Buffalo, compiling "The American Word Book," he began to read law, and, in 1859, was admitted to the bar. He was appointed assistant district attorney of Erie county in 1863, but in 1865 he was defeated for the district attorneyship of the same county. Thereupon he became a member of a Buffalo law firm. In 1871 he was elected sheriff of Erie county. At the close of this term he helped to form the firm of Bass, Cleveland & Bissel. In 1881 he was elected mayor of Buffalo by the largest majority to a mayoralty candidate ever given in that city. In 1882 he was made governor of the state of New York. He was nominated as Democratic candidate for the presidency in 1884, was elected, and inaugurated on March 4, 1885. His term of office was notable on account of his exercising the veto power beyond all precedent. He vetoed one hundred and fifteen out of nine hundred and eighty-seven bills, which had passed both houses, one hundred and two of these being private pension bills. On June 2, 1886, he was married, in the White House, to Frances Folsom, the daughter of one of his former law partners. In 1888 Mr. Cleveland was candidate for a second term as president, but was defeated by Benjamin Harrison. In 1892 he was again a candidate, and this time he was elected. Mr. Cleveland was without doubt the most popular Democrat of his time when running for the presidency. He is an enthusiastic devotee of gun and rod, an ideal host, and even those who differ with him politically admit his statesmanship.

WILLIAM PIERCE FRYE.

William Pierce Frye, who, since 1861, has been United States senator from Maine, was born at Lewiston, Maine, September 2, 1831. His father was Colonel John N. Frye and his mother Alice N. (Davis) Frye. Graduating from Bowdoin college in 1850, he subsequently carried out the wishes of his family and the trend of his own inclinations by following a legal career, in which he was eminently successful. Becoming a member of the Maine legislature in 1861, he was mayor of Lewiston from 1866 to 1867, and afterward held a variety of political offices, including the attorney-generalship of Maine from 1867 to 1869, presidential elector 1864, was made a member of congress in 1871, which office he held for ten years, was chairman of the commerce committee of the senate and member of the peace commission in Paris, 1898; was president pro tem, of the senate from 1896 to 1901, and after the death of Vice-President Hobart discharged the duties of that office during the Fifty-sixth congress. He is now acting chairman of the committee on foreign relations. Mr. Frye married Caroline Spears, who died in 1900. His life history is one that has for its moral the power of integrity when welded to unceasing effort.

JOHN HAY.

John Hay, who, since 1890, has been secretary of state of the United States, first saw the light at Salem, Indiana, on October 8, 1838. His father was Dr. Charles Hay, and John was educated in the common schools at Warsaw, Illinois, and in the academy at Springfield, Illinois. He graduated from Brown university in 1858, and after a preparatory period in a local law school was admitted to the Illinois bar. Mr. Hay was one of the private secretaries of President Lincoln. He was breveted colonel of United States Volunteers and was also assistant adjutant-general during the Civil war. He has also been secretary of legation at Paris, Madrid and Vienna and was charge d'affaires at Vienna. From 1879 to 1881 he acted as first assistant secretary of state. During the international sanitary conference of 1881 he was made its president. His services as ambassador to England from 1897 to 1898 will be long remembered in connection with his tactful and dignified diplomacy. Mr. Hay, notwithstanding his many and onerous official duties has found time to write books of both prose and poetry. His Castilian Days and Pike County Ballads are among the most popular of these. In 1874 he married Clara Stone, of Cleveland, Ohio.

GEORGE FRISBIE HOAR.

A commanding figure among the Republican forces in the United States senate, not alone from his personality and ability, but also because of his attitude on trust legislation and on the Philippine question, is George Frisbie Hoar, Massachusetts. Mr. Hoar was born in Concord, Massachusetts, August 29, 1826. A graduate of Harvard in 1846, aged twenty, and later of Harvard law school, he has retained his interest in higher education, and in scholarly matters. He has been an overseer of Harvard college from 1874 to 1880, at various times regent of the Smithsonian Institute, a trustee of the Leicester academy and the Peabody Museum of Archæology, and officer of various national and state societies. He settled in Worcester, Massachusetts, after graduating and practiced law. He has been married twice, his first wife being Mary Louisa Spurr and his second Ruth A. Miller. His service in the senate, since 1877, is exceeded by but few fellow-members, and he represents that body's best traditions. He was elected because, as legislator from 1852 to 1856, as state senator in 1856, and as member of congress from 1869 until he was sent to the senate, he had shown marked ability, an unfailing watchfulness for public welfare and an unswerving honesty as rare as it is desirable. Senator Hoar is a striking example of how irreproachable integrity can take active and prominent part in party politics. He has kept his influence in his party and in general legislation in spite of sometimes opposing leaders of his own party, when his conscience and judgment bade him do so.

HENRY CABOT LODGE.

Henry Cabot Lodge was born in Boston, Massachusetts, May 12, 1850. He prepared for college in Dixwell Latin school, and, entering Harvard, was graduated in 1876. After his graduation he spent a year in traveling. Returning to America in 1872, he entered the Harvard law school. In January, 1874, he became assistant editor of the North American Review, which position he held until November, 1876. In 1875 he was a lecturer on The History of the American Colonies, in Harvard. From 1879 to 1882 he was associate editor of the International Review of Boston. During the same period he was elected member of the Massachusetts house of representatives. In 1881 he was the Republican candidate for the state senate, but was defeated. He was nominated for congress in 1884, but was again defeated. In

1886, however, being nominated again, he was successful and was re-elected for three successive congresses, but resigned after his last election on account of having been made a United States senator, January 17, 1893. In the senate he has made his mark. Mr. Lodge is an orator of much ability, a far-sighted political executive, and a writer of considerable merit. Among his books are: A Short History of the English Colonies, Life of Washington, Daniel Webster, History of Boston, and he has contributed to the Encyclopædia Britannica and other works. He is a fluent lecturer. He is a member of the Massachusetts Historical Society, the American Academy of Arts and Sciences, trustee of the Boston Athenaeum, a member of the American Antiquarian Society, and a member of the New England Historic Genealogical Society. In 1874 he was elected an overseer of Harvard university, and was offered the degree of LL.D. in 1875. He married, on June 29, 1871, Anna, daughter of Rear Admiral Charles S. Davis, and has three children by her.

RICHARD OLNEY.

Richard Olney was born in Oxford, Massachusetts, September 15, 1835, and is of English ancestry. He received his preliminary education at Leicester academy, and graduated with high honors at Brown university in 1856. He was graduated with the degree of bachelor of laws from Harvard law school in 1858, and was admitted to the bar in the following year, entering the office of Judge Benjamin F. Thomas, with whom he was associated for ten years. Mr. Olney made a specialty of the laws relative to wills, estates and corporations. In 1893 he was appointed attorney-general by President Cleveland. By his advice Mr. Cleveland called out regular troops, July, 1894, to suppress the rioting that followed on the Chicago American railway union strike. In March, 1895, he successfully defended that action in an argument before the Supreme Court in the habeas corpus proceedings brought by Eugene V. Debs, who had been convicted of inciting the strikers. Upon the death of Walter Q. Gresham, Mr. Olney was appointed secretary of state and took office June 10, 1895. He was married, in 1861, to Agnes Park, daughter of Benjamin F. Thomas, of Boston.

ELIHU ROOT.

Elihu Root, secretary of war of the United States and one of the most successful lawyers of his generation, was born at Clinton, New York, February 15, 1845. His father was Orin Root, who was for many years professor of mathematics at Hamilton college, from which institution young Root graduated in 1864. For a year or more he was a teacher in Rome, New York, academy. Coming to New York, he studied in the University law school until 1867, when he was admitted to the bar, beginning to practice forthwith. He lost no time in getting into the current of affairs in the metropolis, and soon began to attract attention on account of his earnestness and ability, and so, while still a very young man, was retained on important cases. President Arthur appointed him United States attorney for the southern district of New York in 1883. He was delegate-at-large at the state constitutional convention in 1894, was appointed secretary of war, August 1, 1899, by President McKinley, and was reappointed in 1901. As a corporation lawyer he has had to do with some historical legal cases, such as the Hocking Valley suit, in which the amount involved was $8,000,000. A few years ago he erected in the Hamilton college grounds the Root Hall of Science as a memorial to his father. He is married and has three children—two boys and a girl.

INDUSTRIAL LEADERS.

E. G. ACHESON.

E. G. Acheson, the inventor of carborundum, which may be called an artificial gem that, unlike the majority of gems, is much more useful than ornamental, has proven that for a man of ideas and ability the world of to-day is as full of opportunities as it was in those periods which are somewhat vaguely alluded to by less successful men as "the good old times." Mr. Acheson was born at Washington, Pennsylvania, in 1854, and after receiving a public school, college and technical training, entered the employ of Edison, the inventor. From the first he was a persistent and somewhat daring experimentalist, one of his scientific fads being the manufacture of artificial diamonds, and it was during the investigations made by him in relation thereunto that carborundum—a substance which has revolutionized some industries and incidentally brought fame and fortune to its discoverer and his associates—was obtained. The principle of the electric furnace, by means of which the substance in question is manufactured, was in existence many years before Mr. Acheson began to use it in connection with his experimental work, but other scientists had failed to recognize its possibilities. Carborundum is produced by fusing carbon and silicon by means of a huge electric arc, the result being a mass of beautifully colored crystals which are harder than any known substance except diamonds. Carborundum is rapidly taking the place of emery for abrasive purposes. Another product of the electric furnace—artificial graphite—is also a discovery of Mr. Acheson, and which is of great value in many of the arts and sciences.

CHARLES HENRY CRAMP.

"He did not cease to be a student when he left school." This fact to a very great extent accounts for the achievements of Charles H. Cramp, who is the president of the largest shipbuilding enterprise in the United States. He was born in Philadelphia, May 9, 1828, and is the oldest son of William Cramp, who was the founder of the industry which bears his name. After receiving a thorough schooling and graduating from the Philadelphia high school, he learned the shipbuilding trade with his father. He is now recognized as the head of naval architecture on the American continent. Mr. Cramp's services in the reconstruction of the navy and in connection with the revival of the American merchant marine alone entitle him to permanent distinction. Beginning in 1887 his firm built, in rapid succession, the Yorktown (gunboat), the Vesuvius (dynamite torpedo vessel), Baltimore (protected cruiser), Philadelphia (protected cruiser), New York (armored cruiser), Columbia (protected cruiser), Minneapolis (protected cruiser), Indiana (battleship), Massachusetts (battleship), Brooklyn (armored cruiser), and the Iowa (seagoing battleship). The fleet has an aggregate of nearly eighty thousand tons of displacement and one hundred and forty-seven thousand indicated horse-power. The shipyard covers thirty acres of ground, employs six thousand men and was capitalized at $5,000,000 in 1894. The William Cramp & Sons Ship and Engine Building Co., from a simple shipyard, has reached the status of the greatest and most complete naval arsenal in the western hemisphere.

CHARLES RANLETT FLINT.

The personality of Charles R. Flint does not suggest the strenuous nature of his life, past and present; yet but few men in this country have shouldered or for that matter are shouldering so many business responsibilities as he is doing—and of large caliber at that. Mr. Flint's successes on the lines indicated are due to system, and system only. With him there is a place for each responsibility and each responsibility occupies its place in the total scheme of his business existence. He was born at Thomaston, Maine, January 24, 1850, graduated from the Polytechnic institute, Brooklyn, in 1868, and in 1883 married E. Kate, daughter of Joseph F. Simmons, of Troy, N. Y. To catalogue the industries and enterprises which Mr. Flint has organized or is connected with would be an undertaking in itself. Suffice it that he is prominently identified with the rubber and lumber industries, is interested in street railways in New York state, is a director in several banks, has organized iron and steel, steamship, starch, caramel and general export companies, has acted as United States consul in Central American countries, in 1893 fitted out a fleet of war vessels for the Brazilian republic, bought for and delivered to Japan a cruiser during the China-Japan war, and, in 1898, was the confidential agent of the United States in negotiating for the purchase of war vessels.

CHARLES MELVILLE HAYS.

It is a good thing for the world at large that human talents are of a diversified nature. It is an equally excellent thing that the possession of special gift on the part of an individual is recognized by those with whom he comes in contact. A case in point is furnished by Charles M. Hays, who, until lately, was president of the Southern Pacific railroad. Mr. Hays' work in life seems to have been that of turning unprofitable railroad systems into permanently paying propositions. He was born May 16, 1856, at Rock Island, Illinois, his parents being in fairly comfortable circumstances. After a common school training he entered the railroad service in 1873, his first position being in the passenger department of the St. Louis, Atlantic & Pacific railroad. The rungs of the ladder of his subsequent upward climb are something in this order: Prompted to a clerkship in the auditor's office, he was at length placed in the general superintendent's office on the same line; next he is heard of as secretary of the general manager of the Missouri Pacific railroad, and in 1886 he was made assistant general manager of the Wabash, St. Louis & Pacific railroad; three years later he was appointed general manager of the Wabash & Western railroad, and was afterward made manager of the Wabash system, which was the outcome of the consolidation of the Wabash Western and Wabash railroads. He has also been general manager of the Grand Trunk system, and, as already intimated, was, until recently, the president of the Southern railroad. When Mr. Hays took hold of the Wabash lines they were in about as bad a condition as railroad lines can be. The same remark applies to the Grand Trunk system. When Mr. Hays severed his connection with these corporations they were in a flourishing condition—popular with the public and paying as to dividends. He created their prosperity by the industrious exercise of his special talents. The lesson may be taken to heart.

JOHN B. HERRESHOFF.

The person who is handicapped in the struggle for existence by physical infirmities excites our sympathy, but when such an one achieves as well as or far better than the normal individual, we regard him with an admiration that is akin to wonder. John B. Herreshoff, the famous blind yacht and boat designer, is such an individual. He is a marvel such as the world has never seen before, and is not likely to witness for some time to come. He is the admitted head of a profession which as one would believe calls for keen eyes as a preliminary. Yet Mr. Herreshoff has set all precedent at naught. It would almost seem that his blindness, so far from being a handicap, is of positive value to him, for it is certain that those exquisite floating creations of his, have never yet been duplicated by the owners of eyesight. When, in August, 1851, the America won the famous "Queen's Cup," which has ever since remained on this side of the water, two youngsters were playing on a farm at Point Pleasant, at Bristol, Rhode Island. John, the oldest, was then a blue-eyed boy of ten. As soon as he could use a knife he began to whittle boats, and when fourteen years of age built a usable craft, which was said to be a marvel of beauty by local experts. At fifteen, blindness descended upon him, but he nevertheless continued to study boats and build them. His younger brother, Nathaniel, also had a love for boats, and together the two brothers lived and ruled and had their being in an atmosphere of boats. Both boys were educated at local schools, and John, with the assistance of his mother, managed to keep pace with his fellow pupils. Nathaniel became a civil engineer and made a name for himself in his profession. In the meantime the reputation of John had so extended that in 1863 he founded the Herreshoff Manufacturing Co., and fourteen years later Nathaniel became a partner in the concern and is now its superintendent. The fame of the Herreshoffs is perhaps best known to the public in connection with their construction of several of the defenders of the "Queens," or, as it is better known on this side of the water, "The America Cup." John B. Herreshoff, on being asked what the elements of success are, said: "Concentration, decision, industry, economy, together with an invincible determination and persistence, will always place a man in the position which he desires."

LEWIS NIXON.

"Four letters sum up my idea of how to make a success in life; they are W-O-R-K (work)." These are the sentiments of Lewis Nixon, who starting life as a poor boy, has by sheer determination won social position, fame, wealth and political honor before he was forty. His story is a simple one, but none the less helpful. Born in Leesburg, Virginia, April 7, 1861, he was the son of Joel Lewis and Mary Frances (Turner) Nixon. His parents were in poor circumstances. His diligence in the public schools interested General Eppa Hunton (then representative from Virginia), who secured for him an appointment to the United States Naval academy at Annapolis as midshipman, and in 1882 he graduated at the head of his class. Going to England, he took a course in naval architecture and marine engineering. Upon returning to this country, he was appointed to the staff of the chief constructor of the navy and served as superintendent of construction at the Cramp yards and the New York navy yard. In 1890 he designed, in ninety days, the battleships Indiana, the Massachusetts and the Oregon. After resigning from the navy department, he became superintending constructor of the Cramps' yard, Philadelphia, but soon after resigned that position and opened a shipyard of his own at Elizabeth, New Jersey. He has built the gunboats Annapolis, Josephine, Mangro and others, besides the submarine torpedo boat Holland. He was married in Washington, January 29, 1891, to Sallie Lewis Wood. Mr. Nixon is a member of the New England organization of architects and marine engineers, the chamber of commerce, and is a member of the Democratic club, Press club, Army and Navy club of Washington and others. He takes an active part in Democratic politics.

JOHN H. PATTERSON.

John H. Patterson, the president of the International Cash Register Co., of Dayton, Ohio, is a specimen of what, happily for this country, is not an infrequent young American, whose original capital being that of brains and industry, pays interest in the shape of great enterprises and a large fortune. Mr. Patterson's parents were farmers. After a public school education he went to Miami university, and afterward to Dartmouth college. On graduating he began life without any definite plans, clerked, saved money and pushed ahead until he became manager of a coal mine. It was while he was holding this position that he heard of the then almost unknown cash register, bought two of them and saw that there was a field for their development and use. Together with his brother, Frank R. Patterson, he bought the patent of the machine and began to manufacture the registers. In 1894, after ten years of effort, and with success apparently in sight, the brothers were confronted with the complete failure of one of their new inventions and the return from England of a carload of broken machines, instead of an expected draft for $30,000. Nothing daunted, Mr. Patterson began to analyze the causes of the setback and came to the conclusion that the successful manufacture of the machines depended on the faithfulness of his workmen, which had to rest upon the mutual goodwill of employer and employe. This belief led him to adopt an industrial system which is probably unique in the annals of manufacturing enterprises. Briefly, it consists of developing the mechanical talents of the workmen by prizes and promotions; by making schools, clubs, libraries, choral societies and the like a part of the economy of the factory and by remembering that all work makes Jack and his bosses very dull boys indeed. That the principle is a sound one seems to be certain, if one may judge by the general use of the Patterson cash register.

MANUFACTURERS.

HUGH CHISHOLM.

The individual who begins life as a poor newsboy, and in the full flush of his manhood is found to be the head of an industry created by himself in which untold millions are invested, and which is of supreme importance to the community, serves his generation in more ways than one. If he has done nothing else he has acted as an exemplar for the faint-hearted, as a beacon for the persevering, and as a type of American manhood, and all that lies before it. Such an individual is Hugh Chisholm, who has brought into existence a corporation which is making paper for nearly all the newspapers of the United States. When it is said that one New York newspaper buys six thousand dollars worth of paper every day, some idea may be gained of the vast proportions of the industry. Mr. Chisholm was born at Niagara-on-the-Lake, Canada, May 2, 1847, and began life as a train newsboy on the Grand Trunk railroad, studying meanwhile in evening classes of business colleges in Toronto. When the Civil war broke out, the lad, who is of Scotch descent, with the shrewdness of his race, realized the possibilities of the situation and pushed his wares to the utmost, sometimes holding them at a premium. He at length was able to hire some other boys to sell newspapers for him. He next obtained from the railroad company the exclusive right to sell newspapers on the division east of Toronto. He extended his "combinations," and when he was twenty-five years of age had the exclusive news routes over four thousand miles of railroad, and had two hundred and fifty men on his payroll. Selling out his interests to his brothers, who had similar interests in New

England, he purchased the latter and located in Portland, Maine, where he added publishing to his business. Foreseeing a growth of the newspaper trade, and realizing that there would be a huge consequent demand for white paper, he organized the Somerset Fiber Company, the manufacturing of wood pulp at Fairfield. Later he established a number of pulp mills in Maine. Next he devised a plan of business consolidations and a few years ago the Chisholm properties and a score of other mills in New England, New York and Canada were merged into one company. The output of the mills is more than 1,500 tons per day and is increasing rapidly. In 1872 he married Henrietta Mason, of Portland.

THEODORE LOWE DE VINNE.

From a country printer boy to the head of one of the greatest printing establishments in the metropolis—this in brief is the story of the career of Theodore Lowe De Vinne. He was born in Stamford, Connecticut, December 25, 1828, being the second son of Daniel and Joanna Augusta De Vinne. His parents were of Holland extraction. His father was a Methodist minister, who was an uncompromising opponent of slavery. Theodore secured a common school education at Catskill, White Plains, and Amenia, New York, and at the age of fourteen entered the office of the Gazette, Newburgh, New York, to learn the printing trade. After he had gotten a general knowledge of the business he went to New York city in 1848. Two years later he obtained employment in the establishment of Francis Hart & Co. and rose to the position of foreman. In 1858 he became a junior partner in the firm and five years after the death of Mr. Hart, which took place in 1883, he changed the name of the firm to Theodore L. De Vinne & Co., making his only son, Theodore L. De Vinne, Jr., his partner. He now occupies one of the largest buildings in the United States, which is wholly devoted to the printing business. Mr. De Vinne has marked ability as an organizer, having, with the assistance of the late Peter C. Baker, formed the society now known as the Typothetæ. In 1850 he married Grace, daughter of Joseph Brockbant. He is the author of the Printers' Price List, The Invention of Printing, Historic Types and Printing Types. Mr. De Vinne has done much to elevate the standard of typography. As early as 1863 the American institute awarded his firm a medal for the best book printing. The firm has published St. Nicholas and the Century since 1874.

WILLIAM LOUIS DOUGLAS.

William Louis Douglas, of Brockton, Massachusetts, who, through the medium of his widely advertised shoes, is probably one of the most easily recognized men in the United States, was born in Plymouth, Massachusetts, August 22, 1845. The career of Mr. Douglas emphasizes the fact that the days of opportunity for young men without money or influence are by no means over. He was an orphan, handicapped by lack of schooling, a victim of injustice and apparently without any prospects in life whatever. Now he is the owner of a vast fortune, a great business, an honorable place among honored men, and has influence for good in laboring circles, and no small power politically. When Mr. Douglas was five years of age, his father was lost at sea. At the age of seven he was apprenticed to his uncle to learn the shoemaking trade. The uncle proved to be a hard taskmaster, and at the expiration of his apprenticeship William found himself the owner of just ten dollars and remembrances of many hard knocks. Subsequently he tried several ways of getting a livelihood, from driving ox teams in Nebraska to working at his trade. In conjunction with a Mr. Studley, he opened a boot store at Golden, Colorado. The venture did not pay, and returning to Massachusetts he took to shoemaking again until 1870, when he removed to Brockton to become superintendent of the shoe factory of Porter & Southworth. In 1876, with a borrowed capital of $375, he went into business for himself. Successful from the start, he, six years later, built a four-story factory, which had a capacity of 1,440 pairs of boots daily. In 1884 he placed on the market his well-known $3 shoe, with which his name and his face are so prominently identified. He has broken away from the old traditions of manufacturers by establishing retail stores, where he sells direct to the public. The Douglas factory of to-day was erected in 1892, and has a capacity of 10,240 pairs of boots daily. There are 2,724 employes. Mr. Douglas is Democratic in politics. He has been a member of the common council of Brockton several times and was its mayor in 1890. It was through his efforts that a bill was enacted in the state legislature of Massachusetts for the establishment of a board of arbitration and conciliation. Labor troubles are practically unknown in the Douglas factory. Mr. Douglas is also the author of the weekly payment law that observes in Massachusetts, is president of the people's savings bank of Brockton, a director in the Home national bank and ex-president of the Brockton, Taunton & Bridgewater street railroad.

CHARLES EASTMAN.

Charles Eastman was born at Waterville, New York, July 12, 1854. Photographers, especially amateurs, need not be told who Mr. Eastman is, inasmuch as he has done much to popularize the camera and all that to it belongs. He was educated at Rochester, New York. Becoming interested in amateur photography, he began a source of exhausted experiments to the end of making dry plates and secured results which prompted him to make further investigations. These latter were successful also, and from this preliminary work rose the great business with which he is now identified. The kodak, which is probably the most popular of cameras in the world, is his invention also. He is manager of the Eastman Kodak Company, of Rochester, and of London, England; president of the General Aristo Company, of Rochester, and is the head of the so-called camera trust. Mr. Eastman is a member of many social and scientific organizations, and gives liberally to charitable institutions.

ALBERT AUGUST POPE.

The name of Colonel Albert August Pope is identified with the popularizing of the bicycle in this country, for he it was who, more than any other, gave it the impetus which made it a prime favorite with the public. Apart from that, however, he has furnished us with yet another example of the power of push, perseverance and probity. Colonel Pope was born in Boston, May 10, 1843, of poor parents. He had to leave school early in life in order to earn a livelihood. When ten years of age he peddled fruit, and it is said by persons who knew him in those days that he made it a rule to pay every debt as soon as it was due. After years of hard work young Pope, then nineteen, accepted a junior second lieutenancy in Company I, of the Thirty-sixth Massachusetts Volunteers. His record during the war was most brilliant, and he came out of it with the rank of colonel. He then went into business for himself and built up a profitable trade. It was in the centennial exposition in 1876 that he first saw a bicycle. Realizing the future of the machine, he in 1877 placed an order for "an importation of English wheels." In the same year he organized the Pope Manufacturing Company. The vast nature of the business done by the corporation is a matter of familiarity to all those who were or are interested in bicycles. He also founded the publication entitled The Wheelman, putting upward of sixty thousand dollars in the enterprise. It is known to-day under the name of Outing. It was mainly through his efforts that public parks and boulevards were thrown open to the uses of bicycles, and that the machine was put upon the same footing as any other vehicle. When the bicycle interest began to wane, Colonel Pope turned his attention to the manufacture of automobiles. He also has a large interest in banks and other corporations. He is a member of the Loyal Legion and a visitor to Wellesley college, and the Lawrence scientific school. In 1871 he married Abbie Lyndon, of Newton, Mass.

C. W. POST.

The name of C. W. Post is identified with an industry that has only come into existence within the past few years, but which, nevertheless, has assumed tremendous proportions, and is remarkable in many ways, not the least of which is that it puts cereals to uses which were absolutely unknown a generation ago. Postum cereal coffee, for example, has only been before the public since 1895. Yet recently Mr. Post and his associates declined an offer of ten millions of dollars for the factories which made the coffee and its associated products of the wheat field. Mr. Post's life story is that of a boy with a light purse, boundless ambition and a determination to reach the goal of large successes. He was born October 26, 1854, in Springfield, Illinois. After a common school education he entered the University of Illinois when thirteen years of age, took a military course, and remained there until he was fifteen, when the spirit of independence which has been a characteristic of his career throughout asserted itself. To use his own words, "I became weary of depending on my father's money." Leaving the university, he obtained a position with a manufacturer of farm machinery, which he sold and put in operation for the purchasers. After a couple of years of this work, he began business for himself in conjunction with a partner in the appropriately named town of Independence, Kansas. The firm dealt in hardware and farm machinery. But too little capital hampered his efforts, so he sold out and again took up drumming. Later he became manager of a wholesale machinery house in Kansas City. Returning to Illinois, he organized a company for the manufacturing of plows and cultivators, was quite successful, but his health breaking down, chaos resulted, and he lost all his savings. After dabbling in real estate in California, he ranched in Texas, fell ill again, recovered, and then bought twenty-seven acres of ground at Battle Creek, Michigan. Here it was that he began to make the famous coffee, to which allusion has been made. Here, too, he experimented with prepared, and finally placed upon the market those cooked and semi-cooked cereal foods with which we are familiar at the breakfast-table. The first year that the Post products were before the public, there was a profit of $175,000, the second year showed a loss of over $40,000—this being due to profits being sunk in advertising—and the third year there was a clear gain of $384,000. From that time on the business has been most profitable. It is stated that the concern is now preparing to spend one million dollars a year for advertising. Two years ago Mr. Post retired from the active conduct of the concern. He now divides his time between the offices in this country and abroad, and the chain of factories in the west. He is president of the association of American advertisers, and maintains at his own expense the Post check currency bureau at Washington.

JOHN WILSON WHEELER.

John Wilson Wheeler, whose name is familiar to every housewife who owns or wants to own a sewing machine, was born in Orange, Franklin county, Massachusetts, November 20, 1832, being the second of nine children. He was the son of a carpenter-farmer, and was educated in a district school. When about fourteen years of age he began to follow the trade of his father, and continued to do so until he was twenty-three years old. But he was not satisfied with his narrow surroundings, and so when the opportunity came for him to accept a place in a little grocery store in Fitchburg at one hundred and twenty-five dollars a year and his board he gladly accepted it. Returning to Orange some time later, he became a clerk in the store of one Daniel Pomeroy, finally succeeding the latter in the business, which he conducted for three years longer. Selling out, he became clerk in the claim agency of D. E. Chency, one of the leading men of the village. By this time he had established a reputation for ability and integrity, and so it came about that Mr. Chency and another of his friends loaned him two thousand dollars on his personal security to buy a grocery store. The venture was successful and was only given up in 1867, in order that Mr. Wheeler might become a partner in the firm of A. E. Johnson & Co. that had just started in a small way to make sewing machines. After some years of struggling the firm was turned into a corporation under the name of the Gold Medal Sewing Machine Company, Mr. Wheeler being secretary and treasurer. In 1882 the name was again changed to that of the New Home Sewing Machine Company. Of this corporation Mr. Wheeler was vice-president, as well as secretary and treasurer. He later became president, but subsequently resigned, but retained the office of treasurer, as well as being a member of the board of directors. How the business has grown from small beginnings to its present extensive status is a story that is familiar to everyone who knows somewhat of the sewing machine industry. The company employs nearly six hundred men and turns out about four hundred machines daily. Mr. Wheeler is also president of the Orange savings bank and of the Orange national bank, and has been president of the Orange Power company and the Orange board of trade. He has furthermore held office with the Boston mutual life insurance company, is the director of the Athol and Orange City railway company, is president of the Leabitt Machine company, of the Orange good government club and is vice-president of the Home Market club. He married Almira E. Johnson, by whom he had three daughters, only one of whom survives. He is the owner of much real estate, and is erecting a mansion near Orange at the cost of $150,000.

TRANSPORTATION LEADERS.

GEORGE F. BAER.

George F. Baer, when a boy, worked on his father's farm in Somerset county, Pennsylvania. He was recently chosen president of the Philadelphia & Reading and New Jersey Central railroad systems, two of the most important transportation corporations in the country. He is also identified with many enterprises of a diversified and extensive nature. He is still in the prime of life, and the secret of his so attaining is an open one—he did not waste time. Young Baer attended school for but a few years, and then entered the office of the Somerset Democrat to learn the printing trade. But he did not permit himself to retrograde in his studies, but instead pored over books and practiced writing at night. When sixteen years of age he managed to get a year's tuition in the Somerset academy and afterward secured a position as clerk in the Ashtola Mills, near Johnstown, Pennsylvania. At the end of twelve months he was made chief clerk. Resigning, he entered the sophomore class at Franklin and Marshall colleges. Next, and in conjunction with his older brother, he bought the Democrat. Then the war broke out and the brother enlisted. Mr. Baer, then hardly nineteen years of age, ran the paper alone. In 1862 he, too, got the war spirit and went to the front. He was mustered out in 1863 and forthwith began to read law with his two brothers. After practicing in Somerset for four years, he went to Reading, where he was retained by the attorney of certain railroads that were trying to compete with the Philadelphia & Reading railroad. The opposing company finally decided that he was worth more for them than against them and so made him its legal adviser. From that time up to his election as president of the corporation he had been its solicitor. He is also interested in coal mines, paper manufacture, banks and insurance corporations, is married and has five daughters.

AUGUST BELMONT.

August Belmont, builder of the New York City subway, began his career with the handicap of great wealth. His father, August Belmont, senior, was one of the richest and best known American bankers. His son August was graduated from Harvard University in 1875, and for a time gave himself up in large measure to the usual occupations of the youth of fortune. But as he grew older he interested himself more and more in the great banking business established by his father. In the course of a few years he became, on his own account, a power in the financial world. He is now an officer or director in many banking, railway, manufacturing and other corporations. In addition to these he has been a strong supporter of the best art, literary, patriotic and other American activities, being a member of numerous associations devoted to such movements. He has taken an active part in politics, and is much interested in the breeding of thoroughbred race-horses. His most conspicuous activity, however, has been the building of the subway, which has added so greatly to the transportation facilities of the metropolis.

ALEXANDER JOHNSTON CASSATT.

Another railroad man who has risen from a place of obscurity to a position of prominence is Alexander Johnston Cassatt, who has been president of the Pennsylvania railroad company since June, 1899. Like George H. Daniels, of the New York Central railroad, he started life as a rodman, in 1861, in the employ of the corporation of which he is now the head. Mr. Cassatt preferred to begin at the foot of the ladder for the sake of the knowledge of the primary details of the business which his so doing gave him, instead of making use of the influence as he probably could have obtained in order to assure him a less humble position. He was born in Pittsburg, December 8, 1839, and was educated at the University of Heidelberg and the Rensselaer Polytechnique institute. After his experiences as rodman, by force of sheer industry and integrity, he rose from place to place until, in 1871, he was made general superintendent of the Pennsylvania system and general manager of the lines east of Pittsburg. Between 1874 and 1882 he held the offices of third vice-president and second vice-president, was elected director in 1883 and was made president of the road in 1899. "Thoroughly ground yourself in the elementaries of your chosen business, and then stick to it," is Mr. Cassatt's advice to young men. He is a thorough believer in the old axiom that "a rolling stone gathers no moss."

GEORGE HENRY DANIELS.

George Henry Daniels, who in his capacity of general passenger agent of the New York Central and Hudson River railroad, is probably better known personally or by repute to the traveling public, than any other man in this country, was born in Hampshire, Kane county, Illinois, December 1, 1842. He began his railroad career as a rodman in the engineering corps of the Northern Missouri railroads, and from that humble position has risen, not rapidly perhaps, but slowly and certainly, until he has the passenger transportation responsibilities on his hands of what is probably the greatest railroad in the United States. After some years of strenuous work, he became, in 1872, the general freight and passenger agent of the Chicago and Pacific railroad, and in 1880 was made ticket agent of the Wabash, St. Louis and Pacific road. After a number of varied experiences, all of which were in the west, and were connected with positions of great responsibility, he acted as assistant commissioner or commissioner for several roads, and in April, 1889, was rewarded for his years of faithful service by being appointed to the position which he now holds. No small portion of Mr. Daniels's success is due to his personal tactfulness and unfailing courtesy; or, as someone has put it, he knows how to grant a favor without placing the grantee under an obligation, and he knows how to refuse a request without offending the individual who makes it.

GEORGE JAY GOULD.

George Jay Gould, whose name is so generally identified with high finance, is the son of the late Jay and Helen Day (Miller) Gould. He was born in New York in 1858 and received his education at the hands of private tutors or in private schools. Inheriting a genius for finance and an instinct for railroading, he has succeeded in successfully conducting those vast enterprises and investments which were brought into existence by his father. Mr. Gould is an ardent devotee of field sports, particularly those of which horses are a part and portion. He married Miss Edith Kingdon, who was at one time a member of Augustin Daly's Dramatic Company in this city. By her he has two sons, both of whom are as fond of strenuous sports as is their father. Nevertheless he does not permit his pastimes to interfere with his business affairs, and is a familiar figure in the financial districts of New York City. He has been president of the Little Rock and Fort Worth railroad, Texas and Pacific railroad, International and Great Northern railroad, Manhattan Elevated railroad, Missouri Pacific railroad, and the St. Louis and Iron Mountain and Southern railroad. Mr. Gould is a good specimen of the young American who does not let his great wealth hamper his activities.

CLEMENT ACTON GRISCOM.

The placing of young men in positions of extreme responsibility seems to be peculiar to this country. Abroad such positions are usually held by persons of mature or advanced years. That the commercial world of America does not suffer from its departure from European customs in the respect cited is evidenced by its commercial and mercantile progress. Clement Acton Griscom, Jr., manager of the great American line of steamers is a case in point. He was born in 1868 and graduated from the University of Pennsylvania in 1887. His father is Clement Acton Griscom, Sr., president of the line. Griscom, the manager, entered the service of the company the day following his last examination at college and two weeks before he received his diploma. He first worked as office boy in the freight department at a salary of $3.00 per week, and, as the story goes, although a college graduate and the son of the president, the other employes treated him exactly as they did the other boys. His business progress then was something in this order: junior clerk at $5.00 per week; junior clerk in the passenger department, $7.00 per week; clerk in the ticket department, dock clerk from 7 a. m. until 6 p. m., assistant to the manager of the Chicago office, assistant to the general manager in New York, supervisor at the head of the purchasing board steward departments, and finally manager. It will be seen that young Griscom had to "hoe his own row" completely, and, although at the time he, like the ordinary boy, objected to so doing, he now recognizes the wisdom of his father in compelling him to learn all there was to be learned. Under Mr. Griscom's management, the American Line flourishes. He is also president of the James Riley repair and supply company, a director of the Maritime Exchange and is interested in a number of other enterprises. He married the daughter of General William Ludlow, and his friends say that his home life has had a determining influence on his career in general.

JAMES J. HILL.

Intimates of James J. Hill, the transportation giant of the northwest, say that the ambition of his life is to encircle the world with a system of railroads and steamships, all of which shall be under his guiding hand. He has nearly attained it. He owns the Great Northern railway, which stretches from Seattle, Washington, to St. Paul and Duluth, Minnesota. He is proprietor of the line of steamers which ply between Duluth and Buffalo. He is largely interested in the Baltimore & Ohio railroad, which covers the territory between Chicago, Philadelphia and New York. He is organizing, in Europe, a steamship company whose vessels shall have for their terminal ports Seattle, Washington, on the one side, and Vladivostok, Yokohama and Hong Kong on the other. He is now reaching out across the Pacific to Seattle, intending to connect his Great Northern road with the Trans-Siberian road, and the man who controls all these huge enterprises earned them from humble beginnings, and asserts that the principle that has enabled him to reach power and affluence is simply that of economy. When he earned five dollars a week he saved; now that he is the owner of an income the size of which he can hardly pass upon, he saves, not in miserly fashion, but he detests unnecessary expenditure. Mr. Hill was born near Guelph, Upper Canada, September 16, 1838. He was educated at Rockwood academy and started life in a steamboat office in St. Paul, Minnesota. Hard and continuous work brought its reward in the shape of his being made agent for the Northwestern Packet company in 1865. Then he branched out for himself, establishing a fuel and transportation business on his own account. From that time on his rise was rapid. He founded the Red River Transportation company, 1875; organized the syndicate which secured control of the St. Paul and Pacific railroad, became the president of the organized road and finally merged it with other lines into the Great Northern system of which he is now president. Mr. Hill is married and has several sons, all of whom are following the railroad business.

MELVILLE EZRA INGALLS.

One of the many railroad presidents who began life on a farm is Melville Ezra Ingalls. He was born at Harrison, Maine, September 6, 1842. Brought up on his father's farm, he had his full share of hard work during boyhood. He was first educated at Burlington academy, later at Bowdoin college, and graduated from the Harvard law school in 1863. Establishing himself in practice in Gray, Maine, he soon found that the village was too small for his hopes and ambitions, so he removed to Boston. There he became identified with political affairs and was elected a member of the Massachusetts senate in 1867. In 1870 he was made the president of the Indianapolis, Cincinnati and Lafayette railroad, which was then in a bankrupt condition. A year later he was made receiver for the road. Then it was that Mr. Ingalls' genius for railroading began to show itself. With the aid of the organization in 1873 and 1880, he put the successor of the road, which was the Cincinnati, Indianapolis, St. Louis and Chicago, on a sound footing, subsequently consolidating it with other roads under its final title of the Cleveland, Cincinnati, Chicago and St. Louis railroad, now known as the "Big Four" system. Mr. Ingalls is president of the road, and up to February, 1900, was also president of the Chesapeake and Ohio railroad. Mr. Ingalls' successes have left him the same charitable, genial and approachable individual that he was when a struggling lawyer in a little village in Maine.

INVENTORS.

ALEXANDER GRAHAM BELL.

Alexander Graham Bell, whose name is so clearly associated with the invention and the development of the telephone, was born in Edinburgh, Scotland, March 3, 1847. He was educated at the Edinburgh and London universities, and on graduating went to Canada in 1870, in which country he spent two years endeavoring to decide on a vocation. Later he located in Boston, where he became professor of vocal physiology at the Boston university. It was during this period that he became interested in and made an exhaustive series of experiments culminating in an application for a patent which was granted February 14, 1876. The history of the invention, which is second in importance only to the electric telegraph, is well known to the public. Without going into details, it is only necessary to say that Mr. Bell, like all other successful inventors, had to face and overcome the popular prejudices, and had to protect his rights in the courts through interminable law suits. The place that the telephone fills in the social and commercial economy of the world to-day is also too well known to need emphasis. Professor Bell is also the inventor of the photophone, and is interested in the current scientific efforts of the American association to promote the teaching of the deaf and dumb. Scientific honors have been showered upon him in connection with his inventions. In 1881 the French government awarded him the Volta prize, and he is the founder of the Volta bureau. He is also the author of many scientific and educational monographs.

CHARLES FRANCIS BRUSH.

The development and general use of the "arc" electric light is to a very great extent the outcome of the researches of Charles F. Brush. While the "arc" was by no means unknown to electricians prior to Mr. Brush's development of it, it was he who was responsible for its becoming a commercial possibility. Mr. Brush was born in Euclid, Cuyahoga county, Ohio, March 17, 1849. His father was Colonel Isaac Elbert Brush, his mother being Delia Wissner (Phillips) Brush. Both parents came from old lines of American families. After periods spent in public schools in Ohio, Mr. Brush attended the Cleveland high school and graduated from the University of Michigan in 1869. From the first he displayed a fondness for electricity and chemistry, and subsequent to his graduating became an analytical chemist and consulting chemical expert in Cleveland. All this time, however, he was studying electricity, foreseeing the time when it would be one of the chief factors of modern civilization. In 1877 he devoted himself entirely to electrical affairs and a year later presented to the public the light with which his name is identified. In 1880 the Brush Electric Company was formed and the "arc" light grew in favor. A year later it was introduced into England and on the continent. Nevertheless Mr. Brush had the usual experience of inventors, but was successful in litigation and has the satisfaction of knowing that his claims of priority of invention have been recognized by the leading scientific societies in the world. He is interested in a number of electrical enterprises, is a member of many clubs and scientific and charitable institutions. In 1875 he married Mary E. Morris, of Cleveland, by whom he has three children.

SANTOS DUMONT.

Santos Dumont, who has attained world wide publicity in connection with his daring and novel experiments in ærostatics, is still a young man. He was born in Brazil in 1873 and is of French ancestry, although his father was also a Brazilian by birth. The Santos Dumont plantations at San Paulo are said to be the largest in the country in question, so large indeed that a small railroad runs around it, which is used for the transportation of labor and products. At an early age Santos Dumont developed a taste for mechanics and the railroad was his constant study and delight. When still a boy he was sent to France to be educated, and in that country, some thirteen years since, began to experiment with automobiles, abandoning them, however, in 1893, for ærostatics. His first ascents were made in spherical balloons, but he quickly adopted those of cylindrical form. He has practically invented the dirigible balloon of to-day through the medium of his ingenious arrangement of screws, rudders, motors, cars, shifting weights, etc. He was the first to give up the net and attach his car to the balloon itself. On July 12, 1901, he sailed from St. Cloud to the Eiffel Tower and around in Paris. He has made over half a dozen machines and is engaged on others. During his experiments he has had more than one narrow escape from death, but these have had little or no effect upon his nerve or his enthusiasm.

PETER COOPER HEWITT.

Peter C. Hewitt—who is much in the eye of the scientific world by reason of his invention of an electric "convertor" and his discovery of a wonderful method of electric lighting—is the grandson of the late Peter Cooper, the philanthropist. Mr. Hewitt was born in New York city in 1861, his father being

Abram Stevens Hewitt, who held the office of mayor of the metropolis from 1887 to 1889. After being educated by private tutors, he entered the Columbia university, New York city, and on graduating therefrom studied for some years in a technical school in New Jersey. Afterward he became connected with the glue factory established by his grandfather and owned by his father. But that bent toward scientific investigations which seems to have been born in him, prompted him to devote himself to experimental work in the laboratory. A portion of the result of such work has already been alluded to. There are not wanting indications that the electric light devised by Mr. Hewitt will, to a very great extent, take the place of that now furnished by the arc or incandescent filament. It is described as "soft sunlight." Mr. Hewitt is married, his wife being Lucy, daughter of the late Frank Work. He is popular socially, and his private charities prove that he has inherited his grandfather's great-heartedness to no small degree.

JOHN P. HOLLAND.

John P. Holland, the inventor of the submarine boat which bears his name, is an Irishman by birth. He is now about sixty years of age, hale, hearty and devoted to the task of improving the wonderful craft of which he is the creator. Mr. Holland reached this country early in the 70's, but long before that he had come to the conclusion that much of the naval warfare of the future would be done beneath the water rather than on its surface. He states that his convictions in this respect were the outcome of a newspaper account of the fight between the Monitor and Merrimac, which he read about two weeks after the occurrence of that historical conflict. From that time on, he began to form plans and make models for submarine torpedo boats or destroyers. He not only had to contend with great mechanical difficulties, but even when his boat was so far perfected that it could be submitted to the authorities, he encountered prejudices and opposition of the strongest. As the matter now stands, the most conservative of naval experts have become convinced of the importance of the Holland submarine, that, too, not only in this country but abroad. The United States now owns a number of the boats, as does Great Britain. Mr. Holland, when he first came to this country, was a school teacher, and, like the majority of inventors who are not capitalists, had a hard time of it for many years. He was at length fortunate enough to interest some moneyed men in his invention and was enabled to devote himself entirely to it. It is said that his creations provide for every contingency, both above and below water. It was only after prolonged tests of their efficiency that the U. S. government added them to the navy.

WILLIAM MARCONI.

This is eminently the age of young men, and William Marconi is a case in point. He was born at Marzabotto, Italy, September 23, 1875, his father being an Italian and his mother an Englishwoman. After being educated at the universities of Bologna and Padua, he, at a very early age, began to evidence a liking for scientific pursuits. Happily for the world at large, Marconi's father was so placed financially that he could permit of his son following his inclinations to the utmost. After some preliminary work, young Marconi instituted a series of experiments in order to test the theory, which at that time was a theory only, that electric currents under certain conditions are able to pass through any known substance. The result was that when but fifteen years of age he invented an apparatus for wireless telegraphy, which attracted the attention of Sir William Henry Preece, engineer and electrician-in-chief of the English postal service. The apparatus was tested in England and with success. For the next few years Marconi was engaged in perfecting his system. Public attention was called to his further successes in 1897 by messages being sent from Queen Victoria on land to the Prince of Wales (now King Edward), some miles distant on the Royal yacht. Later the British government engaged Marconi to install a number of wireless stations around the southern coast of England, and from that time on, wireless telegraphy has become an accepted fact with civilized governments all the world over. He came to this country in 1889, where he made more experiments and organized and incorporated a company for the commercial use of his methods. At the present writing messages have been successfully sent between England and America, a greater number of liners are equipped with the Marconi apparatus, and the same remark applies to the warships of the United States and European powers.

GEORGE WESTINGHOUSE.

George Westinghouse was born at Central Bridge, New York, October 6, 1846. Ten years later his parents removed to Schenectady, where he was educated in the public and high schools, spending much of his time in his father's machine-shop. During the Civil war he served in the Union army. At its close he attended Union college, Schenectady, for two years. In 1865 he invented the device for replacing railroad cars on the track. In 1868 he invented and successfully introduced the Westinghouse air-brake. From time to time he has modified and improved this, one of the most notable of his inventions. He is also the inventor of many other devices connected with railroads, such as signals, automatic and otherwise, electric devices of several sorts and other things which make for the efficiency of transportation in general. He is the president of twelve corporations, a member of many scientific societies, and is also the recipient of medals and decorations from the king of Italy, the king of Belgium and other European notables. It is not too much to say that without the Westinghouse inventions railroading as we know of it to-day would hardly be possible. Apart from adding much to the safety of railroad travel, the Westinghouse brake permits paradoxically enough of speeds being attained which would not be possible under old-time conditions. Mr. Westinghouse's inventive genius has been largely rewarded in a financial manner.

MERCHANTS.

EDWARD COOPER.

Edward Cooper, one of the more prominent merchants of New York, was born October 26th, 1824. He is the son of Peter Cooper, the philanthropist, and, like his father, has, during the course of a busy life, done much for the well being of the people of the municipality in which he lives. Mr. Cooper was educated in New York public schools and is a graduate of Columbia university. Throughout his life he has been more or less active in New York political affairs, and, while a consistent Democrat, has had no hesitation in putting principle before party. He was one of the leaders of the successful movement which overthrew the infamous Tweed ring. From 1879 to 1881 he was mayor of New York and added to his reputation by the honesty and energy of his administration. Mr. Cooper is associated with his brother-in-law, Abram S. Hewitt, in the conduct of the Trenton Iron Works, New Jersey Steel Works and other enterprises of a like nature. He is a good example of the man who does not permit his business affairs or his wealth to interfere with his obligations as a citizen.

ROBERT CURTIS OGDEN.

Robert Curtis Ogden was born at Philadelphia, July 20th, 1836, and is the son of the late Jonathan Curtis Ogden. He was educated in private schools in the city of his birth. On March 1st, 1860, he married Ellen Elizabeth Lewis, of Brooklyn. Since 1885 he has been a partner in the firm of John Wanamaker. His business acumen, as well as his bent toward philanthropic and religious work, has eminently fitted him to hold the responsible position which he occupies in the firm's affairs. In spite of the many commercial duties which are part and portion of Mr. Ogden's every-day life, he nevertheless finds time to attend to the many philanthropic enterprises in which he is interested. In 1889 he acted as a member of the State Johnstown Flood Relief Commission, which accomplished much in the way of relieving the sufferers from the disaster in question. He is also a director of the Union Hill Theological seminary, trustee of the Tuskegee Institute of Alabama and is first vice-president of the Pennsylvania Society of New York. Mr. Ogden takes an active part in church matters and is the author of several books and pamphlets, including "Pew Rentals and the New Testament—Can They Be Reconciled?" "Sunday School Teaching," etc. As a contributor to the magazines, he is well known, some of the articles from his pen which have attracted much attention being "Getting and Keeping a Business Position" and "Ethics of Modern Retailing." Mr. Ogden takes an active interest in the welfare of the young people employed by him and his partners.

HENRY SIEGEL.

Henry Siegel, whose name is identified with those huge so-called department stores, which are cities of commerce inclosed within four walls, was born March 17, 1852, at Enbighein, Germany. His father was the burgomaster of the village, and he himself was one of a family of eight children. Two of his brothers, on attaining manhood, came to this country and were fairly prosperous. The letters that they sent home acted as fuel to the ambitions of Henry, and so when seventeen years of age he sailed for America, and obtained a position in Washington, District of Columbia, in a dry goods house at a salary of three dollars per week. By dint of hard study at night schools he managed to get a fair English education and next became traveler for a clothing house. After some years of hard work, he and his brothers began business for themselves in Chicago and fortune followed their efforts. In 1887 he founded the well-known firm of Siegel, Cooper & Co., of Chicago, again prospered, and in 1896, together with his partners, opened a vast store on Sixth avenue, New York. In 1901 he sold out his interest in the New York enterprise, but immediately acquired the old-established firm of Simpson, Crawford & Co. He simultaneously disposed of his interest in the Chicago concern. A year later he bought a half-interest in the firm of Schlessinger & Mayer, of Chicago. Not content with these undertakings, early in 1903, he began to build a store at Thirty-fourth street and Broadway, New York, and also purchased an entire block in Boston on which he proposes to erect a building which shall dwarf those of which he is already the owner. And so the little German who began life as an errand boy is now one of the merchant princes of America.

FRANK W. WOOLWORTH.

Frank W. Woolworth was born at Rodman, New York, April 13, 1852. He passed his boyhood on his parents' farm, was educated at a district school, and graduated from the Commercial college at Watertown, New York. His start in life was as a clerk in a dry goods store at Watertown. In 1878 he originated the popular five and ten-cent store, which, thanks to his energy and acumen, has attained such marvelous popularity. His employers, Moore & Smith, at his suggestion, bought $50 worth of the cheapest sort of goods and put them with other old shop-worn goods on the counter, displaying the sign "Any article on this counter five cents." The stock was sold the first day, and Mr. Woolworth then decided to have a five and ten-cent store of his own. Borrowing $325, he opened a place in Utica, New York. The public patronized him and at the end of six weeks he had a net profit of $139.50. In

1869 he removed to Lancaster, Pennsylvania, where he opened a store, and next another at Harrisburg, Pennsylvania. Both of these ventures were successful and he now has stores in nearly every large city in the country, there being eight of such in New York alone. He was married, in 1876, to Jennie, daughter of Thomas Creighton, of Pictou, Ontario, Canada, and has three daughters. Mr. Woolworth's career is a practical commentary on the value of the maxim that it is unwise to "despise the day of small things."

FINANCIERS.

WILLIAM WALDORF ASTOR.

William Waldorf Astor, the capitalist and author, born in New York city, March 31, 1848 is the son of the noted John Jacob and Charlotte Augusta (Gibbs) Astor. He was educated chiefly by private tutors, among whom was a professor of the University of Marburg. At the age of 23 he was taken into the offices of the Astor estate in order to master the details of each department. Recognizing the need of a thorough legal education, he studied for two years in the Columbia Law School, being admitted to the bar in May, 1875. His father being convinced of the son's exceptional business ability, subsequently gave him absolute control over all of his property. In 1877 Mr. Astor was elected a member of the New York state legislature from the Eleventh Assembly District, defeating the Tammany Hall and the Independent Democratic candidates. In 1879 he was elected to the state senate and in 1881 was nominated for congress in the district formerly represented by Levi P. Morton, but was defeated by Roswell P. Flower. In August, 1882, President Chester A. Arthur appointed Mr. Astor Minister to Italy. While in Rome he spent much time in studying the early history of the country, and on returning home, in 1885, published his novel, Valentino, which embodies his researches in the mediæval history of Italy. His later novel, Sforza, also deals with Italy in the Middle Ages. Mr. Astor has built the New Netherlands hotel, on Fifth avenue and Fifty-ninth street, New York city, and Hotel Waldorf Astoria, the latter on the site of the old Astor residence. In September, 1890, Mr. Astor moved to London, England, where he has entered upon a notable career in journalism. He now owns the Pall Mall Gazette, and has founded the Pall Mall Magazine. He is and has been a stockholder and director in several American railroads. He has other interests outside of his vast real estate holdings. On June 6, 1878, he was married to Mary Dahlgren, daughter of James W. Paul, of Philadelphia, Pa. Mrs. Astor died in 1894.

HENRY CLEWS.

When the long-sought-for opportunity to become a banker came to the ambitious young man, now the financier, Henry Clews, he did not let his chances pass him. He was born in Staffordshire, England, August 14, 1840, coming of a good old English family. His father, an able business man, intended Henry for the ministry of the Established Church of England. But at the age of fifteen the boy, visiting America with his father, became so interested in the country and its people that he gave up all idea of becoming a clergyman, and, with his parents' consent, settled in the United States. His first position in this country was as a clerk with an importing firm, in which he rose to a position of responsibility. In 1859 he became a member of the firm of Stout, Clews & Mason, which subsequently became Livermore, Clews & Co. At the outbreak of the Civil War Secretary Chase invited him to become agent for selling government bonds. His unfaltering faith in their worth was shown by his subscribing to the National loan at the rate of five million or ten million dollars per day, even going into debt by borrowing on the bonds. This materially strengthened the public confidence in the government's course of action. When Mr. Chase was congratulated upon his success in placing the war loans, he said: "I deserve no credit; had it not been for the exertion of Jay Cooke and Henry Clews I could never have succeeded." Mr. Clews founded and organized the famous "Committee of Seventy" that successfully disposed of the "Tweed Ring." After the Civil War, besides establishing a distinctive banking business, he became one of the largest negotiators of railroad loans in America or Europe. The present firm of Henry Clews & Co. was established in 1877, its members pledging themselves never to take any speculative risks. Mr. Clews has for many years been treasurer of the "Society for Prevention of Cruelty to Animals," and is also connected with many city institutions and financial corporations. He married Lucy Madison, of Worthington, Kentucky, a grandniece of ex-President Madison. He is a frequent contributor to newspapers and magazines and the author of Twenty-eight Years in Wall Street.

MRS. HETTY GREEN.

America's richest woman, Mrs. Hetty Green, is like the majority of wealthy persons, not only able to keep, but to increase her riches. Her genius for finance is admittedly equal to that possessed by any of those individuals whose names are identified with vast and progressive wealth. She was born November 21, 1835, in New Bedford, Mass., her maiden name being Hetty Howland Robinson. Not long after her birth her father, Edward Mott Robinson, died, leaving her a large fortune. She was educated at the Mrs. Lowell's school in Boston. In 1876 she married E. H. Green, of New York City. From thence on she began that financial career which has made her famous. Mrs. Green is said to be interested in nearly every large corporation all over the world. She also has large real estate holdings in a number of cities in this country, and is interested in many enterprises of a general nature. She personally manages her business affairs, and is a familiar figure in Wall Street, and "downtown" New York. Her formula for getting rich is that "Economy is the secret of making money."

JOHN PIERPONT MORGAN.

John Pierpont Morgan was born at Hartford, Conn., April 17, 1837. His mother was a daughter of the Rev. John Pierpont, a noted clergyman, poet, author and temperance worker. He was educated at the English high school at Boston and at the University of Gottingen, Germany, from whence he graduated in 1857. On returning to the United States he became associated with the banking house of Duncan, Sherman & Co., of New York city. In 1860 he severed his connection with that firm and began business for himself. In 1864 he formed the firm of Dabney, Morgan & Co. Meantime he had become representative of the house of George Peabody & Co., of London, and during the Civil War he was able, through this connection, to render substantial assistance to the Federal government. In 1871 he organized the firm of Drexel, Morgan & Co., and by the death of Mr. Drexel, in 1893, he became senior partner. In 1895 the firm title was changed to J. P. Morgan & Co. He is also head of the firms of J. P. Morgan & Co., of London; Morgan, Hayes & Co., of Paris, and Drexel & Co., of Philadelphia. Mr. Morgan is generally known as the "King of Trust Magnates," on account of his having engineered so many mercantile and financial consolidations; in fact, he has been instrumental in forming the majority of the great corporations or trusts. He gives large sums to charity, is a liberal patron of art, and is a member of all the leading clubs of New York and other cities. In 1865 he was married to Frances Louise, daughter of John Tracy. He has one son, John Pierpont Morgan, Jr., and three daughters. Mr. Morgan's vast operations are not confined to this country. He is an active power in English and Continental financial circles.

JOHN DAVISON ROCKEFELLER.

The owner of what is believed to be the largest individual income in the world began his business life as a poorly paid clerk in a small provincial firm. John Davison Rockefeller was born at Richford, New York, on July 8th, 1839. He was educated in the local public schools. In 1853 his parents moved to Cleveland, Ohio, where, while still a boy, he obtained a position as clerk in a general commission house. When nineteen he went into business for himself by becoming a partner in the firm of Clark & Rockefeller, general commission merchants. Subsequently the firm admitted another partner, and under the title of Andrews, Clark & Co., engaged in the oil business. Its so doing, so it is said, was due to the sagacity of Mr. Rockefeller, who was one of the few men of the period who recognized the future and gigantic possibilities of the oil industry. Later changes were made in the organization of the firm, and in 1865, under the name of William Rockefeller & Co., it built the Standard Oil Works at Cleveland. In 1870 the works were consolidated with others and were then known as the Standard Oil Company. From time to time other oil interests were acquired, and in 1882 all were merged into the Standard Oil Trust. Ten years later, however, the trust was dissolved, and from that time to the present the various companies of which it was composed are operated separately, with Mr. Rockefeller at the head of the business as a whole.

CHARLES TYSON YERKES.

The Yerkes family is of Dutch origin, and Charles Tyson Yerkes was born June 25, 1837, in Philadelphia, Pennsylvania. He was educated at the Friends' School and the Central High School in his native city, and entered business life as clerk in a flour and grain commission house. He worked without salary, since, in those days, it was counted a privilege to be connected with first-class houses. Because of his close attention to his duties he was presented with fifty dollars at the end of his first year's service. In 1859 he opened a stock broker's office in Philadelphia. During the Civil War he dealt heavily in government, state and city bonds. The panic occasioned by the Chicago fire caught him heavily indebted to the city for bonds sold for it. The authorities demanded settlement; but, being unable to pay in full, he made an assignment. In 1873 he commenced the recuperation of his fortune, and with success. In 1880 he made a trip to Chicago, and, becoming convinced of the opportunities the west offered to financiers, he joined an "improvement syndicate," of which he later became sole owner. Subsequently he sold his interest in it and opened a banking house in Chicago. In 1886 he obtained control of the North Chicago Railway Company. He added other systems, and finally united several corporations under the title of the Chicago Consolidated Traction Company. Mr. Yerkes was a chief factor in getting the Columbian Exposition for Chicago. He is a devoted lover of art, and possesses a unique collection of pictures. His successful efforts to introduce New World street transportation methods into England are a matter of recent record. In 1861 Mr. Yerkes was married to Mary Adelaide Moore, of Philadelphia.

POLITICAL LEADERS.

NELSON WILMARTH ALDRICH.

The republican leader in the senate, Nelson Wilmarth Aldrich, was born in Foster, Rhode Island, November 6, 1841. After having received a common school and academy education, he became engaged in mercantile pursuits in Providence, being entirely successful therein. While a very young man, Mr. Aldrich became interested in the conduct and welfare of public schools. He became so prominent in connection with efforts looking to school improvements that in 1871 he was elected president of the Providence common council. In 1873 he was a member of the Rhode Island legislature, and at 1876 was its speaker. It was about this period that Mr. Aldrich began to take an active part in national politics, in consequence of which he was made member of congress in 1879, holding that office until 1883, when he resigned in order to take a seat in the senate. Since that time he has been more or less continuously in the public eye. He is chairman of the committee of rules of the Fiftieth congress, and is, as already stated, republican leader in the senate. While Mr. Aldrich is not a brilliant orator, he has a remarkable instinct for organization, and it is that faculty more than any other that has obtained for him the prominent position in the Republican party which is now his.

WILLIAM JENNINGS BRYAN.

William Jennings Bryan was born in Salem, Marion county, Illinois, March 19, 1860. He got an elementary education at home from his mother until he was ten, and then attended public school until his fifteenth year, studying thereafter for two years at Whipple academy, Jacksonville, which he left in order to enter Illinois college. During his college course he was prominent in literary and debating societies and on his graduation, in 1881, delivered the valedictory of his class. For the next two years he studied law in the Union law college, and in the office of Lyman Trumbull, and upon his admission to the bar began to practice at Jacksonville. In 1884 he removed to Lincoln, Nebraska, and became a member of the law firm of Talbot & Bryan. He soon became active in politics, his first public reputation being made in the campaign of 1888. In 1890 he was sent to congress. In 1892 he was renominated and again elected. In 1896 he was a delegate from Nebraska to the national convention of the Democratic party at Chicago, where his brilliant speech in defense of free silver caused his nomination as candidate to the presidency of the United States. After a most remarkable campaign he was defeated. He was a colonel of the Third Nebraska Volunteers during the Spanish-American war, and at its termination returned to Nebraska, resuming his political activities. He edits and publishes The Commoner, a weekly periodical, in which he sets forth his political principles. Mary E. Baird, of Perry, Illinois, whom he married in 1884, has borne him three children.

ARTHUR PUE GORMAN.

There are very few people who begin political life as early as Arthur Pue Gorman. He was born March 11, 1839, and at thirteen years of age became a page in the United States senate. In 1866 he was appointed revenue collector in Maryland, which office he held until 1869, when U. S. Grant became president. From 1875 to 1879 he was state senator, and from 1881 to 1899 he was United States senator from Maryland. From 1869 to 1875 he was member of the Maryland House of Delegates. In spite of his limited schooling, he managed by wide and careful reading and practical experience to secure an education in general and in public matters in particular, which has procured for him the position of a notable political leader. It was largely through Mr. Gorman's management that Grover Cleveland was elected to the presidency after an uninterrupted series of democratic defeats for a quarter of a century. Calmness of temper, courage, self-reliance and honesty are the qualities which he possesses, which, too, inspire respect and which win him triumphs. He is an able speaker and a master of parliamentary law. He has strikingly impressed himself upon national affairs, and his name has often been voiced in the press as a fit candidate for the presidency.

MARCUS ALONZO HANNA.

Marcus Alonzo Hanna, one of the most prominent figures in national republican affairs, was born September 24, 1837, at New Lisbon (now Lisbon), Ohio. His father was a grocer in that village. Young Hanna was educated at local schools, and in the Western Reserve college and Kenyon college, Ohio. When not in school he was helping his father in the latter's store, and cut short his academic course in order to clerk for his father, who had decided on opening a place of business in Cleveland. Until he was twenty he thus worked, receiving a small salary for so doing. In 1861 his father died, and young Hanna became heir to the business, which he continued to run until 1867. During that year he sold out and laid the foundations of the vast fortune which he now possesses. Mr. Hanna is interested in banks, railroads, mines of many sorts, especially coal, steamship lines, etc. At a comparatively early age he became interested in political questions, into the solving of which he threw himself with characteristic earnestness. For many years he has been chairman of the republican national committee, and in that capacity he secured the nomination of the late President McKinley, as well as obtaining a second term for him. Mr. Hanna is United States senator from Ohio, having been elected to that office in 1897. In his own words, his success may be explained thus: "I was never penniless, because I always saved. I was never hopeless, because I would not be discouraged, and I always felt assured that present endeavors would bring forth future fruit."

CARTER HENRY HARRISON, JR.

Carter Henry Harrison, Jr., was born in Chicago, April 23, 1860. He is the son of the late Carter Henry Harrison, one of the builders of the City of Chicago, who was its mayor five times. Carter Henry Harrison, Jr., was educated in the public schools, in educational establishments in Altenburg, Germany, at St. Ignatius college, Chicago, and the Yale law school, from which he graduated in 1883. On December 14, 1887, he was married to Edith, daughter of Robert N. Ogden, of the Court of Appeals, New Orleans. He followed his father's profession of law and the real estate business. He also was the publisher of the Chicago Times, 1891 and 1893; was elected mayor of Chicago as a democrat, April 6, 1897, 1899, 1901 and 1903. Mr. Harrison has the courage of vigorous opinions politically, municipally and in other ways. While some may differ from him as to his beliefs and methods, even these admit his possession of those qualities which enable him to successfully fulfil duties that are usually relegated to much older men.

JOSEPH WINGATE FOLK.

One of the most prominent and promising young men in the political life in the United States is Joseph Wingate Folk, who was elected governor of Missouri in the fall of 1904. Though Governor Folk's rise has been a very rapid one, it has been the result of qualities which make for the most substantial and enduring kind of political success. Dominating factors of Governor Folk's career have been honesty and a rigid performance of duty. For these he has courted defeat and failure, has even undergone danger to his life. He has refused to listen for a moment to some of the largest financial offers that have ever been made to tempt a servant of the people to betray his trust. Not only has the power of money, but also the corrupt personal influence of many able men, been brought to bear upon him in his work as circuit attorney in St. Louis. Many of his friends, even, endeavored to persuade him that his course of action toward the political leaders in St. Louis would result only in disaster to himself. But Governor Folk's invariable answer was that he accepted public office for no other purpose than to do his duty.

The result has been a great surprise to both his friends and enemies, and the introduction of an uplifting influence in American politics. Governor Folk has won a great personal triumph in his election to the governorship of Missouri, and the indications are that he will rise to still greater heights. His prominence and influence are rendered all the more notable by the fact that he is only thirty-five years old, and rose from the position of an obscure lawyer to American leadership in the short space of four years.

Governor Folk was born in the town of Brownsville, Tenn., in 1869. He finished his college education at Vanderbilt University, where he was known as a clever, whole-souled young man who devoted much attention to his books, but by no means neglected athletics and the general life of a college boy. He was admitted to the bar in 1890, and began the practice of law in St. Louis, where for some years his experiences were those of the average struggling young attorney. During this period of his career he became a friend of Henry W. Hawes, who was afterward one of his bitterest political enemies. Hawes rapidly rose to a position of considerable power in St. Louis, and when, in 1900, he was asked by the Democratic boss of the city, Edward Butler, to suggest a likely man for the place of circuit attorney, he at once recommended his friend Folk. Butler knew very little of the young lawyer, but on the strength of Hawes' word he accepted him as being sufficiently pliable to serve the corrupt uses of the political machine.

Folk was elected and immediately inaugurated the now celebrated campaign against the corrupt practices of both his political supporters and his enemies. It was the former who suffered chiefly in the execution of Governor Folk's ideas as to his duty. They were at first astonished, then incensed, and finally panic-stricken. Many of those who helped to elect him to office were sent to prison. Others were compelled to take flight to avoid the same fate. The St. Louis political machine, one of the most corrupt in existence, was shattered. It was a herculean task which Governor Folk had mapped out for himself, but his courage, steadfastness and ability carried him to a triumphant conclusion of it, and now he stands before the country as a political leader of the highest type.

LAWYERS AND JURISTS.

FRANK SWETT BLACK.

Frank Swett Black was born at Limington, Maine, March 8, 1853. He graduated from Dartmouth, 1875. He entered professional life as the editor of the Johnstown, New York, Journal. Later he became reporter of the Troy Whig, New York. He was a clerk in the registry department of the Troy postoffice, during which time he studied law and was admitted to the bar in 1879. He was a member of congress in 1895 to 1897, and in 1897 was elected by the republicans as governor of New York state. He also won distinction as a trial lawyer and has defended a number of notable cases, among which was the celebrated case of Rollin B. Molineaux.

FREDERICK RENÉ COUDERT.

The young man who wishes to succeed in the profession of law would do well to study the life of the lawyer, Frederick René Coudert, whose every act has been marked by fairness and courtesy. He was born of French parentage in the city of New York in 1832, receiving his early education at his father's school in that city. At the age of fourteen he entered Columbia college, graduating with highest honors in 1850, his address on that occasion calling forth much comment from the press. During the next few years he busied himself with newspaper work, teaching and translations, besides studying law; and at the age of twenty-one was admitted to the New York bar. His brothers, Lewis and Charles Coudert, Jr., joining him in the practice of law, they formed the firm of Coudert Brothers, one of the oldest and largest law firms of New York city, and of which Frederick R. Coudert is the recognized head. He has achieved quite a reputation as a speaker and lecturer; and among his most notable addresses might be mentioned one at the centennial celebration of Columbia college, 1887; an eloquent speech in favor of the Democratic union during the campaign of Tilden in 1879, and his public addresses on the arrival of Bartholdi's statue of liberty and the statues of Lafayette and Bolivar. He has been quite active in the political work of the democratic party, but avoiding, rather than asking, public functions, several times having declined nominations which signified election to the bench of the Supreme Court. Mr. Coudert played a prominent part in the election of President Cleveland in 1884. Mr. Coudert's abilities have been of great service in other fields. He was the first president of the United States Catholic Historical Society, holding the office several terms; for years president of the Columbia college alumni association; for years government director of the Union Pacific railroad; for a long time trustee of Columbia and Barnard colleges and of Seton Hall College, New Jersey, besides being the director in numerous social and charitable organizations. In 1880 Seton college awarded him the degree of LL.D., which degree was also given by Fordham college in 1884, and, in 1887, he received from Columbia college the degree of J. U. D. As a mark of recognition the French government presented him with the Cross of the Legion of Honor, which decoration he has also received from the governments of Italy and Bolivia.

JAMES BROOKS DILL.

A sturdy Scotch ancestry has given to the lawyer, James Brooks Dill, that pertinacity and determination which successfully overcomes all obstacles. He was born in Spencerport, New York,

July 25, 1854, the oldest child of the Rev. James Horton and Catherine (Brooks) Dill. Four years after his birth his parents removed to Chicago, but upon the death of his father, in 1863, he removed with his mother to New Haven, Connecticut, continuing his studies in the elementary branches. After studying at Oberlin, Ohio, from 1868 to 1872, he entered Yale, graduating in the class of 1876. He now taught school and studied law, and in 1877 came to New York, where he obtained a position as instructor in Stevens' Institute, Hoboken. Mr. Dill was graduated with the degree of LL.D. from the University law school in 1878, as salutatorian, and was then admitted to the bar of New York. Corporation law was made one of his special studies, and, in 1879, he won an important corporation case which soon established his reputation as a corporation lawyer and an authority on this particular subject. His marked business ability, combined with a clear legal mind, made his services sought by the many large and influential corporate interests. He was married in 1880 to Miss Mary W. Hansell, daughter of a Philadelphia merchant, thereupon removing to Orange, New Jersey. He became an active worker in the municipal and social improvement of the Oranges, organizing a People's Bank, of which he has always been a director and counsel. He also assisted in establishing the Savings Investment and Trust Co., becoming director and vice-president. He is now director in the Seventh National Bank of New York City, the Corporation Trust Company of New Jersey, the American School of Architecture at Rome, the New England State Railway Company of Boston, the Central Teresa Sugar Company and others.

MELVILLE WESTON FULLER.

The most notable figure of the judiciary of this country is undoubtedly Chief Justice Melville Weston Fuller, of the Supreme Court of the United States. He is in every way the ideal dignitary of the bench, impressive as to appearance, forceful in forensic oratory, learned in the law and unblemished as to reputation, personal and professional. He was born February 11, 1833, at Augusta, Maine, coming of sterling New England stock. Graduating from Bowdoin college in 1853, and later educated at Harvard law school, he, in 1855, was admitted to the bar. Forming a law partnership in the town of his birth, he later established there a Democratic paper known as The Age, of which he became assistant editor. The venture was successful and The Age became a power in political circles in Maine. Young Fuller was also elected president of the common council, and city attorney for the town. But Augusta was too small a sphere for the rising young lawyer, so in 1859 he went to Chicago, where he opened a law office. Simultaneously he took an active part in Illinois politics. It was not long before he became a recognized political leader locally. In 1863 he became a member of the Illinois legislature, in which capacity he confirmed the beliefs of those who regarded him as a coming man. He was delegate to a number of Democratic national conventions, in each of which he was a prominent figure. President Cleveland appointed him chief justice on April 30, 1888, and he was confirmed and seated the year following.

JOHN WILLIAM GRIGGS.

John William Griggs was born at Newton, New Jersey, July 10, 1849. He was graduated from Lafayette college in 1868, and, after studying law, was admitted to the bar in 1871. He practiced law at Paterson until 1876, in which year he was elected a member of the New Jersey general assembly. In 1886 he was president of the New Jersey senate. He was elected governor of New Jersey in 1896, which office he resigned to accept the office of attorney-general of the United States. He resigned the attorney-generalship in 1901.

OLIVER WENDELL HOLMES.

Oliver Wendell Holmes, the son of Dr. Oliver Wendell Holmes, the poet and essayist, was born at Boston, March 8, 1841. He graduated from Harvard in 1861, and from the Harvard law school in 1866. During the Civil war he served three years with the Massachusetts volunteers, and was wounded in the breast in the battle of Balls Bluff, and again wounded at the battle of Antietam. At the close of the war he engaged in the practice of law in Boston, and was editor of the Law Review from 1870 to 1873. In 1882 he became professor at the Harvard law school. In the same year he was made assistant justice in the Supreme judicial court, Massachusetts, and on August 2, 1899, he was made chief justice of the same court.

WILLIAM TRAVERS JEROME.

William Travers Jerome, who, by reason of being the district attorney of the metropolis, his power of pungent political oratory and his strenuous work as a municipal reformer, is one of the best known and decidedly one of the most interesting figures in the current history of New York, is still a young man. He was born April 18, 1859, in Lawrence, Massachusetts, receiving his initial education at the local public school and from private tutors; he took a classical course at Amherst college, and next was a student at the Columbia university law school of New York city. He was admitted to the bar in 1884 and became connected with a New York law firm. From the first he gave evidence of being the possessor of those qualities which later made him famous. As a lawyer his learnedly aggressive methods brought him popularity and many fees. As a justice of the court of special sessions, he lived up to the reputation that he had established on the bench. When, a few years since, he threw himself into the political whirlpool, he gave the country-at-large an excellent example of the man who has waited for his opportunity, recognizes it when he sees it and grasps it forthwith. It is not too much to say that Mr. Jerome did more than any one man, or, for that matter, any one group of men to free New York from certain evil influences which had fastened themselves upon it and its citizens. Here is what he says relative to his political success, but his remarks apply equally to success of all kinds: "A young man must have strong convictions of the right kind, hold to them through thick and thin, be willing to accept defeats smilingly, if necessary begin his work all over again, but still stick to it—and victory is assured."

JOSEPH MCKENNA.

Another of the numerous successful jurists whose ancestry is Irish. He was the son of John and Mary McKenna, his father being from Ireland and his mother from England. He was born at Philadelphia, August 10, 1843, and was educated in the public schools and at St. Joseph college until 1855, when the family removed to Benicia, California, where he entered St. Augustine college and took up the study of law. Directly afterward he graduated and was admitted to the bar. In 1865 he was elected district attorney of Solano county. He served in this capacity for two terms. In 1873 he was elected to the legislature, and one year later the republicans nominated him for congress, but he was defeated, and not only on this occasion but again in 1878. In 1884, however, he was elected, and a year later entered congress, where he remained, by re-election, until 1891. As a member of the ways and means committee he had a great deal to do with important tariff legislation. In 1892 President Harrison appointed him circuit judge. In 1897 he entered McKinley's cabinet as attorney-general, but in December of the same year was appointed judge of the Supreme Court of the United States to succeed Justice Field.

He was married in San Francisco, 1869, to Amanda Borneman.

ALTON BROOKS PARKER.

Alton Brooks Parker comes from good old New England stock. He was born in Worcester, Massachusetts, May 14, 1851. Later his family moved to Cortland, New York, in which place he was educated, graduating from the normal school at that place. He spent three years in teaching, and then entered a law school at Kingston, New York, and afterward took a course at the Albany law school, where he was graduated in 1872. After being admitted to the bar, he formed a partnership with W. S. Kenyon at Kingston, New York. In 1877 Mr. Parker was elected surrogate of Ulster county, and was again re-elected in 1883. Two years later he was appointed, by Governor Hill, justice of the Supreme Court to fill the vacancy occasioned by the death of Hon. Theodoric R. Westbrook. At the end of the year he was elected justice for the full term. In January, 1889, the second division of the Court of Appeals was created, and Judge Parker was appointed to it, he being the youngest member who ever sat in the Court of Appeals in New York city. The second division court was dissolved in 1892, and at that time Governor Hill appointed him member of the general term of the first department, where he continued until 1895. He has always been active in politics and has been a delegate to nearly every state convention, and also to the national convention in 1884 which nominated Grover Cleveland. In 1895 he was chairman of the Democratic state executive committee. In 1897 he was elected by a majority of over sixty thousand to the office of chief justice of the Court of Appeals, the highest judicial office in the state of New York. He has often been mentioned as a possible candidate for president by the Democratic party. He was married October 16, 1873, to Mary L. Schoonmaker.

SOLDIERS AND SAILORS.

ADNA ROMANZA CHAFFEE.

Adna Romanza Chaffee was born at Orwell, Ohio, April 14, 1842. He was educated in the public schools and entered the army July 22, 1861, serving first as a private, but the close of the war, March 31, 1865, found him a captain. In 1868, in fighting the Comanche Indians on Paint Tree creek, Texas, he was made a major for gallantry in that and other campaigns, and was finally made lieutenant-colonel. At the breaking out of the Spanish-American war he was appointed brigadier-general of the United States volunteers, commanding the third brigade, fifth corps, in the Santiago campaign. He was promoted to major-general United States volunteers, July 8, 1898, and was honorably discharged as major-general, April 13, 1899, but was again appointed brigadier-general United States volunteers, one year later and assigned to the command of the United States forces for the relief of the United States legation at Pekin, China. In 1901 he was made a major-general United States army.

GEORGE DEWEY.

George Dewey, the third admiral of the United States navy, was born at Montpelier, Vermont, December 26, 1837. His father, Julius Yemans Dewey, was a physician. George attended school in Montpelier and at Johnson, Vermont. In 1853 he entered the University of Norwich, Vermont, but, instead of completing his course, he secured an appointment in the United States naval academy in 1854. He was graduated with honors in 1858 and was attached to the steam frigate Wabash. In 1861 he was commissioned a lieutenant and assigned to the steam sloop Mississippi, of the West Gulf squadron. He saw his first service under fire with Farragut in 1862, served with distinction all through the Civil war, and, at the close, he was commissioned lieutenant-commander. From 1868 to 1870 he was an instructor in the naval academy. Promoted to a captaincy in 1884, he was placed in command of the Dolphin, but in 1895 was returned to the European station in command of the flagship Pensacola; there he remained until 1888, when he was ordered home and appointed chief of the bureau of equipment, ranking as commander. On February 26, 1896, he was commissioned commander and made president of the board of inspection and survey, which position he held until January, 1898, when he was given command of the Asiatic station. While at Hongkong Prince Henry of Germany gave a banquet, at which he proposed a toast to the various countries represented, but omitted the United States, whereupon Commander Dewey left the room without ceremony. Three days after the beginning of the war with Spain President McKinley cabled him at Hongkong: "Proceed at once to the Philippine Islands. Commence operations, particularly against the Spanish fleet. You must capture or destroy the vessels. Use utmost endeavor." Dewey's success in carrying out these orders is known to all the world. President McKinley yielded to the popular demand that the rank of rear-admiral be revived in favor of Dewey. Accordingly, on March 3, 1899, the appointment was confirmed in executive session of the United States senate. He was married at Portsmouth, New Hampshire, October 24, 1867, to Susan B., daughter of ex-Governor Ichabod Goodwin, who died in December, 1872; he was again married to Mrs. Mildred Hazen in Washington on November 9, 1899.

ROBLEY DUNGLISON EVANS.

Robley Dunglison Evans, better known as Fighting Bob Evans, was born at Floyd Courthouse, Virginia, August 18, 1847. His father was a physician and a farmer, his mother being the daughter of John Jackson, of Fairfax county, and sister of James Jackson, who shot Colonel Ellsworth for capturing a Confederate flag on the roof of his hotel. Robley was educated at a country school and Gonzaga classical school, Washington, D. C. On September 20, 1860, he was appointed to the United States naval academy by Congressman William R. Hooper, from the Utah Territory. He was made a midshipman in 1860, and promoted to ensign in 1863. In 1864 and 1865 he served with his ship in the North Atlantic blockade squadron. He saw considerable service in the West Indies, and, in the attack on Fort Fisher, in 1865, received rifle shot wounds which disabled him for a time. In 1866 he was commissioned lieutenant; in 1868 was made lieutenant commander, and was later assigned to duty at the navy yard, Washington, and still later at the naval academy, Annapolis. From 1877 to 1881 he was in command of the training ship Saratoga, and later was promoted to commander. In 1891-'92 he was in command of the United States naval force at the Behring Sea to suppress sealing. In 1893 he was promoted to captain. During the Spanish-American war Captain Evans was in command of the battleship Iowa, which achieved distinction during the battle of Santiago, when the fleet of Admiral Cervera made an attempt to run the blockade. He served all through the Spanish-American war, and, in 1898, by his own request, he was detached from the command of the Iowa and was assigned to duty as a member of the board of inspection and survey. He was married in 1860 to Charlotte, daughter of Frank Taylor, of Washington, District of Columbia.

FRED FUNSTON.

Fred Funston was born in Ohio, November 9, 1865. His father was a prominent public man and one time a member of congress from Kansas. He was graduated in 1886 from the high school at Iola, Kansas, and later studied for two years in the state university at Lawrence, but was not graduated. In 1890 he was a reporter in Kansas City, and his first public work was done as botanist in the United States death valley expedition in 1891. Returning he was made a commissioner in the department of agriculture and was assigned to explore Alaska and report on its flora. In 1893 he floated down the Yukon alone in a canoe. He served eighteen months in the insurgent army in Cuba, and upon his return to the United States, in 1896, was commissioned a colonel in the Twentieth Kansas volunteers. In 1898 he went to the Philippines and took part in several battles. He crossed the Rio Grande river at Calumpit on a small bamboo raft under heavy fire and established a rope ferry by which the United States troops were enabled to cross and win the battle. For this deed of valor he was promoted to brigadier-general of the United States volunteers May 2, 1899. He remained in active service in the Philippines and organized the expedition which succeeded in the capture of Aguinaldo. For this he was promoted to brigadier-general United States army, March 20, 1901.

RICHMOND PEARSON HOBSON.

Many of our naval and army officers are of southern birth. Richmond Pearson Hobson is a case in point, since he was born at Greensboro, Alabama, August 17, 1870. His ancestors were English and many of them were members of the nobility. Young Hobson, after a course in the public schools and the Southern university at Greensboro, entered the United States naval academy at Annapolis in 1889. He was immediately appointed a midshipman on the Chicago, under command of Rear-Admiral Walker and ordered to the European station. Upon his return he received the compliment of an appointment as one of the United States officers permitted by the British government to receive a course of instructions at the Royal navy college, Woolwich, England. Here he remained three years, taking a special study in naval architecture. On returning home he received an appointment to the navy department at Washington, and discharged his duties with such fidelity and intelligence that he was given an appointment as assistant naval constructor. He was later ordered to the Brooklyn navy yard, where he remained one year. Next he went to Newport News to inspect the battleships Kearsarge and Kentucky, which were under construction there. He then became instructor in the post-graduate course in naval instruction, which he inaugurated at the naval academy in 1897. In 1898 he, with his pupils, was ordered to join Sampson's fleet at Key West, with which he remained until the performance of the remarkable and historic feat of bottling up Cervera in the harbor of Santiago de Cuba. He received a great deal of deserved honor for this achievement, and was nominated by President McKinley March 1, 1899, to be advanced ten numbers from number one from the list of naval constructors for extraordinary heroism. This is said to be the greatest possible promotion in the naval service for gallant conduct in the face of the enemy. Hobson has done subsequent excellent work and is the author of a number of works on subjects relative to his profession.

WINFIELD SCOTT SCHLEY.

Winfield Scott Schley was born in Frederick, Maryland, October 9, 1839. After being educated in the public schools he entered the naval academy at Annapolis, September 20, 1856, and was graduated in 1860. During the Civil war he served in various capacities, and at its close he was commissioned lieutenant-commander and was made instructor in languages at the United States naval academy. In 1884 he volunteered for, and was placed in command of, the relief expedition sent to the arctic regions in search of Lieutenant Greely and his companions. Two other attempts to relieve Lieutenant Greely had been failures, but Commander Schley's determination and intrepidity carried his expedition to success, and the seven survivors of the expedition were found and brought back, together with the bodies of those who had perished. In recognition of this achievement, the Maryland legislature presented him with a gold watch and a vote of thanks, and the Massachusetts Humane Society gave him a gold medal, and a territory west of Cape Sabine was named Schley land. He was also commissioned to carry, to Sweden, the remains of John Erickson, for which King Oscar awarded him a gold medal. In 1898 he was made commodore. Previous to the outbreak of the Spanish-American war he was given command of the "Flying Squadron." On May 19 he was ordered by Sampson to blockade Cienfuegos. On May 29, he had been ordered to Santiago by the navy department and there he discovered the Spanish fleet in the harbor. At 8:45 of that day Sampson steamed eastward to Siboney, thus placing Schley in command. Scarcely an hour later the Spaniards emerged from the harbor, the Brooklyn, Schley's ship, signalling, "clear ship for action," "the enemy escaping to westward" and "close action," and steamed forward to meet the advancing enemy. One after another the Teresa, Oquondo, Biscaya and Colon were run aground under a storm of American projectiles. The credit of this victory was claimed by Sampson, but as he was absent at the time, it became ultimately recognized by the American people that Schley had fought and won the victory. His ship was nearest to the Spanish squadron at the time of action and was the most badly injured of all the American fleet. At the close of the war he was placed on waiting orders. He was married in Annapolis, Maryland,

September 10, 1863, to Anna Rebecca, daughter of George E. and Marie Caroline Franklin.

WILLIAM RUFUS SHAFTER.

William Rufus Shafter was born at Galesburg, Michigan, October 16, 1835. He was brought up on a farm and received a common school education. He entered the Union army as first lieutenant of the Seventh Michigan infantry. He rose in rank, and when mustered out of the volunteer service, in 1865, entered the regular army as lieutenant colonel. In 1867 he was breveted colonel and given congressional honor for gallant conduct at the battle of Fair Oaks, Virginia. He was made a brigadier-general May 3, 1897, in charge of the department of California and later a major-general of volunteers; May, 1898, he went to Tampa, Florida; afterward to Cuba, where he commanded the military operations which ended in the surrender of Santiago de Cuba in July, 1898, while at the close of the war he received his share of criticism for some incidents of the campaign, yet his personal gallantry and technical skill have never been questioned. His success in his chosen profession may be traced to his putting into practice the ruling axiom of his life, which he formulates thus: "I think that, when a man once finds the thing he likes, and for which he is best fitted, he is bound to like it always, and stick to it."

JOSEPH WHEELER.

General Joseph Wheeler gained "three stars" on his coat-collar, in contending for the "Lost Cause." He now has the two stars of a United States major-general in the Cuban war. General Wheeler was, from boyhood, a careful and painstaking student of the profession which he adopted. He was born at Augusta,

Georgia, September 10, 1836, and was sent to West Point at seventeen. While others were passing their leisure moments in sport, young Wheeler could be found in the library, poring, with deepest interest, over those volumes which spoke of campaigns and battles, both ancient and modern, and examining military maps and plans of battle of distinguished generals. From the cavalry school at Carlisle, Pennsylvania, he went, in the spring of 1860, to New Mexico, and, in March, 1861, returned to Georgia. He became a first lieutenant of Confederate artillery at Pensacola, and led the Nineteenth Alabama infantry regiment as colonel. At Shiloh he had two horses shot under him, and is said to have carried the regimental colors in his own hands. On the retreat from Kentucky, Colonel Wheeler, as chief of cavalry, covered the movement. During this campaign, he met the enemy in thirty fights and skirmishes. Having been made a brigadier-general, on recommendation of Bragg, Polk, Hardee and Buckner, he was sent to Middle Tennessee. The Union troops at that time reported that "not a nubbin of corn was obtained without fighting for it." Here he received the *sobriquet* of "The Little Hero." General Wheeler was sick when the American troops attacked Santiago, but he hastened on a litter to the point of danger, and by his words and example stimulated his men to victory. He was retired as brigadier-general September 10, 1900.

EXPLORERS.

EVELYN BRIGGS BALDWIN.

Evelyn B. Baldwin, the well-known arctic explorer, was born in Springfield, Missouri, July 2, 1862. He is the son of Elias Briggs Baldwin, who served with distinction during the Civil war. The subject of this sketch was educated at the public schools in Dupage county, Illinois, and, on graduating from the Northwestern college, Naperville, Illinois, taught in district schools for some time. After an experience as professional pedestrian and bicyclist in Europe, he returned to this country and was appointed principal of high schools and superintendent of city schools in Kansas. Next we hear of him as attached to the United States weather bureau and becoming inspector-at-large of the signal corps of the United States army. In 1883 he was a member of the Peary expedition to North Greenland in the capacity of meteorologist. In 1897 he made a voyage to the Andree balloon station in Spitzbergen, hoping to join that ill-fated scientist, but arrived a few days too late. In 1898 he accompanied Wellman's polar expedition as meteorologist, and secured valuable data in connection with same. He also organized and commanded the Baldwin-Ziegler polar expedition in 1901. He is the author of several works on arctic exploration and is the member of a number of scientific societies.

FREDERICK ALBERT COOK.

Dr. Frederick A. Cook, physician by profession and explorer by inclination, was born in Callicoon Depot, Sullivan county, New York, on June 10, 1865. He is the son of Dr. Theodore Albert Cook and was first educated in Brooklyn, graduated from the University of the City of New York in 1890, and received his medical degree from that institution in the same year. His work of exploration has been confined to the arctic regions. He was surgeon of the Peary expedition in 1891 and acted in the like capacity for the Belgium antarctic expedition in 1897. Dr. Cook has a fertile pen, and it is mainly through its efforts that he is as well known to the American people as he is. He has contributed liberally to the leading magazines, writing on the problems of the north and south poles; is the author of a monograph on the Patagonians, and has published a work entitled The First Antarctic Night. He is a member of a number of scientific societies, has been decorated by King Leopold of Belgium and has received medals from foreign geological societies as a recognition of his services in the lines indicated.

SVEN ANDERS HEDIN.

The ancient Norseman's desire to wander and to conquer still stirs the blood of many of his modern descendants. Happily nowadays, the wandering is done for the benefit of humanity and the conquests are those of peace and not of the "Swan Path." Sven Anders Hedin, explorer and geographer, is a case in point. He was born at Stockholm, February 19, 1865, and is the son of Ludwig Hedin, official chief architect of Stockholm. When a mere child he exhibited the traits that distinguished his later years, and there are many stories told of how his parents were kept on the alert to prevent their baby—for he was not much more—from playing truant, which he did whenever the opportunity offered. The boy was indeed father to the man, and his parents, on his finishing his education, had the wisdom not to attempt to thwart his expressed desire to become an explorer. Had they done so the world would possess much less geographical knowledge than it now does. After courses in the universities of Stockholm, Upsala, Berlin and Halle, he began his travels. The Orient attracted him, and he made journeys through Persia and Mesopotamia. In 1895 he was a member of King Oscar's embassy to the Shah of Persia. He is best known in connection with his explorations in Asia, those of Khorasan, Turkestan and Thibet being especially notable. Hedin is the author of many works on travel and has contributed largely to those journals which are published in the interest of science of geography.

E. BURTON HOLMES.

E. Burton Holmes, who is well known to the American public through his lectures on foreign countries, was born in Chicago, January 8, 1870. He is the son of Ira and Virginia (Burton) Holmes. Educated at first in the Allen academy, and subsequently in the Harvard school, Chicago, he, not long after his graduation, began to evince that uncontrollable desire to see the world which is innate in the breast of the born explorer. Notwithstanding that he is still a comparatively young man, Mr. Holmes has managed, since he attained his majority, to visit Japan, Algeria, Corsica, Greece and Thessaly. He has also taken part in an expedition sent under the auspices of a scientific organization to Fez, Morocco. All of the continental countries of Europe are known to him, as are the Hawaiian Islands, the Philippine Islands and China. He has visited the Yellowstone Park and the Grand Canyon of the Colorado river. His first appearance on the lecture platform was in 1890, and since then he has appeared in nearly all of the

American cities. Mr. Holmes has graphic powers of description, which explains the popularity of his addresses. His lectures have been published in book form.

A. H. SAVAGE LANDOR.

The power of purpose is emphasized in the career of A. H. Savage Landor, artist and explorer. Son of Charles Savage Landor, and the grandson of Walter Savage Landor, author and poet, he was born in Florence, Italy; was educated in that city, and afterward went to Paris to study art. There he entered the studio of Julian, one of whose favorite pupils he soon became. There is every likelihood that he would have become prominent in art circles had it not been for his keen desire for travel. So deserting the easel for the knapsack, he visited Japan, China, Corea, Mongolia, India, Napaul, Thibet, America, Australia, Africa and other countries. He lived for some time among a curious race of aborigines known as the Hairy Ainu, in the wilds of Northern Japan. Mr. Landor is best known to the reading public by reason of his explorations in Thibet and the remarkable book which was the fruit thereof. During his sojourn in "The Forbidden Country" he underwent incredible hardships, and as a result of the tortures inflicted upon him by the natives who held him prisoner for some time, he will probably be a sufferer to the end of his days. A man, who when riding on a saddle studded with sharp spikes, can take note of the physical features of the surrounding country and can calculate the height of the plateau over which he is passing in agony must be molded from that kind of stuff of which hero adventurers are made. Likewise does he show the power of a purpose over the dangers and difficulties that threaten to thwart it.

FRIDTJOF NANSEN.

Of the several explorers who have endeavored to solve the mysteries of the Arctic regions, none perhaps is better known than Fridtjof Nansen, a descendant of the old Vikings. He was born in Christiania, October 10, 1861, and is the son of a lawyer well known in Norwegian legal circles. After an education, which began at home, he graduated from the University of Christiania, and immediately began to exhibit those nomadic tendencies which distinguish the born explorer. His first trip to the far north was in 1882, when he made a voyage to the seas surrounding Greenland. Returning with much valuable geological and zoological data, he was appointed curator of the natural history museum at Bergen. In 1889 he took his second trip to the Arctic, when he succeeded in crossing Greenland. Subsequent thereto he was made curator of the Museum of Comparative Anatomy of Christiania university. His most memorable undertaking, however, was in 1893, when he endeavored to reach the North Pole. Although he did not accomplish his object, he succeeded in getting nearer to it than had any of his predecessors. On that occasion he spent three years in the Arctic region, and again returned laden with data which, from a scientific standpoint, was invaluable. He was next appointed professor of zoology of the Christiania university. Nansen has published several books dealing with his life work, including Esquimaux Life, Across Greenland and Farthest North. He has also written a number of articles for magazines. He married Eva Sears, who was well known in musical circles of the continent.

ROBERT EDWIN PEARY.

Robert Edwin Peary, the brilliant Arctic explorer, was born at Cresson, Pennsylvania, May 6, 1856. After a course in public schools he entered Bowdoin college, graduating therefrom in 1877. In 1881 he was appointed civil engineer to the United States navy. From 1884 to 1885 he acted as assistant engineer in the surveys for the Nicaraugua ship canal, and from 1887 to 1888 was engineer in charge of further surveys for the same project. In this connection he invented the rolling lock-gate for canals. He inaugurated his career as Arctic explorer in 1886, when he made his famous reconnaissance of the Greenland inland ice cap, a thing that none of his predecessors had attempted. In 1891 he undertook another expedition to the north under the auspices of the Academy of Natural Sciences of Philadelphia. He also determined the insularity of Greenland, for which he received medals from a number of scientific organizations. Still another voyage was made in 1893, and a year later he discovered the famous Iron Mountain, which proved to consist of three meteorites, one of them weighing ninety tons. Some of the meteorites he brought back with him during a summer trip made in 1896. In 1898 he again started north in an endeavor to reach the North Pole, but was not successful. Lieutenant Peary married Josephine Diebitsch in 1888. He is the author of several books on his work in the arctic regions and of a great many papers in geological journals and popular magazines. He once remarked that even Polar ice would melt "by heat of effort," meaning that any obstacle can be destroyed by enthusiasm and persistency.

HENRY MORTON STANLEY.

The career of Sir Henry M. Stanley is not only of a more or less romantic nature, but furnishes lessons that are as obvious as they are useful. Beginning life as an unknown boy, he is now one of the best-known, as he is the most highly honored of men. And he has thus achieved, through the medium of his stalwart mental and physical attributes. Sir Henry was born in Denbigh, Wales, and emigrated to the United States in 1856. He was adopted by a New Orleans merchant, whose name he now bears. Coming north, he became connected with the New York Herald, and in 1870 was sent to Africa by that newspaper, in order to explore some of the then unknown sections of that country. Returning to America, in 1874, he was ordered at brief notice by James Gordon Bennett, of the Herald, to find Dr. Livingston, the late famous traveler and missionary, from whom no tidings had been heard for some time. Stanley successfully carried out the instructions. Subsequently he discovered the source of the Congo, and still later his explorations, undertaken at the request of the King of Belgium, resulted in the foundation of the Congo Free State. He also commanded the Emin Pasha relief expedition. Since 1895 he has been a member of the British parliament. His books are many and have for the most part to do with his adventures and experiences in Africa. He was knighted by the late Queen Victoria for his services to science as explorer.

WALTER WELLMAN.

Walter Wellman, journalist and explorer, was born in Mentor, Ohio, November 5, 1858. He was educated in the district schools, and during his boyhood gave evidence of his journalistic instincts, for when but fourteen years of age he established a weekly newspaper at Sutton, Nebraska. When he attained his majority, he founded the Cincinnati Evening Post, the venture being of a successful nature. For many years he was political and Washington correspondent of the Chicago Herald and Times-Herald. Mr. Wellman, in 1892, succeeded in locating the landing place of Christopher Columbus, on Watling Island, in the Bahamas, and erected a monument upon the spot. In 1894 he took his initial trip to the Arctic regions, making explorations on the northeastern coast of Spitzbergen. Four years later he explored Franz Josef Land, where he discovered many new islands and made valuable contributions to Arctic geography. As a writer on subjects connected with the frozen north, he is well known by reason of his articles in leading magazines. He has also written on political and general topics.

EDUCATORS.

ELISHA BENJAMIN ANDREWS.

Elisha Benjamin Andrews was born at Hinsdale, New Hampshire, January 10, 1844. He received a public school education, meantime working on a farm. At the outbreak of the Civil war, although only seventeen years of age, he enlisted and served with distinction, being promoted to the rank of second lieutenant. A severe wound destroyed the sight of his left eye, and he received his honorable discharge in 1864. Forthwith preparing for college at Powers institute, he later studied at Wesleyan academy, entered Brown university and was graduated in the class of 1870. During the two years following he was principal of the Connecticut Literary institute at Suffield. In 1874 he graduated from the Newton Theological institution and was the same year ordained pastor of the First Baptist church, Beverly, Massachusetts. One year after he accepted the presidency of Denison university, Granville, Ohio. Afterward he held the professorship of homoletics, pastoral theology and church polity in Newton Theological institution, where he remained three years, and after studying a year in Germany, he filled the chair of professor of history and economy in Brown university. In 1889 he was elected president of Brown university. He has always been noted for his interest in public questions and has been a liberal contributor to magazines and other periodicals. He has published several books on history, philosophy and economics. In 1870 he married Ella A. Allen, of Boston, and has had two children by her.

NICHOLAS MURRAY BUTLER.

Nicholas Murray Butler was born at Paterson, New Jersey, April 2, 1862. He was educated in the public schools of his native city, where his father for many years had been president of the board of education. At sixteen he entered Columbia College, New York, and was graduated in 1882. The following year he received the degree of A.M. from his alma mater, and in 1884 the degree of Ph.D. The same year he visited Europe, studying at the universities of Berlin and Paris. Upon returning to America, in 1886, he became an instructor in philosophy in Columbia college. In 1890 he was made professor of philosophy, ethics and psychology. For a number of years he was president of the board ofeducation of Paterson, New Jersey, and in 1887 he organized the New York college for the training of teachers, and which is now the Teachers' college, Columbia university. In 1891 he founded the magazine Educational Review, which he has edited ever since and which is probably the foremost educational publication in the world. He is also the editor of the Teachers' Professional Library and has published numerous educational essays and addresses. In 1894 he became an examiner for the state of New York, and in the same year was elected president of the National Educational association. In September, 1901, he was elected president of Columbia university to succeed Seth Low. On February 7, 1887, he married Susanna Edwards Schuyler. One daughter is the issue of the union.

CHARLES WILLIAM ELIOT.

Charles William Eliot was born in Boston March 20, 1834. After a period spent in the public schools he was prepared for college at the Boston Latin school, and entering Harvard he graduated in 1852. After graduation he took a position as tutor of mathematics in Harvard and went through an advanced course in chemistry with Professor Josiah P. Cook. In 1858 he undertook a trip to Europe to investigate its educational methods and make a further study of chemistry. From 1865 to 1869 he was professor of analytical chemistry in the Massachusetts institute of technology. In 1867 he was elected a fellow of the American academy of arts and sciences, and also became a member of the American philosophical society. He has delivered many noteworthy addresses on educational and scientific subjects and has written a number of text books, essays and educational contributions to periodicals. His principal works are text-books on chemistry, which were written in conjunction with Professor Francis H. Storer. In 1869 he was elected president of Harvard university. He is a member of many scientific societies and is regarded as an authority on abstruse questions and problems of chemistry and allied sciences.

WILLIAM HERBERT PERRY FAUNCE.

The Rev. W. H. P. Faunce, D.D., the new president of Brown university, Providence, Rhode Island, is not an example of success under difficulties. He has never experienced reverses, and he has always improved his opportunities. His father, Thomas Faunce, was a prominent clergyman at Worcester, Massachusetts, and had preached in Plymouth, in that state, which is the home of many generations of the family. I called upon Dr. Faunce, and was invited into his study. He is only forty years of age, a courteous, broad-minded gentleman. "I was born in Worcester," he said, "but received a public school education at Concord and at Lynn, and in 1876 entered Brown university. After I was graduated, I taught for a year in mathematics, during the absence of a professor in Europe. I always intended to become a minister, and I entered Newton Theological Seminary. Eight months before graduation, I preached one Sunday in the State Street Baptist church, of Springfield, Massachusetts. It was a large church, having a membership of seven hundred and fifty. I did not know that the pulpit was vacant, and, peculiarly enough, chose for my text the sentence, 'I that speak unto you am He.' At the close of the services, I was asked to be their pastor, and, after I was graduated from the seminary, I was ordained. It was in 1889 that I was asked to preach as a candidate in the Fifth Avenue Baptist church, of New York, which I regret to leave. I refused to be a candidate; but members continually came to Springfield to hear me, and finally I was called. All along I have been more or less identified with college work, and my congregation tell me they have been expecting I would leave and devote myself to educational lines. For a number of years, I have been one of a board of preachers at Harvard, preaching there three weeks in the autumn, and three in the winter, and for six weeks each summer (the summer quarter), at the University of Chicago, where I also taught in theology. Again, I have preached quite regularly at Cornell, Amherst, Wellesley and Brown." "Have other colleges asked you to become president?" "Yes; that is, two official boards of two colleges have sounded and invited me, but I considered that my work here was too important. Brown, however, is my alma mater." "You must spend much time in study," I remarked. "I have always kept my studies up," replied Dr. Faunce. "I have been abroad three times to study German, French and philosophy. I am a great believer in constant work." "Success? you ask. Why, success involves the complete expression of all of one's powers, and every one leaves a lasting impression on the life of the world. The man who is sincere in the expressing of himself, in whatever line it may be, becomes a factor in the world. Genuine success is the kind that is helpful to others, as well as to the one who is striving. Every other kind falls short of the mark and becomes stale. How to achieve success? you ask. Show strong, absolute whole-heartedness in whatever you undertake; throw yourself, body, mind and soul, into whatever you do. Patiently master details. Most of the men that I know who have failed have ignored details,—have considered them petty and insignificant. They have not realized the importance of small things." "Do you think the average man appreciates this?" I asked. "No." Here Dr. Faunce was called away for a moment, and I picked up a book of Browning's poems. These lines in "Christmas Eve" were marked:

Whom do you count the Worse man upon earth?
Be sure he knows, in his conscience, more
Of what Right is, than arrives at birth.

When he returned I asked: "Do you think that the worse individual, a useless member of society, can elevate himself and be of consequence?" "Most decidedly, and through work, congenial work. The happiest hours of a man's life should be when he is working. A man will not succeed who is continually looking for the end of the day. Vacations are necessary, but they are for the sake of work and success."

ARTHUR TWINING HADLEY.

The father of Arthur Twining Hadley, now president of Yale, was Professor James Hadley, a Yale graduate of 1842. He was a tutor at Yale three years, and, in 1857, he took President Woolsey's place as professor of Greek. This place he held until his death, in 1872. His mother was Ann Twining, an intellectual woman, who completed the full Yale course in mathematics before the days of the "new woman." Thus, young Hadley was, as Oliver Wendell Holmes might say, "fortunate in the choice of his parents." He first saw the light at New Haven, April 23, 1856. Becoming a Yale graduate, in 1876, he was the valedictorian of his class. He spent some years in Berlin, and became a tutor in 1879, a lecturer at Yale (and Harvard) on political science in 1883, and a professor in 1886. He had also done journalistic work on several newspapers. His work on "Railway legislation" has been translated into French and German, and twice into Russian. He made two reports as commissioner of labor statistics for Connecticut, in 1885 and 1886. He wrote, at the Harpers' solicitation, the article on "Yale" in their well-known volume, "Four Universities." In 1891 he married Helen Harrison, daughter of Governor Luzon B. Morris, of Connecticut. President Hadley is the ideal educator, learned, sympathetic, progressive and possessing an intimate acquaintance with the details and duties of his onerous position.

WILLIAM TORREY HARRIS.

William Torrey Harris was born North Killingly, Connecticut, September 10, 1835. He was educated in local common schools and academies, and for two and a half years was a member of the Yale college class of 1858, but left before graduating. In 1857 he went to St. Louis, where, for some time, he acted as teacher, principal, assistant superintendent and superintendent of public schools. At the Paris exposition of 1878 thirteen volumes of reports prepared by Mr. Harris, and contributed to the educational exhibit of the United States, attracted such attention that he was given the honorary title of officier de l'Academie. The reports were placed in the pedagogical library of the Paris ministry of public instructions. When Mr. Harris resigned, in 1880, on account of failing health, the city of St. Louis presented him with a gold medal and a purse of $1000. He next visited Europe, representing the United States bureau of education at the international congress of educators held at Brussels in 1880. In 1889 he again represented the United States bureau of education at the Paris exposition, and on December 12 of the same year he was appointed United States commissioner of education and removed to Washington, D. C. Mr. Harris has contributed many educational articles to the magazines and was the founder of the Journal of Speculative Philosophy.

HENRY MITCHELL MCCRACKEN.

Henry Mitchell McCracken was born at Oxford, Ohio, September 28, 1840. His early education was obtained in the public schools and later at Miami university, from whence he graduated in 1857. He also studied at the United Presbyterian theological seminary at Zenia, Ohio, at the Princeton theological seminary, and at Tubingen and Berlin universities. His first professional work was that of a teacher of classics and a public school superintendent. From 1857 to 1860 he was pastor of the Westminster church at Columbus, Ohio, and later of the Presbyterian church at Toledo, Ohio. In 1868, he was elected chancellor of the Western university, at Pittsburg, and in 1880 was made vice-chancellor and professor of philosophy in the New York university, which position he held until 1891, when he was made chancellor. He is the author of numerous educational and theological works. In 1872 he married Catherine Hubbard. Chancellor McCracken's life work has had a dominating influence on educational theories and methods in this country. His powers of professional expansion have enabled him to keep pace with the drift of modern thought and sentiment.

WOODROW WILSON.

Woodrow Wilson was born at Staunton, Virginia, December 28, 1856. He is of Scotch ancestry. After being trained in private schools of Augusta, Georgia, and Columbia, South Carolina, he graduated from Princeton in 1879, and then studied law at the University of Virginia. Being admitted to the bar, he practiced for a year in Atlanta, Georgia, and later entered Johns Hopkins university for a graduating course in history and politics. In 1885 he was chosen as an instructor in history and politics at

Bryn Mawr college and in 1886 he received the degree of Ph.D. from Johns Hopkins university. In 1888 he was a member of the faculty in Wesleyan university, and in 1890 was called as the chair of jurisprudence at Princeton. In August, 1902, he was elected president of Princeton to succeed President Patton. He has published a number of educational text-books and historical, biographical and political works. His most recent and perhaps most important work is a history of the American people, issued in five volumes. President Wilson is well known as a lecturer on military and political subjects, through the medium of his contributions to various periodicals.

EDITORS.

HENRY MILLS ALDEN.

Harper's Magazine is one of the classics in the vast library of monthly publications. Magazines, like people, have their periods of elevation and depression. But Harper's has maintained a steady level of high-class individuality, this being due in no small degree to the work of Henry Mills Alden, who, since 1869, has been its editor-in-chief. Mr. Alden was born at Mount Tabor, near Danby, Vermont, November 11, 1836. He attended public school at Hoosick Falls, New York, graduated from Williams college in 1857, and from the Andover theological seminary in 1860, but he never took orders. His literary bent was made manifest early in life, and, after much general work with his pen, he became managing editor of Harper's Weekly, which position he held until he was put in charge of the magazine. For some time he was lecturer at the Lowell institute, Boston. He is the author of some religious books, and also of Harper's Pictorial History of the Great Revolution, Mr. A. H. Guernsey being associated with him in the production of that work. Mr. Alden's life story is that of a man who, having a purpose, hopes on and works on, ceasing not until his hopes are lost in full fruition.

EDWARD WILLIAM BOK.

Edward William Bok, who, since 1888, has been the editor of the Ladies' Home Journal, was born in Helder, Holland, October 9, 1863. He came to this country with his parents when six years of age and was educated in the public schools of Brooklyn. He then learned stenography and entered the employ of the Western Union Telegraph Company. Finding that his position had no future for him, he, in 1884, became connected with the firm of Henry Holt & Co., publishers, and later with the Scribner firm, with which he remained. His industry and integrity gained for him the respect of his employers, and when finally he became desirous of securing the control of the publication of which he is now owner, he had no difficulty in obtaining the needed capital with which to accomplish his desires. Mr. Bok is married and is the author of "A Young Man In Business," "Successward," etc.

JAMES MONROE BUCKLEY.

Of the several publications which voice the views of the religious world, perhaps none is better known or more generally read than is the New York Christian Advocate. Under the editorship of the Rev. Dr. James M. Buckley, the Advocate has become more than a mere reflex of the opinions of its contributors. It is a power for good and the extent of its usefulness is only bounded by the limits of its circulation, which are world-wide. Dr. Buckley was born in Rahway, New Jersey, December 16, 1836, his father being the Rev. John Buckley. Educated at first in Pennington, New Jersey, seminary, he later spent a year in the Wesleyan university, and afterward studied theology at Exeter, New Hampshire. He became a member of the New Hampshire conference of the Methodist Episcopal church in 1858, was called to Troy in 1863, and to Brooklyn three years later. Dr. Buckley has traveled extensively, and no small portion of the popularity of his work on the Advocate is due to the wide experience of men and manners which he acquired during his wanderings abroad and in this country. He is the author of several books, including Travels on Three Continents, Land of the Czar and the Nihilists, The History of Methodism in the United States and others. Dr.

Buckley's literary work in general is distinguished by a breadth of view and a charity of spirit which are only possible to the man of large mind and wide horizons.

RICHARD WATSON GILDER.

If a magazine contributor was asked what, in his opinion, represented the ultimate happiness of his ilk, he would probably reply, "the editorship of the Century." That enviable position is at present held by Richard W. Gilder, and that Mr. Gilder has done honor to the wisdom which placed him in the editorial chair, is made manifest by the body matter of the magazine itself. He was born in Bordentown, New Jersey, February 8, 1844, his father being the Rev. William H. Gilder, and he was educated in the seminary established by his father at Flushing, Long Island. In 1863 he became a private in Landis' Philadelphia battery, and, at the expiration of his term of service, had a year's experience as a railroad man. Later he was correspondent, and afterward managing editor, of the Newark (New Jersey) Advertiser. From that time on Mr. Gilder has lived in an editorial atmosphere. In connection with Newton Crane he established the Newark Register, next edited the defunct New York monthly publication called Powers at Home, made his mark while so doing, attracted the notice of the Scribner management, and was made managing editor of its magazine in 1870 and editor-in-chief in 1881. Mr. Gilder has taken a prominent part in movements and organizations which had for their object the improvement of municipal conditions. He has held office as chairman of the New York tenement house commission, was the first president of the New York kindergarten association and is president of the Public Art League of the United States. He is also a member of the City club and of the Civil Service Reform league. His published books of poems include The Celestial Passion, Five Books of Songs and Two Worlds.

GEORGE BURTON MCCLELLAN HARVEY.

One of the most prominent, as well as one of the youngest occupants of an editorial chair is George Burton McClellan Harvey, who is president of the famous publishing firm of Harper & Brothers and editor of the North American Review. He was born at Peachan, Vermont, February 16, 1864, being the son of Duncan and Margaret S. (Varnum) Harvey. Educated at Peachan Academy, Mr. Harvey began his journalistic life by becoming reporter on the Springfield (Massachusetts) Republican. Subsequently he was on the reportorial staff of the Chicago News and the New York Herald, of which latter newspaper he was eventually made managing editor. He bought the North American Review in March, 1899, and was placed in charge of Harper & Brothers' affairs a year later. Notwithstanding the onerous nature of his editorial duties, Mr. Harvey finds time to act as president of several electric railroads, in the construction of which he was also interested. Governors Green and Abbott, of New Jersey, respectively appointed him colonel and aide-de-camp on their staffs. The irresistible force of character and ability properly directed is shown by the career of Mr. Harvey.

GEORGE HOWARD LORIMER.

Horace Greeley is credited with the aphorism that "It is the man and not the machine, the editor and not the newspaper, that brings about the smooth running of the first and the popularity of the second." George Howard Lorimer, editor-in-chief of the Saturday Evening Post, furnishes an excellent illustration of the verity of Greeley's assertion. Under his management, the Post has, during the past few years, attained a popularity which was forbidden to it before he took charge of its affairs. The Post was founded by Benjamin Franklin, and it is the policy of Mr. Lorimer to retain somewhat of the quaint features of its earlier issues, but he weds them to modern methods. By means of this policy he has succeeded in galvanizing a moribund publication into active and prosperous life. Mr. Lorimer was born in Louisville, Kentucky, October 6, 1868, and is the son of the Rev. Dr. George and Belle (Burford) Lorimer. He was educated at the Moseley high school in Chicago, and took courses at Colby and Yale universities. In 1893 he married Alma Viola, daughter of Judge Alfred Ennis, of Chicago. Mr. Lorimer has, through the medium of the Saturday Evening Post, proven that literary matter of a helpful and elevating nature can be made as attractive to the average reader as so-called "popular fiction."

WHITELAW REID.

Whitelaw Reid, the editor of the New York Tribune, was born in Xenia, Ohio, October 27, 1837, and is a graduate of Miami university, Oxford, Ohio. After leaving college Mr. Reid entered journalism, becoming editor of the Xenia News. In 1860 he was legislative correspondent, and a year later was war correspondent for several newspapers. In 1862 he became Washington representative of the Cincinnati Gazette. After a period spent in the service of the government, including the acting as librarian in the House of Representatives, Mr. Reid in 1866 tried his hand at cotton planting in Louisiana. But the newspaper instinct was too strong in him to warrant his being anything but a writer. In 1868, therefore, he became a member of the editorial staff of the Tribune; in 1869 he was appointed its managing editor and has been its editor-in-chief and practical proprietor since 1872. In 1877 he declined the appointment of UnitedStates minister to Germany and again in 1881. In 1889 he was United States minister to France, was special ambassador from this country to Queen Victoria's Jubilee in 1897, and was a member of the Peace commission in Paris in 1898. He was nominated for the vice-presidency in 1892. Mr. Reid is the author of a number of books on political and journalistic questions. His life has been full of many but faithfully discharged duties.

ALBERT SHAW.

Albert Shaw, editor of the American Review of Reviews, was born in Shandon, Butler county, Ohio, July 23, 1857. He is the son of Dr. Griffin and Susan (Fisher) Shaw. Graduating from Iowa college, Grinnell, Iowa, in 1879, he became part owner of the Grinnell Herald, while taking a post-graduate course in constitutional history and economic science. He also studied history and political science at the Johns Hopkins university. All this was preparatory to entering the profession which he had chosen as his life work. Next he became editorial writer on the Minneapolis Tribune in 1882, studied journalism in Europe for a year, and in 1891 began to conduct the well-known publication with which he is now identified. Mr. Shaw is the author of a number of works on municipal government and political science, on which subjects he is accepted as an authority. He is a member of many learned societies and is well known on the lecture platforms of the universities and colleges of this country. Mr. Shaw is an excellent example of the value of thorough preparatory work looking to a given career.

HENRY WATTERSON.

Henry Watterson, who is responsible for the editorial policy of the Louisville Courier-Journal, was born in Washington, D. C., February 16, 1840. He was educated by private tutors, this owing to his being threatened with blindness. During the war he acted as staff officer in the Confederate army. When peace was established he at once engaged in newspaper work, and has ever since been more or less conspicuous in the field of journalism. Elected a member of congress in 1875, he has since, although repeatedly offered office, uniformly declined it. He was delegate-at-large from Kentucky for six Democratic national conventions. Mr. Watterson is not only distinguished as a journalist and author, but he has a well-deserved reputation as an orator. His command of the English language, allied to his general wit and braininess, have made his editorials famous throughout the country. He is the author of works on the Civil war and others. In 1865 he married the daughter of the Hon. Andrew Ewing, of Tennessee.

PUBLISHERS.

FRANK NELSON DOUBLEDAY.

The founder of the flourishing publishing house of Doubleday, Page & Co., of New York, is Frank Nelson Doubleday, who was born in Brooklyn in 1862, being the son of W. E. Doubleday. He was educated at the Polytechnic institute of the City of Churches, and during his school days gave indications of his future career, for before he had finished his studies he had established quite a flourishing job printing business among his schoolmates and friends. When fifteen years of age he got a position with the Scribners as errand boy, remaining with the firm for many years in a number of capacities. He founded the publication entitled "The Book Buyer," and when Scribner's Magazine was started he was made its manager and publisher. The average young man would have been contented with this position, which was honorable, professionally, and lucrative, financially. But young Doubleday was ambitious, and so in 1897 he joined the S. S. McClure Company. After a brief stay with them, he formed the Doubleday & McClure Co., book publishers. The firm flourished and published many works of well-known authors, including Rudyard Kipling's "Day's Work." It was at this time that a close friendship was formed between Mr. Doubleday and the famous author. In 1900 Doubleday, Page & Co. came into existence, associated with the senior partner being W. H. Page, former editor of the Atlantic, and H. W. Lanier, who is a son of the poet, Sydney Lanier, and others. The firm established World's Work, a magazine that achieved an immediate success. Another venture of the company was "Country Life in America," which is typographically and artistically very beautiful. This magazine, too, was an emphatic success. He married Neltje de Graff, a descendant of a historic Dutch family. Mrs. Doubleday is the author of a number of works, many of which have to do with natural history subjects, including "Bird Neighbors" and "Nature's Garden," both of which are well known to students of nature.

ISAAC KAUFFMAN FUNK.

Originality has been a powerful factor in the career of the noted clergyman, editor and publisher, the Rev. Dr. Isaac Kauffman Funk. He was born at Clifton, Greene county, Ohio, September 10, 1839. His parents, John and Martha (Kauffman) Funk, were descendants of early Holland-Swiss emigrants to Pennsylvania. Graduating from Whittenberg college, Springfield, Ohio, with the degree of D.D., he from this same institution, in 1896, received the degree of LL.D. From 1861 to 1872 he was engaged in active work in the Lutheran ministry. At the end of that time he resigned his pastorate and traveled extensively in Europe, Egypt and Palestine. Upon returning to America he became associate editor of the Christian Radical. In 1876 he founded and published in New York city the Metropolitan Pulpit, now the Homiletic Review, acting as its editor-in-chief. His former college classmate, Adam W. Wagnalls, a lawyer of Atchison, Kansas, became in 1877 his partner, and the firm name was changed to I. K. Funk & Co., and later, in 1891, to Funk & Wagnalls Co. Their several branch houses in Canada and England, as well as their many published books which have met with public favor, testified to the business successes of the members of the concern. Dr. Funk is the founder of some well-known periodicals, among which The Voice, The Literary Digest and The Missionary Review are the most important. He also published a standard dictionary of the English language, of which he was editor-in-chief. The production of this work was a gigantic undertaking, costing nearly one million dollars.

WILLIAM RANDOLPH HEARST.

It is usually supposed, and rightly so, that a young man who inherits much wealth is not very likely to make his mark in the world. The career of William Randolph Hearst furnishes an exception to the general rule, however, for, in spite of being handicapped by a comfortable fortune, he has achieved no small reputation as a newspaper editor and publisher. Mr. Hearst was born in San Francisco, California, and is the son of the late United States Senator George F. Hearst. He is the owner of the San Francisco Examiner and other well-known newspapers. In 1895 he bought the New York Journal, later purchasing the Advertiser and consolidating it with the Journal to secure a franchise. In 1900 he founded the Chicago American, which paper has the largest morning circulation in the city in which it is published. At present Mr. Hearst is publishing altogether five large newspapers: two in New York, two in Chicago and one in San Francisco. He is a firm believer in the theory of so-called "yellow journalism," claiming that with its help he reaches the masses. His papers are noted chiefly for their brilliant editorials. Mr. Hearst advocates the cause of the laboring classes, is a member of congress, has been mentioned as a possible candidate for the Presidential nomination on the Democratic ticket in 1904.

EDWARD EVERETT HIGGINS.

If you should ask Edward E. Higgins, the publisher of Success, what are the characteristics which have given him his present position in the publishing world, he would doubtless reply, "Courage, persistence and patience." He has had an unusually varied training and experience. He was born on April 4, 1864, in Chelsea, Massachusetts, and, after a preliminary education in the local grammar and high schools, which were then considered among the best in the state, he entered the Massachusetts Institute of Technology and was graduated as an electrical engineer in 1886. He obtained there the mathematical training which has remained with him ever since, and which has contributed not a little to his acknowledged power of distinguishing between the possible and the impossible in both engineering and business matters. Foreseeing the great future of the electric street railroad, he became associated, in its earliest development, with the Sprague and Edison companies, and it was largely through his efforts that electricity was first introduced into Buffalo and other cities of New York state. Acquiring a large fund of information on street railroad matters at home and abroad, Mr. Higgins became, in 1893, the editor of the Street Railway Journal, and has won an international reputation as a statistical, engineering and financial expert on street railway matters. In 1899 he perceived an opportunity to develop a large and important home publication from what was then a small and struggling periodical—Success—and acquired an interest, intending that it should be merely a side issue. But the phenomenally rapid growth of Success soon called for Mr. Higgins' entire time, and the result is seen in the fact that Success, with its circulation of over 300,000, now, after only four years' time, is one of the first half-dozen American magazines in circulation, prestige and general standing, and no paper is more useful or valuable in the home.

LOUIS KLOPSCH.

No better example of the zealous religious worker, disinterested benefactor and talented journalist can be cited than the subject of this sketch, Louis Klopsch. He was born in Germany, March 26, 1852, receiving only a common school education. In 1886, after having removed to New York, he married May E., daughter of the Rev. Stephen Merritt. Becoming interested in newspaper work, he became the proprietor of the Daily Reporter, New York. He was also owner of the Pictorial Associated Press from 1884 to 1890, and has had charge of the Talmage sermon syndicate since 1885. On his return from Palestine, in 1890, he became connected with the Christian Herald, which he purchased in 1892. Since that time he has, through his paper, raised and distributed nearly $2,000,000 in international charities. In recognition of his relief work, during the Russian famine of 1892, he was received by the Czar of Russia, and in 1898 the English and Indian governments extended official thanks to him for his services in behalf of famine-stricken India. President McKinley appointed him one of the three commissioners in charge of the relief of the starving Reconcentradoes in Cuba, and for this purpose he raised nearly $200,000. In the spring of 1900, accompanied by Gilson Willets, Mr. Klopsch visited the famine and cholera fields of India, and through his paper, in six months' time, secured a fund of $700,000 for their relief. He has also guaranteed the support of five thousand famine orphans in India.

SAMUEL SIDNEY MCCLURE.

One of the leading magazine publishers of to-day, Samuel Sidney McClure, was born in County Antrim, Ireland, February 17, 1857. Being an ambitious youth, he naturally turned to America, "the land of opportunity." By his own earnest efforts he succeeded in securing a liberal education, being graduated from Knox college, Illinois, in 1882, obtaining the degree of A. M. in 1887. September 4, 1883, he was married to Harriet, daughter of Professor Albert Hurd, of Knox college, Galesburg, Illinois. He established, in November, 1884, a newspaper syndicate, and in 1893 he founded McClure's Magazine, which ranks among the most popular periodicals of the day. His national reputation is largely due to this enterprise. His executive ability has made him the president of the S. S. McClure Company, and he has been a trustee of Knox college since 1894. Mr. McClure has discovered and recognized a human need, and by filling that need is realizing his well-merited success.

FRANK ANDREW MUNSEY.

The rise of Frank A. Munsey from a poor postoffice clerk in Augusta, Maine, to the head of one of the most profitable publishing houses in the world has been as rapid as it is remarkable. His only capital when he began his current business were his ideas and his nerve; yet, in less than ten years, he has made a fortune. Mr. Munsey was born in Mercer, Maine, August 21, 1854, the son of Andrew C. and Mary J. Munsey. After securing an ordinary education in the public schools of Maine, he began his business career in a country store, and later became manager of the Western Union telegraph office of Augusta, Maine. When, in 1882, he went to New York and started the Golden Argosy, a juvenile weekly (now the adult monthly, The Argosy), his friends thought he was as unwise as he was reckless. It is said that some of them actually proposed an inquiry into his sanity. Having made money by The Argosy, he invested it, in 1890, in a magazine, launching Munsey's Weekly, which he converted October, 1891, into Munsey's Magazine. He now also publishes The Puritan and the Junior Munsey, besides newspapers in New York and Washington. Although more widely known as a publisher than an author, he has written several books, including Afloat in a Great City, 1887; Boy Broker, 1888; Tragedy of Errors, 1889; Under Fire, 1890, and Deering Forte, 1895.

JOSEPH PULITZER.

Extraordinary energy and executive ability and a Napoleonic faculty of perceiving and utilizing the talents of others, are the qualities upon which the journalist and publisher, Joseph Pulitzer, has built his reputation and his fortune. He was born in Buda-Pesth, Hungary, April 10, 1847, and, after receiving a classical education in his native city, came to the United States at the age of sixteen. For two years he served as a private soldier in the Federal Army, and, afterward, failing to gain a foothold in New York city, he went to St. Louis, where he became a reporter on the Westliche Post, a German newspaper then edited by Carl Schurz. Studying law, he was next admitted to the bar of Missouri. Then he was made managing editor of the Post, and in 1869 was sent to the Missouri legislature. In 1878 he bought the St. Louis Dispatch, uniting it with the Evening Post as the St. Louis Post-Dispatch, which is now one of the most successful publications of the west. In 1883 Mr. Pulitzer purchased the New York World, which, thanks to his journalistic genius, is now one of the most widely read newspapers published in New York city. He was elected to congress in New York for the term of 1885 to 1887. In 1890 he erected in Park Row one of the most striking and costly newspaper buildings in the United States. In 1896 he was a strong advocate of the National (gold standard) Democratic party. Mr. Pulitzer has always been distinguished by his generous and courteous treatment of his subordinates.

JOHN BRISBEN WALKER.

Among the leading magazine editors of to-day is John Brisben Walker, the author and publisher of the Cosmopolitan Magazine, who is also the founder of Cosmopolitan university. He was born in western Pennsylvania, September 10, 1847, and is the son of John and Anna (Krepps) Walker, and his early education was received at Gonzaga Classical School, Washington, D. C. In 1863, he entered Georgetown university, remaining there until he received appointment to the United States military academy at West Point, in 1865. In 1868, however, he entered the Chinese military service, in which he remained for two years. Returning to America, he was married, in 1870, to Emily, daughter of General David Hunter Strother. For the next three years he was engaged in manufacturing in western Pennsylvania. In 1872 he was a candidate for congress on the Republican ticket, but was defeated. During the panic of 1873 his entire fortune was swept away. But, in spite of political and financial failure, Mr. Walker rapidly forged to the front again. He next entered in journalism, and for three years was managing editor of the Washington (D. C.) Chronicle. Then he moved to Colorado, and for about nine years was a successful alfalfa farmer in that State. In 1889 he located in New York, and bought the Cosmopolitan Magazine, of which he is still the editor. The entire plant was moved to Irvington-on-Hudson in 1895. While Mr. Walker has achieved notable success in the magazine business, the most notable work of his life was the founding of the Cosmopolitan university in 1896.

ORATORS.

ALBERT J. BEVERIDGE.

When the Indiana legislature elected Albert J. Beveridge to the United States senate in 1898, he was but thirty-six years of age, and with one exception was the youngest member of the distinguished body in question. Mr. Beveridge was born October 6, 1862, in a log cabin of Highland county, Ohio, his father being a small farmer. When the war broke out the year preceding his birth, his father and his four half-brothers entered the army, while his mother volunteered as a nurse. Moving to Illinois, they settled near Sullivan, renting a small farm there. At the age of ten the future senator was a full-fledged farm hand. At fourteen he was a railroad laborer and at sixteen joined a logging camp. Whenever he could find no work he attended school. At the age of seventeen young Beveridge heard that the district cadetship for West Point was to be filled by competitive examination. He was one of the competitors, and, although practically self-educated, took second place on a list of twenty-five. In 1881 he managed to enter De Paw university, his capital consisting of $50. By wheat-cutting in the summer, serving as a steward in the college club, and winning money prizes offered to students, he managed to pay his way. Graduating from college with high honors, he went direct to Indianapolis, called on General Benjamin Harrison and asked permission to study law with him. Failing in this, he obtained employment with Messrs. McDonald, Butler & Mason, well-known lawyers at the Indiana capital, and soon became a third partner in the firm. In 1889 he opened an office of his own, and his first fee was from Governor Hovey. His initial political speech was in 1884, and, as someone has put it, he turned out to be "a revelation, a dream of oratory and a trip-hammer of argument." His fame as a speaker being established, he was in demand in all directions. His subsequent career is well-known to the public at large. In 1887 he married Miss Catherine Maud Langsdale, daughter of George J. Langsdale, the editor of a well-known paper in Indiana.

CHAMP CLARK.

Through the medium of a highly successful career, Champ Clark, who has a national reputation as stump speaker and forensic orator, furnishes yet another illustration of the possibilities that lie before the young American who determines to "get there." Mr. Clark was born in Anderson county, Kentucky, March 7, 1850. First educated in the local schools, he later studied at the Kentucky university, Bethany college and the Cincinnati law school. In order to support himself while acquiring his education, he worked as a farm hand, a clerk in a country store, an editor of a country newspaper, and finally as a lawyer. Not long after he had begun to practice law for a livelihood he commenced to take an active interest in political affairs and was at length elected city attorney of Louisiana, Mo., and later for Bowling Green, Mo. He has served as prosecuting attorney of Pike county, and since 1893, has been a member of congress from the Ninth Missouri district. Mr. Clark's eloquence, apart from his other notable qualities, makes him a prominent figure in congressional affairs.

WILLIAM BOURKE COCKRAN.

W. B. Cockran, the well-known lawyer and politician, who is also one of the most popular orators before the public, was born in Ireland, February 28, 1854. He was educated in that country, and later in France. When he landed in New York in 1871, he knew no one in America and had exactly one hundred dollars in his wallet. But he was well educated, of marked ability, and ambitious to the highest degree. Failing to secure something better, he became clerk in A. T. Stewart's store. A month later, however, he obtained a position as teacher in a public school on Rutgers street, where he taught French, Latin and history. Still later he accepted an appointment as principal in a public school in Westchester. But at this period Mr. Cockran had mapped out his future. He had determined to become a lawyer, and when on Saturdays his time was his own, he studied law in the office of the late Chauncey Schaffer. Saving some money, he resigned as school principal, and for nearly a year did nothing but read. In 1890 he was admitted to the bar of New York. His rise thenceforward was rapid. Very soon he became known as a man of great ability as an advocate and of supreme eloquence as a speaker. It was not long before he had a lucrative practice, and took a foremost place among the best lawyers of the metropolis. In the meantime his repute as an orator had attracted the attention of democratic leaders, and hence it was that Mr. Cockran was in demand at national democratic conventions and "on the stump." He was elected member of congress in 1891, serving in that capacity until 1895. In 1896, however, he refused to accept the 16 to 1 theory of the Democratic party and did his utmost to elect McKinley. Some will call Mr. Cockran a fortunate man, but as a matter of fact his fortune, professional and financial, is the outcome of his persistent industry and sincerity.

JOHN WARWICK DANIELS.

John Warwick Daniels was born at Lynchburg, Virginia, September 5, 1842. He was educated in the public schools of the town, at Lynchburg college, and also at Dr. Gessner Harrison's university school. During the Civil war he was an adjutant-general in the Confederate army, serving on the staff of General Early. At the close of the conflict he took up the study of law at the University of Virginia and graduated in 1866. He has practiced ever since at Memphis, Va. He was elected to the state senate in 1875 and was a member of the Virginia House of Delegates from 1869 to 1872. In 1881 he was democratic candidate for governor of Virginia, but was defeated. As member of congress in 1885 to 1887, and since 1887 as United States senator he has been much in the eye of the public. He is one of the most eloquent of forensic orators in America, as well as being the author of several well-known legal works.

CARL SCHURZ.

The riper years of Carl Schurz are so generally identified with the peaceful and progressive things that are the fruits of the rostrum of the orator and the sanctum of the editor that it seems hard to associate him with the stormy and romantic incidents that crowded his youth. Born in Liblar, Rhenish Prussia, on March 2, 1829, he was educated at the Cologne gymnasium, and at the age of seventeen entered the University of Bonn. When, in 1848, the revolutionary spirit became actively in evidence, he, together with Gottfried Kinkel, a professor of the university, started a liberal newspaper. As the consequence, the young men were forced to flee from Bonn. Later, Schurz received a commission as adjutant in the revolutionary army, and upon the fall of Badstadt was compelled to fly to Switzerland. His friend Kinkel was captured and sentenced to twenty years' imprisonment. Schurz, however, did not desert his friend, but returning to Germany, by the exercise of marvelous courage and ingenuity, liberated Kinkel, and went with him to Scotland. Subsequently, and in Paris, Mr. Schurz entered the journalistic profession. In 1855 he, accompanied by his young wife, whom he had married while under the ban of the German authorities, came to America and settled in Philadelphia. Afterward he went to Madison, Wisconsin, where he became identified with local political affairs. He soon became a prominent figure in state politics. In the interval he had been admitted to the bar and now opened an office in Milwaukee. In 1860 he was a member of the national republican convention, and when Lincoln became president he was made minister to Spain. During the Civil war he served with distinction under General Franz Sigel, who had been his old commander in Germany. In 1866 he was made Washington correspondent of the New York Tribune. Later he established the Detroit Post. He disposed of his interest in it, and in 1867 removed to St. Louis, where he became editor of the Westliche Post. In January, 1869, Mr. Schurz was made United States senator for Missouri. He has taken an active and even strenuous part in presidential campaigns for many years. In 1884, 1888 and 1892 he supported Mr. Cleveland. When he visited Europe, in 1888, he was cordially received by Prince Bismarck and other German leaders. He is an author, having published several books, including a life of Henry Clay and an essay on Abraham Lincoln. His screeds are often seen in periodical literature.

MUSICIANS.

WALTER JOHANNES DAMROSCH.

It is questionable if there is a better method of giving intellectual pleasure to a large number of people than by teaching them concerted singing. More than that, music is admittedly one of the most powerful factors in the bringing into being those finer qualities which are identified with the higher civilizations. It follows, then, that the man who devotes his life to cultivating a love of music among the masses is a public benefactor. Such an individual is Walter J. Damrosch, who is both well known and popular in this country in connection with his work on the lines alluded to. Mr. Damrosch was born at Breslau, Prussia, January 30, 1862. His father was Dr. Leopold Damrosch, his reputation as a conductor being of an international nature, led to his coming to this country in 1871 to become director of the Oratorio society and Symphony society of New York. In the meantime Walter had received a thorough musical training under his father, and, when the latter died, in 1885, he succeeded to the directorship of the organizations named. Since that period his continuous and conscientious work for the popularizing of vocal music has borne fruit not only in New York, but in many other cities of the United States. Mr. Damrosch was also the director of German opera at the Metropolitan Opera House and added to his reputation in connection therewith. Mr. Walter J. Damrosch is married to Margaret, daughter of the late James G. Blaine.

HENRY LEWIS REGINALD DE KOVEN.

When individuality is allied to talent the world stands ready to recognize, applaud and recompense. But the welding process is not to be accomplished without faithful and constant effort. The results approximate genius so closely that the division between it and mere talent is more theoretical than absolute. All this applies to Henry L. R. De Koven, the composer, who is one of the younger, and, at the same time, one of the most successful of American musicians. Comic operas there are and comic operas there will be, but in most instances the end of their vogue marks also the end of their existence. In the case of Robin Hood, The Highwayman, and other of Mr. De Koven's works, it is otherwise. Those named and others bid fair to remain popular beyond the limits of this generation. The composer was born at Littleton, Connecticut, April 5, 1861, his father being a clergyman. At first educated in public schools, he later went abroad, and was graduated from Oxford, England, in 1880. Like other successful composers, he gave indications of his love of music at an early age, and, during his college course, fostered his special gifts by constant study. After graduating, he studied still further under masters at Stuttgart, Florence, Paris and Vienna. On returning to this country he acted as musical critic on various publications coincidently with his work as a composer. Apart from his many operas he has written a number of songs. In 1884 he married Anna Farwell.

MAURICE GRAU.

Maurice Grau, who for many years was prominently identified with the exploiting of grand opera in this country, was born in Brünn, Austria, in 1849, and came to New York with his parents at the age of fifteen. He graduated from the Free Academy, New York, in 1867, attended the Columbia law school and later was for two years an employee of a law firm. Mr. Grau, however, was gifted with foresight. He saw that the citizens of this country, on recovering from the stress and strain of the Civil war, would not only be possessed of money with which to gratify their artistic instincts, but that these same instincts would come into active being. In other words, in his own way, Mr. Grau had faith in the recuperative powers of the United States. In 1872, therefore, he became manager for Aimée, the opera bouffe prima donna, and was also the manager of Rubenstein, pianist; Clara Louise Kellogg company, Salvini and other foreign musical and dramatic stars. Finally he became a member of the firm of Abbey, Schoeffel & Grau. Sarah Bernhardt, Patti, Henry Irving, Coquelin, Jane Hading, Maunet-Sully and Mlle. Rejane were exploited by the firm. Until 1902 he was managing director of the Maurice Grau opera company and lessee of the Metropolitan opera house, New York, in which capacity he annually produced for some years standard grand operas, the casts of which included the most famous singers of the present generation. He furthermore has acted as managing director of the Royal opera house, Covent Garden. On 1903 Mr. Grau severed his connection with the Metropolitan opera house, much to the regret of those to whose musical taste he had so successfully catered.

VICTOR HERBERT.

The secret of success, as far as those who cater to public amusement is concerned, is the placing of one's fingers upon the pulse of the public and shape one's methods and manners in accordance with the knowledge so obtained. Victor Herbert, the composer, has so shaped his career, and, while his work is more or less identified with the lighter forms of comic opera, he nevertheless has exhibited unmistakable musical genius.

Mr. Herbert was born in Dublin, Ireland, February 1, 1859, and is the grandson of Samuel Lever, the author of Handy Andy, and other Irish novels. He began to study music in Germany when but seven years of age, and took lessons from a number of masters. While yet a boy, he was appointed the principal 'celloist of the court orchestra in Stuttgart. After more study and a prolonged tour in Europe, he came to this country as 'cello soloist of the Metropolitan opera house orchestra in New York. During his career of almost uninterrupted professional successes, he has been connected with the Thomas, Seidl and other orchestras in the capacities of 'celloist and director. He has also been bandmaster of the Twenty-second Regiment of the national guard of the state of New York, and, in 1898, was made conductor of the Pittsburg (Pennsylvania) orchestra. Among the many comic operas which he has written are The Wizard of the Nile, The Viceroy and The Idol's Eye. He is also the author of a number of orchestral compositions. In 1886 he married Theresa Foerester, a prima donna.

LEONORA JACKSON.

Of the many American girls who have made riches and reputations as violinists, none is better known to the musical world of this country and abroad than Leonora Jackson. Still a girl as far as years go, she has acquired a reputation as a virtuoso that usually comes to one in the sere and yellow times of life. She was born in Boston, February 20, 1879. After an education received in Chicago public schools, during which time she studied her favorite instrument, she went abroad and became a pupil in the Royal school of music, Berlin. While still a child, she made her début in Europe and scored an instantaneous success. She has appeared in concerts with Paderewski, Patti and other famous singers and musicians and has added to her reputation by scores of performances before musical societies in America and on the continent. Audiences of the Boston symphony orchestra concerts know her well. During the season of 1900 and 1901 she gave one hundred and sixty concerts in the United States, securing for herself in this connection a national reputation. Queen Victoria decorated her as a recognition of her talents. Miss Jackson has also appeared before the German empress and many other notables of Europe.

FRANZ KNEISEL.

Boston musical circles have a sincere affection for Franz Kneisel, not only on account of his musical gifts but in connection with the work that he has done for the Boston symphony orchestra. Apart from that, however, some of his admirers aver that as a violin soloist he has no equal in this country and but few rivals abroad. Be that as it may, it is certain that his gifts are of a remarkable nature, and, like all successful men, he has cultivated them, constantly and conscientiously. Franz Kneisel was born in Roumania, in 1865, of German parents. From a child he studied music and violin instruction under Grun and Hellmsburger and early gave indications of the successes that awaited him in the future. For some years he was concert master of the Hoffburg theatre orchestra of Vienna, and later of Bilse's orchestra in Berlin. While filling these positions he acquired the reputation which led to his being invited to America. On reaching this country he at once became concert master of the Boston organization and director of the Kneisel quartet. He maintains his reputation as a violoncellist, however, in spite of the demands made upon his time by his other duties.

MAUD POWELL.

The popularity of Maud Powell, the violinist, amongst musically inclined people is not altogether due to a recognition of her genius. Those who know her life story know, too, that the place which she now occupies in the eye of the public has been obtained at the expense of a tremendous amount of work, in the face of many obstacles. Besides that, she is a typical American girl, which means that she is the possessor of the pluck independence and perseverance which are supposed to be characteristic of the citizens of the United States. Miss Powell was born in Peru, Illinois, August 22, 1868. She studied in the common schools at Aurora, Illinois, and, after some preliminary instruction on the violin in this country, took an advanced course of study in Leipzig, Paris and Berlin. As a pupil of the famous Joachim she gave promises of a brilliant future. Miss Powell is best known to the American public through the medium of her solos given in connection with orchestral concerts of Thomas, Seidl, Gericke, Nikisch, Damrosch and others. In 1892 she toured Australia and Germany with the New York Arion society, and, in 1896, on the strength of the popularity which she had established in her preceding tour, made another and most successful visit to Europe. She has contributed liberally on musical topics to a number of periodicals. Yet, as far as the American public is concerned, the fame of Maud Powell is permanently identified with her violin, rather than with her pen.

THEODORE THOMAS.

Like many of the well-known musicians of to-day, Theodore Thomas not only inherited his talents from his father, but was a pupil of the latter. Mr. Thomas shares with Damrosch and some other conductors the credit of making music, not only familiar to, but popular with, the masses in this country. He was born at Esens, Hanover, Germany, October 11, 1835, and at the age of ten made his first appearance in public as a violinist. Shortly after that he came to the United States, and for a number of years gave performances in New York. After a successful tour in the south, which extended over two years, he returned to New York and appeared in concerts and opera, first as violinist and later as orchestra conductor. In connection with other musicians he organized an annual series of chamber concerts. In 1867 he founded the Thomas orchestra and maintained it until 1888. He also acted as conductor for the Brooklyn and New York Philharmonic societies. In 1891 he moved to Chicago, and since then has been conductor of the Chicago orchestra. He is director of the Cincinnati college of music, was musical director of the Chicago exposition and has held other prominent positions in the musical world. He has been married twice, his second wife being Rose Fay, of Chicago.

SINGERS.

DAVID SCULL BISPHAM.

David Scull Bispham is another of those wise ones who recognized the call of his career and followed it. Originally intended for a business life, he found that his vocation was on the operatic stage, and in spite of the apparently insurmountable obstacles that intervened, he at length reached the goal of his desires. Mr. Bispham was born in Philadelphia January 5, 1857, and graduated in 1876 from Haverford college, a Quaker institution near Philadelphia. When not very much more than a baby he gave evidence of his musical taste, and when at college his connection with the glee club developed and fostered his gifts. Finally, after some years of experience as an amateur, he became a soloist in Philadelphia churches and in 1884 went to Italy to study and then appeared in concert in London. In 1892 he was intrusted with the rôle of "Tristan" at the Covent Garden Opera House, London, taking the audience of the British metropolis by storm. Since that time he has sung in all the great cities of the continent and of the United States, adding to his laurels meantime both as singer and actor. He is almost unexcelled as an oratorio vocalist, and is an exponent of classical ballads. Mr. Bispham was married in 1895 to Caroline, daughter of the late General Charles S. Russell. He is now the principal baritone of the Covent Garden Opera, London.

EMMA CALVÉ.

This generation seems to be particularly fortunate in regard to the number and the quality of its singers. Not the least prominent among these is Emma Calvé, the well-known prima donna, who has sung, so it is said, in every civilized or semi-civilized country in the world and in each and every instance has vindicated her professional reputation. She was born in France in 1866 and was educated at a convent. After some years of study under continental masters, she made her début in grand opera in 1882 at the Theater De la Monnaie, Brussels, where she appeared in Massenet's Herodiade. Since then she has been intrusted with a number of responsible operatic rôles and is well known in the United States. No small portion of her current reputation rests upon the success that she achieved in connection with her appearance in Mascagni's "Cavalleria Rusticana."

ZELIE DE LUSSAN.

Among the younger prima donnas who have attracted nearly as much attention abroad as they have in this country is Zelie de Lussan. She is an American girl by birth and received her musical training in New York and Boston. Subsequently she studied abroad, and after some concert work in France and Germany, returned to the United States, where she appeared in English and grand opera. Her successes from the inception of her artistic career were almost continuous. Besides her vocal gifts she owns histrionic talents of a high order. Subsequent to her last New York appearance, she was again called to Europe, and in that connection has given renewed assurance of her abilities. She is one of the several American girls who have succeeded in a profession which bristles with difficulties.

EDOUARD DE RESZKE.

Edouard de Reszke was born at Vasevie, Poland, in 1853. He is the brother of Jean de Reszke, and with him shares vocal gifts of a high order and a permanent popularity among musically inclined people. He studied music and singing under Ciaffei and Celetti, making his début as an operatic singer in Paris in 1876 as the king in "Aida." Since then he has been before the public more or less constantly, and his reputation has not waned by reason of his many years of professional life. He is a favorite in grand opera rôles in Europe and has appeared in every city of importance in the United States. He is the owner of a basso of remarkable purity and timbre.

JEAN DE RESZKE.

A triple alliance of magnificent vocal gifts, a commanding personality and a robust physique are responsible for the long and brilliant career of the operatic singer, Jean de Reszke. He was born in Vasevie, Poland. January 14, 1850, and studied under the masters, Ciaffei, Cotogni and Sbriglia. His début as baritone singer was made in Favorita, Venice, January, 1874, and his début as tenor singer in Madrid, 1879. Mr. de Reszke has appeared in leading rôles in grand opera both in the United States and Europe, one of his most popular characters being Tristan, in Tristan and Isolde. He was married to the Countess Marie de Goulaine, and now makes his home in New York city.

EMMA EAMES.

It is not often that one compasses one's ambition to the full. More frequently it will be found that those whom the world calls successful are successful in part only, and that much is left unfilled. It is open to question, however, whether the man who has fully realized his hope is more happy than he to whom somewhat remains for which to crave and struggle. The answer to the question involved could hardly be given by Emma Eames, prima donna, for humanly speaking, she seems to have achieved the ambitions and the purposes of her life. The singer was born in Shanghai, China, August 13, 1867, of American parentage. Her childhood was spent in Boston, her musical education being at first under the direction of her mother and later under Miss Munyard, a well-known teacher of vocalism. While singing in a church choir in Boston, she attracted the attention of Prof. Gericke, then leader of the Boston symphony orchestra, and Prof. Paine, of Harvard, both of whom became interested in her. It was under their direction that the technical foundation of her future fame was laid. By their advice and with their assistance, she took lessons from Mme. Marchesi, of Paris, for two years and later, after instruction in operatic rôles by Prof. Gevart, chief of the Brussels conservatory of music, she made her début in Paris in Gounod's Romeo and Juliet. A pronounced and spontaneous success was hers, and the news that a comparatively unknown American girl had become famous in a night excited the interest of musically inclined people all over the world. Gounod himself declared that she was his ideal Juliet. During her engagement in Paris, Miss Eames was the recipient of many social and official attentions, the president of the French republic honoring her with a decoration. In 1891 and the year following, she appeared in grand opera at the Covent Garden opera house, London, where she also scored. In 1893 and 1894 she gave New York audiences a taste of her quality by appearing in opera at the Metropolitan opera house and won immediate popular favor. She is installed a permanent favorite in musical circles of this country. In 1891 she married Julian, son of W. W. Story, the sculptor.

LILLIAN NORDICA.

Lillian Nordica, one of the most popular of American prima donnas, was born in Farmingdale, Maine, in 1859, her family name being Norton. Her musical education began early and was of a very thorough sort. After a period spent in local public schools, she became a student in the New England conservatory, her teacher being John O'Neil. Later she studied under San Giovanni at Milan, Italy. After preliminary work in concerts abroad, she made her operatic début at Brescia, Italy, in La Traviata, and scored instantaneously and emphatically. In 1887 she made a successful appearance in London, and later visited Paris, St. Petersburg and other European capitals. In each and every instance she repeated her initial successes. She has been twice married, her first husband being a Mr. Gower, and her second Herr Zoltan Done. The prima donna's repertoire embraces the leading rôles of forty operas, and includes nearly all the standard oratorios. She is best known to the public in connection with Wagnerian parts, and has appeared in grand opera in this country on several occasions. Mme. Nordica has a charming personality, and her professional successes have by no means estranged her from the friends of her childhood.

ADELINA PATTI.

Theoretically the uses of poverty are many, tending to the development of varied virtues. As a matter of fact, poverty is the mother of much meanness and many crimes. The struggle for mere existence among the poor is so keen that it absorbs their mental and physical vitality. So it is that he or she who passes from the twilight of penury into the sunlight of prosperity must be rarely gifted. Such an individual is Adelina Patti, whose fame as a great singer is not only yet undimmed, but bids fair to last as long as music itself. Patti was born in Madrid, Spain, February 19, 1843, her mother being a prima donna at the Grand theater. In 1844 the family came to this country, the father being appointed one of the managers of the then Italian opera house on Chambers street, New York. Little Adelina received her preliminary musical training from her half-brother, Ettore Barilli. Owing to the financial stresses in which her parents then were, she, although only seven years of age, was allowed to make her début in concert at Tripler's hall, New York, on which occasion her undeveloped but phenomenal voice attracted general attention. In 1859 she made her début in grand opera at the Academy of Music, New York, when she appeared in Lucia di Lammermoor. Her audience gave her a most cordial welcome. But, as it turned out, her struggles were only beginning. As far as the mere cultivation of her voice was concerned, her natural gifts were of such a nature that she had no difficulty in overcoming the technical obstacles of her art, but the spirit of jealousy and suspicion which success usually arouses in the breasts of the unknown, prevented her talents from being duly recognized, or, to put it in another way, she was so belittled by her rivals that she had to individually satisfy every great city in America that she had not been overrated. Patti was deeply wounded by these unlooked-for conditions, but nevertheless she bravely faced the sneers and unkind criticisms and overcame them, and for many years has occupied a place in the estimation of the public, which probably no other prima donna in the history of civilization has attained. Twice during her career she has been threatened with the total loss of her voice, but happily the "nightingale in her throat" is as yet unsilenced. To the end of her days she will reap the reward of the self-denial and persistent attention to duty and art which she gave them during the years of her childhood. She has been as successful abroad as she has in this country. In grand opera she has assumed nearly all existing prominent rôles. For some years past she made her home abroad. In 1881, Patti revisited the United States, when she received $5,000 per night, which is said to be the largest amount ever paid to a singer or actor for one performance. Married three times, her last husband was Baron Rolf Cedarstrom. She is the owner of a castle at Craig-y-Nos, Wales. During her last and most recent visit to this country, the American public gave her ample proof that she still occupies a warm place in its affection.

MARCELLA STENGEL SEMBRICH.

Marcella Stengel Sembrich is one of the several prima donnas to whom the American music-loving public has remained loyal for many years. As an artist she ranks with the foremost singers of to-day, while her domestic life is of an ideal nature. As a rule, the law of compensation takes greatly where it gives freely, and so the woman of talent who devotes herself to the service of the public is apt to be the loser as far as home life is concerned. In Mme. Sembrich's case it is otherwise, however, and her social popularity, too, is no less than is her vogue on the operatic stage. The songstress was born at Lemberg, Galatia, February 18, 1858. Her early musical education was obtained in the Conservatory of Lemberg, after which she studied at Vienna and Milan. Her marvelous vocal gifts assured the success of her début as Elvira, in I Puritani, at the Royal theater, Athens. After a season spent on the continent in opera she, in 1883, came to this country under the management of Henry Abbey. Her reception here was of the warmest nature, and from that time on she has been a constant favorite with the American public. She has made a number of tours in the United States and has been uniformly successful in connection therewith. In 1877 she married Prof. Wilhelm Stengel, who had formerly been her teacher at Lemberg.

ACTORS.

WILLIAM H. CRANE.

A tireless worker and devoted to his calling, William H. Crane is without doubt one of the foremost comedians of the day. Mr. Crane was born in Leicester, Massachusetts, April 30, 1845. At the age of eighteen he made his professional début at Utica, New York. His first permanent engagement was with the Harriet Holman's opera company, with which organization he remained for seven years. His first part, with this company, was that of the Orator, in The Child of the Regiment; later he filled the rôles of Beppo, in Fra Diavolo; Mephisto, in Faust; Hugh Challoner, in Ours; Dr. Dalcomora, in The Elixir of Love. Leaving the Holmans, he joined the Alice Oates opera company, becoming its leading comedian. Later, after creating the part of Le Blanc, in Evangeline, he, in 1874, became a member of the stock company playing at Hooley's theater, Chicago. His first appearance in New York city was at Niblo's theater, in 1876, and it was in the same year that at the Park Theater, he won distinct recognition as a comedian of exceptional talent by his impersonation of Dick Swiveler to The Marchioness. During this time an acquaintance with Stuart Robson resulted in the two actors collaborating in Our Boarding House, which was given its initial presentation at the Park theater, New York city, October 11, 1877. This engagement being ended, they formed a partnership that lasted for twelve years. Since 1899 he has appeared in star rôles in The Senator, On Probation, For Money, Brother John, A Fool of Fortune, A Virginia Courtship, and other plays. Mr. Crane has accumulated a comfortable fortune, and in the intervals of his professional labor enjoys a pleasant home life with his wife and children at Cohasset, Massachusetts.

JOHN DREW.

John Drew is an excellent example of a man finding his vocation and filling it. While it is true that he inherited his histrionic talent, his father, John Drew, Sr., having been a noted Irish comedian and his mother, Louise Lane Drew, also having been a great favorite on the stage—yet he has achieved success because of his personal efforts looking to its development. The prime requisite for advancement in any field is, first, find your talent, then bend every energy toward its development. The subject of this sketch was born in Philadelphia, Pennsylvania, November 13, 1853, and early showed a preference for the boards. He was educated at the Episcopal academy and by private tutors, making his first appearance behind the footlights at the Arch street theater, Philadelphia, as Plumper, in As Cool as a Cucumber. Although only nineteen, his efforts met with almost immediate success, and at twenty-one he joined Mr. Daly's famous company soon quickly becoming the most popular member of the organization. Since 1892 he has been starring in his own company. Although Mr. Drew excels in society plays, he has also made a brilliant record in classical drama, and especially in Shakespearian rôles. Petruchio, in Taming of the Shrew, is his favorite character, and it is the most difficult and exacting of any he assumes. He has brought out in yearly succession The Butterflies, The Bauble Shop, Christopher, Jr., Rosemary, A Marriage of Convenience, One Summer Day, and The Liars. Commenting upon Mr. Drew, William Winter, the well-known critic, wrote "that he possesses drollery, the talent of apparent spontaneity, and the faculty of crisp emotion. He has surpassed all young actors of his day as a gay cavalier and the bantering farceur of the drawing-room drama of modern social life. He is thoroughly in earnest, and his attitude toward his art is that of intellectual purpose and authority."

WILLIAM HOOKER GILLETTE.

We sometimes speak and often hear of an instantaneous success, but in reality there is no such thing as success or failure being immediate. Every real achievement is the culmination of weeks and months, and even years, of earnest and unremitting toil. The popular actor and well-known author, William Hooker Gillette, furnishes a case in point. The structure of his reputation bids fair to last indefinitely, but it rests on foundations of preparatory work of which the public knows but little. He was born in Hartford, Connecticut, July 24, 1855, being the son of Francis G. (late United States senator from Connecticut), and Elizabeth Daggett (Hooker) Gillette. Graduating from the Hartford high school at the age of twenty, he afterward attended the New York university for two years. From a lad he had given evidence of his love for the stage. While at the university he obtained a minor position in one of the theaters. In 1876, becoming a student in the Boston university, he followed the same plan of studying by day and playing in small parts at night. In this way he made himself thoroughly acquainted with the "business" of the stage, as well as the first principles of acting. Mr. Gillette made his first palpable hit in the title rôle of A Private Secretary by playing a part which required a particular delicacy of treatment.

NATHANIEL C. GOODWIN.

Even as a schoolboy the famous comedian, Nat. C. Goodwin, by his clever imitations of leading actors, displayed signs of his future greatness. He was born in Boston, July 25, 1857, and educated in the public schools of that city. His parents intended that he should follow a commercial career, but he early decided for the stage as against a business life. His mirth-provoking powers were finally recognized by Stuart Robson, who engaged young Goodwin at a salary of $5 a week to play the part of the Bootblack, in Law in New York. Mr. Goodwin's reputation was quickly established, and the next season he contracted with Josh Hart to appear in the Eagle theater in New York city, at a salary of $150 a week. In 1876 he played Captain Dietrich in Evangeline, and three years later entered upon his career as a star, a practically unbroken line of successes having followed both here and abroad, for when, in 1890, he filled a long engagement in London, he was received with every manifestation of approval. Mr. Goodwin has been married three times, the last wife being Maxine Elliott.

JAMES KETELTAS HACKETT.

James Keteltas Hackett, one of the youngest of the prominent actors of America, and certainly the youngest actor-manager of note in this country, was born at Wolfe Island, Ontario, Canada, September 6, 1869. He is the son of the late James Henry Hackett, who in his time was also a notable figure of the American boards. After graduating from the College of the City of New York in 1891, he studied in the New York law school, but his inclination for the stage, which manifested itself almost as soon as he could talk, became more and more marked, and, abandoning the legal career which it had been intended he should follow, he gave himself up to studying for the stage. In 1892 he made his début in New York in the A. M. Palmer stock company. From the very first he gave unmistakable indications of his subsequent success. In four years—being then twenty-six years of age—he was leading man of the company in question, and was a star in the dramatic firmament of New York. From that time on his progress in his chosen profession has been unceasing. For some years he was under the management of Mr. Daniel Frohman, during which period he made distinctive hits in The Prisoner of Zenda and its sequel, Rupert of Hentzau, and The Pride of Jennico. Leaving Mr. Frohman's management, he branched out for himself. As already intimated, he is as successful as he is popular. He married Mary Mannering, a well-known actress, whom he met during his association with the Frohman forces.

SIR HENRY BRODRIBB IRVING.

Sir Henry Brodribb Irving, who has created an era in theatrical art, did not attain his ambitions until he had experienced a full share of disappointments and privations. His name is now associated with all that makes for the splendor of the drama, spectacular and intellectual. But the time was with Sir Henry when the next meal was an unknown quantity, when his wardrobe was carried on his back, and when his future seemed to be without promise professionally or otherwise. But with him, as with other successful men, his belief in himself enabled him to combat stress of troubles and finally landed him at the goal of success. Apart from all else he has, through the medium of his masterly productions of Shakespeare's plays, done more to revive an intelligent interest in the "Immortal Bard" than has any other manager-actor of this generation. His keenest critics admit his genius, even while they comment on his methods. Like most men of his type he has a marked individuality, and for this reason he has been accused of mannerisms. On the other hand, his admirers claim that his individuality is responsible for no small portion of the charm and power of his work. The actor was born in Keinton, near Glastonbury, England, February 6, 1838, his actual name being Brodribb. By permission of the English authorities in 1887 he was authorized, however, to continue the use of the adopted name of Irving. Educated in private schools in London, he, in 1856, went on the stage in the provinces. His first appearance before a public was a failure, pure, simple and absolute. The London stage first knew him in 1859; then he returned to the provinces, remaining therein until 1866, when he once more came to London, playing in several different theaters, but in minor rôles. At about this period his talents began to assert themselves, and since 1871 Sir Henry Irving has been successfully before the public at the Lyceum Theater, London, of which he was lessee and manager from 1878 until 1899. He is well known to play-goers in this country by reason of his several tours here. In recognition of his work for the betterment of the stage he was knighted by Queen Victoria in 1895. Sir Henry Irving is also an author, his most notable work being The Drama.

JOSEPH JEFFERSON.

Many ancestors of Joseph Jefferson followed the profession of acting. Both his father and mother were players. He was born at Philadelphia, February 20, 1829, was educated at home and first appeared on the stage as a child in the old-time favorite play of Pizarro. In 1843 his father died, and he joined a party of strolling players, who traveled through Texas and followed the United States army to Mexico. His first prominent rôle was that of Asa Trenchard, in Our American Cousin, which was first presented October 18, 1858, and continued for one hundred and fifty consecutive nights at Laura Keene's theater in New York city. His other notable parts have been Newman Noggs, in Nicholas Nickelby; Caleb Plummer, in The Cricket on the Hearth; Dr. Pangloss, in The Heir-at-Law; and Dr. Ollapod, in The Poor Gentleman. But the public chiefly identify him with the title rôle of Rip Van Winkle, which he has played in every city in the United States, and also in England and Australia. He enjoys the distinction of having presented the character more times than any other actor has ever played a single character in the history of dramatics. Besides being one of the most popular actors of his times, Mr. Jefferson is a painter of considerable ability and is an author of some note. His "autobiography" is his most important work, but he has also contributed many articles to the magazines. He married, in 1848, Margaret Lockyer, and after her death took to wife Sarah Warren, in 1867.

EDWARD H. SOTHERN.

How many failures in life are caused by misfit occupations! The world would have perhaps never known of Edward H. Sothern if he had followed the wishes of his father in choosing a life career. This man, who has attained such prominence in the histrionic profession would probably have been doomed to obscurity had he become a painter. He was born in New Orleans, Louisiana, December 6, 1859, being the second son of Edward Askew Sothern, the famous comedian. At the age of five he was taken to London, where he received his education. He studied drawing for some time, his father wishing him to become an artist, but he seems to have inherited a predilection for the stage. It was during his two visits to the United States with his father in 1875 and 1879, that, in spite of his parents' objections, he decided to become an actor, which he did, making his début as a cabman, in Sam, at the Park theater, New York city. Later he joined his father's company, but shortly after resigned in order to become a member of John McCullough's company. In 1883, after appearing for two years at the Criterion, Standard, Royalty and other London theaters, and traveling one year, in company with his brother, Lytton Sothern, he returned to this country, again entered the company of John McCullough, becoming its leading comedian. Subsequently Mr. Sothern played with Helen Daubray, in One of Our Girls; he first took a leading rôle as Jack Hammerton, in The Highest Bidder. Since that time he has starred with his own company in Lord Chumley, The Maister of Woodbarrow, Prisoner of Zenda, Under the Red Robe, etc. He married Virginia Harned, his leading woman. Mr. Sothern has had an adequate professional training and his creditable work proclaims him a master of his art.

ACTRESSES.

MAUDE ADAMS.

Maude Adams is descended from a long line of theatrical people. She was born at Salt Lake City, Utah, November 11, 1872. Her mother was the leading woman of a stock company in that city, and at a very early age Miss Adams appeared on the stage in child's parts. Her school days were scarcely over when she joined the E. H. Sothern Company. She afterward became a member of Charles Frohman's stock company, and still later was leading lady for John Drew. Her most pronounced success was as Babbie, in The Little Minister and another as the title rôle of l'Aiglon. She also received much publicity as the model for the silver statue which was exhibited at the World's Fair, Chicago. Miss Maude Adams has established herself permanently in the good-will of American play-goers.

VIOLA ALLEN.

Viola Allen was born in the south, but went to Boston when three years of age. She was educated in that city and at the Bishop Strachan school, Toronto, Canada. Her début was made at the Madison Square theater, New York, in Esmeralda, in 1882. During the season of 1883 and 1884 she was leading lady for John McCullough, and afterward played classical and Shakespearian rôles. She was a member of the Empire theater stock company in 1892, but her principal success was in creating the character of Gloria Quayle, in The Christian, which had a long run in New

York in 1898, succeeded by a tour through the principal cities of the country. Miss Allen's private charities are many, and she is identified with those phases of church work which have to do with the bettering of the conditions of the poor.

ETHEL BARRYMORE.

Ethel Barrymore, one of the youngest stars in the theatrical profession, was born in Philadelphia in 1880. She comes of a professional family, and when, while yet a child, gave to those who were responsible for her first appearance behind the footlights assurance of innate talent. Miss Barrymore was by no means unknown to Metropolitan play-goers prior to the time when, under Mr. Charles Frohman's management, she made her stellar début a few years since. The young actress is a finished comedienne and is a member of that modern school of comedy that cultivates repressed effort.

MRS. LESLIE CARTER.

David Belasco, playwright and manager, has been uniformly successful with his plays and his stars. A case in point is that of Mrs. Leslie Carter, who has been connected in a professional capacity with Mr. Belasco for some years. Stepping from social circles in Chicago to the stage, she was in the first instance a somewhat indifferent specimen of the crude amateur actress, but Mr. Belasco detected in her undeveloped talent, and the rest is professional history. Under his guidance as tutor and manager she holds a prominent place in the theatrical world. Her first success was made in the Heart of Maryland and her last and most notable in Du Barry.

ELEANORA DUSE.

Eleanora Duse, the Italian tragedienne, who is Signora Cecci in private life, was born, in 1861, in Vigovano, Italy. At an early age she gave indications of those histrionic talents which subsequently made her famous. For many years she was one of the most notable figures on the stage of her country. She made her American début in 1893 at the Fifth Avenue theater, New York. While there is no gainsaying the sincerity and finish of her art, yet at the same time there are not a few critics who take exception to it on the score of the sombre plays and methods of the actress. Since her début she has visited the United States on more than one occasion, and in each instance her following in this country have accorded her the welcome which is due to her as an artiste and a woman.

MAY IRWIN.

"Blessed are the laughmakers," is one of the later beatitudes, and on that score May Irwin will certainly receive her share of blessings. She was born at Whitby, Ontario, Canada, in 1862, and made her début at the Adelphi theater, Buffalo, in February, 1876. Later, with her sister Flora, she became a member of Tony Pastor's company, and shortly afterward joined Augustin Daly's company. She ranks as one of the wholesome mirth-making actresses of the American stage. The plays in which she has starred include The Widow Jones, The Swell Miss Fitzgerald, Courted Into Court, Kate Kip, Buyer, and other farcical comedies. In 1878 she was married to Frederick W. Keller, of St. Louis, who died in 1886.

VIRGINIA HARNED.

Virginia Harned was born at Boston, and, at the age of sixteen, made her début as Lady Despar, in The Corsican Brothers. She first played in New York city in 1890 at the Fourteenth street theater in a play entitled "A Long Lane or Green Meadow." In this play she made so good an impression that she was engaged by Daniel Frohman as leading woman for E. A. Sothern. In 1896 she was married to Mr. Sothern and has since appeared in leading parts in his company. Probably her greatest success was in the creation of the title rôle of Trilby.

MRS. LILLIE LANGTRY.

Mrs. Lillie Langtry, if she has done nothing else, has proven that a woman can command admiration even when she is no longer in the first flush of her youth or in the full bloom of her womanhood. This statement is made in view of the public regard which she still enjoys as an actress, in spite of the fact that she first saw the light in 1852, in Jersey, Great Britain. Her father was connected with the Established church of England. She married an officer in the English army and subsequently settled in London. Domestic differences ensuing, she went upon the stage. Her American début, as an actress, was made in 1893 at the Fifth avenue theater, New York. Since then she has visited this country on two or three occasions. Mrs. Langtry is popularly known as the Jersey Lily. She was married for the second time in 1899.

JULIA MARLOWE.

That tender and graceful exponent of some of Shakespeare's women, Julia Marlowe, was born at Coldbeck, Cumberlandshire, England, August 17, 1870. She came with her parents to this country when she was five years of age. After a period spent in Kansas, the family removed to Cincinnati, where she attended public school until she was twelve years of age. She then became a member of a juvenile opera company which produced Pinafore, Chimes of Normandy, etc. After several years of arduous work and study, she appeared in New York, but was a failure. Not discouraged, however, she went to work to study again, and in the spring of 1897 attained that recognition from a metropolitan audience for which she had striven so faithfully. Since that time she has advanced in her profession and has secured a prominent place among the leading actresses of to-day.

ORGANIZERS AND LECTURERS.

CYNTHIA MAY WESTOVER ALDEN.

Mrs. Cynthia May Westover Alden is an example of the possibilities of journalism as a vocation for women. She was born at Afton, Iowa, May 31, 1862, being the daughter of Oliver S. and Lucilda (Lewis) Westover. After a period spent in local common schools, she graduated from the Colorado state university and the Denver business college. Subsequently she taught geology, book-keeping and vocal and instrumental music. The owner of an excellent voice, she was for some years a soprano soloist in several church choirs in New York. In 1887 she was appointed United States inspector of customs at the port of New York, and during her term of service as such made many important seizures. She was also secretary in a municipal department of New York, and for a time was an employee of the New York state museum of natural history, resigning therefrom to engage in journalism. After editing the woman's department of the New York Recorder, she took charge of a similar department on the New York Tribune. She is now on the editorial staff of the Ladies' Home Journal. Mrs. Alden is also the founder and president-general of the International Sunshine society. Her life has been as busy as useful, and she has made for herself a large circle of friends who, though not knowing her personally, are nevertheless acquainted with her through the medium of the kindly and helpful journalism with which she is so generally identified.

CLARA BARTON.

That most noted and beloved of humanitarians, Clara Barton, is of Puritan ancestry, being born in Oxford, Massachusetts, in 1830. She was the daughter of Captain Stephen and Sally Stone Barton, and was educated at Clinton, New York. When still very young she founded a seminary for girls at Elizabethtown, New Jersey. Later, she became principal of the first public school in Bordentown, New Jersey, resigned through sickness and was the first woman to hold a regular clerical position under the government, afterward being appointed to the patent office at Washington, District of Columbia. During the Civil war she was instrumental in forming the famous sanitary commission which did such magnificent work for the sick and wounded at Bull Run, Antietam, Spottsylvania and many other battlefields of the war. When the Andersonville prisoners were released they received timely aid through her relief work, and by her earnest efforts the fate of over thirty thousand missing men was ascertained by means of the bureau of records which she organized at Washington. During the Franco-Prussian war she and her assistants nursed the sick and wounded in Strasburg and Metz. In the days of the Commune she entered Paris, distributing food and clothing to the hungry and starving. On her return to the United States in 1873, she started the successful movement to obtain recognition of the projected Red Cross society from the government. In 1882 the society was organized and she became its first president. In that capacity she has superintended the work of giving help to sufferers from the Michigan forest fires, the earthquake at Charleston, floods on the Ohio and Mississippi, 1884; the Johnstown flood, the Galveston disaster, 1900, etc. Wherever there has been a cry from the sufferer, Clara Barton, often in the face of almost insurmountable difficulties and constant danger, has ever responded to the call of duty.

FRANCIS EDWARD CLARK.

Francis Edward Clark, the president of the United Societies of Christian Endeavor comes of New England stock, although he was born in Aylmer, province of Quebec, September 12, 1851. His parents died when he was a child, and his uncle, the Rev. E. W. Clark, adopted him and took him to Claremont, New Hampshire. Thus it was that he acquired a new name and country. Education and home influence inclined him to the ministry, and he early decided to become a clergyman. After an academic and college course—the latter at Dartmouth—he studied theology for three years at Andover, and was later appointed pastor of Williston church, Portland, Maine, a small mission from which he built a large Congregational church. One of his many ideas was the exaction of a pledge of faithful Christian endeavor from the members of his Bible classes. The results were of so marked a nature that the well-known society of which he is president was a consequence thereof. Churches of many denominations endorsed the idea, and within a few years national conventions of the organization were held which made the world think that a tidal wave of religious enthusiasm was sweeping over it. An organ of the movement was founded, entitled "The Golden Rule," with Dr. Clark as editor-in-chief. The work continued to grow, and finally he was compelled to resign from the pastorate in order to devote himself to the needs of the society. The movement has extended all over the world, and in connection with it he has organized other societies, such as The Tenth Legions, The Macedonian Phalanx, The Christian Association, and Quiet Hour. Dr. Clark was married in 1876 to Harriet E. Abbott. He is the author of several books dealing with his life work.

MARY LOWE DICKINSON.

Mrs. Mary Lowe Dickinson, the well-known authoress, was born in Fitchburg, Massachusetts, in 1897. She received a preparatory education in the common schools, then was placed under the instruction of private tutors, and subsequently studied art and literature abroad. Returning to this country, she became head assistant in the Chapman school, Boston, taught for some time in the Hartford female seminary and finally was made principal of the Van Norman institute, New York. Marrying John B. Dickinson, a New York banker, she on his death some years since became professor of belles lettres, emeritus professor and lecturer at Denver university. She is now connected in an official capacity with a number of philanthropic and religious institutions, is the editor of Lend a Hand Magazine, and for ten years has edited The Silver Cross. She has written poems and works of fiction which are illustrative of various lines of philanthropic work.

THOMAS DIXON, JR.

Thomas Dixon, Jr., lecturer, writer and clergyman, was born in Shelby, North Carolina, January 11, 1864, his father being the Rev. Thomas Dixon. He graduated from Wake Forest college, North Carolina, in 1883, from the Greensboro, North Carolina, law school in 1886, and from Johns Hopkins university in 1899. Harriet Bussey became his wife on March 3, 1886, in Montgomery, Alabama. He was a member of the North Carolina legislature from 1884 to 1886. Resigning in order to enter the ministry, he was ordained a Baptist clergyman in 1887, taking a pastorate at Raleigh, North Carolina, and late in the same year accepted a call to Boston. Two years later he came to New York, where he has become noted by reason of his pulpit treatment of topics of the day in a manner uniquely his own. He is the author of several works on religious and social problems, one of which, The Failure of Protestantism in New York, whichwas published in 1897, has attracted much attention. Mr. Dixon is a forceful speaker, a man of magnetic presence, and possesses the courage of his convictions to a high degree.

HERBERT HUNGERFORD.

Herbert Hungerford was born at Binghamton, New York, February 22, 1874. He was brought up on a farm, obtained the groundwork of his education in district schools, and graduated from the academy at Windsor, New York, in 1895. The following year he entered Syracuse university, but was compelled to leave at the close of the freshman year on account of illness. Serving as a private in the First Regiment of New York volunteer infantry during the Spanish-American war, he, while the regiment was stationed at Honolulu, Hawaiian Islands, established, edited and published the News Muster, which was a unique contribution to the curiosities of journalism, being the first illustrated newspaper published by a body of soldiers in the field. At the close of the war he returned to Binghamton and there organized the initial branches of the Success league. Later he was called to New York to further and take charge of the development of the organization in question, which is a federation of literary, debating and self-culture societies. The league has developed rapidly under his direction, now having branches in every state and in nearly every city and town of importance in the United States. He was married, in 1898, to Grace M. Whipple, of Binghamton, New York.

JOHN MITCHELL.

The story of the early struggles of the labor leader, John Mitchell, is both pathetic and inspiring. A son of the common people, he has risen from being a poor door-boy in the coal mines of Illinois, to a position of great trust and general honor. Mr. Mitchell was born in Braidwood, Brill county, Illinois, February 4, 1869, being the son of Robert and Martha Mitchell. Compelled to leave school at the age of ten, his subsequent education was obtained by night study. He afterward studied law, worked on a farm, became coal miner and was finally attracted to the labor movement, which at that time was directed by the Knights of Labor. In 1888 he took an active part in trade union affairs as president of the local organization of the Knights. Knowing that knowledge is power, he read everything that came within his reach and joined debating societies, athletic associations, independent political reform clubs and various other organizations, in order to take advantage of the several opportunities that they presented to him. When, in January, 1890, the order of United Mine Workers of America was organized, he was among the first to be enrolled, and in January, 1898, was elected its vice-president. He has been re-elected every year since, is also second vice-president of the American Federation of Labor and a member of various committees at the National Civic Federation. During the five years of his leadership the union has grown from a membership of forty-three thousand to a membership of over three hundred thousand. He has brought about many reforms in the interests of labor. His chiefest achievement is that of securing a settlement of the recent great coal mine strike through the arbitration commission appointed by President Roosevelt. He has demonstrated anew the force of the maxim that "It is to him only who has conquered himself it is given to conquer."

LITTLE VISITS WITH GREAT AMERICANS

ERNEST THOMPSON-SETON.

Historians of the Wild—of the denizens of fields and woods and rivers—there are and have been, but in the majority of instances their work has been confined to mere descriptions of the personalities of birds and beasts and fish from the standpoint of the museum, rather than from that of the interested, if unscientific, observer. Ernest Thompson-Seton, however, naturalist and artist, has, through the medium of his books, managed to so wed popular interest and scientific data that the result is fascinating in the extreme. He has shown, too, that to a man of talent there is always a new field to be discovered amid the old ones, which, apart from all else, is a lesson that no one can afford to ignore. Thompson-Seton was born in South Shields, England, August 14, 1860. He is a descendant of the famous Setons of Scotland, Thompson being a *nom de plume*. Coming to this country when a boy, he at first lived in the backwoods of Canada and also had experiences on the plains of the then far west. He was educated at the Toronto collegiate institute and also at the Royal academy, London, England. In 1896 he married Grace, daughter of Albert Gallatin, of San Francisco. His qualifications as a naturalist becoming known to the government of Manitoba, he was made official naturalist therefor, subsequently publishing works on the birds and mammals of that territory. He studied art in Paris and was at one time one of the chief illustrators of the Century dictionary. His works on natural history topics are well known. Thompson-Seton is what may be called a psychological naturalist, inasmuch as he analyzes the mentalities of his subjects. The results are seen in such books as The Biography of a Grizzly, The Trail of the Sand Hill Stag, Wild Animals I Have Known, etc.

CANADIANS.

SIR WILFRID LAURIER.

The man who stands before the world as Canada's most distinguished statesman is Sir Wilfrid Laurier, Premier of the Dominion. Sir Wilfrid has very broad and very optimistic ideas as to the destiny of Canada, and these he expresses with a poetic eloquence which never fails to arouse enthusiasm. His oratory takes lofty flights.

Sir Wilfrid was born in the Province of Quebec in 1841. French was the language of his childhood. He went to school in his native parish, and later took the classical course at L'Assomption College. He began in 1860 to study law in the office of the late Hon. R. Laflamme, Q. C., who was Minister of Justice for the Dominion and one of Sir Wilfrid's colleagues at Ottawa, when the latter became a member of Parliament. He was admitted to the bar in 1864. Eager to succeed, he devoted himself so zealously to his legal work that after three years of practice his health gave way, and he was forced to retire to the country. In the town of L'Avena he became editor of *Le Defrecheur*, a journal devoted to political and social reform. It was in this work that he first actively interested himself in politics. His articles in the journal were full of the earnestness, enthusiasm and eloquence which have since brought him fame.

Country air agreed with the young lawyer and writer. He regained his health, and opened a law office at St. Cristophe, now Arthabaskaville, where he made his home until he removed to Ottawa as Prime Minister of Canada. He first held office in 1871, when he was elected to the Quebec Assembly. He resigned his seat in the general elections of 1874, was elected by the same constituency to the Dominion House of Commons, and when Parliament assembled was given the honor of seconding the address in reply to the speech from the Throne. His burst of oratory on the occasion attracted wide attention and caused prophecies to be freely made that he was destined for great things.

It was only two years afterward, in 1876, that he attained the distinction of a position in the Cabinet, being appointed Minister of the Internal Revenue in the Mackenzie administration. His constituency did not support him in the next general election, but he was returned to Parliament from Quebec East, which constituency has ever since been his political sponsor. When the Mackenzie government was defeated in the elections of 1878, Mr. Laurier, who had by this time become the acknowledged leader of the Liberal party in Quebec, joined his friends in Opposition and waited for eighteen years for his party's return to power. This came in 1896. Mr. Laurier was then supreme in the House of Commons, and was called upon to organize a new government. Thus it was that he rose to the exalted position of Premier of Canada and found the opportunities which have given him so high a place among the world's statesmen.

Perhaps the most important policy which he inaugurated upon his rise to power was that of a preferential tariff in favor of Great Britain. It was due to this policy, as well as to his high position in the affairs of Canada, that when he went to England upon the occasion of the Queen's Diamond Jubilee in 1897 he was received with distinguished honor. The Queen made him a Knight Grand Cross of the Order of St. Michael and St. George. Oxford and Cambridge Universities conferred upon him honorary degrees. Upon a visit to the Continent of Europe during this trip abroad he was entertained by President Faure of France and was received by the Pope at Rome. When he returned to Canada he was greeted with great enthusiasm by all classes. In the general election of 1904 Sir Wilfrid's administration gained a triumphant endorsement at the polls.

LORD STRATHCONA.

One of the foremost of Canada's great workers is Lord Strathcona, who, as Donald Smith, was born in Scotland in 1820. He received his preliminary education in the common schools. He gave up the law, and became, when he was eighteen, an employee of the Hudson Bay Company on the bleak coast of Labrador.

Here he remained for thirteen years, becoming one of the company's most valued traders. From Labrador he went, in 1851, into the wilderness of the Northwest, where he rose through the grades of trader, chief trader, factor and chief factor. In 1869 he reached the top rung of the ladder in the Hudson Bay Company, receiving the appointment of resident governor.

He established himself in Montreal, but when the half breeds and Indians under the leadership of Louis Riel rose in rebellion against the project of transferring to the Crown the vast tracts of territory belonging to the Hudson Bay Company, Donald Smith again utilized his remarkable skill and experience in dealing with these children of nature. He went to the seat of the trouble at Red River Settlement, where he was made a prisoner and threatened with death. He obtained his liberty, and through his strong but adroit attitude toward the rebels was able to keep them in check until the arrival of troops. As a reward for this achievement he was elected to the Dominion House of Commons, and became a zealous supporter of the administration of Sir John McDonald.

In the early seventies Donald Smith undertook to raise the very large amount of capital necessary for the new Canadian Pacific railroad across the continent. On more than one occasion the enterprise threatened ruin for those connected with it, but Donald Smith eventually triumphed, and in 1885 the road was completed to the Pacific. The man who had commenced life as an humble trader had become by this time a celebrated and very important man in Canada, and in recognition of his services Queen Victoria bestowed on him in 1886 the Grand Cross of the Order of St. Michael and St. George. Upon the occasion of the Queen's Jubilee in 1897, being then Lord High Commissioner of Canada, Sir Donald was raised to the peerage, and became Lord Strathcona. In commemoration of the Jubilee he gave in the same year, jointly with Lord Mount Stephen, the sum of one million dollars to the Royal Victoria Hospital in Montreal, and eight hundred thousand dollars more to endow the institution, which, through his generosity, has become one of the best equipped hospitals on the continent. Lord Strathcona has also given at least a million dollars to education in Canada, most of the money going to McGill University. He has also contributed largely to the Royal Victoria Hospital for Women in Montreal. Lord Strathcona's philanthropy is made the more notable by the fact that while he has large means, he does not possess the immense wealth of some of the American financiers. In addition to his railway and numerous other interests in Canada, he is president of the Bank of Montreal, which is one of the largest banking institutions in the world.

At the outbreak of the war between Great Britain and the Boers Lord Strathcona further increased his usefulness to Canada and the Empire by the organization of a body of mounted troops called "the Strathcona Horse." These men, many of whom were recruited from the Northwest, and who represented the flower of Canadian horsemanship and valor, went to South Africa, and greatly distinguished themselves in the service of the Queen. Their work at the front was not as important, however, as was their influence in the direction of solidifying the union between the mother country and the colony.

In spite of the fact that he is now eighty-four years old, Lord Strathcona is still a restless and energetic spirit. He has residences in Montreal, Winnipeg, Nova Scotia, Scotland and London, and divides his time between them. In London he is fond of entertaining the leaders in political and commercial life. He spends much of his time in Canada, however, and often makes trips across the continent. In many respects he is Canada's most remarkable citizen.

ILLUSTRATORS.

WILLIAM DE LEFTWICH DODGE.

Among the American mural decorators who have achieved a reputation which is not confined to the land of their birth, is William de Leftwich Dodge. Some of the principal decorations of the Boston public library and the capitol of Washington are the outcome of his genius. He has also executed a number of private commissions, and in each and every instance has given evidence of fertile imagination and forceful execution. It is perhaps too much to say that Mr. Dodge has inaugurated or suggested a new school of mural art, but it is certain that he has so modified accepted methods that the results are practically without precedent as far as his special line of work is concerned. He was born in Liberty, Virginia, and, after a preliminary art education in this country, studied in Paris and Munich. He began his career proper as an illustrator, but it was not long before he realized that his future lay along the lines of decoration rather than in the pages of publications, and, as has been intimated, his successes have vindicated the wisdom of his decision. He has been awarded the third medal of the Concours d'Atelier, Paris; the gold medal, Prize Fund exposition, 1886; three medals Cours Yvon, 1887; Prix d'Atelier, 1888, and medal of the Columbian exposition, 1893.

CHARLES MENTE.

Charles Mente, a popular illustrator, comes of a musical family, and so narrowly escaped being a musician instead of an artist. He was born in New York city, educated in the public schools and afterward learned wood-carving, making figureheads and ornamental work on furniture. This work was not to his taste, however, so he entered the credit department of A. T. Stewart's store, New York city. This was even more distasteful, and, resigning, he spent his evenings attending Cooper institute art classes, and later the art students' league. At that time all illustrations were drawn on wood. Mr. Mente's first drawing was for Harper & Brothers, and was successful, and for two years he worked for that firm. By the end of that period he had managed to save about $1,500, with which he went abroad to study in Munich at the Royal academy. There he received a medal, with honorable mention. Coming back to New York, he was engaged as a teacher of painting at the Gotham art students' league, but gave up this position to devote himself to painting and illustration. He has received first prize at the exposition of the Chicago society of artists, a gold medal of the Art club of Philadelphia in 1895, and a diploma of excellence and silver medal at the Cotton States' international exposition, Atlanta, Georgia, in 1895. Mr. Mente's reputation rests to a great extent on his pictures based on inspirational subjects.

THURE DE THULSTRUP.

The vigor of the work of Thure de Thulstrup is known to the reading public mainly through his illustrations in metropolitan magazines, but he has also painted a number of canvases which show that he is as much at home with the brush as with the crayon or pencil. Thulstrup was born in Stockholm, Sweden, and, after graduating from the Royal Swedish military academy, was commissioned a lieutenant of artillery in the army of that country. But being of an adventurous spirit, he went to Algiers, where he enlisted in the First Zouave Regiment of the French army, saw some service in Northern Africa, and was afterward given a commission in the Foreign Legion. While a member of that body, he took part in the Franco-German war of 1870-'71, and also assisted in crushing the Commune in Paris. In 1872 he set sail for Canada, where he obtained a position as civil engineer. From his boyhood he had delighted in sketching, and it was about this time that he determined to put his artistic gifts to practical use. His début as an illustrator was with the New York Daily Graphic in the 70's. Subsequently he became connected with the Frank Leslie Magazine and with Harper & Brothers, and it was his work with the last named firm that established his reputation as an illustrator. He has painted a number of military pictures, including a series of twelve which have to do with stirring events of the Civil war in this country. Recently he has been engaged on canvases which illustrate cavalier life in Virginia in the middle of the eighteenth century. He has drawn the pictures of a number of books.

CARTOONISTS.

T. S. ALLEN.

One of the artists whose purpose in life seems to be smile-breeding is T. S. Allen. Well known in connection with his work in the columns of the New York American, his studies of and contingent jokes on "tough" youngsters under the caption of "Just Kids" are full of genuine humor. Mr. Allen was born in 1869, in Lexington, Kentucky, and was educated at Transylvania university, of that state. After some years spent in writing jokes, jingles, etc., for local and New York newspapers, he began to illustrate the same in a manner which quickly caught the attention of editors. To-day he has an established reputation as a graphic humorist, and his work finds a ready and remunerative market.

CHARLES G. BUSH.

Charles G. Bush, the cartoonist of the New York World, is an example of success achieved comparatively late in life. His early work consisted for the most part of magazine illustrations of a serious nature. After studying in Paris, under Bonnat, he, on his return to America, endeavored to follow a career of painting, but fate willed it otherwise. In 1895 Mr. Bush drew a cartoon in which David B. Hill was the principal figure. The New York Herald accepted the picture, and the next morning Mr. Bush woke up to find himself famous as a cartoonist. From thence on his career has been one of more or less constant successes.

LOUIS DALRYMPLE.

Louis Dalrymple, the illustrator and cartoonist, was born at Cambridge, Illinois, January 19, 1861. After receiving a common school education, he entered the Pennsylvania academy of fine arts, graduated from it with credit and later studied at the art students' league of New York. Subsequently he branched out for himself and began to submit drawings to the metropolitan comic publications and newspapers. Work of this kind secures immediate recognition for anartist who can comply with the public demands of the moment. Mr. Dalrymple being not only clever but shrewd, it came about that within a very short time he was kept busy in executing commissions. His work is characterized by a delicacy and acumen that prove that he thinks as well as he draws.

SYDNEY B. GRIFFIN.

When the modern daily newspaper began to add to its news columns the so-called supplement, there was a coincident demand for artists who had the gift of humor. Sydney B. Griffin was one of such, and for some years past his supply of unique ideas seems to have been inexhaustible. He was born October 15, 1854, of English and Scotch parents, attended public schools at Detroit, Michigan, and, in 1888, came to New York. When his first ideas were presented to Puck they were declined, but upon his taking them to Judge they were accepted forthwith. Mr. Griffin took the trouble to inform the Puck people of his success with their rivals, whereupon he was told that his work had been refused for the simple reason that it was so excellent that it was feared that it was not original. However, Puck made the amende honorable by engaging him forthwith. Mr. Griffin's style is bold and slashing and his drawings are full of point and power.

R. F. OUTCAULT.

In the world of illustrators, the man who can originate an idea which excites the laughter and holds the attention of the public is indeed fortunate. Such an individual is R. F. Outcault, the artistic father of the "Buster Brown" series which appear in the Sunday New York Herald. He is also the author of the "Yellow Kid" and "Hogan's Alley" pictures of the Sunday New York World, and of equally laughable creations in the New York American and other publications. Born in Lancaster, Ohio, January 14, 1853, he was educated in that town. In 1888 he secured a position with Edison, and went to Paris in the inventor's employ. Returning to this country, he illustrated for some time with a fair degree of success, but it was not until 1894 that he made his first distinctive hit as a comic artist. Mr. Outcault's personal description of his daily life is interesting. He says: "I have flowers, a garden, a dog and a cat, good music, good books, light stories, draw pictures, smoke a pipe, talk single tax theories, am a member of a couple of clubs, lead the Simple Life."

CARL E. SCHULTZE.

Humor, strenuous and wholesome, marks the work of Carl E. Schultze. His name is literally a household word in this country by reason of that quaint conceit, "Foxy Grandpa," of which he is the creator. He was born on May 25, 1866, Lexington, New York, and was educated in the public schools of that town and at Cassel, Germany. On his return to America he studied art under Walter Satterlee, of New York. For some time later he seems to have been undecided as to how to apply his gifts, but an accidental sketch submitted to a Chicago paper, resulted in his being forthwith engaged by that publication. After remaining in Chicago on several newspapers for some years, he took a trip to California, doing further artistic work in San Francisco. At length he determined to beard the metropolitan journalist lions in their dens. After a struggle, during which he did work on Judge and other New York publications, he became a member of the staff of the Herald, where, thanks to an accidental inspiration, "Foxy Grandpa" came into existence. Later he became connected with the New York American. Mr. Schultze is a man of magnificent physique, and is held in high esteem by those who know him. He is the author of several works of comic drawings, and "Foxy Grandpa" has been dramatized.

EUGENE ZIMMERMAN.

Eugene Zimmerman's cartoons in Judge are characterized by an insight into the political questions of the hour which is assisted rather than hindered by the sheer humor of his work. He was born at Basel, Switzerland, May 25, 1862. While yet a baby his parents came to the United States and settled at Paterson, New Jersey, where he received his education in the public schools. After leaving school, he was in turn a farmer's boy, an errand boy in a store, a fish peddler, a baker and a sign painter, but sketched and drew continuously. In 1882 he secured a position in the art rooms of Puck, and after doing considerable work for that publication left it in order to join Judge. He has also illustrated books and articles by Bill Nye and James Whitcomb Riley. As a caricaturist pure and proper he is almost without a rival in this country.

HUMORISTS.

GEORGE ADE.

George Ade has an established reputation among those who are lovers of wholesome humor. His sketches, given in a picturesque dialect, are characterized by a freshness of observation which is aided rather than marred by the so-called slang in which they are written. Born at Kentland, Newton county, Indiana, February 9, 1866, he graduated from the University of Lafayette, Indiana, and subsequently became reporter and telegraph editor on the Lafayette Evening Call. In 1891 he went to Chicago, as a member of the staff of the Daily News of that city, and afterward joined the forces of the Tribune. After establishing a reputation as a humorist, he turned playwright and has scored several metropolitan successes. His Fables in Slang, issued in 1899, and More Fables are the best known of his pen products.

JOHN KENDRICK BANGS.

John Kendrick Bangs occupies a distinctive position in the domain of humor. To use the vernacular, he is in a class by himself, and so the products of his pen can hardly be referred to or compared with that of any other of the writers of to-day. He was born in Yonkers, New York, May 27, 1862, his father being Francis N. Bangs, who for many years was the president of the Bar association of New York. Mr. Bangs graduated from Columbia university in 1883 and entered his father's office, but his humor would not down, and so it was that he shortly deserted the law in order to become the associate editor of Life. This was in 1884. Since that time he has held many responsible journalistic positions in New York, and in his present capacity as editor of Harper's Weekly has added much to the reputation which is deservedly his.

SAMUEL LANGHORN CLEMENS.

Samuel L. Clemens, who is better known as "Mark Twain," was born in Monroe county, Missouri, November 30, 1835, and received his education at the village schools. On his father's death, which took place when he was twelve years of age, he went to work in order to contribute to the support of his mother and little brothers and sisters. As an apprentice in the office of the Hannibal (Missouri) Courier, he laid the foundations of his reputation as author and journalist. Within the following twenty-five years he was steamboat pilot, soldier, miner and editor. His first contributions under his famous nom-de-plume appeared in 1862, in the newspaper, The Virginia City Enterprise. Since 1872 he has devoted himself to literary work, lecturing occasionally, and making frequent trips to Europe. It is said that nearly a million copies of his works have been sold. Space will not permit of a full list of them, but Roughing It, The Prince and the Pauper, A Connecticut Yankee in King Arthur's Court, and Pudden-Head Wilson are classics whose popularity bids fair to last as long as American literature itself.

FINLEY PETER DUNNE.

The author of the immortal "Mr. Dooley" is Finley Peter Dunne, who began life as a Chicago reporter, but is now under contract to Harper Brothers to write exclusively for their publications. He was born at Chicago, July 10, 1867, was educated in local public schools and began his reportorial life in 1885. After serving on the staffs of several Chicago papers he became editor of the Journal of that city in 1897. It was about this time that he conceived "Mr. Dooley." The reputation which that unique character brought him resulted in his being engaged to contribute to a syndicate of New York, Chicago and San Francisco newspapers, and later to form his current connection with the Harpers.

SIMEON FORD.

Simeon Ford, the after-dinner speaker and raconteur who, so it is said, can look more sad and at the same time talk more humorously than any other man before the American public, was born in Lafayette, Indiana, in 1856. After an education received in the public schools of the town of his birth he studied law, but finding that there was but little merriment in Blackstone and briefs, abandoned his first intentions, and after plunges into various businesses, drifted to New York, where, in 1883, he fell in love with and married Julia Shaw, the daughter of the proprietor of the Grand Union hotel. He forthwith became a partner with his father-in-law, and from thence on has been as successful as a hotel manager as he is famous as an after-dinner speaker.

ELIZABETH MERIWETHER GILMER.

Elizabeth Meriwether Gilmer, whose nom-de-plume is "Dorothy Dix," was born in Montgomery county, Tennessee, November 18, 1870. She was married November 21, 1888, to George O. Gilmer. In 1896 she became the editor of the woman's department of the New Orleans Picayune, and contributed to that paper a series of articles called Dorothy Dix Talks, which won her immediate recognition as a humorist. In 1900 she joined the New York American and Journal staff as a writer on special topics, which she treats in a breezy, snappy fashion.

GEORGE V. HOBART.

George V. Hobart, the humorist and librettist, who is well known to the newspaper public under his nom-de-plume of Dinkelspiel, was born at Cape Breton, Nova Scotia. When a boy he studied telegraphy and obtained a position as an operator on one of the Cumberland (Maryland) newspapers. One day between the clicks of his instrument he wrote a humorous story, and handed it to the editor, who remarked, "I want more of that." That was the beginning of the famous Dinkelspiel sketches. Mr. W. R. Hearst, of the New York American, saw Hobart's work, called him to New York. He is the author of several comedies and books of musical productions.

MELVIN DE LANCY LANDON.

Melvin De Lancy Landon, "Eli Perkins," was born at Eaton, New York, September 7, 1839. After a course of preparation in the public schools he entered Union college and graduated in 1861. One week later he received an appointment from the United States treasury, but soon resigned his position to enlist in the Union army to take part in the Civil war. He left the army, in 1864, with the rank of major. Next he became a cotton planter in Arkansas and Louisiana. Later he traveled in Europe and was secretary of the United States legation at St. Petersburg. In 1877 he was married to Emily Louise Smith. He has written copiously for magazines and other publications. But it is his books, Wit, Humor and Pathos, Franco-Prussian War, Wit and Humor of the Age, Kings of Platform and Pulpit, and Thirty Years of Wit, upon which his reputation as a humorist rests.

JOURNALISTS AND WRITERS.

STEPHEN BONSAL.

A most industrious contributor to magazines and writer of short stories is Stephen Bonsal. He was born in Virginia in 1863, and educated in St. Paul's school, Concord, New Hampshire. After finishing his studies in this country he went to Gottingen and Heidelberg, Germany. Returning to this country, he entered journalism. In this connection he is best known as representing the New York Herald during the Bulgarian-Servian war. In the service of that newspaper, he also went to Macedonia, Morocco and Cuba. Leaving newspaper work, he next entered the United States diplomatic service and was secretary of legation and chargé d'affaires in Pekin, Madrid, Tokio and Corea from 1890 to 1896. Besides his magazine work, he is the author of several books, including Morocco As It Is and The Real Condition of Cuba.

RICHARD HARDING DAVIS.

Like many other authors, Richard Harding Davis comes of literary stock, his father being S. Clark Davis, editor of the Philadelphia Public Ledger, and his mother Rebecca Harding Davis, whose works of fiction have brought her a certain amount of public notice. After graduating from the Lehigh university of Pennsylvania, Mr. Davis made a reputation for himself in newspaper circles in his native city. He is a versatile writer and prefers fiction to fact. He first attained prominence through the medium of his Van Bibber Sketches. War correspondent as well as novelist, his life has been filled with stirring incident. Mr. Davis has been charged with egotism by his critics, but every man who is conscious of his individuality is subject to such attacks. Married Cecil Clark, daughter of J. M. Clark, of Chicago, April 4, 1899.

HAMLIN GARLAND.

One of the best-known makers of magazine literature is Hamlin Garland, who was born in West Salem, Wisconsin, September 16, 1860, of English-Dutch parentage. In 1881 his studies were completed in Cedar Valley seminary, Wisconsin, and he next spent some years in traveling and teaching in the east. Later he took the lecture platform, was an occasional writer of sketches and short stories, and spent some time in Boston studying and teaching. He is an ardent advocate of the single tax doctrine and several of his works have to do with the struggles of the poor against existing conditions. He has also written a number of books of fiction.

DAVID G. PHILLIPS.

David G. Phillips, one of the latest of American authors to achieve a measurable success and to give promises of a literary future, was born in Indianapolis in 1866, his father being a banker in that city. After a season spent in the local public schools and a preparatory collegiate course, Mr. Phillips went to Yale, and while there determined to become either a journalist or an author. On graduating he decided to go into newspaper work and so became a member of the reportorial staff of the New York World. It was not long before he attracted the attention of Mr. Joseph Pulitzer, the proprietor of the World. Mr. Phillips was in consequence given an editorial position. After some time spent in the service of the World, Mr. Phillips resigned in order to turn his attention to novel writing. Of his books A Golden Fleece and The Great God Success have been fairly well received, but his last work, The Confessions of a Crœsus, is distinctly the best thing that he has done in the way of pure literature.

CHARLES GEORGE DOUGLAS ROBERTS.

C. G. D. Roberts inherited his literary instinct. His father was the Rev. G. Goodrich Roberts, and he is a cousin of Bliss Carman, the poet, while several of his ancestors were professors in English universities. He was born in Canada in 1860. Graduating from the university of Brunswick, in 1879, he afterward and for several years taught in educational establishments in Canada, but in 1895 devoted himself exclusively to literary work. In 1897 he became associate editor of the Illustrated American, but is best known as a writer of nature stories, several of which have passed through two or three editions.

WILLIAM THOMAS STEAD.

William T. Stead, the founder of the Review of Reviews, and a constant contributor to a number of American newspapers, was born on July 3, 1849, at Embleton, England, being the son of the Rev. W. Stead, a Congregational minister. When fourteen years of age he was apprenticed to a merchant at Newcastle-on-Tyne, England, and began to contribute to local newspapers. His journalistic promptings at length became so imperative that he deserted the commercial world, and after a preliminary struggle became assistant editor of the Pall Mall Gazette. Later he founded the Review of Reviews, and subsequently the American Review of Reviews. He takes an active interest in the larger questions of the day, such as international arbitration, psychological problems, etc. Mr. Stead has a place in his generation and fills it admirably.

VANCE THOMPSON.

Vance Thompson, a well known journalist, author and playwright, was born on April 17, 1863. He graduated from Princeton in 1883, and was subsequently a student of the University of Jena in Germany. He is well known in metropolitan journalism, having held the position of dramatic critic for more than one New York newspaper, and he has also contributed liberally to leading magazines and daily publications in general. He is also known as a musical critic. Mr. Thompson founded a fortnightly publication entitled Madamoiselle New York, which was characteristic of both him and his, and is the author of several plays, pantomimes and books. In 1890 he married Lillian Spencer, of New York.

STEWART EDWARD WHITE.

Stewart Edward White, the author, was born at Grand Rapids, Michigan, March 2, 1873. He studied at the high school of the town of his birth and graduated from the University of Michigan in 1895. Subsequently he came east and took a course in the Columbia law school. Mr. White is still a bachelor, is a fruitful contributor to magazines, and has written some novels which have been given a respectful hearing, these including The Westerners and The Claim Jumpers.

OWEN WISTER.

Owen Wister, who is best known to the public through the medium of his novel, The Virginian, was born at Philadelphia

July 14, 1860. He prepared for college at St. Paul's school, Concord, New Hampshire, and was graduated from Harvard in 1892, being admitted to the Philadelphia bar some years later. Instead of following the profession of a lawyer, however, he engaged in literary work. Apart from his novels, he has been a prolific contributor to magazines and other periodicals. His books are eminently readable, if they are nothing else.

POETS.

THOMAS BAILEY ALDRICH.

Judging from "The Story of a Bad Boy," which is partly autobiographical, Thomas Bailey Aldrich spent his boyhood just as all wholesome-minded, healthy boys do, in having a good time. He was born in Portsmouth, New Hampshire, November 11, 1836. While he was still a baby, his family went to New Orleans, but he was sent back to his native town to be educated. After a common school course, he prepared to enter Harvard, but his father failed in business and soon afterward died. Although young Aldrich's relatives were prepared to pay the expenses of his college course, he preferred to be independent and decided to begin a business career. So it came about that he entered the offices of his uncle in New York city at the age of sixteen. About this time he began to contribute articles in prose and verse to Putnam's Magazine, The Knickerbocker Magazine and other periodicals. His literary ability finally got him a place in a publishing house as reader of manuscripts and of proof. His first book, The Bells, did not attract much attention, but in 1856 he published The Ballad of Baby Bell and Other Poems, which struck the popular fancy. About the year 1860 he became an independent writer, contributing to various publications, but chiefly to the Atlantic Monthly. In 1870 he became editor of Every Saturday, a high-class literary weekly, which was founded in Boston and effectively edited, yet only lived four years. In 1881 he succeeded Mr. Howells in the editorial chair of the Atlantic Monthly. In this same year both Mr. Howells and Mr. Aldrich received from Yale university the degree of LL.D. Mr. Aldrich retired from the Atlantic Monthly in 1890. In 1865 he was married to Miss Lillian Woodman, of New York city. Several children were born to him.

BLISS CARMAN.

Bliss Carman is a native of New Brunswick and began life as a civil engineer and school teacher. The muse won him, however, almost from boyhood, and he has written steadily, slowly and safely, which is equivalent to saying that he has written progressively. Like many of the Canadian writers, he came to the United States to seek recognition. Here he met three other Canadians—C. G. D. Roberts, James Clarence Harvey and the late Richard Hovey. They formed a talented quartet of struggling poets, and their little world known as "Vagabondia," was one of the most fascinating centers of American Bohemianism of the better type. Literary and artistic people coveted the privilege of entering therein. Mr. Carman and Mr. Hovey published several volumes of songs from "Vagabondia." The subject of this sketch is best known by his Coronation Ode and his Sapphic Fragments. There is a fine and tender quality in Mr. Carman's poems that accounts for their popularity among people possessing that which is known as the "artistic temperament."

RICHARD LE GALLIENNE.

Richard Le Gallienne, who has a personality which accords with that of the traditional poet, is an Irishman by birth. In spite of his critics, his place in the world of letters is assured, mainly by reason of his poems, of which he has issued three volumes. Robert Louis Stevenson, an Elegy, is one of the best known of Mr. Le Gallienne's works, and ranks among the classic elegies of the English language. It is not too much to say that it compares favorably with Gray's Elegy in a Country Churchyard,

Swinburne's Ave Et Vale, and Morris' Wordsworth's Grave. In Mr. Le Gallienne's verses, love, romance and dainty imagery are effectively mingled, and, as a rule, the results appeal to both heart and ear. His more ambitious works are those that have to do with literary criticism. He has also written books on Kipling and Meredith, which for vivid, close-range studies of the lives and purposes of two writers whose ideals are diametrically opposed, have rarely been equalled. The output of so-called literary criticism is so voluminous that it "tires by vastness," yet the demand for the product of Mr. Le Gallienne's pen still exists. He is also the author of a number of novels. That he is of industrious habits is proven by the fact that, while only thirty-six years of age, he has produced thirty works, the last being an English rendition of the odes of the Persian poet, Hafiz. Mr. Le Gallienne is an example of the possibilities that are inherent in every man, who, having determined on a given line of work, proceeds to follow it to success. He has never been to college, but has educated himself and so possesses all that belongs to a college curriculum. He has undergone the disappointments, deferred hopes, and all the rest of the unpleasant things that belong to the struggling literary man, and has conquered. The moral is obvious.

ROBERT MACKAY.

Robert Mackay, who is one of the youngest, but none the less promising of America's poets, was born in Virginia City, Nevada, 1871. His father, who is among the oldest of the living "Comstockers," settled in Nevada over fifty years ago, when the state was practically unknown to white men. The subject of this sketch began his literary work when a mere boy as a reporter on the San Francisco Chronicle. Subsequently he was editor and assistant editor of several papers on the Pacific coast. In 1895 he determined to travel over the world. The trip occupied the greater portion of five years, during which period he visited lands where white men were seldom seen. Naturally he gathered many experiences, and much valuable data. While Mr. Mackay has written a great many poems he has never compiled them in book form. He has a theory that too many young writers throw themselves on the mercy of a public which do not know them and necessarily do not care for their callow wares. He therefore proposes to mature his work until he is satisfied that it has a fighting chance for public favor. Nevertheless he is by no means a stranger to the public. Those poems of his that have appeared in a number of periodicals have made him many friends. Mr. Mackay's verses are finely fibered. Technically correct, they are acceptable to those critics who place mechanism on the same plane with motive. But they are more than finished specimens of the verse-maker's art. With deft and tender fingers he plays upon the heart chords of humanity, and these ring responsive to his sympathetic touch. His themes are those that are as old as the race, and as imperishable. Mother love, wedded love, patriotism, the eternal yearning for the higher life, the eternal problem of the hereafter—such they are—and they are treated by him with a facile sincerity that marks him as a true poet—one who writes not for the sake of writing, but because of inner spiritual promptings that will not be denied.

CINCINNATUS HEINE MILLER.

The personality of Cincinnatus Heine Miller, better known as "Joaquin" Miller, is as picturesque as has been his career. In turn a miner, lawyer, express rider, editor, poet and newspaper man, Mr. Miller has amassed a fund of experiences such as rarely falls to the lot of the ordinary individual. That his literary gifts enable him to reproduce in vivid fashion many of these same happenings is a matter for self-congratulation on the part of the reading public. What is yet more fortunate is that he preserves in his poems the breath of the prairie, the air of the mountains and the "tang" of that west that is rapidly passing into nothingness. The poet was born in the Wabash district of Indiana, November 10, 1841. In 1850 his parents removed to Oregon, and there is but little doubt that the wild and beautiful scenery amid which he spent his childhood had had much to do with fostering his then undeveloped poetical instincts. When the famous rush of gold seekers to the Pacific coast took place in 1859, young Miller was among the Argonauts. He does not appear to have been particularly successful in his hunt for gold, and returned to Oregon in 1860. Then he began to study law, supporting himself in the meantime by acting as express rider in Idaho. In 1863 he started the Eugene (Ore.) Democratic Register, which, however, had a brief existence. Later he opened a law office in Canon City, and in 1866 went to London, where he remained until 1870. It was in that city that he published his first book of poems. It received a most favorable reception, and established him as a poet of a unique type and quality. Returning to this country, he did some years of newspaper work in Washington, D. C., but finally drifted back to the Pacific coast, and devoted himself entirely to literature. In 1897, acting as correspondent for the New York newspaper, he visited the Klondike to compare modern miners with those of '59. Some of his best known books of poems are Songs of the Sierras, Pacific Palms, The One Fair Woman, Songs of the Sunland, etc. He is also a playwright. One of the most important and successful of his dramas is The Danites. He lives in a picturesque home, known as the Heights, at Oakland, California.

HENRY VAN DYKE.

"Life is an arrow; therefore you must know
What mark to aim at and how to use the bow,
Then draw it to the head and let it go."

These words, as well as the career of the well-known author and clergyman, the Rev. Dr. Henry Van Dyke, emphasize the fact that he has successfully pursued his all-absorbing ideal. He was born at Germantown, Pennsylvania, November 10, 1852, his father being the Rev. Henry Jackson Van Dyke, who is of Dutch colonial blood. At the age of sixteen, and after graduating from the Brooklyn Polytechnic Institute, young Van Dyke entered Princeton college and received the degree of A.B., with highest honors, in 1873. While an undergraduate he was awarded the junior oration prize and senior prize in English literature. He was also reception orator on class day, and on commencement delivered the salutatory and belles lettres. Upon graduating in the theological course from Princeton seminary, in 1876, he delivered the master oration. Later he went to Germany to pursue his studies in divinity at the University of Berlin, and, in 1878, returned to the United States, becoming pastor of the United Congregational church, Newport, Rhode Island, and remained there for four years. In 1882 he accepted a call to the Old Brick Presbyterian church, Fifth avenue and Thirty-seventh street, New York, which was founded in 1767. At that time the church membership was small and its financial condition far from satisfactory. But, thanks to the untiring efforts of the new pastor, it became one of importance, spiritually and in other ways. Since 1900 he has been professor in English literature at Princeton university. He is the author of numerous books of wide circulation.

CANADIANS.

DR. WILLIAM OSLER.

The most eminent medical man of Canada, and perhaps of the world, is Dr. William Osler, who has recently been appointed by King Edward to the exalted position of Regis Professor of Medicine at Oxford University, England. This means that Dr. Osler will be the chairman of the faculty of this great university. He will be its head. No greater distinction than this could come to any medical man. Aside from the honor of his appointment and the salary of $10,000 per year, his position will bring Dr. Osler a private practice which will make him one of the most highly compensated physicians in the world.

Dr. Osler was born at Bondhead, Ontario, July 12, 1849. His father was a minister of the Church of England. Dr. Osler went to school at Port Hope, Ont., and afterward entered Trinity University in Toronto, where he received his academic degree. The only distinction he attained at college was the reputation of being a hard student. He followed out then the injunction which he has since often made to students of his own, namely, "love to labor."

After leaving the University, Dr. Osler entered the office of Dr. Bonell in Toronto as an assistant. Here he studied three years and then entered McGill University at Montreal, where he was graduated in 1872. He then went abroad, and returning to Canada in 1875 was elected to the chair of Institute of Medicine at McGill. Some remarks of his apropos of his first plunging into teaching are worth quoting. "My first appearance before the class filled me with tremulous uneasiness and an overwhelming sense of embarrassment. I soon forgot this, however, in my interest in the work. Whatever success I achieved then and throughout my subsequent career has been due to enthusiasm and constitutional energy."

Four years after Dr. Osler became connected with McGill he was appointed a member of the visiting staff of the Montreal General Hospital. In 1883 he was elected a fellow of the Royal College of Physicians of London, England.

Dr. Osler became in 1884 professor of medicine at the University of Pennsylvania. He was invited in 1889 to create the chair of Professor of the Practice and Principles of Medicine at the Johns Hopkins Medical School at Baltimore. It was his work here that lifted him into world-wide prominence as a physician. In 1890 he was elected dean of the medical faculty of Johns Hopkins. Meanwhile he had built up a very large private practice, and was one of the doctors called upon to treat President McKinley after he had been shot in Buffalo.

In spite of the fact that Dr. Osler's great powers of concentration have been one of the factors in his remarkable success in his profession, he is a strong believer in having a broad outlook, and avoiding too great an absorption in any one line of work. He has said in an address to students:

"Do not become so absorbed in your profession as to exclude all outside interests. Success in my profession depends as much upon the man as upon the physician. The more you see of life, outside the circle of your work, the better equipped you will be for the struggle. While medicine is to be your calling, see to it that you have also some intellectual task which will keep you in touch with the world of art and letters. When tired of anatomy refresh your mind with Oliver Wendell Holmes, Keats, Shelley and Shakespeare.

"I advise you to have no ambition higher than to join the noble band of general practitioners. These are generous hearted men, with well balanced, cool heads, who are not scientific always, but are learned in the wisdom of the sick room. No man can stand higher in the love and respect of the community, and wield a more potent influence, than the family doctor....

"As to your work, I have a single bit of advice which I give with the earnest conviction of its paramount influence in any success which may have attended my efforts in life: Take no thought of the morrow. Live neither in the past nor the future, but let each day's work absorb your entire energy and satisfy your widest ambition."

SIR GEORGE A. DRUMMOND.

A high and representative type of the Scotchmen who have done so much for Canada is Sir George Alexander Drummond, who for many years has been very actively identified with the best elements in Canadian commercial and social life. Sir George was born in Edinburgh in 1829, and in 1854, after graduation from Edinburgh University, came to Canada to assume the management of the extensive sugar refinery which had been established in Montreal by the late John Redpath. Though the refinery was for some years very successful under the direction of Sir George, it was closed in 1874 because of the appalling effects of a high tariff. It was reopened, however, in 1879, when Sir George founded the Canadian Sugar Refining Company, which has exerted a strong influence in the upbuilding of the prosperity of the Dominion. Sir George steadily grew in commercial power. He became a director of the Bank of Montreal in 1882 and vice-president of the institution in 1887. For two years he was president of the Montreal Board of Trade. He also assumed the presidency of the company which owns very valuable coal and iron mining properties at Londonderry, Nova Scotia, and he has been connected with many other enterprises of importance.

His activities, however, have been by no means confined to commerce. He has been president of the Art Association of Montreal, and possesses one of the finest art collections on the continent. He is an enthusiastic golfer and has been president of the Canada Golf Association. He has busied himself with philanthropic projects and was made one of the trustees of Victoria Order of Nurses in 1897. He was called to the Senate of Canada by the Marquis of Lorne and was knighted by the Queen.

AUTHORS.

JAMES LANE ALLEN.

Among the many literary lights which the south has given us is James Lane Allen. He was born in Lexington, Kentucky, in 1849, and comes of one of the old Virginia families. Shortly after the Civil war broke out Mr. Allen's father lost his fortune, and James in consequence had to work and attend school simultaneously. He graduated with honors from the Transylvania university, Lexington, in 1872. Then he began to teach for a livelihood. Subsequently he was called to a professorship in Transylvania university, and later was a professor of Latin and higher English at Bethany college, West Virginia. In 1884 he went to New York to make literature his profession. He was then unknown in that city, but soon gained recognition as one of the most poetic and dramatic of American novelists. Of his many books The Choir Invisible, A Summer in Arcady, and Aftermath, are perhaps the most in demand by the reading public.

GEORGE WASHINGTON CABLE.

A novelist who works on original lines is George W. Cable. He was born in New Orleans, October 12, 1844. At the age of fourteen necessity compelled him to seek employment in a store. In 1863 he joined the Confederate army, serving until the close of the war. Returning to New Orleans, he became an employee of a mercantile house, and later studied civil engineering. It was at this time that he began to contribute to the New Orleans

Picayune and was at length given a position on its editorial staff. He returned to business life, writing in the meantime, however, for Scribner's and other magazines. His sketches of Creole life were so well received that he finally decided to devote himself to literature. He has produced a number of works whose chief characters are almost all of the Creole type, is a successful lecturer, and takes an active interest in religious affairs.

WINSTON CHURCHILL.

Winston Churchill, the novelist, was born in St. Louis, Missouri, November 10, 1871. He received his early education at the Smith academy in that city, and when seventeen years of age was appointed a cadet of the United States naval academy at Annapolis. Graduating therefrom in 1891, he joined the cruiser San Francisco, but his tastes being more literary than naval he resigned and became a member of the staff of the Army and Navy Journal, of New York. In 1895 he was made editor of the Cosmopolitan magazine, but a few months later resolved to identify himself with independent work on original lines. His first book, The Celebrity, won recognition and a certain amount of popularity. Mr. Churchill's reputation as a novelist rests for the most part on Richard Carvel and its sequel, The Crisis, which is hardly less popular than was its predecessor.

FRANCIS MARION CRAWFORD.

A clever and popular writer is Francis M. Crawford, who was born at Bagni-di-Lucca, Italy, August 2, 1854. He is a son of Thomas Crawford, the sculptor, and comes of a long line of literary and artistic ancestors. Francis was educated in New York schools, subsequently entering Harvard, but did not complete his course there. He was also a student at Cambridge university,

England, and at the universities of Karlsruhe and Heidelberg, Germany, and the university of Rome, where he gave special attention to Sanscrit. In 1873 Mr. Crawford was compelled by circumstances to adopt journalism as a means of livelihood. Some years later he turned his attention to literature proper, his first book, Mr. Isaacs, appearing in 1882. Among his other well-known works are A Cigarette Maker's Romance, The Three Fates, Zoroaster, etc. He is also an artist of considerable ability and has traveled extensively. He and his wife and children live near Sorrento, Italy.

RUDYARD KIPLING.

Rudyard Kipling, the poet and novelist who, perhaps more than any other writer of this generation, has voiced the militant spirit of the British empire, was born at Bombay, India, December 30, 1865. His father was John Lockwood Kipling. Rudyard was educated at the United Services college, Devonshire, England. Returning to India at the end of his school days, he became the assistant editor of the Civil-Military Gazette, and subsequently was connected with the staff of the Pioneer, a prominent newspaper of the country. The well-known Soldiers Three series and those other of his works which have to do with army life in India were the outcome of his Pioneer experiences. In 1892 he married Caroline Balestier at Brattleboro, Vermont. Mr. Kipling has not only a marvelous faculty of describing things as they actually are, but he also has the prophetic instinct of the true poet. As a case in point may be cited his famous Recessional, written at the end of Queen Victoria's Jubilee. The full significance of the poem was only realized by the British during the disastrous and humiliating periods of the Boer war. In prose and poetry he has been alike fruitful.

THOMAS NELSON PAGE.

Thomas N. Page was born in Oakland, Hanover county, Virginia, April 23, 1853. The Civil war interfered with his education, and left the Page family in an impoverished condition. Nevertheless he, during this period, was gathering material which resulted in the production of those two delightful books of his, Marse Chan and Meh Lady. Later he managed to secure a course at Washington and Lee university. At the law school of the University of Virginia he secured his degree in a year, and, after being admitted to the bar, practiced in Richmond from 1875 to 1893. During his leisure hours he did work which placed him on a high eminence as lecturer and literary man. His books are many, and for the most part have to do with the war between north and south and the reconstruction period following its close.

CHARLES MAJOR.

Charles Major, the novelist, was born at Indianapolis, Indiana, July 25, 1856. He was educated at the common schools at Shelbyville and Indianapolis, after which he studied law and engaged in practice at Shelbyville. But his literary tastes were stronger than his legal inclinations, and he began to contribute to magazines and to write novels. His most famous book, When Knighthood was in Flower, was issued in 1898, and reached an edition of several hundred thousand. In 1885 he was married to Alice Shaw.

NOVELISTS.

GERTRUDE FRANKLIN ATHERTON.

One of the most vivid and entertaining interpreters of the complex characteristics of American womanhood is the versatile and entertaining writer, Gertrude Franklin Atherton. She was born on Rincon Hill, San Francisco, California, October 30, 1859, daughter of Thomas Lyman Horn, of German descent, and on her mother's side descended from a brother of Benjamin Franklin. She was educated at St. Mary's Hall, Benicia, California, also at Sayre Institute, Lexington, Kentucky, and by private tutors. In addition to this, she had obtained a good foundation in the classics, English especially, from the teachings of her grandfather. Before leaving school she was married to George Henry Bowen Atherton, a native of Valparaiso, Chili. After his death, in 1888, Mrs. Atherton went directly to New York city, beginning literary work in earnest. As she never received courteous treatment from the press of her own country, she settled in London in 1895, and there met with gratifying recognition. Some of her most important works are: "The Doomswoman," 1902; "Patience Sparhawk and Her Times," 1897; "His Fortunate Grace," 1897; "American Wives and English Husbands," 1898; "The Californians," 1898; "A Daughter of the Vine," 1899; "Senator North," 1900. The latter is the first attempt in American fiction at a purely national novel, disregarding section. The Leeds Mercury styled "The Californians" an oasis in fiction, while the British Weekly declared Mrs. Atherton to be the ablest writer of fiction now living. The brilliancy of her portraiture and the humor and freshness of her dialogues are undeniable. A western writer says,

"The early days of the missions and Spanish rule have given her a most congenial field, and she has successfully reproduced their atmosphere in her best novels; against the background of their romantic traditions she paints the world, old, strong of passion, vague, dreamy, idyllic, yet strong and elemental."

AMELIA EDITH BARR.

Amelia Edith Barr was born at Ulverton, Lancashire, England, March 29, 1831. She was the daughter of the Rev. William Huddleston. Her mother's family were among the followers of the noted evangelist, George Fox. She was educated in several good schools and colleges and was graduated, at the age of nineteen, from Glasgow high school. In 1850 she was married to Robert Barr, son of a minister of the Scottish Free Kirk. In 1854 Mr. and Mrs. Barr came to America, settling at Austin, and later at Galveston, Texas. Her husband and three sons died in 1857 of yellow fever and Mrs. Barr was obliged to support herself and three daughters with her pen. Two years after Mr. Barr's death she came to New York city and received immediate encouragement from Mr. Beecher, of the Christian Union, and Robert Bonner, of the New York Ledger. She taught school for two years, meanwhile writing various sketches and miscellaneous articles for magazines and newspapers. The work which gave her the greatest fame, "A Bow of Orange Ribbon," appeared in serial form in the Ledger. Since 1884 she has devoted her time almost entirely to the writing of novels and short stories.

FRANCES HODGSON BURNETT.

There are very few who are not acquainted with "Little Lord Fauntleroy," one of the sweetest children's stories ever written, but not so many perhaps are acquainted with the interesting life story of its author, Frances Hodgson Burnett. She was born November 24, 1849, in Manchester, England, and while yet attending school she developed a talent for writing short stories and poems and even novels. When her father died her mother brought the family to America in 1865, settling at Newmarket, but a year later removing to Knoxville, Tennessee. She then completed a story which was planned in her thirteenth year, and succeeded in disposing of it to Godey's Lady's Book, in which it was published in 1867. Other interesting short stories followed in this and in Peterson's Magazine, but the turning point of her literary success was "Surly Tim's Trouble," which appeared in Scribner's Monthly in 1872, attracting a great deal of attention. At the invitation of the editor more of her publications were published in Scribner's, one of the most popular being "That Lass o' Lowries," which appeared later in 1877 in book form. Mrs. Hodgson has been twice married, the first time, in 1873, to Dr. Swan M. Burnett, from whom she obtained a divorce in 1898, and the second time, in 1900, to Stephen Townsend, an English author. Mrs. Burnett, by winning a suit against the unauthorized dramatization of "Fauntleroy," secured for authors of England the control of dramatic rights in their stories, for which Reade and Dickens had spent thousands of pounds in vain.

PEARL MARY THERESA CRAIGIE.

The authoress, Pearl Mary Theresa Craigie, more familiarly known as John Oliver Hobbes, was born in Boston, Massachusetts, November 3, 1867, daughter of John Morgan and Laura Hortense (Arnold) Richards. She is descended from early settlers of New York. After being educated under private tutors, Miss Richards, in 1883, went to Europe, continuing her studies in Paris. In 1887 she was enrolled as a student at University College, London, where, under the tuition of Professor Goodwin, she obtained an adequate knowledge of the classics and philosophy. In early childhood she was fond of writing. One of her first stories, entitled "Lost, A Dog," appeared in Dr. Joseph Parker's paper, The Fountain. This story was signed Pearl Richards, aged nine. Another of her stories, entitled "How Mark Puddler Became an Innkeeper," appeared in The Fountain of February 10, 1881. At the age of eighteen she decided to make literature her profession and immediately took up a special study of style, especially dramatic dialogues. Her first book, entitled "Some Emotions and a Moral," 1891, is an excellent example of success under difficulties. This book was composed during months of weary illness and amid the strain of domestic anxiety, but its success was immediate, for over eighty thousand copies were sold in a short time. Since then she has written several other novels.

MARY ELEANOR WILKINS-FREEMAN.

"Wonderful in concentrated intensity, tremendous in power," this record of the heart tragedies of a dozen men and women is not surpassed in our literature for its beauty of style, the delicacy of its character delineations, and the enthralling interest of its narrative. It is the praise merited by "Pembroke," the greatest work that has come from the pen of the author, Mary Eleanor Wilkins. She was born of Puritan ancestors January 7, 1862, in Randolph, Norfolk county, Massachusetts, and received her early education in Randolph, later removing to Brattleboro, Vermont. She afterward attended Mount Holyoke seminary, South Hadley, Massachusetts, but previous to this she had already begun her literary work, writing poems and then prose for Youth's Companion, St. Nicholas, Harper's Bazar and finally for Harper's Magazine. "A Humble Romance and Other Stories," 1887, placed Miss Wilkins in the class with Mrs. Stowe, Miss Jewett and other conspicuous authors as a delineator of New England character. The simplicity and the astonishing reality of her story brought a new revelation to New England itself. Her literary style displays a fearlessness of the critic and the dominating thought to be true to her ideal. "The Pot of Gold and Other Stories," 1891, and "Young Lucretia," 1892, are among her popular juveniles. "The New England Nun and Other Stories," called forth the most lavish praise. Her next work of importance, as well as her first novel, was "Jane Field," 1892. When "Pembroke" appeared, in 1894, it was praised almost indiscriminately in England, some critics even venturing to say that George Eliot had never produced anything finer.

ANNA KATHERINE GREENE.

The simple stories and poems, written in her childhood, were the beginning of the career of the authoress, Anna Katherine Greene, who was born in Brooklyn, New York, November 11, 1846, daughter of James Wilson and Anna Katherine Greene. Her early education was obtained in the public schools of New York city and Buffalo, and she completed her course of study in Ripley Female College, Poultney, Vermont, graduating in 1867. Returning to her native city, she engaged in literary work, and, in 1878, produced her first important novel, "The Leavenworth Case." She attracted immediate attention in literary circles. It had been carefully prepared and was given to the public only after repeated revisions. It had a phenomenal sale—already, in 1894, exceeding seven hundred and fifty thousand copies. From that time on there was a great demand from the publishers for books from her pen, and during the next seventeen years she wrote and published fifteen novels. The story of "The Leavenworth Case" was dramatized and produced during the season of 1891 and 1892, her husband, Charles Rohlfs, to whom she had been married in 1884, sustaining the leading part, Harwell. The book is also used as a text-book in Yale university to demonstrate the fallacy of circumstantial evidence.

SARAH ORNE JEWETT.

A writer paid a just tribute to the subject of this sketch when she wrote: "The secret of Sarah Jewett's great success outside of its artistic perfection, is the spirit of loving kindness and tender mercy that pervades it." She was born at South Berwick, Maine, September 3, 1849, daughter of Theodore Herman Jewett. Her parents were both descendants of early English emigrants to Massachusetts. Sarah, owing to delicate health in childhood, spent much of her time communing with nature, where she received material and the inspiration that eventually made her such a popular writer. She was educated at Berwick academy, in her native city. When a mere girl she began her career as an author by contributing to Riverside Magazine and Our Young Folks. At nineteen she sent a story to the Atlantic Monthly, and has been averaging nearly a book a year ever since. Miss Jewett adopted the pseudonym "Alice Elliott" in 1881, but after that she used her own name instead.

CONSTANCE CARY HARRISON.

Constance Cary Harrison, who is better known to the reading public as Mrs. Burton Harrison, was born in Fairfax county, Virginia, April 25, 1846. She was educated by private governesses, and while under their tuition gave proofs of being the possessor of literary ability. During the Civil war she lived with her family in Richmond, Virginia. At the end of the conflict she went abroad with her mother to complete her studies in music and languages. Mrs. Harrison has traveled much and has lived in nearly all of the continental capitals. She married Burton Harrison, a well-known New York lawyer, and since her union to him has resided in the metropolis. Her works are many and range from children's fairy stories to works on social questions, and again from small comedies to books on municipal problems.

ELIZABETH STUART PHELPS WARD.

Heredity and environment conspired to make Elizabeth Stuart Phelps Ward a woman of letters. Her father, the Rev. Austin Phelps, was pastor of the Pine Street Congregational church of Boston at the time of her birth, August 31, 1844. In 1848 he became a professor in the theological seminary at Andover, Massachusetts, and thus his daughter Elizabeth grew up among a circle of thinkers and writers. She received most of her education from her father, but also attended the private school at Andover and the seminary of Mrs. Prof. Edwards, where she took a course of study equal to that of the men's colleges of to-day. At the age of nineteen she left school and engaged in mission work at Abbott Village and Factory Settlement, a short distance from her home. It was here she began an acquaintance with the lives and needs of working people, which resulted in books such as "Hedged In" and "Jack, the Fisherman." Her first story was published in the Youth's Companion when she was only thirteen years old. In 1864 she published "A Sacrifice Consumed," in Harper's Magazine, which earned her right to the title "author." The book which has given her greatest fame, "The Gates Ajar," was begun in 1862 and was published in 1868. Nearly one hundred thousand copies were sold in the United States, and more than that number in Great Britain. It was also translated into a number of foreign languages. Probably Mrs. Ward has written more books worth while than any other woman writer of her time. In 1888 Miss Phelps was married to Herbert D. Ward, and has co-operated with him in writing several romances.

REFORMERS.

GEORGE THORNDIKE ANGELL.

George Thorndike Angell was born at Southbridge, Massachusetts, June 5, 1823. He was educated in the public schools and graduated from Dartmouth College in 1846. After study at the Harvard law school he was admitted to the bar in 1851. For thirty-four years he has headed the work for the humane treatment of animals and helpless human beings. In 1868, when a young man of twenty-two, he founded the Massachusetts society for the prevention of cruelty to animals. He has served as its president since its inception, no one being better fitted to fill the position. He has propagated his ideas on humanity to animals by many organizations, and forty-four thousand "bands of mercy" speak for his efficient and zealous management. As an editor and publisher, his activity has been enormous, for in one year his societies sent out 117,000,000 pages of literature. His work for dumb brutes is so well known that it has overshadowed those other forms of philanthropy with which he has to do, and which in the case of an ordinary man would have made him a reputation. The work of the Social Science Association, of which Mr. Angell is a director, is of a varied nature, and ranges from the prevention of crime to the detection of food adulteration, or from the betterment of tenement houses to obtaining a higher standard of citizenship.

SUSAN BROWNELL ANTHONY.

Susan Brownell Anthony was born at Adams, Massachusetts, February 15, 1820. Her father, a Quaker, was a cotton manufacturer and gave her a liberal education. When she was seventeen years old her father failed in business and she had to support herself by school teaching, which profession she followed for thirteen years. Aroused at the injustice of the inequality of wages paid to women teachers, she made a public speech on the subject at the New York Teachers' Association, which attracted wide attention. She continued to work in the teachers' association for equal recognition continuously and enthusiastically. In 1849 she began to speak for the temperance cause, but soon became convinced that women had no power to change the condition of things without being able to vote at the polls, and from that time on she identified herself with the suffrage movement. She has written a great many tracts and was at one time the editor of a weekly paper called the Revolution. Her work, The History of Woman's Suffrage, which she prepared in conjunction with Elizabeth Cady Stanton and Matilda Joslyn Gage, attracted wide attention.

FREDERICK ST. GEORGE DE LAUTOUR BOOTH-TUCKER.

Frederick St. George de Lautour Booth-Tucker was born at Monghyr, India, March 21, 1853. He was educated at the Cheltenham college, England, and, after passing the Indian civil service examination, was appointed assistant commanding magistrate in the Punjab. He resigned in order to join the Salvation army in 1881, inaugurated the Salvation Army work in India in 1882, and had charge of the work of the army there until

1891, when he was made secretary for the international work of the organization in London. Since 1896 he has been in charge of the affairs of the army in the United States, in conjunction with his wife, Emma Moss Booth, whom he married, after which he adopted the name of Booth-Tucker. He is the author of a number of religious and other works and has considerable ability as an orator and organizer. Mr. Booth-Tucker has a magnetic personality, and with the practical side of his nature stands him in good stead in connection with his chosen walk in life.

ANTHONY COMSTOCK.

Anthony Comstock, who has been described as the most honest and the best-hated man in New York city, was born in New Canaan, Connecticut, March 7, 1844. He received his education in district schools and academy and later at the High School at New Britain, Connecticut. Early in life he began to earn his own livelihood, and in order to do so followed several vocations in succession. His brother Samuel was killed fighting for the Union cause at Gettysburg, and Anthony, volunteering to fill his place in the regiment, enlisted in the Seventeenth Volunteer Connecticut Infantry and saw much service during the war. He was mustered out in July, 1865. On January 25, 1871, he married Margaret Hamilton. In 1873 he was appointed postmaster inspector in New York, later became prominent in Young Men's Christian Association affairs, and finally identified himself with the New York society for the suppression of vice. Mr. Comstock's services in connection with what is his life work are too well known to be recapitulated. Possessing courage, moral and physical, of the highest order and a keen sense of his duties to the community in his official capacity, Mr. Comstock has for years been a terror to evil-doers, especially those who pander to vicious instincts. He has brought nearly 3,000 criminals to justice and has destroyed over 80 tons of obscene literature, pictures, etc. Altogether he is a notable figure in the complex life of New York, and the making of bitter enemies has necessarily followed on Mr. Comstock's career. But these, many and influential as they are, have never successfully attacked his motives or his integrity.

WILBUR FISKE CRAFTS.

The Rev. Wilbur Fiske Crafts was born at Fryeburg, Maine, January 12, 1850. His father was the Rev. A. C. Crafts. In 1869 the future author, lecturer and clergyman graduated from Wesleyan University, Connecticut, subsequently taking the post-graduate course in Boston University. On leaving college he became a minister of the Methodist Episcopal Church, holding charges for several years therein and laying the foundation for the reputation which now attaches to him. Later, however, Mr. Crafts decided that the tenets of the Congregational denomination were more to his liking, and accordingly accepted a call to a Congregational church in Brooklyn. Still later he became a Presbyterian pastor in New York. Resigning from the ministry, he was made superintendent of the International Reform Bureau, the object of which is to secure moral legislation in the United States and Canada with the assistance of lectures, literature and personal example and influence. He is the author of many works, the majority of which are of a religious nature, or deal with social questions.

ELBRIDGE THOMAS GERRY.

Elbridge Thomas Gerry, born in New York city, December 25, 1837, was named after his grandfather, who was one of the vice-presidents of the United States and a signer of the Declaration of Independence. Mr. Gerry was educated in the New York public schools, and graduated from Columbia college in 1858. He was admitted to the bar in 1860. He acted as vice-president, until 1899, of the American society for the prevention of cruelty to animals. He was chairman of the New York state commission on capital punishment from 1886 to 1888. Since 1891 he has been president of the annual convention of the New York societies for prevention of cruelty. He is trustee of the general theological seminary of the Presbyterian-Episcopal church and also trustee of the American museum of natural history, and of the New York Mutual Life Insurance company. Besides that, he is a member and director of various corporations and societies. Since 1876 he has been president of the New York society for the prevention of cruelty to children, which society is generally known as the Gerry Society. He has one of the largest private law libraries in the United States. Mr. Gerry is one of those conscientious citizens whose work for the public good has been as continuous as it has been successful.

WILLIAM REUBEN GEORGE.

William R. George was born at West Dryden, New York, June 4, 1866. He was educated in the common schools. His parents came to New York city in 1880, where he later engaged in business. Becoming interested in poor boys and girls, he, during the seasons of 1890 to 1894, took two hundred of them to the country for from two weeks to a month to spend a portion of their school vacations with him. Impressed with the large number of children endeavoring to live by charity, he conceived, in 1894, the plan of requiring payment in labor for every favor the youngsters received, and, in addition, instituted a system of self-government. This was the beginning of a junior republic, which was put into practical operation in 1895 and has continued successfully ever since. He was married November 14, 1896, to Esther B. George, of New York. To Mr. George belongs the credit of inaugurating a novel and praiseworthy method of fostering good citizenship.

CHARLES HENRY PARKHURST.

The Rev. Dr. Charles Henry Parkhurst was born in Framingham, Massachusetts, April 17, 1842. His father worked on a farm in summer and taught school in winter. Until sixteen years of age Charles was a pupil of the Clinton (Mass.) grammar school. The two years following he acted as clerk in a dry goods store. At the age of eighteen he began to prepare for college at Lancaster academy. At the end of the course there, he went to Amherst, from whence he graduated in 1866. The following year he became principal of the Amherst high school, remaining there until 1870, when he visited Germany. On his return he became professor of Greek and Latin in Williston seminary, holding that position for two years, during which period he married a Miss Bodman, a pupil of his while a teacher at Amherst. Accompanied by his wife, he next made a trip to Europe to study at Halle, Leipzig, and Bonn. Again in this country he received a call to the pastorate of the First Congregational church in Lenox, Massachusetts, where he soon gained a reputation as an original and forceful pulpit orator. On March 9, 1880, he became pastor of the Madison Square Presbyterian church, New York city, the call being the outcome of his work at Lenox. He immediately began to take a lively interest in city and national politics, and one of his sermons attracted the attention of Dr. Howard Crosby, president of the society for the prevention of crime, in which society Dr. Parkhurst was invited to become a director. A few months later Dr. Crosby died and Dr. Parkhurst was chosen as his successor. Dr. Parkhurst has done more for reform in New York city than any other single individual. His courageous course in connection with the Lexow investigation of certain phases of life in New York will not be readily forgotten.

ELIZABETH CADY STANTON.

That which is popularly, if somewhat vaguely, characterized as the "Cause of women" in this country, is closely identified with the name of Elizabeth Cady Stanton. Many years of her life were spent in promoting the cause of her sex politically and legally, and that her work has not been fruitless is proven by the fact that as long ago as 1840 she advocated the passage of the Married Woman's Property bill, which became a law in 1848. That measure alone is sufficient to obtain for Mrs. Stanton the gratitude of her sex. She was born in Johnstown, New York, November 12, 1815, being the daughter of Daniel C. Cady, judge of the New York State Supreme Court. She obtained her education at the Johnstown academy and the Emma Willard seminary, Troy, New York, graduating from the latter institution in 1832. Eight years later she married Henry Brewster Stanton, a state senator, anti-slavery orator and lawyer. From the first Mrs. Stanton identified herself with "Woman's Rights," and she it was who called the first woman's rights convention, the meeting taking place at Seneca Falls, New York, in July, 1848. Continually working on the lines indicated, she has for the last quarter of a century annually addressed congress in favor of embodying woman suffrage in the constitution of the United States. In 1861 she was president of the Woman's Loyal League, and through the medium of her personality made it a power in the land. From 1865 to 1893 she held the office of president of the Woman Suffrage Association. In 1868 she was a candidate for congress. Her eightieth birthday, which took place in 1895, was celebrated under the auspices of the National Council of Women, three hundred delegates attending the convention.

PHILANTHROPISTS.

MRS. PHOEBE APPERSIN HEARST.

Mrs. Phoebe Appersin Hearst was born in 1840. After an education in the public schools she became a teacher in them until 1861, when she married the late United States Senator George F. Hearst from California, who died, in 1891, leaving her and her son, William Randolph Hearst, a fortune of many millions. W. R. Hearst is the well-known newspaper owner and publisher. Mrs. Hearst has established kindergarten classes and the manual training school in San Francisco, kindergartens and the kindergarten training school in Washington, District of Columbia; has made donations to the American university at Washington, gave $200,000 to build a national cathedral school for girls, has established working girls' clubs in San Francisco, is the patron of a school for mining engineers at the University of California, and, as a memorial to her husband, has built and endowed libraries in a number of mining towns in the west. In connection with the plans for the projected University of California, she has also agreed to erect two buildings to cost between three and four million of dollars.

DANIEL KIMBALL PEARSONS.

Daniel K. Pearsons was born at Bedford, Vermont, April 14, 1820, and was educated in the public schools. Entered college at Woodstock, Vermont, and was graduated as a physician, practicing in Chicopee, Massachusetts, until 1857. He removed to Ogle county, Illinois, and became a farmer, 1857 to 1860, and in the latter year began the real estate business in Chicago, which he continued until 1887, when he retired from business but remained a director of the Chicago City Railway Company and other corporations. He has made handsome donations to various colleges and charities there, including $280,000 to the Chicago theological seminary and $200,000 to Beloit college. He has also contributed to the treasuries of several other educational establishments. Mr. Pearsons seems to be a pupil of Mr. Andrew Carnegie in some respects, inasmuch as he has a profound belief in the wisdom of distributing his money for praiseworthy purposes during his lifetime.

MRS. HENRY CODMAN POTTER.

The dominant quality of the character of the wife of Bishop Henry Codman Potter, of the diocese of New York, is undoubtedly charity. Her maiden name was Elizabeth L. Scriven, and she was born in 1849 in New York, coming of good American stock. She has been married twice, her first husband being Alfred Corning Clark, who in his lifetime controlled the Singer sewing machine interests and who also had extensive real estate holdings in the metropolis. When Mr. Clark died he left an estate of an estimated value of about $30,000,000, the bulk of which, after a liberal allowance made to his four children, went to his widow. All her life Mrs. Potter has given largely to charity and philanthropic enterprises. She has done excellent work in New York in connection with improvements in tenement houses, those that she owns being ideal dwellings in regard to construction, light, ventilation and sanitary arrangements. At Cooperstown, New York, which is her home, Mrs. Potter has spent large sums of money in beautifying the village. She gives annually a dinner to a thousand poor persons, and has a long list of private pensioners. Her marriage to Bishop Potter took place on October 1, 1902, at Cooperstown.

MRS. THEODORE ROOSEVELT.

The maiden name of the wife of President Roosevelt was Edith Kermit Carow, and she, like her husband, comes of one of the most distinguished of the older families of New York. Born in the metropolis in the old Carow mansion, Fourteenth street and Union square, her father was Charles Carow, and her grandfather General Tyler Carow, of Norwich, Connecticut. She was educated at a school kept by a Miss Comstock on West Fortieth street. She was married to the President on December 2, 1886, at St. George's church, Hanover square, London, the ceremony being performed by Canon Cammadge, who is a cousin of Mrs. Roosevelt. Fortune has never been more kind to Mr. Roosevelt than when she gave him the amiable and beautiful woman who bears his name. The Roosevelt children seem to have inherited many of the attractive qualities of their mother.

MRS. RUSSELL SAGE.

Mrs. Russell Sage was born at Syracuse, New York, in 1828. She was the daughter of the Hon. Joseph Slocum. Educated at first in private schools of Syracuse, it had been intended that she should go to college later, but financial disaster altered the plans of the family. After working at home to help her mother for some time, she started for Mount Holyoke college, intending to do housework in that institution in order to pay for her board. On her way thither she was taken sick in Troy, and when she recovered she, at the request of her uncle, entered the Troy female seminary. In 1869 she became the second wife of Russell Sage, the financier. Mrs. Sage's charities are large; she has built a dormitory costing $120,000 in the Emma Willard seminary and gives annually large sums of money to various hospitals and other praiseworthy institutions.

MRS. LELAND STANFORD.

Mrs. Jane Lathrop Stanford was born at Albany, New York, August 25, 1825. Was educated in the public schools there, and in 1848 married Leland Stanford. In 1855 she went with her husband to California. Mr. Stanford took a prominent part in the public affairs of the state, and in 1861 was elected its governor. A son was born, who died when sixteen years of age in Florence, Italy. Mr. Stanford founded the university which bears his name, in memory of his boy. Since her husband's demise Mrs. Stanford has given further endowments to the institution, the total amount of which is said to be several million dollars. She has also given liberally to other educational institutions.

ANSON PHELPS STOKES, SR.

Anson Phelps Stokes, Sr., financier and public-spirited citizen, was born in New York, February 22, 1838, being the son of James and Caroline (Phelps) Stokes. He was educated in private schools and in 1855 married Helen Louise, daughter of Isaac Newton Phelps. Becoming connected with the firm of Phelps, Dodge & Co., merchants, he afterward became a partner in the banking firm of Phelps, Stokes & Co., of New York. He is director and trustee of a number of philanthropic institutions and hospitals, owns interests in varied corporations and is a prominent member of several clubs whose objects it is to promote municipal and legislative reform. Mr. Stokes has written two books on financial questions.

DIVINES.

LYMAN ABBOTT.

Dr. Lyman Abbott is an illustration of the fact that a young man who is gifted with more than ordinary intellect and even genius need not be discouraged, even if his first intentions regarding his life work come to naught by force of circumstances or unlooked-for developments within himself. He was born December 18, 1835, in Roxbury, Massachusetts, being the son of Jacob and Harriet Abbott. Graduating from the College of the City of New York in 1853, he took a course at Harvard, after which, and in accordance with his prearranged plans, he took a law course, was admitted to the bar and began to practice. But his literary instincts and religious convictions resulted in his finally abandoning the law. After a good deal of writing for a number of publications and more theological studies, he was finally ordained a Congregational minister in 1860, being made pastor of a church at Terre Haute, Indiana, in the same year. Leaving Indiana, he came to New York and took charge of the New England Congregational Church in that city. In 1869 he resigned the pastorate in order to devote himself to literature. He edited the Literary Record Department of Harper's Magazine and was associate editor with Henry Ward Beecher on the Christian Union. He succeeded Mr. Beecher as pastor of Plymouth Church, Brooklyn, in May, 1888, but resigned in 1898 and is once more prominent in religious literary circles. On October 14, 1857, he married Abby F. Hamlin, daughter of Hannibal Hamlin, of Boston. He is the author of a great many works of a religious nature and of others which deal with social problems. At present he is editor of The Outlook, of New York city.

THEODORE LEDYARD CUYLER.

Theodore Ledyard Cuyler, the clergyman whose striking sermons have made him famous the world over, was born at Aurora, New York, January 10, 1822. He was educated at Manheim, New Jersey, and Princeton college, from which he graduated in 1841. After spending a brief period in traveling in Europe, he entered the theological seminary at Princeton, from which he graduated in 1846, and was ordained by the presbytery in 1848. His first charge was at a small church near Wilkesbarre, Pennsylvania, where he remained for six months. He was then called to the Presbyterian church of Burlington, New Jersey. In 1849 he became pastor of the Third Presbyterian church of Trenton, New Jersey, and in 1853 he was invited to the Market Street Dutch Reformed Church, New York city. He was one of the leaders in the great revival of 1858, and in 1860 he was called to the Lafayette Avenue Presbyterian church, Brooklyn. This was a young church and was not in a very prosperous condition, but the new pastor infused life into it from the first, and, in 1861, his congregation commenced the building of a new church at the corner of Lafayette avenue and South Oxford street. This building was completed in March, 1862, and cost $60,000. In 1893 Dr. Cuyler withdrew from active charge of the church and determined to devote the remainder of his years to the ministry at large. Dr. Cuyler was married, in 1853, to Annie E. Mathist, of Newark, Ohio, and has two children. His writings and printed sermons have been widely circulated. Among them are: Thought Hives, Stray Arrows, The Empty Crib, The Cedar Christian. One of his most famous tracts, Somebody's Son, had a circulation of over one hundred thousand copies. Many of his articles and tracts have been translated into several languages, and his contributions to the religious press have been more numerous than those of any living writer.

EDWARD EVERETT HALE.

Edward Everett Hale was born in Boston, April 3, 1822, and after passing through the public schools entered the Boston Latin school. He was graduated from Harvard in 1839, and for two years acted as usher in the Latin school, studying theology in the meantime. On October 13, 1852, he married, at Hartford, Connecticut, Emily Baldwin Perkins. He has been a prominent promoter of Chautauqua circles and was the founder of the "Lend-a-Hand" clubs. He has probably traveled as much and delivered more lectures than any other man in this country. The fact that the catalogue of Harvard university lists more than one hundred and thirty titles of books and pamphlets on varied subjects of which he is the author shows how prolific has been his pen. Fiction, drama, narrative, poetry, theology, philosophy, politics—all are treated by him in a masterly way. He is never dull or common-place, but invariably suggestive and practical. One of his masterpieces is A Man Without a Country, which was written in war time. This story alone would have given him lasting fame. Yet it is not as an author, a great scholar, a great teacher, a great orator, or a great statesman that Dr. Hale will be remembered, but, as William Dean Howells has said, his name will go down in history as "a great American citizen."

BENJAMIN FAY MILLS.

Benjamin Fay Mills was born at Rahway, New Jersey, June 4, 1857. His father was a clergyman. Educated in the public schools and at Phillips academy, Andover, he graduated from Lake Forest university, Illinois, in 1879. In the same year he married Mary Russell, and in the year following he was ordained pastor of the

Congregational church at Rutland, Vermont. From 1886 to 1897 he acted in an evangelistic capacity and conducted meetings throughout the country. In 1897 he withdrew from the orthodox church and inaugurated independent religious movements in the Boston music hall and Hollis street theatre. Since 1889 he has been the pastor of the First Unitarian church, Oakland, California. He is eloquent, magnetic and convincing and has the gift of playing on the emotions of an audience in a manner possessed by few speakers within or without the church.

HENRY CODMAN POTTER.

There have been a great many clergymen in the Potter family, and doubtless the Right Reverend Henry Codman Potter, bishop of the diocese of New York, had an inclination for the pulpit which was an ancestral inheritance. He is the son of Bishop Alonzo Potter, of Pennsylvania, and was born at Schenectady, New York, May 25, 1835. He was educated at the Philadelphia Academy of the Protestant Episcopal church, and later at the theological seminary in Virginia. Graduating therefrom in 1857, he was at once made a deacon and one year later was ordained to the priesthood. Until 1859 he had charge of Christ P. E. church, Greensburg, Pennsylvania, when he was transferred to St. John's, P. E. church, Troy, New York; for seven years he was rector of that parish. He then became an assistant of Trinity P. E. church, Boston, and in May, 1868, was made rector of Grace P. E. church, New York. For sixteen years he was identified with the affairs of that famous church. In 1883 he was elected an assistant to his uncle, Bishop Horatio Potter, who presided over the diocese of New York. A short time after entering on his duties as such, his uncle withdrew from active work and the care of the diocese fell upon the younger man. On January 2, 1887, Bishop Horatio Potter died and was succeeded by his nephew. His diocese is the largest in point of population in the United States. Eloquent, earnest and devoted to his life work, Bishop Potter commands the love and respect of all of those with whom he comes in contact.

WILLIAM TAYLOR.

William Taylor was born in Virginia May 2, 1821. Reared on a farm, he learned the tanning business. He entered the Methodist ministry in 1842. Going to California with the "Forty-niners" as a missionary, he remained there until 1856. He next spent a number of years traveling in Canada, New England and Europe. After conducting missionary services in Australia, New Zealand and Tasmania, he visited South Africa and converted many Kaffirs to Christianity. From 1872 to 1876 he organized a number of churches in India and in South America. He also established mission stations on the Congo and elsewhere in Africa. He has written a number of books, the most interesting of which is, without doubt, The Story of My Life. In 1884 he was made missionary bishop for Africa.

JOHN HEYL VINCENT.

John Heyl Vincent, bishop of the Methodist Episcopal Church and chancellor of the Chautauqua system, was born in Tuscaloosa, Alabama, February 23, 1832. He was educated at Lewisburg and Milton, Pennsylvania, and as a mere boy gave evidence of the religious trend of his nature. When only eighteen years of age he was a preacher, and many of his then sermons are said to have been both eloquent and convincing. After studying in the Wesleyan Institute of Newark, New Jersey, he joined the New Jersey Conference in 1853, was ordained deacon and four years later was made pastor. He had several charges in Illinois between 1857 and 1865, and during the next fourteen years brought into being a number of Sunday school publications. He was one of the founders of the Chautauqua Assembly and was the organizer of the Chautauqua Literary and Scientific Circle, of which he has held office of chancellor since its inception. In 1900 he was made resident bishop in charge of the European work of the church with which he was associated. He is preacher to Harvard, Yale, Cornell, Wellesley and other colleges. As an author of helpful and interesting religious works, Dr. Vincent is well known to all students of American literature.

CANADIANS.

WILLIAM PETERSON.

One of the influential educators in Canada is Dr. William Peterson, President of that powerful and progressive educational institution, McGill University. Dr. Peterson's policy in the conduct of the university is to maintain a harmonious relationship between classical education and the scientific training which is now so greatly in demand. That the university is kept well abreast of the times in scientific teaching and equipment is indicated by the fact that a recent addition to the institution has been a school for instruction in all branches of railroading. Dr. Peterson keenly realizes that the future development of Canada will depend in a very considerable measure upon the extension of the Dominion's railway system—that in the railroad business there will, perhaps, be more and greater opportunities for young Canadians than in any other one branch of industry. Another proof of the scientific thoroughness at McGill is the high standing held by the University's medical and engineering schools, but Dr. Peterson holds fast to the belief that no education is complete without a familiarity with the classics. He is himself an accomplished classical scholar.

After spending his boyhood in the city of Edinburgh, Scotland, where he was born in 1856, he became a student at the Edinburgh University, and there distinguished himself. He won the Greek travelling fellowship, and continued his classical study at the University of Göttingen. Returning to Scotland, he was elected to the Mackenzie scholarship in the University of Edinburgh and went to Oxford University, where he added to his scholastic laurels. He became assistant Professor of Humanity in Edinburgh University, and in 1882 was appointed Professor of Classical and Ancient History and head of the faculty in University College, Dundee. Here he remained until 1885, when he was chosen to succeed Sir J. W. Dawson as Principal of McGill University, Montreal. He has received honorary degrees from St. Andrews and Princeton universities, and is regarded not only as a scholar of unusual attainments, but as a man possessing in marked degree the executive ability necessary to successfully conduct the affairs of a great university.

GEORGE A. COX.

Perhaps the most important financier in Canada is Senator George A. Cox of Toronto, who is regarded as the Dominion's closest parallel, in financial activity, to J. Pierpont Morgan of New York. His interests are extensive and widely varied. He is the president of the Canadian Life Assurance Company, president of two fire insurance companies, president of the Central Canadian Loan and Savings Company, and is one of the ruling spirits in the great project to build the Grand Trunk Pacific Railway across the continent to the Pacific Ocean. He has a very considerable amount of capital invested in the United States.

Senator Cox was born sixty-four years ago in the village of Colborne. His father was a shoemaker in humble circumstances. The ability of Senator Cox, as a boy, attracted the attention of a neighbor, who educated him. When he became a young man he went to the town of Peterboro and embarked in the photographic business. He afterwards became an express agent, and also occupied himself with soliciting insurance for the Canadian Life Assurance Company. He engaged in politics, and for seven years was mayor of Peterboro. When the Midland Railway became involved in financial difficulties, he was one of the Canadians asked to reorganize the road. He at once became the dominating factor in this work and in 1878 was made president of the Midland line. The vigor and ability which he brought to his task soon put the decrepit railway company on its feet again. It afterward became the Midland Division of the Grand Trunk Railway. Besides his insurance and railway affiliations Senator Cox is largely interested in Canadian banks and lands.

Senator Cox attributes much of his success to the fact that he is a good judge of human nature. He has long made a point of surrounding himself with clever young men who are able to develop and zealously put into operation the hints which he freely gives them. Senator Cox's personality is of a kind which inspires enthusiasm on the part of those who are working with and for him. He is genial and never stands on formality in his contact with the young men whom he has around him. In this respect he more closely resembles Andrew Carnegie than any other captain of industry. Senator Cox lives in modest style in Toronto. He is quiet in his tastes, and greatly dislikes anything suggestive of display or self-aggrandizement. He is a close personal friend of most of the political leaders in the Canadian Liberal Party, and of many of the financial powers in the United States. The Earl of Aberdeen appointed him to the Senate of Canada in 1896. He is a prominent member of the Methodist Church, and has long interested himself in the welfare of Victoria University in Toronto.

TIMOTHY EATON.

The most important retail merchant in Canada is Timothy Eaton. He began his career as an apprentice in a small shop in a village in Ireland, and now has an establishment which employs the services of six thousand persons, and which is by far the largest and best equipped retail store in the Dominion.

It was in a shop in the town of Port Gleone, in the north of Ireland, that Mr. Eaton obtained his first experience as a storekeeper. Here he served an apprenticeship of five years, receiving no pay until the end of his term of service, when he was given the sum of one hundred pounds. To convey an idea of the long hours that he used to devote to the services of his employer in Ireland, Mr. Eaton likes to tell about how he used to watch the donkey carts passing through the village streets to the market-town of Ballymena at five o'clock every morning, when he was taking down the shutters. While he had very little time in those days to devote to anything but his regular work, he was fond of books, and read *Chambers's Journal*, an unusual literary selection for a lad of his education and position. In this publication he read one day an article on the then almost unknown process of manufacturing artificial gas. This so interested him that with the help of a companion he made with his own hands a small gas plant, and by means of it succeeded in lighting the store. Before that there had been no gas light in that section of Ireland. The innovation of the young apprentice aroused great interest and curiosity on the part of the people of the countryside. They flocked to the shop to view the miracle of the new light. This proved to be a valuable advertisement for the establishment, and it lifted young Eaton into a position of prominence in the community.

He felt, however, that there were no chances in Ireland for the degree of success of which he dreamed. The potato famine and other misfortunes had laid the country prostrate. Everybody was talking about the golden prospects in America, and great numbers were emigrating to the promised land. One of Timothy Eaton's elder brothers decided to join the exodus, and Timothy himself lost no time in making up his mind to go with him.

After crossing the Atlantic they made their way to the town of St. Marys, in Ontario, and there started a very small store, being glad to accept produce in payment for their goods. Another brother came to St. Marys. One of these remained there permanently, while Timothy Eaton, not satisfied with the possibilities in St. Marys of the mercantile expansion which he had in mind, went to Toronto, and started a modest store on one of the lower streets. This was in 1869. In 1883 he had a larger establishment. In 1887 he had added to his general store equipment a small factory for the purpose of eliminating the charges of middlemen and thus conserving the interests of his customers by reduced prices. The factory was an unqualified success. By means of it, and through Mr. Eaton's general methods, the establishment steadily grew until, at the present time, he has a store which from a comparative point of view may be regarded, perhaps, as the most successful in the world. Mr. Eaton's pay roll includes nearly six thousand names, while the largest retail store on earth, which is located in Chicago, where the population is many times greater than that which can be reached by Mr. Eaton, employs only about twenty-five hundred more persons. It will be seen that this Chicago establishment is only one-half larger than the Eaton store. Indeed, the factories of the latter are larger than those of any establishment which deals directly with retail buyers.

The two leading elements in Mr. Eaton's remarkable success have been his store-system, regarded by leading retail merchants as a model, and his constant endeavor to save money for his customers. It is to this end that he conducts his business on a cash basis, and that he has established his factories. He is a very firm believer in bringing goods direct from the maker to the consumer. In a single department in his manufacturing section, for instance, there are over a thousand sewing machines which produce nearly seven thousand garments a day for sale exclusively in the store. The money which Mr. Eaton has been able to save by this policy of producing his own goods is directly applied to the reduction of prices. The fact that his patrons feel that they are obtaining maximum value at minimum cost is the chief reason of the store's great and constantly growing trade.

Another very prominent factor in his success has been his strict rule of allowing absolutely no misrepresentation. He very strongly feels that truth is a most important element in any permanent success in storekeeping and in life in general. In addition to Mr. Eaton's constant vigilance in the interest of his patrons, he has always in mind the well-being of his employees. He was one of the pioneers in the movement for shorter hours, believing that opportunities for legitimate rest and recreation give those who are in his service an added zeal and energy which materially increase the satisfaction of buyers and has a direct beneficial effect upon the profits and progress of the store.

While Mr. Eaton is proud of his success, he by no means takes all the credit to himself. It is his idea that the quality which has chiefly enabled him to build up this great commercial unit lies in his ability to pick out the right man for the right place. Each employee is held to a personal responsibility, and is given to understand that he or she is considered a possibility for the higher positions in the establishment. Every clerk understands that promotion is to be obtained not by favoritism, but on the strength alone of conscientious and intelligent effort.

A celebrated department store proprietor in New York City not long ago remarked to a Canadian merchant who informed him that he had come to the New York establishment to obtain hints on the best system of store management, "Why, it is not at all necessary for you to come down here for this information. You have a man in Canada, Timothy Eaton, who can tell you a good deal more about this than most of us can. In fact, we always keep our eyes on him with a view of obtaining fresh suggestions as to methods."

SIR THOMAS G. SHAUGHNESSY.

One of the most successful railroad men of this continent is Sir Thomas G. Shaughnessy, president of the Canadian Pacific Railroad. By means of a particularly virile personality and a remarkable capacity for hard work, Sir Thomas has raised himself to his present high position from the bottom of the ladder. He owes absolutely nothing to the extraneous circumstances of birth or fortune. His education has been chiefly obtained in the school of experience; yet Sir Thomas adds to his conspicuous knowledge of man and affairs a culture that would do credit to a university graduate.

Though Sir Thomas is always associated in the public mind with Canada for the reason that his most important work has been done in the Dominion, he was born in 1853 in Milwaukee. His school days ended at the age of sixteen, when he obtained a place in the office of the Milwaukee & St. Paul Railway as a clerk in the purchasing department. During a period of ten years the young man slowly rose in this department until, on the strength of his ability and alertness, he was promoted to the place of a general storekeeper for the railroad. Mr. Shaughnessy took hold with an acceleration of the powers which had brought him his steady promotion. Work in the office began to move more swiftly than ever before. Each man was held to a very strict accountability in the performance of all his duties, and yet with a new spirit of contentment and zeal for the reason that Mr. Shaughnessy was very considerate to those under his direction. He was quick to criticise, but was equally quick to praise. No man who had ever held a position of authority in the company was more popular with his subordinates.

But Mr. Shaughnessy's abilities were too great for his position. William C. Van Horne, who had recently become general manager of the young Canadian Pacific Railway, had known Mr. Shaughnessy in Milwaukee, and asked him to take a place of purchasing agent in the new company. This was in 1882. He became assistant to the general manager in 1884, and the next year was promoted to the office of assistant to the president. He became a full-fledged vice-president in 1891. Mr. Shaughnessy was the right-hand man of the president of the road, Sir William C. Van Horne, and when the latter resigned the presidency in 1899 it was obvious that the man in all respects best equipped to succeed him in the very important position of executive head of the longest railroad in the world was Mr. Shaughnessy. The latter was knighted by the Prince of Wales, then Duke of York, in Ottawa, Canada, 1901.

The work of Sir Thomas as president has been notable. He has had a careful regard not only for the interest of the line, but also of Canada. During his incumbency of the presidency the Canadian Pacific system has been greatly extended. It now employs over thirty-five thousand persons and buys products of the labor of fifty thousand more. Within the last two years it has paid Canadians over one hundred millions. The progressive management of the line under the direction of Sir Thomas Shaughnessy has greatly stimulated the prosperity of the Dominion, and on this account the Canadians feel that Sir Thomas has been one of the Dominion's most valuable citizens.

WILLIAM S. FIELDING.

The Hon. William Stevens Fielding, considered one of Canada's ablest men, stands high in the administration of Sir Wilfrid Laurier, holding the important place of Minister of Finance. He attained distinction by the path of newspaper work. Mr. Fielding was born in Halifax of English parentage in 1848, and at the age of sixteen entered the business office of the *Morning Chronicle*. This was perhaps the most influential newspaper of the Maritime Provinces, and counted among its contributors numerous men of intellect and influence. It was from them that young Fielding imbibed his political views and became imbued with the spirit of broad patriotism which has since distinguished him.

Soon after he formed his connection with the *Chronicle* he was promoted to a place as reporter, and was most zealous and thorough in this sphere. Before he was twenty he had commenced to write editorials. For two decades Mr. Fielding remained with the *Chronicle*, rising by degrees to the place of editor, and at the same time taking an active part in the political campaigns in Halifax. He was elected in the elections of 1882 to a seat in the Nova Scotia

Legislature, and rose so rapidly that within a few months he was offered the premiership of the Province. He declined the honor on this occasion, but soon afterward organized a government at the request of some of the other leaders, and took upon himself the duties of provincial secretary, which also involved the work of financial administrator. His government was so effective that for years it controlled the affairs of the Province. When Sir Wilfrid Laurier became premier of the Dominion in 1896 he appointed Mr. Fielding Minister of Finance, and the latter was returned by the constituency of Shelbourne and Queens to the Dominion House of Commons. It was Mr. Fielding who introduced the measure for the preferential tariff which has been so conspicuous a feature of the Laurier administration. Mr. Fielding is regarded as one of the strongest members of the cabinet.

CHARLES FITZPATRICK.

The Hon. Charles Fitzpatrick, Minister of Justice in the Canadian Government, and one of the ablest of the Dominion's lawyers and political leaders, was born of Irish parentage in the Province of Quebec in 1851. His father was a lumber merchant. He was graduated from Laval University in Quebec, studied law and began practice in the city of Quebec, where he rapidly rose to prominence. He had acquired such a reputation at the bar when he was thirty-four years old, that the half-breeds and others who rallied to the support of Louis Riel when the latter was imprisoned and about to be tried for his life, retained Mr. Fitzpatrick as the man best fitted to defend their leader. In this case he opposed a number of the ablest lawyers in Canada, and while his client, Riel, was condemned to death, Mr. Fitzpatrick's eloquence and command of legal principles attracted wide attention. He has since appeared in many of the most important cases that have been tried within the Dominion.

Mr. Fitzpatrick's entry into public life was made in 1891,

when he was elected a member of the House of Commons of the Province of Quebec, representing his native county. He held this seat until 1896, when he was a successful candidate for the Dominion House of Commons. His general ability and his attainments as a lawyer had by this time become so conspicuous that when in the same year Sir Wilfrid Laurier organized his government he appointed Mr. Fitzpatrick to the position of Solicitor General. In 1900 he was re-elected, by a large majority, a Liberal member from Quebec, in a constituency that was largely Conservative. In 1902, on the elevation of the Hon. David Mills to the Supreme Court bench, Mr. Fitzpatrick was called to his present post of Minister of Justice.

The political success of Mr. Fitzpatrick is made the more notable by the fact that ninety per cent. of the voters of Quebec are French Canadians, while he himself is an Irishman.

In addition to his powers as an orator, his grasp of legal principles and his strong personal magnetism, one of his predominant traits is energy. It has been said of him that in the days of his youth he was in the habit of rising so early in the morning that he had his cases carefully analyzed and his plan of action formulated before other lawyers were out of bed. At present his most absorbing interest is the project for the Grand Trunk Pacific Railway line across the continent. It was he who drew up the contract for the undertaking, and he has been its chief defender, in its legal aspects, against the many attacks to which it has been subjected by the opponents of the government of Sir Wilfrid Laurier.

Mr. Fitzpatrick attributes his zest for work to the fact that he has always been an outdoor man. During his early years his reputation as an athlete was as great in Quebec as was his fame as a lawyer. He married a daughter of the late Lieutenant Carors, and thus became intimately identified with one of the oldest of the French-Canadian families, which dates back to the early days in Canadian history.

There is no more enthusiastic believer in the future of Canada than Mr. Fitzpatrick. In 1903 he made a tour of the Northwest, and has expressed himself as astonished at its marvelous resources. It is his opinion that the projected Grand Trunk Pacific line, adding another railway to the transportation facilities of this territory, will develop it into one of the richest and most productive regions, not only in grain, but in minerals, the world has ever known.

GEORGE WILLIAM ROSS.

The Hon. George William Ross, Premier of the Province of Ontario, was born near London, Ontario, in 1841. His father was a Scotchman, who, after migrating to Canada, became a prosperous farmer. Mr. Ross began his active life as a country school teacher. The government of the Province of Ontario established in 1871 a system of school inspectors, and he was appointed to one of these places. In the general election of the following year, Mr. Ross was chosen to represent the Conservative party in the western division of his native county, and was elected to the Dominion House of Commons. It was particularly his ability as an orator that brought him this honor. He was a member at the time of the Sons of Temperance, and it was at the meetings of this society that he seized his first opportunities to develop and display his gifts as a public speaker. He has said since that this experience in talking on his feet was invaluable to him, and he advises all young men who desire to acquire the gift of public speaking to join a debating society or other organization whose members are willing to listen to budding eloquence.

Mr. Ross was made Minister of Education for the Province of Ontario in 1883, and in 1887 succeeded in having passed a law for the federation of the denominational colleges of Toronto into a single unit, The University of Toronto. He inaugurated other educational reforms, and materially raised the standard of public education in the Province. Mr. Ross relinquished his work in this special field in 1900 to become Premier of Ontario. He has been prominently identified with movements in the cause of temperance, and holds honorary degrees in five Canadian universities. One of his distinguishing qualities is versatility. He is interested in astronomy, and has a marked literary bent, having written biographical sketches and some poetry.

LORD MOUNT STEPHEN.

In spite of the fact that Lord Mount Stephen has not resided in Canada for a number of years, he must be included in any group of important workers in the Dominion. He played a leading part in the upbuilding of the Canadian commonwealth. The vital importance of his work for the Canadian Pacific Railway cannot be overlooked. Lord Mount Stephen and Lord Strathcona were the two great personalities which carried the project of the transcontinental line through a dark period of financial storm and stress. Lord Mount Stephen reorganized or built several other railroads in Canada, and was very closely identified with many of the Dominion's most important commercial movements.

Like so many other men who have achieved remarkable success in Canada, Lord Mount Stephen is a Scotchman, having been born in that country in 1829. In his childhood he was a herdboy on the Highlands, and served as an apprentice in Aberdeen. He afterward obtained employment in London, and in 1850 migrated to Canada, where his uncle, William Stephen, was engaged in the woolen business. The young man was taken into partnership, and upon his uncle's death bought his interest in the firm, which steadily grew in importance in the manufacture of woolen goods. Lord Mount Stephen's financial standing at this time is indicated by the fact that he became a director in Canada's leading banking institution, the Bank of Montreal, of which he was afterward vice-president. It was owing to this financial eminence, as well as to his great ability, that he was able to build a magnificent structure of success out of what appeared at that time to be the wreck of the project for the Canadian Pacific Railroad. In recognition of his services for her domain across the ocean, Queen Victoria knighted him in 1886, and a few years afterwards raised him to the peerage with the title of Lord Mount Stephen, a title suggested by the peak in the Rockies called Mount Stephen, which itself had been named after the able Scotchman. Lord Mount Stephen retired from the presidency of the Canadian Pacific Railroad in 1888, and has spent most of his time since then in England. He has, however, retained some of his interests in Canada, and has remembered numerous hospitals and other institutions with generous contributions.

www.ingramcontent.com/pod-product-compliance
Lightning Source LLC
Chambersburg PA
CBHW021239240426
43673CB00057B/617